mUSiC+
reVOLutiOn

For Josephine Barone, my mother, whose love for music
and life drives me every day.

And for my students — may their music create a revolution of its own

mUSiC+ reVOLUtiOn

GREENWICH VILLAGE IN THE 1960s

RICHARD BARONE

Backbeat
Books

Guilford, Connecticut

Backbeat Books
An imprint of The Rowman & Littlefield Publishing Group, Inc.
4501 Forbes Blvd., Ste. 200
Lanham, MD 20706
www.rowman.com

Distributed by NATIONAL BOOK NETWORK

Images are from The David Gahr Archive/DavidGahr.com, unless otherwise noted.
Additional photography by the author.

British Library Cataloguing in Publication Information available

Library of Congress Cataloging-in-Publication Data

Names: Barone, Richard, author.
Title: Music + revolution : Greenwich Village in the 1960s / Richard Barone.
Other titles: Music and revolution
Description: Guilford, Connecticut : Backbeat, 2022. | Includes index.
Identifiers: LCCN 2022001901 (print) | LCCN 2022001902 (ebook) | ISBN 9781493063017 (paperback) | ISBN 9781493063024 (epub)
Subjects: LCSH: Folk music--New York (State)--New York--History and criticism. | Folk musicians--New York (State)--New York--Social life and customs. | Popular music--New York (State)--New York--1961-1970--History and criticism. | Greenwich Village (New York, N.Y.)--Social life and customs. | Nineteen sixties.
Classification: LCC ML3551.8.N49 B37 2022 (print) | LCC ML3551.8.N49 (ebook) | DDC 781.62/1307471--dc23
LC record available at https://lccn.loc.gov/2022001901
LC ebook record available at https://lccn.loc.gov/2022001902

The paper used in this publication meets the minimum requirements of American National Standard for Information Sciences—Permanence of Paper for Printed Library Materials, ANSI/NISO Z39.48-1992

The Village was . . . authentic. Its oldness was new.

For all its history, the Village was new with life and new with thought and new with passions of all varieties.

Contents

06 Preface

08 Foreword

12 Timeline: Setting the Stage

16 Chapter One: The Hammer Song

38 Chapter Two: Folksingers

58 Chapter Three: 1960

80 Chapter Four: The Beatnik Riot

102 Chapter Five: Folk Messiah

120 Chapter Six: Two Bearded Prophets and a Blonde-and-a-Half

140 Chapter Seven: An Artistic Revolution

162 Chapter Eight: Power and the Glory

186 Chapter Nine: 1965

210 Chapter Ten: The Exploding, The Plastic, and the Inevitable

236 Chapter Eleven: Season of the Witch

260 Chapter Twelve: Another Age

288 Acknowledgments

289 Permissions

293 Sources

295 Index of Subjects

298 Index of Songs

preface

When I gaze out of my window at the townhouses of Waverly Place, they appear almost exactly the way they might have looked in 1961. It makes sense, as Greenwich Village has been preserved as a historic district since 1969. But, even before that, the Village always seemed to hold on to its history, adding without deleting much of it—like a brick-and-cobblestone computer with unlimited space on its hard drive.

Though I arrived two decades after the events of this book took place, the music and the stories still lingered. Then, in 2016, at the suggestion of music writer Mitchell Cohen, I made an album, *Sorrows & Promises,* celebrating the explosive fusion of music and message that occurred here in the 1960s. That led to a deep dive into the era, a series of panel discussions at the Jefferson Market Library, live concerts that included one in Central Park, and creating the course Music + Revolution: Greenwich Village in the 1960s, at the New School's School of Jazz and Contemporary Music, in the Village. Sharing this history with my students and sensing its relevance today, through them, convinced me to write this book.

I became immersed in the richness of the era and location: the many colorful personalities, the lyrics and music they wrote, and the unique mixing of genres—particularly in the musical melting pot of Washington Square Park. But even with all the preparation, I was not ready for the emotional journey that would take place as I wrote. There were many ghosts. In the middle of a global pandemic, the Village streets were quiet, abandoned, so the ghosts could roam freely. I imagined them with me, watching over me at my desk as I wrote, making sure I got it right—with my guitar always next to me so I could strum the chords to the songs I was writing about. That's the only way to really get inside this music and understand it.

When I got stuck for words or had a question, regardless of the hour, I would step outside and walk along Waverly Place to the blocks just around Washington Square. There I found the answers written in invisible hieroglyphics on the streets and buildings. One night, standing in the middle of MacDougal Street and looking uptown, I observed that the street was perfectly aligned with the Empire State Building thirty blocks away, in the same way that Stonehenge is aligned with the sun.

I often texted with Scottish folksinging superstar Donovan who, while not a Villager himself, was a keen observer of the scene and a favorite songwriter among many who performed here. He gave me invaluable advice, reminding me, "Ricardo, write about the ones nobody has ever heard of. That's where the story is." He was right, and it became my desire to illuminate those who are lesser known but no less interesting.

I knew that I wanted this book to feature the photography of the legendary David Gahr, whose pictures masterfully captured the beauty and intensity of Greenwich Village musicians. I was fortunate to work with David in the 1990s, and we became fast friends. David taught me about the sixties scene and generously showed me his stunning images from that time, many of which illuminate these pages.

For all that has remained the same in the Village, the world of the 2020s is a very different place. Still, as seriously divided as our society is now, *Rolling Stone* editor Anthony DeCurtis reminded me that culture was equally polarized then. Nothing has really been resolved. The word "revolution" itself, once used to describe a class struggle to lead to progressive political change, is now sometimes used to describe an opposite movement to revert to a previous time of restrictions that limit rights and freedoms. We're through the looking glass.

One final note: When I reference *Billboard* chart positions in these pages, it is for the purpose of illustrating how many people a song or album was reaching via broadcast radio and sales, not as an indication of merit or quality. It is important to remember, too, the limited number of television and radio networks in the 1960s, compared to the endless streaming channels of today. A musician being seen on a show like the *Ed Sullivan Show* could go viral overnight, simply by word of mouth.

With many tears, laughs, and early morning suns coming up, the story you are about to read unfolded. It has been a remarkable experience, and it is my delight to share it with you now.

Richard Barone
Greenwich Village, NYC

**The author, photographed by David Gahr on
MacDougal Street in the 1990s.**

foreWord

What I like most about *Music + Revolution: Greenwich Village in the 1960s*

is how fully—and how satisfyingly—it expresses all of Richard Barone's many virtues. I've been Richard's friend for many years, since *Numbers With Wings*, the second album by his band the Bongos, came out. The Bongos were playing the underground club 688 in Atlanta, where I was living at the time, and I interviewed him for a short piece in *Record* magazine. Richard was ill and huddled on the band's tour bus before going on stage, but gamely went ahead with the interview nonetheless. Over the years I would have many more reasons to admire and feel grateful for that determination and work ethic. The Bongos, of course, were one of the indie bands that helped make Hoboken, NJ, a musical hotspot. What I particularly enjoyed about the Bongos was their lovely melodic sense and Richard's beautifully evocative lyrics. For that band, being excited by punk did not preclude being gripped by the Beatles. They were willing to respond to whatever was good and incorporate it into their own highly distinctive sound—a sound shaped, in large part, by Richard's scintillating guitar playing and his wonderfully emotive vocals.

After my stint in Atlanta, I moved back to New York, where I had been born and grown up, and since then I've happily had many occasions to encounter Richard and even to collaborate with him. I've had the privilege of writing about Richard's music; have seen him perform many times; have interviewed him for my Lou Reed biography; have sung background on a Tiny Tim project he produced; have performed Lou Reed and Velvet Underground songs with him; have visited his classes at the New School for Social Research; and, as I write this, I'm looking forward to Richard visiting the David Bowie class I'm teaching at the University of Pennsylvania and performing a set of Bowie songs at an event sponsored by the creative writing program.

Writing lyrics, needless to say, is closer to writing poetry than writing prose, so I only discovered how skilled a prose writer Richard is when he published his memoir *Frontman: Surviving the Rock Star Myth* in 2007. But Richard has outdone himself with *Music + Revolution*. As the activities I've cataloged would indicate, Richard has incredible musical range, and that quality serves him extremely well here. The folk revival of the early 1960s is well-worn territory, to be sure, but Richard's extensive knowledge and enthusiasm bring both the era and the environment vividly to life.

That Richard is not a "professional" writer dutifully executing (in all senses of the term) his latest project holds him in very good stead here. Throughout the book he responds to his own passions and interests, moving deftly from cogent bios of key figures on the scene to insightful musical analysis drawing on his background as a musician to moving reminiscences about his personal encounters with the people he's writing about. It all makes for a lively, irresistible read—and a surprising one, too. Richard is not following a literary formula here. He's inventing one.

Richard has lived in Greenwich Village for decades, and you can feel the rhythm of its streets in the pace of his prose. I can say this with confidence because I grew up in the Village—quite literally born on Bleecker Street—and lived there through the 1950s, 1960s, and early 1970s, the very period Richard addresses in this book. Underage though I was, I was able to see shows at clubs like the Bitter End and the Café Au Go Go, and later at the Dom, the Village Theatre, and the Fillmore East. I saw and later, after I became a music writer, was able to interview many of the artists Richard writes about here.

For all those reasons, this book has been an unalloyed pleasure to read. Richard brings his characteristic generosity to every aspect of this book—from the definition of revolution to who deserves recognition as a singer-songwriter (rightly including the likes of Buddy Holly and Lou Reed) to the very boundaries of the Village, which is as much an emotional and imaginative landscape as a physical one. Which is just another way of saying that Richard thinks like a musician and an artist. He's less interested in overly strict definitions than in sources of inspiration and matters of the heart. Richard has learned all the most meaningful lessons of true revolution and of life in Greenwich Village, in other words, and he imparts them here to all of us.

Anthony DeCurtis
New York City
Spring 2022

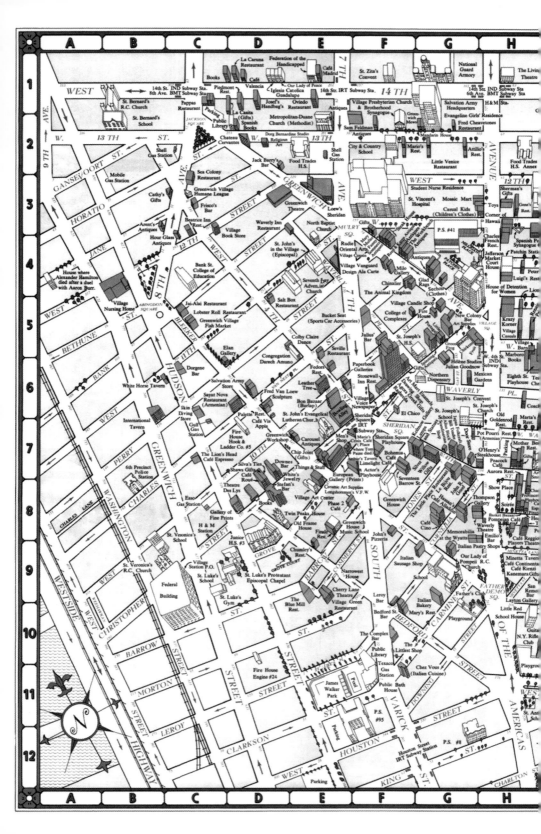

MAP
of the
GREENWICH VILLAGE
SECTION OF NEW YORK CITY

SCALE 1:3,100

200   0   200   400   600 Feet

Public buildings are shown in white, all others in red.

DRAWN & PUBLISHED BY
LAWRENCE FAHEY, CARTOGRAPHER

SECOND EDITION 1961

Copyright
No part of this map may
be reproduced without the
written permission of
the publisher.

Copies of this map may
be obtained by sending
$1.50 to L. Fahey, P.O.
Box #112, Village Station,
NY 14, NY.

setting the stage (1600-1939)

The question is: "Why was it Washington Square?
How did it become a 'churnin', burnin', yearnin' center?"
—Steve Berkowitz, Producer, Columbia Records

The known history of Greenwich Village dates back to the sixteenth century, when it was a marshland where the Native American Lenape tribe camped and fished. It is said that when the Dutch first arrived, in the seventeenth century, their relationship with the Lenape was amicable. But in 1626, following the much-mythologized land-purchase transaction, Dutch colonists took over the Lenape island of Manahatta, settled in its southernmost tip, and renamed it New Amsterdam. They built a wall around their settlement to protect themselves from the Lenape and the British. Now the site of Wall Street, this community marked the beginning of the forced, mass migration of the Lenape from their homeland.

Besides "Manhattan," many Lenape words still remain as street names, such as Minetta Lane, which was once Minetta Brook, a fishing stream that the Lenape called *Mannette*, or "spirit water." What is now the West Village and Meatpacking District was planted with tobacco, and the Lenape name for the Village, *Sapokanikan*, meant "tobacco field." The Dutch called it Groenwijk, or "green district."

1643 Between 1643 and 1716, former slaves of the Dutch West India Company, after successfully petitioning for their freedom in the first Black legal protest in America, were granted land in the area comprising present-day Greenwich Village and SoHo, from just north of Washington Square down to Canal Street. The area, used primarily for farming, became the first free Black settlement in North America and was known as "Land of the Blacks."

1664 When the British seized New Amsterdam from the Dutch in 1664, they renamed it New York City in honor of the Duke of York. Groenwijk was anglicized to "Greenwich Village," echoing the name of the posh London district. With Dutch, English, German, and French immigrants arriving in greater numbers, the city became increasingly diverse, but the freed slaves lost their farm properties after the British takeover.

1785 Surviving the Revolutionary War, New York City became the first capital of the United States—from 1785 to 1790. George Washington was inaugurated here. Greenwich Village, at that time, was still a rural countryside, a few miles to the north of the center of things, with the city steadily inching closer.

1797 In 1797, New York State's first penitentiary, Newgate Prison, was built at the end of West Tenth Street, near the Christopher Street Pier, on the Hudson River. To be sent "up the river" was to be sent to Newgate. Riots and violence ensued on the waterfront as the prison was crammed to nearly twice its capacity. As such, there were sometimes fifty prisoners released into the Village per day.

1799   That same year (1797), Washington Square Park was purchased by the Common Council of New York and became a potter's field. More than twenty thousand bodies are still buried there, and tombstones unearthed in recent years date back to 1799.

1811   In 1811, New York City instituted a strict, uniform grid for the island of Manhattan, essentially with avenues running north and south and streets east and west, creating perfectly shaped rectangular blocks. But when it came to the Village, its residents refused. They sought to keep the well-established, irregular street plan that had been based on Native American trails, as well as property lines and paths laid out by the Dutch settlers in the early seventeenth century. City officials conceded, and the streets remained as they were.

1826   In 1826, Washington Square, at the center of the Village, was converted into a military parade ground. Soon, elegant homes and the buildings of New York University sprang up along its perimeter.

1832   The influx of artists to the Village began in 1832, when Samuel F. B. Morse, inventor of the telegraph and Morse code, became the first professor of painting and sculpture in America, at New York University. In 1835, Morse moved into NYU's new, neo-Gothic University Building on Washington Square East, acquiring studio space for himself and his students.

1857   In 1857, a new attraction began drawing artists to the Village—the Tenth Street Studio Building, at 51 West Tenth Street between Fifth and Sixth Avenues, which opened as the first modern facility designed solely to serve the needs of artists. The brainchild of real estate speculator James Boorman Johnston, its unique design by architect Richard Morris Hunt housed three floors of studios with a central, glass-ceilinged gallery for exhibitions. It would remain a creative hub for nearly a century, until it was finally razed in 1956.

1859   In 1859, Brooklyn poet Walt Whitman began frequenting Pfaff's Beer Cellar, a gay-friendly, bohemian hangout located at 647 Broadway, at Bleecker Street in the Village. Literary readings, critiques, and debates would last well into the night. Whitman's poems often explored themes of male-male intimacy, relationships, and self-identity.

1860   On February 27, 1860, just a few blocks east of Washington Square and within earshot of Pfaff's, Abraham Lincoln delivered his watershed Cooper Union address denouncing slavery and, according to Lincoln historian Harold Holzer, transformed himself "from a regional leader into a national phenomenon." Legend has it that, after the speech, Lincoln walked over to McSorley's Ale House, at 15 East Seventh Street, for a beer.

1860 On October 1, 1860, the first Women's Library, located in the University Building—the very building that was home to Samuel Morse's artist studio on Washington Square Park—officially opened its doors. This predated the New York Public Library system and ran counter to private libraries, which routinely excluded women. Reporting at the time indicated that it was the first and only library of its kind.

1880 From the 1880s to the late 1910s, the area around the Minettas—Minetta Lane, Street, and Place—became known as "Little Africa." Although predominantly Black, the neighborhood—now urbanized with tenement dwellings—showed signs of integration (then rare) between Black and white residents, especially at its popular "Black and tan" saloons.

1892 In 1892, a triumphal, seventy-seven-foot-tall white marble arch with two poses of George Washington—one portraying "War" and the other "Peace"—was designed and built by architect Stanford White. Inspired by the Arc de Triomphe in Paris, it replaced a temporary one that had been constructed for Washington's Centennial in 1889. The Arch still serves as the gateway to Washington Square Park.

1910 By 1910, Left-leaning poets, journalists, socialists, and playwrights were congregating in the Village, declaring it an American bohemia, a center of defiant nonconformity.

1911 In 1911, an innovative, monthly journal of arts and politics, *The Masses*, was launched in Greenwich Village, with offices at 91 West Twelfth Street. Featuring poetry and fiction, Marxist and labor articles, columns like "Knowledge and Revolution," and artwork by some of the leading radicals of the time, *The Masses* utilized art and literature as tools of social activism.

At 4:40 on the afternoon of March 25, 1911, the Triangle Shirtwaist Factory, located on the top three floors of the Asch Building just east of Washington Square Park, burst into flames. Locked inside by management, 146 mostly young, female, Italian and Jewish immigrants perished in the blaze or leapt to their deaths. The event and its aftermath triggered major reformation of New York State and national labor laws, workers' rights regulations, and the formation of the International Ladies' Garment Workers' Union.

1916 By 1916, the Provincetown Playhouse, on MacDougal Street between West Third and West Fourth Streets, was boldly staging controversial plays, involving women in all levels of productions, featuring Paul Robeson and other prominent African American actors, and exploring racial themes.

1917 On January 23, 1917, six tipsy, socially prominent Village artists and actors, including Dadaist painter and sculptor Marcel Duchamp and artist John Sloan, climbed to the top of the Washington Square Arch at midnight armed with wine bottles, Chinese lanterns, toy guns, and balloons. From high above Washington Square Park, they theatrically signed a parchment, loudly declaring Greenwich Village "a Free and Independent Republic." While the only real outcome was that the door to the Arch's stairway was permanently locked, Greenwich Village had been formally established as a free and independent republic—of the mind.

1920 In the 1920s and '30s, at the height of the so-called Pansy Craze, elaborate drag balls were held at Webster Hall, located at 125 East Eleventh Street.

1926 A couple of blocks away, in 1926, Columbia Phonograph Company, later Columbia Records, set up its recording studio at 55 Fifth Avenue. John Hammond produced his first recordings there, including, on July 2, 1935, the very first racially integrated recording session that featured clarinetist Benny Goodman, African American swing pianist Teddy Wilson, and jazz vocalist Billie Holiday.

1938 Café Society, the first integrated nightclub in the United States, opened its doors at One Sheridan Square on December 18, 1938, with a performance by Billie Holiday. On that same stage a few months later, in March 1939, Holiday introduced one of the most brutally artful political songs of all time: "Strange Fruit."

1939 Around the same time, Greenwich Village was becoming the center of a renewed interest in folk and rural blues music. A handful of charismatic, impassioned urban folksingers in the Village were embraced by leftist political activists, college students, and folklore enthusiasts. As the music's following expanded, it would inspire a strum heard 'round the world.

And that is where our story begins.

Special thanks to Andrew Berman of the Greenwich Village Society for Historic Preservation for his help in creating this timeline.

Chapter One

the ham So

mer

ng

Pete Seeger, performing at the Village Gate in May 1961.

Folklore inherently rejects all authoritarian notions. It allows for the creative rights of the individual at the same time that it is flexible in its response to community sentiment. Perhaps here lie the reasons that folklore has a staying power unrivaled by even the very greatest of cultivated art.
—Alan Lomax , "America Sings the Saga of America"
New York Times, January 26, 1947

Though it is often viewed as one, monolithic movement,

the American Folk Revival and its dazzling culmination in the 1960s can be seen as happening in at least two distinct waves or two acts in a play, each with its own dramatic arc and unique cast of players, both largely played out against the perfect backdrop that had been built over time in Greenwich Village.

The first wave, beginning in the late 1930s, was the result of a combination of factors stemming from the Great Depression, intertwined with the labor union movement and the leftist politics of the time. For the most part, it shunned overt commercialism and disdained current pop culture. Music performances were often connected to leftist political or union-sanctioned events for which folk music provided an appropriately galvanizing soundtrack. By contrast, the second wave, beginning circa 1960, was a reflection of growing postwar prosperity, the doubling of the number of college students in the United States, and a whole new set of political issues, in particular the civil rights movement and, later, the war in Vietnam. Many of the musicians of the second wave grew to embrace commerciality. And, even at its most political, the music was rarely beholden to a particular organization or doctrine. It was therefore at liberty to express itself through a far wider range of topics and to appeal to a far wider, more general audience.

By the time of the second wave, the seeds had been planted by the first, and the listening public had acquired a taste and appreciation for folk music on its own terms, as musical entertainment. There was, of course, some overlapping of the two waves, and a few of the key players provided a thread of continuity. But though both waves were born of the same primordial soup, their paths evolved in very different ways

Essential to the actual discovery and exposure of the music that started it all, and that might have otherwise been lost to history, was the extraordinary father-and-son archivist team of John and Alan Lomax. Making revolutionary, remote field recordings in the American South and Midwest for the Library of Congress's Archive of Folk Song starting in the 1930s, they uncovered, frequently far from urban centers, thousands of songs and discovered artists like Muddy Waters and Son House, who are now considered seminal. But what they really found, in my opinion as a guitar-wielding lover of three chords and a story, was the origin not only of folk music but of multiple genres of American popular music that followed. They recorded work songs, sung in the fields to pass the time, in the mines, and on the chain gangs. They collected Cajun music in Louisiana and blues from the Mississippi Delta. You name it—songs of hope and despair, violence and retribution, attraction and rejection; sea shanties and Celtic folk ballads that had made their way across the Atlantic and mixed with African songs and instruments. The banjo, the great symbol of American folk music that had its origins in West Africa, was refined and reworked in the Caribbean islands and found its way to the rural South. African American musicians interpreting European folk songs in their own styles, often interlacing church music and field hollers, and all the handing down and reinterpreting of this music evolved into multiple new forms, most obviously the blues, country, jazz, and—yes—rock and roll. Primordial soup and musical big bang all rolled into one.

Alan Lomax, himself a Left-leaning musician (father John was far more conservative), was able to deftly straddle the political and broader social worlds, spreading the word and the music in a variety of broadcast media and concert events and through record labels. By 1937, Alan had taken over for his father at the Library of Congress, becoming "assistant in charge," and he continued to create recordings for the Library of Congress until 1942. "What Lomax found, the recordings he made in the 1930s and '40s, were filled with the forms and language that would be used to create the music of the 1960s," producer/engineer Steve Rosenthal told me. "He was able to capture it before it disappeared." Rosenthal, a four-time Grammy winner, restored over one hundred CDs of these recordings for the Alan Lomax Collection that were released on Rounder Records starting in 1997.

With his proto-hipster goatee, easygoing charm, and evangelical zeal, Alan Lomax became one of the greatest proponents of folk and blues music in history. In Pete Seeger's words, "Lomax didn't just collect—he *preached* and *converted*." As a CBS radio host in the early 1940s, he brought this music to millions. It should be added here that actor/folksinger Burl Ives was also on national radio at this time with his show, *The Wandering Stranger*, playing a more refined, sophisticated brand of folk music. From Canada, folksinger Oscar Brand brought folk to the masses via the medium of radio on his *Oscar Brand's Folksong Festival*, a show launched in 1945 that would run for nearly seventy years on New York's WNYC-AM. Both Ives and Brand were essential figures in the folk revival.

Today, there are some who question Alan Lomax's methods—such as adding his name to songwriting credits and claiming publishing copyrights—and who criticize as imperious his self-appointed role as gatekeeper and chief authority of the folk canon. At the time of Lomax's passing in 2002, American music critic Dave Marsh wrote, "Sometime soon, we need to figure out why it is that, when it comes to cultures like those of Mississippi Black people, we celebrate the milkman more than the milk." Regardless, but for his very act of recording and disseminating this music, it could be argued that the rest of this story might not have happened or, at least, not in the way that it did. And, besides, being Alan Lomax put him in the unique position of uniting what I think of as the holy trinity of the folk revival.

The People's Poet

Oklahoma native Woody Guthrie, blown to California like so many others in the region by the winds of the Dust Bowl disaster—a period of severe dust storms that ravaged the Great Plains in the 1930s and was intensified by the devastating impact of the Great Depression—had a particular knack for writing topical songs that reflected current events and attitudes and for delivering them in a manner and visual presence that mirrored the plight of common people. Composing in a style that echoed traditional, rural folk songs gave his work an absolute genuineness, familiarity, timelessness, and a kind of inevitability. With the famous message declaring "**THIS MACHINE KILLS FASCISTS**" prominently displayed on his Gibson Southern Jumbo acoustic guitar, and a metaphorical middle finger aimed at the establishment, Guthrie created an indelible and compelling archetype. In 1940, Guthrie wrote "This Land Is Your Land" as his response to Irving Berlin's "God Bless America," the inescapable hit record of that year sung by Kate Smith that irritated him as he heard it played repeatedly on radios during his cross-country travels. It was a song that Guthrie felt glossed over the tremendous disparity in the distribution of wealth and land that he was observing.

It's complicated though. When "This Land Is Your Land" was performed at the inauguration of President Joe Biden in 2021, some groups were disappointed. Writing in *Smithsonian Folklife*, Native American activist and musician Mali Obomsawin wrote, "In the context of America, a nation-state built by settler colonialism, Woody Guthrie's protest anthem exemplifies the particular blind spot that Americans have in regard to Natives: American patriotism erases us, even if it comes in the form of a leftist protest song. Why? Because this land '*was*' *our* land." Although the song was surely intended by Guthrie to be a message of unity, in the context of a national event such as the inauguration, it may be considered tone-deaf to modern ears.

> *I've roamed and rambled and I followed my footsteps,*
> *To the sparkling sands of her diamond deserts;*
> *And all around me a voice was sounding;*
> *This land was made for you and me.*

It should be noted that the music and melody of "This Land Is Your Land" is indebted to the Carter Family's recording of "When the World's on Fire," recorded in 1930 and credited to A. P. Carter. Exemplifying the nature of folk music being handed down and reworked, the Carter Family was the source of much of the music and playing styles that were in the process of being revived by Guthrie and the others—in particular, Mother Maybelle Carter's unique "Carter scratch" guitar technique.

Recent controversies notwithstanding, "This Land Is Your Land" is now considered by many to be an alternative national anthem and is one of the most widely sung folk songs ever. Even if Guthrie had only written that one song, I would probably still be typing about him today. In fact, he wrote over a thousand songs that provided a kind of continuity throughout the folk revival. Guthrie's influence over future musicians transcended genre and generation.

King of the Twelve-String Guitar

Huddie Ledbetter, better known as Lead Belly, was an imposing, charismatic African American folk-singer with a monumental repertoire of hundreds of songs he had sung for fellow inmates in the Louisiana State Penitentiary at Angola. "How many songs do you know, Huddie?" he was asked on his own WNYC radio show, *Folk Songs of America*, in the 1940s. "Well, I can sing five hundred songs and never go back to the first one." The Lomaxes "discovered" him at the penitentiary in 1933. But it wasn't Lead Belly's first time doing time. He had previously been imprisoned and won an early release by composing and singing a song for the governor of Texas, Pat M. Neff, who commuted Huddie's sentence in 1925. In 1934, the Lomaxes helped him obtain his release from Angola by playing a recording of Lead Belly's second call for mercy, for Louisiana governor O. K. Allen in the governor's office. Again, Lead Belly was granted a reprieve, went to work as an assistant for John Lomax, and arrived in Greenwich Village in 1935. All great fables—like the one of Lead Belly singing his way out of prison—*twice*—should have an air of unbelievability about them, even if they're true. This one does, and it is. Lead Belly himself—along with John Lomax—appeared in a bizarre 1935 *March of Time* newsreel reen-actment in which he depicts himself as a prisoner in stripes being rescued by Lomax. In the 1976 film *Leadbelly*, Black filmmaker, musician, and photojournalist Gordon Parks, creator of the "blaxploitation" film genre with his film *Shaft* (1971), portrayed Lead Belly as a violent but lovable folk superhero.

Like Guthrie, Lead Belly was a witty and prodigious songwriter and social critic who was able to chronicle current events in personalized folk and blues forms. For instance, his first song, written in 1912, "The Titanic," tells the tale of the ship's sinking while adding a wry racial commentary about Black boxer Jack Johnson, the then-current heavyweight champion, who the lyrics falsely claim was not allowed to sail on the doomed ocean liner:

> *Jack Johnson want to get on board,*
> *Captain said, "I ain't hauling no coal,"*
> *Cryin', fare thee, Titanic, fare thee well*

Besides providing a gold mine of material, Lead Belly was a polished and dignified performer with a distinctive way of explaining and commenting on the lyrics, using spoken ad libs within the song itself, between the lines. According to author and historian Benjamin Filene in *American Quarterly* (1991), the Lomaxes presented Lead Belly as a "populist spokesman" but also emphasized the rougher aspects of his convict past, such as in their 1936 biography *Negro Folk Songs as Sung by Lead Belly*, writing of his "career of violence."

I contacted Benjamin Filene, who is now associate director of curatorial affairs for the Smithsonian's National Museum of American History, and asked him bluntly if the Lomaxes, in the 1930s, were in some ways responsible for propagating the "gangsta" image in the marketing of Black musicians, something that was to become so prevalent in more recent years. "I don't think we can or need to say that the Lomaxes created the gangsta image," Filene replied, "but I do think one can say that even as the Lomaxes deeply valued and shaped legacies of African American music, they exoticized its practitioners in ways that built on and helped advance damaging tropes about primitivism, violence, untrammeled emotion, and untutored expression in African American culture."

Conversely, Pete Seeger, quoted in Filene's 1991 article, remembered Lead Belly as "soft-spoken, meticulously dressed" and "wonderful with children." Moses Asch of Folkways Records referred to Lead Belly's "overall aristocratic appearance and demeanor." Historian Stephen Petrus believes the Lomaxes genuinely saw Lead Belly as a "pure, authentic folksinger; an emblem of Americana music."

"His voice in those days was clear, sweet and far-carrying, like a powerful jazz trumpet. Under his magic fingers, his battered twelve-string guitar 'talked like a natural man,'" Alan Lomax would write of Lead Belly in an essay published in his *Selected Writings 1934–1997* (2003). Although Lead Belly performed regularly at the Apollo Theater in Harlem in the mid-1930s, by 1939 he was becoming a fixture downtown on the New York folk scene, performing with Josh White, Sonny Terry, Brownie McGhee, and Woody Guthrie. Usually dressed in a suit and tie, Lead Belly possessed a vocal richness and power together with a percussive playing style. His guitar technique, on a specially made twelve-string Stella with extra bracing to support his heavy-gauge strings, tuned-down two full steps for a heavier sound, earned him the title "King of the Twelve-String Guitar." Lead Belly presented a unique, virile elegance that inspired scores of folk and blues performers, including rock icon Little Richard who, speaking in the 1988 CBS documentary *A Vision Shared: A Tribute to Woody Guthrie and Leadbelly*, called Lead Belly "one of the foundations of music." George Harrison was even more succinct: "No Lead Belly, no Beatles."

America's Tuning Fork

Pete Seeger grew up in an intensely musical household and matured with a profound, lifelong love, knowledge, and *belief* in folk music that rivaled all the fervor and faith of the world's great religions. In it he saw a unique power to communicate, to unify, and to advance positive change in society. His father, Charles Seeger, a fiercely opinionated folklorist, had established the first musicology curriculum in the United States at the University of California in Berkeley and wrote for the communist *Daily Worker* newspaper; his mother, Constance de Clyver Edson, was a concert violinist and then later a teacher at the Juilliard School. Pete would inherit qualities of both, especially a propensity for teaching and the leftist leanings of his father. He attended the same class as future president John F. Kennedy at Harvard University where, drawn by its stance on anti-fascism and support of racial equality, he joined the Young Communist League (YCL), the youth wing of the Communist Party USA (CPUSA), and founded a leftist campus paper, *The Harvard Progressive*. In 1937, when he was eighteen years old, Pete went to work for the Lomaxes at the Library of Congress as their intern, going through recordings and helping them separate authentic folk music from crass commercial imitations.

From Lead Belly, young Pete would learn songs and study his distinctive technique on twelve-string guitar. From mentor Woody Guthrie, he would learn to hop freight trains as he provided guitar and banjo accompaniment, singing in labor union halls and living the life that the songs depicted. Pete was to become not only a master but a champion of the banjo, authoring a landmark instruction book and film, *How to Play the Five-String Banjo* (1948), a staple of the folk revival. In revealing contrast to Guthrie's message that his guitar kills fascists, Pete Seeger's banjo in later years carried the more nonviolent message "This Machine Surrounds Hate and Forces It to Surrender." Similarly, his brand of folk music had a gentle approach. Even his songs of protest were usually allegorical and poetic. Pulitzer Prize–winning writer, poet, and folklorist Carl Sandburg was to dub Pete "America's Tuning Fork." Due in part to his youth, passion, and skills as a performer and communicator, it would be left to Seeger to help guide, steer, and inspire the folk movement through both waves of the revival, though sometimes, by necessity, from behind the scenes.

It could be said that the pivotal "*Grapes of Wrath* Evening for the Benefit of the John Steinbeck Committee for Agricultural Workers"—a concert named for Steinbeck's 1939 novel—is where things got started. Held on March 3, 1940, at the Forrest Theatre on West Forty-Ninth Street, the Hollywood film of the same title had recently opened, and public awareness of the Dust Bowl crisis was high. Proceeds of the concert went to impoverished farmers devastated by the disaster. That night, Alan Lomax introduced a nervous Pete Seeger to his soon-to-be mentor, Woody Guthrie. And Guthrie, who had barely been in New York for a month, was introduced to Lead Belly for the first time. Lomax, one of the concert's presenters, also performed on the bill, along with his sister Bess. But it was Guthrie, with his commandingly unassuming, windblown presence, who stole the show with his Dust Bowl ballads. For many, Lomax included, this concert was a turning point in the American folk music revival. "Go back to that night when Pete first met Woody Guthrie. You can date the renaissance of American folk song from that night," Lomax was to say to a journalist, as later quoted in *The Guardian*. According to Stephen Petrus in his book *Folk City*, the concert not only forged new artistic relationships that would have lasting resonance but it also publicly vitalized the relationship between folk music and leftist politics. "The concert was a distinctively New York affair, an expression of the city's leftist sensibility, though, ironically, only one of the performers, Pete Seeger, was actually born in New York," wrote Petrus.

It was labor songs and left-wing activism that brought Seeger together with folksinger/activist Lee Hays to form the Almanac Singers, circa 1941. Soon Woody Guthrie would join them, along with a revolving door of folksingers that had met at the *Grapes of Wrath* concert, in addition to Burl Ives, Cisco Houston, Josh White, and others. In an energetic, driving style, they sang material that addressed the issues of working people and their support of workers' rights. Consistent with Woody Guthrie's image, the group wore street clothes, unheard of at a time when musical groups were expected to wear more formal attire.

Like labor activist/songwriter Joe Hill (1879–1915), a member of the Industrial Workers of the World (or IWW, known as "Wobblies") before them, Seeger said the mission of the Almanac Singers was to "build a singing labor movement." But Joe Hill was to suffer for his labor activism. He was convicted on what was said to be a false charge and executed by firing squad in Salt Lake City in 1915, famously sending a final telegram to IWW leader Big Bill Haywood: "Goodbye Bill. I die like a true rebel. Don't waste time in mourning. Organize."

The Almanacs set up shop in Greenwich Village, living together and sharing expenses, first at 70 East Twelfth Street, in a building they christened Almanac House, then at Almanac House 2, at 130 West Tenth Street, a slim but sturdy-looking, red-brick townhouse next door to the quaintly Romanesque fire station of Engine Company 18. Off-and-on-again member Bess Lomax—daughter of John and sister of Alan—called it "a commune of the period" when she described their shared living arrangements. Woody Guthrie lived at Almanac House, also, until he eventually got his own place a stone's throw away at 74 Charles Street. Lead Belly's apartment, which he had called home since 1935, was just a few blocks east, at 414 East Tenth Street, and was another popular hangout for musicians in the Village. It was there that Pete Seeger first heard Lead Belly play "Goodnight, Irene."

To help pay the $100 monthly rent on their townhouse, the Almanac Singers began to give weekend "hootenannies" in the basement, charging 35 cents per person. "Hootenanny" was a phrase Pete had picked up while performing at a Seattle political club that used it to describe their musical fundraisers. The word stuck and gained popularity as folk music's equivalent of a jam session in jazz. Participation was the essence of these basement gatherings, with everyone—musicians and audience—joining in. Musicians Cisco Houston, Sonny Terry, and Brownie McGhee would sit in on occasion. As word spread, the Greenwich Village "hoots" caught on.

Besides the *convenience* of hosting the hootenannies in their own basement, it was some-what of a necessity, as options were scarce. Commercial venues for folk music at that time were few and far between, even in Greenwich Village. Max Gordon's Village Vanguard had opened in 1935, first, briefly, at a location on Charles Street and soon moving to its landmark address at 178 Seventh Avenue South, which still thrives in 2022. Through the 1940s, with its red double doors, famous red awning, and small, red neon signage, the Vanguard presented headliner folk artists and poetry readings in a dimly lit, low-ceilinged, wedge-shaped basement space, down a narrow flight of stairs banked by red-enameled walls. The red decor of the Vanguard was, apparently, not by accident. According to Stephen R. Duncan, author of *The Rebel Cafe: Sex, Race, and Politics in Cold War America's Nightclub Underground* (2018), "the club's name itself was a sly nod to the Marxist notion of a revolutionary 'workers' vanguard.'" In those days, jazz jam sessions were relegated to Sunday afternoons, with folk and poetry at night. Lead Belly, Woody Guthrie, and Harry Belafonte, in a breakthrough performance, were among the folk, blues, and calypso artists who performed there, along with, a few years later, revolutionary stand-up comedian and social satirist Lenny Bruce.

Barney Josephson's more expansive basement venue, Café Society, with its policy of equally welcoming Black as well as white patrons (unlike, say, the Cotton Club in Harlem, which wel-comed Black performers on stage but sat Black guests in the back of the audience), was but a scant few blocks away, at One Sheridan Square. The venue's name was satirical, as the club was intended to defy the conventions of the social elite. In its motto, "The wrong place for the Right people," the letter R was purposely capitalized as a jab at conservatives and a message to liberals. It was a place for music as well as leftist political events and fundraisers. But the music at Café Society centered around jazz, swing, and gospel, showcasing African American artists, many having been discovered by the venue's unofficial musical director, John Hammond. Hammond was a producer, director of talent acquisition, vice president of Columbia Records, and one of the most influential figures in the history of popular music. Producer Steve Berkowitz, who began working for Columbia in 1987, described for me the leadership of Columbia Records in the 1940s and '50s: "They were erudite men, mostly white and Protestant, who said, 'We can uplift the taste of civilization with the power of the corporation—television, music, and publishing.' Hammond, for one, didn't need money. He was a Vanderbilt." Born into great wealth, Hammond grew up in a six-story mansion in Manhattan, where he fell in love with music—early classical records heard on the family phonograph and jazz and blues coming from the servants' quarters. "The simple honesty and convincing lyrics of the early blues singers, the rhythm and creative ingenuity of the jazz players, excited me the most," he would later write in *John Hammond on Record: An Autobiography* (1977).

Besides Billie Holiday, Café Society was also responsible for making the influential, eclectic singer/guitarist Josh White a star. In 1940, Hammond produced Josh White's groundbreaking concept album dealing specifically with civil rights, *Chain Gang* (credited to Joshua White and His Carolinians), for Columbia. Tenor Bayard Rustin—later to become a major civil rights activist and memorialized today by the Bayard Rustin Center for Social Justice in Princeton, New Jersey—sang on the album. But Café Society wasn't really a folk venue. As such, besides the basements, public or private, Washington Square Park provided a spacious, free venue in the center of the Village where folk musicians could gather and perform for—and with—the crowd. Especially on Sunday afternoons, while jazz was occupying the Vanguard. But by 1957, as more folk clubs would begin to open in the Village, jazz would become the dominant music at the Vanguard, as it is to this day.

A square-dancing craze that was to peak in the forties gave further exposure to folk music and provided another venue for folk artists to perform. Educator and folk music collector Margot Mayo had spearheaded the folk dancing revival movement, forming the American Square Dance group in 1934

and writing on the subject for books and periodicals. Some of Pete Seeger's earliest performances were for Mayo's dance company. Folksay, a singing and square dance collective affiliated with the American League for Democracy, youth group of CPUSA, was also presenting bimonthly square dances with live accompaniment. Mayo and her troupe appear in the 1947 Seeger documentary film *To Hear Your Banjo Play*, scripted by Lomax. Also that year, she was involved in a conference devoted to city folklore, presenting the vital lore of New York City—street cries, Yiddish folk songs, folk songs from Harlem—organized by Lomax and held at Elisabeth Irwin's aptly named Little Red School House, the city's first progressive school and still a vital Village institution. It was through Margot Mayo, at a square-dancing event in 1939, that Seeger met his future wife, Toshi Aline Ohta. They would marry in 1943, moving in with Toshi's parents at 129 MacDougal Street, less than a block from Washington Square. The parlor-floor apartment is now a storefront café, La Lanterna. Pete and Toshi would go on to be partners not only in raising a family but in producing some of the most consequential happenings of the folk revival. They remained together until Toshi's passing at the age of ninety-one, nine days before what would have been her seventieth wedding anniversary.

In 1945, Israel "Izzy" Young attended his first square dance and became a folk devotee and aficionado for life. "Folk music is the heartbeat of a person," he would tell the *Village Voice*. Young was born in 1928 on the Lower East Side, first living on Ludlow Street, "surrounded by the largest Jewish population in America," as he wrote in *Autobiography*, a 1969 collaboration with photographer David Gahr. He grew up in the Bronx and worked in his father's bakery in Brooklyn before getting into the book business. In May 1957, Izzy Young would open the Folklore Center, the first in the world, strategically located at 110 MacDougal Street, to supply the folk community's needs with items such as guitar strings, capos, picks, sheet music, books, and records. And Young himself was a folksy firebrand who could make things happen. But it was the square-dancing circuit of the 1940s that first drew him in.

World War II put the Almanac Singers on pause, although they did contribute some anti-fascist songs, including the uncharacteristically brutal "Round, Round, Hitler's Grave" (1942), keeping in line with the CPUSA's enthusiastic rallying in favor of the Soviet-American war effort against Nazi Germany. Clearly, the Almanac Singers' overtly political messaging was more akin to the 1960s protest singers than were Pete's and Lee Hays's more commercially successful group that was to follow. Performing solo in 1946, *Billboard* magazine took notice and referred to Seeger as "a trim, slim Sinatra of the folk song clan."

At first, the word "communism" had not yet been fully weaponized. But that was about to change. Postwar communism in America was an ideology that resulted from the perceived failures of capitalism that led to the Great Depression of 1929–1933. It embraced economic and social causes such as the rights of African Americans, workers, and the unemployed, and it appealed to a wide range of Americans, even if, as fellow travelers, they did not actually join the party. "We were against Hitler," Pete Seeger once told me in a phone call, explaining his initial membership at Harvard. But by the late 1930s, there was an anti-communist backlash, sparked by fears of Soviet influence and the totalitarian dictatorship of Joseph Stalin. Even more than warning of the "red menace," anti-communist rhetoric would be used by right-wing politicians as a tool to discredit labor, social activism, and President Roosevelt's liberal New Deal policies.

After the war, during which he served for a time in the army, Seeger, along with Lomax and Hays, formed People's Songs, a nationwide organization with headquarters on both coasts that published a quarterly folk song newsletter, the *People's Songs*, from 1946 to 1950. It contained traditional and newly written contemporary union and folk songs with lyrics, sheet music, and tablature, along with information about upcoming hootenannies and folk dances. In 1950, Seeger and political activist Irwin Silber, who had cofounded Folksay, would use the same format to create the successful *Sing Out!* magazine, which began as a mimeographed fanzine and remained in print until 2014. *People's Songs* supported Progressive Party candidate Henry Wallace's 1948 presidential campaign and, although the effort failed, the publicity helped put folk music in the bright glare of the national spotlight—and, as the Red Scare gained momentum, squarely in the sights of the FBI. The truth is, based on files released to the public in 2015, Seeger had been under investigation by the FBI since his time in the army, and it continued into the 1970s. Apparently, the investigation was triggered by a letter he wrote to the California chapter of the American Legion, signed Pvt. Peter Seeger, protesting their decision to deport Japanese Americans. "If you deport Japanese, why not Germans, Italians, Rumanians, Hungarians, and Bulgarians?" he wrote.

After this letter was reported to the FBI, Seeger's further written correspondence with his fiancée, Toshi, herself a Japanese American, was intercepted and scrutinized by the FBI.

Along with Hays, Ronnie Gilbert, and Fred Hellerman, Seeger reconstituted the Almanacs as the Weavers at the end of 1948. In 1949, Seeger and Hays wrote "If I Had a Hammer (The Hammer Song)," which was first recorded by the Weavers and became an anthem for both waves of the folk revival. Lyrically, Seeger and Hays kept it streamlined and repetitive, making it easier to get audiences to learn and sing along during performances, and culminating in its final verse:

It's the hammer of justice,
It's the bell of freedom
It's the song about love between all of my brothers,
All over this land.

When the song was recorded by Peter, Paul and Mary in 1962, the group rewrote the penul-timate line of each verse to read "My brothers *and my sisters*." Fifty years later, I was having a phone conversation with Pete Seeger when the subject of Peter, Paul and Mary's version of "The Hammer Song" came up. "They made a good song out of it," he said, "a *better* song." But then he asked, "Richard, why do you think they added 'Oooo-oooo-oooo-oooh' between the verses?" From the sound of his voice, it appeared to be something he was not fond of. "Well, maybe it got people singing along?" I proffered. Pete seemed satisfied with that reply. But, in truth, the "ooohs" added a secondary hook that would appear in nearly every subsequent cover version. And there would be many.

A far more polished and commercial group than the rather ragtag Almanacs, the Weavers wore evening clothes onstage, suits and ties for the men and smart outfits for Ronnie Gilbert. The group hit it out of the park with their first single, Lead Belly's "Goodnight, Irene," on Decca Records. But even if the song itself had been introduced by Lead Belly, who had, sadly, passed away the year before, the production was far from what we would now consider a folk record. It was produced by Milt Gabler, who a few years later would produce one of rock and roll's breakthrough hits, "Rock Around the Clock," by Bill Haley and the Comets. The Weavers had been discovered during their successful residency at the Village Vanguard by orchestrator and band leader Gordon Jenkins, famous for his lush string arrangements on records by mainstream artists like Frank Sinatra, Ella Fitzgerald, and Peggy Lee. As was customary at the time, Jenkins arranged a secondary orchestral accompaniment that bathed the Weavers in strings and a choir. Yet there was a bona fide folk song in there that delighted folk fans, and the production helped propel the record to the number one slot, where it stayed for thirteen weeks in 1950. It sold one million copies that year and was played everywhere. As a commercial force, folk music had arrived.

The group's star continued to rise with more hits—such as "On Top of Old Smokey," "Kiss-es Sweeter Than Wine," and "Wimoweh"—and more appearances, and they were even offered their own national television show. With Toshi Seeger as their booking agent, the Weavers headlined not only at the Village Vanguard and Café Society but in premier nightclubs in Hollywood, Houston, Reno, and elsewhere, as well as in posh, uptown venues in New York, like the Blue Angel. The success of the Weavers on Decca also shined a light on the smaller folk labels, like Moe Asch's Folkways, which showcased folk music of the world as well as albums by Guthrie, Lead Belly, and Seeger. In 1952, Folkways would release one of the most important documents of folk music ever compiled, Harry Smith's *Anthology of American Folk Music*, which was to become a favorite among young folksingers and to play a major role in the second wave of the revival.

While demonstrating the commercial viability of folk, and spawning imitation, the Weavers also educated, directly and indirectly, by bringing attention to the entire folk universe. Their success was a shining moment for folk.

But Cold War, anti-communist sentiments were intensifying, spearheaded by the ambitious Republican senator from Wisconsin, Joseph McCarthy, and, separately, by the ironically named House Un-American Activities Committee (HUAC), which counted among its members future president Richard Nixon. Having been under investigation by the FBI since his days in the army, Pete Seeger was already vulnerable to the Red Scare. In 1950, the *Red Channels* pamphlet was published by the right-wing journal *Counterattack*, listing the names of 151 musicians, actors, writers, and broadcast journalists and purporting communist manipulation of the entertainment industry. Due to Seeger's long history of leftist affiliations, his name appeared on the list. The Weavers found themselves blacklisted, banned from radio and television, and dropped by Decca Records at the height of their success. Burl Ives, Oscar Brand, Josh White, Harry Belafonte, and Alan Lomax all found themselves listed, as did some of the biggest names in Hollywood. Lomax moved to England, where he stayed in exile for eight years—though he used the time to travel through the United Kingdom and Europe making field recordings of regional folk music. The Weavers' momentum was lost, and they disbanded in 1952. Of course, they were not the only ones to suffer. Numerous careers were crushed or severely impeded due to the blacklist, some never to recover. Even without a formal, federal mandate, in light of the circulation of *Red Channels*, record labels, media outlets, and venues outside of Greenwich Village were skittish to promote folk music and especially the "named" artists, fearing boycotts or other repercussions. Even in Greenwich Village, folksingers proceeded with caution. However, the Sunday folk gatherings in Washington Square Park, started in 1945 with printer-by-trade George Margolis singing leftist folk songs by the fountain, continued to grow and attract younger musicians.

But blacklist or no, and regardless of which way political winds were blowing, folk music had caught ears and hearts in America and abroad. In England, a brief but influential revival of a related musical trend, "skiffle," was beginning. In late 1955, British artist Lonnie Donegan and his Skiffle Group recorded a fast-tempo version of Lead Belly's "Rock Island Line" (backed by the classic blues folk song "John Henry" on the single's B side) which became a massive hit the following year. The record sold a million copies worldwide. More importantly, the skiffle craze, often using homemade instruments and household objects like washboards for percussion and tea chests for bass, was to inspire a generation of young musicians, including fifteen-year-old John Lennon in Liverpool, who formed his skiffle group the Quarrymen in 1956. Skifflemania brought American folk and blues music to the fore in the UK, and within it were the seeds of the so-called British Invasion that was to happen a few years down the line.

Back in the States, while the postwar 1940s had been an era that valued, rewarded, and downright *enforced* conformity, young people began showing signs of defiance. One such indicator in the mid-1950s was the adulation of the brooding, young method actor James Dean. After making only three films expressing teenage angst, confusion, and passion, Dean died tragically in 1955 at the age of twenty-four while speeding in his Porsche 550 Spyder race car, nicknamed "Little Bastard," and became a martyr and symbol of teenage rebellion. At the same time, rock and roll, with its swaggering sense of subversion and unbridled sexuality, went mainstream. Meaning: white audiences discovered it. Big time. Suddenly there was a whole new batch of teenaged music stars. In fact, suddenly there were *teenagers*. The term was devised in 1944, but by 1955 it was an international buzzword and had a look. Previous teenagers were essentially just younger versions of their parents. Now they had their own defining hairstyles, fashions, tastes, attitudes, and distinct record-buying habits. Elvis Presley's singles and debut album for RCA in 1956 ruled the airwaves and stocked the record stores.

Even so, and even though his name appeared on the blacklist, Harry Belafonte's RCA album *Calypso*, in the style of Caribbean folk music, topped the *Billboard* chart for an astonishing thirty-one weeks in 1956, and was the first LP record album of any genre to sell a million copies, giving Belafonte's RCA labelmate Elvis a serious run for his money. That same year, Greenwich Village folk trio the Tarriers recorded a version of "The Banana Boat Song," Belafonte's soon-to-become signature tune that had appeared on his album as "Day-O." With the Tarriers' version climbing the charts, RCA released Belafonte's as a single and both records were pop hits, peaking at number five and number four, respectively, and triggering a short-lived calypso craze. The Tarriers became the first commercially successful folk trio from the Village, and the group remained popular on the scene. But, the Tarriers' only other top-ten hit was a recording of "Cindy, Oh Cindy," with singer Vince Martin, another Village regular.

Inspired by activist actor and concert artist Paul Robeson, Harry Belafonte managed to negotiate a tricky balancing act: being a key figure on the music scene, an activist in the growing civil rights movement, and a celebrated actor and television personality. His career skyrocketed. On stage, Belafonte was a particularly attractive and sensual performer, often with a shirt opened to the waist that caused Village Vanguard owner Max Gordon to write in his memoir, "I still don't like his unveiled navel." Although now—after decades of shirtless rock and hip-hop stars—it sounds prudish, male sensuality, especially *Black* male sensuality, was rare in American mainstream culture in the 1950s. Belafonte was a potent sex symbol as Josh White had been in the previous decade.

Meanwhile, the burgeoning Beat Generation literary movement, with its groundbreaking expressions of sexuality and politics, was picking up steam. The Beats, including Jack Kerouac, Gregory Corso, Allen Ginsberg, and William S. Burroughs, were drawn to Greenwich Village because of the low rents and the small-town vibe. Poetry readings were held in Washington Square Park and in various small clubs and venues popping up around MacDougal Street, such as the Gaslight Poetry Café, which featured folksingers in between poetry sets. Both Ginsberg and Burroughs were fixtures in the Village—Burroughs living at 69 Bedford Street; Ginsberg and his partner Peter Orlovsky at 408 East Tenth Street—and both experienced obscenity trials resulting from their work. Ginsberg's publisher was poet Lawrence Ferlinghetti, whose City Lights Books, based in San Francisco, was the center of the scene there. When Ginsberg's monumental rant against conformity and censorship, *Howl*, was deemed obscene in 1957, Ferlinghetti was arrested. The widely reported trial gave priceless free publicity to Ginsberg and the Beats, making them household names. In the end, Ferlinghetti, supported by the ACLU, won the case, and *Howl* was found to have "redeeming social importance." The book was therefore ruled "not obscene," and City Lights Books was exonerated. A few years later, an attempt to ban Burroughs's *Naked Lunch* would have similar consequences in Boston.

The freewheeling wordplay of the Beats would inspire complex cadences and layered meanings in folk-style songs to come that were unlike the mostly straightforward lyrical style that characterized traditional folk music. Not to mention, the visual appearance and demeanor of the Beats were to significantly impact the style and image of the early 1960s folk and rock scenes. The Beats had a particular affinity for jazz and bebop music; they wrote and performed their works as if they were playing jazz. Jack Kerouac said of his prose, "I want to be considered a jazz poet blowing a long blues in an afternoon jam session on Sunday." And Kerouac forayed into music, as well. With stalwart Greenwich Village composer and multi-instrumentalist David Amram—who was Leonard Bernstein's first in-house composer for the New York Philharmonic, had impressive jazz credentials, and would perform with many folk artists—Kerouac would collaborate in 1959 to create the definitive beatnik statement, *Pull My Daisy*, a short film by Robert Frank and Alfred Leslie. With Amram's jazz score and improvised narration by Kerouac, the black-and-white film depicted bohemian life in vérité style. Amram, who often reminds me that, at age ninety-one, he is still "a lifetime scholarship student of the University of Hangout-ology," went on to compose the scores of two landmark Hollywood films— *Splendor in the Grass* (1961) and *The Manchurian Candidate* (1962)—before returning to the Village to continue his education in hanging out and collaborating. A perennial beatnik and consummate musician, to this day.

As the new decade approached, a new crop of folk artists who had gravitated to the Village were also beginning to emerge. In 1957, Odetta, whom Dr. Martin Luther King would later call the "Queen of American Folk Music," released her first solo album, *Odetta Sings Ballads and Blues*. Dr. King was right—Odetta's presence was positively regal. Being classically trained in opera set Odetta apart from others in the movement and, as such, she was to become one of the most powerful and engaging folksingers of all. Settling in Greenwich Village in the late fifties, Odetta—born Odetta Holmes but adopting her stepfather's surname Felious and using neither professionally—became a major figure on the scene, raising the bar with her vocal dynamism and social activism and profoundly influencing others. In particular Joan Baez and Bob Dylan fell under her spell, as they often attested. Odetta stole the show when she sang the powerful African American slave work song "Water Boy" on Harry Belafonte's *Revlon Revue: Tonight with Belafonte* television special in 1959, a program that, in 1960, earned Belafonte the first Emmy award ever presented to a Black person. To see such an explosive, young Black woman singing of slavery on national television in 1959—later, she would refer to such songs as "liberation songs"—must have been mind-blowing and inspiring. Child prodigy Janis Ian, watching on her parents' black-and-white television set in New Jersey, would later recognize this performance as a major inspiration. Watching the video now, Odetta's presence is still as startling as it was then and surely played a part in folk music's imminent commercial resurgence.

Odetta's debut album had been released by Tradition Records, a label formed by Paddy Clancy of the Clancy Brothers, from Ireland. The handsomely personable and affable Clancys started out as actors but were to become highly influential figures on the Greenwich Village folk scene, aiding and abetting many careers. At first, their focus was primarily on theatrical work and their record label.

Then, in the mid-1950s, Tom, Paddy, and Liam Clancy began organizing late-night folk concerts to help raise money for their production company at the Cherry Lane Theatre, which they were renting to produce Irish plays. Woody Guthrie, Pete Seeger, and folksinger/Appalachian dulcimer player Jean Ritchie, among others, performed at these gatherings. But after the release and success of their own album, demand for the Clancy Brothers themselves grew and, with the addition of singer Tommy Makem, they shifted focus and became a professional singing group in their own right. The traditional Irish songs they performed would inspire some of the most celebrated folk songs of the second wave, and the Aran fishermen's sweaters they wore, sent by their mother during a particularly brutal New York City winter, would spark a minor fashion craze.

The Weavers performed a triumphant, now-legendary reunion concert at Carnegie Hall on Christmas Eve 1955 and inked a deal with the independent Vanguard label as the first nonclassical signing for the label. Seeger, however, wasn't comfortable with the increasingly commercial direction of the group and, in particular, with a cigarette commercial in which they had participated. He quit the band and was replaced by Erik Darling of the Tarriers. That same year, Seeger was called in to testify under oath to HUAC. With wife Toshi and their kids in attendance, Pete refused to answer questions about his political affiliations, or name names, on grounds of the *First* Amendment—freedom of speech. Speaking in a tone that mirrored the letter he had written to the California American Legion about the mistreatment of Japanese Americans during the war, he suggested that it was their activities that were un-American. "I love my country very dearly, and I greatly resent the implication that some of the places that I have sung and some of the people that I have known, and some of my opinions, whether they are religious or philosophical, make me less of an American," Pete told the Committee.

By contrast, when Burl Ives had been called to testify, Seeger's friend and fellow Alma-nacs singer was a cooperative witness who *did* name names, including Seeger's, in 1952. Sadly but understandably, this ended their friendship, though they were to reconcile in later years. While many careers were thwarted, Ives was rewarded. Ives was able to continue to work and flourish in Holly-wood, landing parts as Sam the sheriff in *East of Eden* with James Dean in 1955, as "Big Daddy" in Tennessee Williams's *Cat on a Hot Tin Roof* with Elizabeth Taylor and Paul Newman in 1956, and as Sam the Snowman in the popular NBC television special *Rudolph the Red-Nosed Reindeer* in 1964. *East of Eden*, which launched the career of James Dean, was a monumental film made by Ives's fellow name-namer and genius director Elia Kazan. Kazan himself, who had attended Communist Party meetings at 35 East Twelfth Street, was harshly criticized by friends and colleagues for his anti-communist testimony, which ended the careers of many former fellow actors as well as playwrights. He was never forgiven. "I was snubbed. People I knew well would look at me but not talk," Kazan was quoted as saying in the *New York Times* forty-seven years later, on March 4, 1999.

Pete Seeger was cited for contempt of Congress and sentenced to a year in prison. Even though the conviction was later overturned, the FBI kept up the pressure and, though he was still able to perform in Greenwich Village, elsewhere Seeger was only able to get gigs performing at grade schools and universities. He was blacklisted from national television and major concert halls for seventeen years.

However painful, it can be viewed that ultimately, as with the Allen Ginsberg trial, the punishment had the opposite of the intended effect. The baby boomers for whom Seeger and other folk musicians were allowed to perform during the blacklist grew up to be the folk artists and folk fans of the 1960s. They were raised on the folk songs sung at summer camps and schools. The sound of folk music itself became a statement on the sanctity of the right to free speech and expression. And Pete was revered, presented with the National Medal of Arts, the country's highest official honor for an artist, at the White House in 1994. The once unstoppable anti-communist senator McCarthy suffered a different fate. Powerless and ineffectual after being censured and condemned by the US Senate in December 1954, McCarthy died less than three years later at the age of forty-eight, the result of severe alcoholic hepatitis and morphine addiction. HUAC, renamed the House Committee for Internal Security, would continue, albeit more surreptitiously, until it finally ended on January 14, 1975, after the resignation of disgraced US president and former Committee member Richard M. Nixon.

Today, watching the grainy, black-and-white film footage of Pete Seeger's testimony to the Committee juxtaposed with his musical performances of that time—everyone in the audience, kids, teens, adults, singing along to "This little light of mine, I'm gonna let it shine"—you can see a social imprint being made that would be stamped on history. The "singing labor movement" Pete had strived for with the Almanac Singers was about to be reincarnated into something much larger; it would transcend labor alone to become a singing *social* movement. Even if they were not always to agree with him, Seeger would become a catalyst, father figure, conscience, and moral compass for the new generation of folk musicians that were amassing in Greenwich Village. After a brief intermission, the second act of the folk music revival was about to begin.

Chapter Two

folks

ngers

Paul Clayton, one of the most recorded young folksingers of his time,
photographed on the streets of the Village in 1959.

> *Fortunately art is a community effort—a small but select community living in a spiritualized world endeavoring to interpret the wars and the solitudes of the flesh.*
>
> —Allen Ginsberg

Harry Belafonte's commercial breakthrough

in 1956, followed by Odetta's debut in 1957, proved that—in spite of the Red Scare hysteria—folk music's heart was still beating. Even if Belafonte's upbeat calypso tunes could be heard superficially as pop music, there was often an underlying message. Calypso music originated in Trinidad in the seventeenth century as a method of secret communication between West African slaves. Its modern form started in the mid-nineteenth century, often with lyrics that mocked British slave owners, called out political corruption, and criticized authoritarian colonial rule. Similar types of telegraphed messages of protest in songs would be demonstrated during Brazil's Tropicália (or Tropicalismo) movement in the late 1960s, which blended African and Brazilian rhythms with American and British folk-rock and pop. In a *PBS* *NewsHour* interview with Gwen Ifill in 2011, Belafonte defined his signature song "Day-O" as "a song about struggle, about Black people in a colonized life doing the most grueling work." Through his celebratory dance music and easygoing persona, Belafonte was beating the blacklist.

Folk music works in mysterious ways. While Belafonte had white and Black audiences singing along to work songs of the oppressed, Odetta's approach was different. Her voice, by its pure power and passion, commanded audiences to shut up and listen. Through their music, both artists allowed audiences to reflect on realities and emotions that would never have been addressed by most mainstream popular music at the time. I mean, the fifties were the decade when "How Much Is That Doggie in the Window?" sung by Patti Page could spend *two full months* at number one on the *Billboard* chart.

Though the struggle for equality in America was nothing new, 1955 is often cited as a turning point and the beginning of the modern civil rights movement. That was the year activist Rosa Parks famously demanded her dignity and refused to give up her seat to a white man on a public bus in Montgomery, Alabama. She and three others were arrested, and the outcry to that action led to the rise of Dr. Martin Luther King Jr., as the leader of the Montgomery Improvement Association. The epoch-making 381-day Montgomery Bus Boycott followed. This all happened a year after the Supreme Court of the United States deemed segregation of public schools illegal under *Brown v. Board of Education*. In 1957, the Little Rock Nine, students trying to attend Central High School, were met and stopped at the school door by the Arkansas National Guard. They tried again to attend school two weeks later, but violence erupted. Finally, federal troops had to be called in to protect them. Thanks to television, for the first time, millions of Americans could watch the struggle for civil rights play out in real time. That year, President Dwight D. Eisenhower signed the Civil Rights Act of 1957, the first major piece of civil rights legislation since Reconstruction. As Dr. King continued to lead the movement in the South, Harry Belafonte was to become one of his closest confidantes and his connection to the folksinging community in Greenwich Village. In subsequent years, Dr. King would call on the support of Pete Seeger, Joan Baez, and others as the movement gained momentum.

Rock and Roll

In all its highly image- and performance-driven glory, rock and roll had shone brightly in its original form and served as a rebellious alternative to the sanitized, middle-of-the-road pop that was dominating radio. It was created and played primarily by pioneering Black artists like Sister Rosetta Tharpe, Little Richard, Ike Turner, Chuck Berry, and others. However, the music was soon commercialized, exploited, imitated, and manufactured and by the late fifties was seen by many as music for the very young, ridiculed by television comics and the media at large. Even at the time of his first national television appearances, the "king" himself, hip-swaying Elvis Presley, was easily mocked by talk- and variety-show hosts and became a target for a laugh. According to author and music critic Anthony DeCurtis, to the ever-growing population of college kids, the sexual stage antics of rock and roll "seemed silly and a little bit embarrassing. It was a puritanical time. Being sexy *privately* was okay," DeCurtis suggested, "but it wasn't so cool to be sexy onstage." And anyway, as the decade was winding down, a parade of prefabricated, predominantly white, teenaged pop stars, all named "Bobby" and posing as rock and rollers, had displaced the originators. By 1958, Elvis was safely confined in the US Army, Little Richard had joined the ministry, and, the next year, Chuck Berry was also out of the picture, having been arrested and convicted on charges of violating the Mann Act.

Music historian Elijah Wald told me that "to the folk aficionado, the lines were drawn by 1958: Electric music was for high school kids. Acoustic music was for college kids. College kid music included the baroque, folk, and jazz music on the Elektra and Vanguard record labels and was LP album driven. High school music was electric rock and roll, and singles driven." Marc Myers, music writer for the *Wall Street Journal*, told me, "What jazz and folk share is that both require an intellectual investment." Wald claims, in the starkest terms, that rock and roll—and for that matter most commercial music, including Elvis Presley and even Frank Sinatra—was considered "stupid people music." At least to the discriminating ears of college-age folk fans. Regardless, by the mid-1960s, when a new breed of folk artist raised on rock and roll walked MacDougal Street, folk and rock would majestically merge, and the dispute between the two would be widely settled. It might have happened several years earlier if tragedy had not violently intervened.

Buddy Holly

Among musicians, the reputation of Greenwich Village as a place where "real" music was played had been growing for decades. Over the next few years, as Anthony DeCurtis describes it, the Village would become "a magnet for rock stars. It was artist renewal," allowing their music to be about "doing interesting things and not just about having hits." Others might have been drawn by the Beat poetry scene or the general vibe. One of the musicians who moved to the Village in 1958 was charmingly gangly, twenty-two-year-old, bespectacled rock and roll star Buddy Holly, from Lubbock, Texas. Having had a string of jangly hits with his band, the Crickets, that defined the two electric guitars, bass, and drums rock lineup, Holly was already an inspiration to the new generation of singer-songwriters soon to arrive in Greenwich Village. Phil Ochs, Paul Simon, and Bob Dylan (who would praise Holly in his acceptance lecture upon receiving the Nobel Prize for Literature in 2017) would all deem Holly a hero. "If I was to go back to the dawning of it all, I guess I'd have to start with Buddy Holly," Dylan would say.

Buddy Holly had met María Elena Santiago, from San Juan, Puerto Rico, who was living in New York with her aunt and was working at the reception desk at the Brill Building offices of Holly's music publisher, Peer-Southern Music. Southern Music had been established in 1928 by Ralph Peer who, like Alan Lomax, had scoured the hills and dales of the South in search of musical treasures but did so for commercial record labels, namely, Okeh and Victor, as a talent scout. After María Elena met Holly and the Crickets for lunch one day at Howard Johnson's, Holly asked her aunt, who also worked at Peer-Southern, for permission to take María Elena out for dinner that evening. He made reservations for P.J. Clarke's, a popular showbiz hangout on Third Avenue. They sat at a booth. Suddenly excusing himself, Buddy rushed from the table. When he returned, he was hiding something behind his back. Then, handing María Elena a single red rose he had purchased from a roving vendor, he proposed to her. "Will you marry me?" he asked. "Oh, do you want to get married now, or *after* dinner?" was her teasing reply. Holly insisted that he was serious. It was their very first date. Nonetheless, they were married less than two months later, on August 15, 1958, in Lubbock, where the couple temporarily settled. But a few months after the wedding, the Crickets disbanded, and the young couple relocated to New York. It was the center of the music industry and Holly wanted to be in the middle of it. In October

1958, they moved into apartment 4H in the Brevoort, a newly built, midcentury modern high-rise at 11 Fifth Avenue at West Eighth Street, just a block north of Washington Square Park. From the terrace of their fourth-floor, one-bedroom apartment, they could observe people walking by along Fifth Avenue below—students from NYU and the New School rushing to classes, and shoppers on West Eighth Street. Having been inspired by rock and roll pioneers like Little Richard and Chuck Berry, Holly was an accomplished songwriter whose songs, such as "That'll Be the Day," "Peggy Sue," "Oh, Boy," and "Not Fade Away," masterfully melded country music and rock with rhythm and blues. In preparation for his next solo project, Holly acquired a reel-to-reel tape recorder from his producer/manager, Norman Petty, and began writing and recording demos of new songs now known as the "Apartment Tapes." The recordings, often punctuated with the domestic sounds of dishes being washed or María Elena's muffled phone calls in the background, show an artist fully at ease with his craft.

The Texas Songbird

Twenty-year-old Carolyn Hester, a fellow Texan, had arrived in New York a few years earlier. Inspired by Pete Seeger and harpist, zitherist, and singer of traditional folk songs Susan Reed—whom a teacher had turned her on to when she was in seventh grade—Hester's pure, expressively soaring soprano earned her the sobriquet the "Texas Songbird" and would help define the female folksinger sound of the late 1950s and early 1960s. Her long-haired, fresh-faced, natural beauty also helped establish the archetype. Once in the Village, Hester was able to visit her childhood inspiration, Susan Reed, at Reed's antique shop on Greenwich Avenue near West Twelfth Street, in the West Village, where Reed had retreated after she, like so many others, had been blacklisted as a communist sympathizer. In Texas, Holly had snapped photos and fellow Cricket Jerry Allison performed on sessions for Hester's debut album, *Scarlet Ribbons*, produced by Norman Petty and released in 1957 on Coral Records, the Decca subsidiary that was also home to Holly. Holly and Hester had further collaborations, including a rumored, unreleased Christmas EP that was arranged by Holly. Hester admits to being influenced by Holly and, apparently, he was in turn affected by Hester's song choices.

At a 1958 concert at London's Trocadero Cinema, Holly surprised audiences by opening with a folk song. Hester described the scene: "When showtime came, the lights dimmed and the audience could hear an organ playing as an old pipe organ rose up from below the stage. Buddy was sitting at the organ, I think with his back to the audience, and he was singing 'Black Is the Color of My True Love's Hair,' an old folk song that was on my Coral album. He was there when I was recording it. Buddy influenced me, surely, so for me to know he'd done anything I did just knocked me out!" Back in New York,

Hester would witness Holly transporting Petty's tape machine up Fifth Avenue to the Brevoort, having picked it up from Petty's secretary, Josie Harper, who also lived in the Village. According to Hester, it was Harper who probably recommended the Brevoort apartment to Holly. Carolyn Hester is a bridge between the 1950s and the 1960s, as she collaborated with defining musical icons from each of the two decades, was a unique conduit between them, and had a musical influence on both. Hester's place in music history, and as Greenwich Village royalty, would be set by the time she would turn twenty-five.

Some days, wearing sunglasses, Buddy Holly would carry his Gibson J-200 acoustic guitar through the arch and into the park to play songs incognito, along with other guitarists gathered there. The Sunday folksinging crowd had continued to grow, and on any day during the week, the park was a central meeting place for musicians. After playing one of his new tunes, someone might ask him, "Hey, man, did you write that?" and he might shyly reply, "Why, yes, I did," the person never knowing the guitarist was one of the biggest rock and roll stars of the decade.

In the evenings, María Elena and Buddy would frequent Village music venues and restaurants, in particular the Village Vanguard and the newly opened Village Gate, where they would see jazz and folk artists and hang out with other musicians, such as Phil Everly of the Everly Brothers, and Waylon Jennings, Holly's bassist at the time, who often slept on their couch. Buddy was also interested in attending poetry readings and had a fascination with flamenco guitar playing. He must have loved the musical and artistic diversity that surrounded him in the Village. He went on to write and record several new songs on Petty's tape machine in his apartment, some with a decidedly acoustic folk feel and somewhat melancholy themes, such as "Crying, Waiting, Hoping" and "Learning the Game."

Hearts that are broken and love that's untrue
These go with learning the game

Buddy Holly, ever conscious of commercial musical trends, would have been keenly aware that acoustic, folk-influenced music could be on its way to becoming the next big thing, and certainly would have picked up that sense around the Village. With the Crickets, Holly had recorded primarily in an unadorned, self-contained way, so adopting the intimate sound of folk music in some way would not have been too much of a stretch. His association with Carolyn Hester had already revealed an affinity for acoustic folk. In radio interviews at the time, Holly was predicting rock and roll's demise in "six or seven months" and saying that he would "prefer singing something a little more quiet, anyhow."

Switching between acoustic and electric guitars on his demos, it might be construed that he was experimenting with mixing folk and rock sounds in a way that suited both himself and the coming trend. Regardless, we are left instead with silence.

In January 1959, Buddy Holly embarked on the twenty-four-date Winter Dance Party tour, by bus. The zigzagging tour also included Dion DiMucci and the Belmonts from the Bronx, seventeen-year-old Mexican American rocker Ritchie Valens, and radio DJ turned pop star J. P. Richardson, a.k.a. the "Big Bopper." Ice and snow conditions, freezing temperatures, and a bus that kept breaking down plagued the tour. Holly and some of the entourage had had enough and chartered a small plane to get to Fargo, North Dakota, for their next gig in adjacent Moorhead, Minnesota. Dion and Waylon Jennings stayed on the bus. For nineteen-year-old Dion, the thirty-six-dollar airfare was just too extravagant. "That was the exact amount of the monthly rent my parents argued over all my life. I couldn't justify spending a month's rent on a plane ride," he told the *Wall Street Journal* in 2012. "Plus I could handle the cold. I told Ritchie [Valens], 'You go.'" It was on the night of February 3, 1959, that the tiny Beechcraft 35 plane carrying Holly, Valens, and the Big Bopper lost control and crashed into an Iowa cornfield due to severe, snowy weather, killing all on board.

This was before the days of next-of-kin notification taking place before announcing tragedies in the media. Holly's mother back home in Lubbock reportedly heard the news on radio, screamed, and collapsed. At home in Greenwich Village, hearing the report on television, María Elena was devastated, a widow after only six months of marriage. Having been a few weeks pregnant, she revealed, she miscarried the couple's child shortly thereafter.

In the often cruel tradition of "the show must go on," the tour, now without its three top stars and with Waylon Jennings standing in to sing Buddy Holly's songs, would trudge on for two more weeks. "I remember sitting alone on the bus after and there was Buddy's guitar; I was in shock," Dion recalled in the *Wall Street Journal*. "It took me a long time to process that loss." Six decades later, María Elena still has the single red rose Buddy gave her at P.J. Clarke's the night he proposed. It has never faded away.

Holly's presence in the Village might have gone unnoticed by many at the time, but his influence on the music to follow would be unmistakable. With his death, one era was coming to its end and a new one beginning.

The Mayor of MacDougal Street

"The last years of the 1950s were a great time to be in the Village," wrote Dave Van Ronk in his memoir. Brooklyn-born, Queens-raised, instigator, iconoclast, brilliant vocalist, and all-round devoted music-making man, Van Ronk was to become one of the most fascinating figures on the scene. But when he first arrived from Queens, with a guitar-playing girlfriend, to attend the Sunday afternoon folksinging circles in Washington Square Park, the fifteen-year-old future "Mayor of MacDougal Street" was not so impressed. "Jesus Christ," he muttered as he emerged from the West Fourth Street subway station, "it looks just like fucking Brooklyn."

Van Ronk was a six foot, three inches tall, sturdy, handsome, "mostly Irish" blues aficionado with a hearty laugh and thick, straight, longish hair combed to one side that seemed to constantly fall in front of his face. Although he could sing with a heightened sensitivity and delicately fingerpick his acoustic guitar, there was a roughness about him that might have had something to do with him shipping out twice as a merchant marine. With a facial expression that seemed simultaneously approachable, inquisitively intelligent, and slightly suspicious, he had strong leftist political views and affiliations, knew leftist history, and often claimed to be an anarchist. More specifically, Van Ronk was a Trotskyist, a follower of the Marxist ideology of *permanent revolution* first introduced by Russian Revolution leader Leon Trotsky (1879–1940). Van Ronk vigorously disapproved of the control that the Communist Party had on folksinging and leftist politics during the previous generation. In his opinion, the Almanacs, Guthrie, and the others had weaponized folk as a tool of the movement, obstructing musical growth and putting musicians at risk in the process. At least one of his biggest influences and musical role models, superstar singer/guitarist Josh White, had fallen to the blacklist. Van Ronk believed in keeping music separate from politics. In the recently launched *Caravan*, another mimeographed fanzine founded in 1957, Van Ronk, using the nom de plume Blind Rafferty, wrote of Pete Seeger, "I think the man is really great, in almost every sense of the word, and it saddens me to constantly find myself in the opposition camp every time he ventures an opinion." But also in the article, he praises Seeger's singing, musicality, and his "living" folklore while others were "embalming" it.

Van Ronk was one of the most supportive friends and mentors to other musicians in the Village, especially those who would start arriving in the next few years. This would continue for decades, even as the music changed. More than any of the others, Van Ronk would become a mainstay in the Village as a teacher and tastemaker. But, for all his lovable charm and good deeds, he was no angel; his quick wit and snappy retorts could prove painful, especially when aimed at those whose intentions he questioned. "Folk is a permanent minority form," he admonished in his raspy timbre. "Those who come seeking fame and fortune should be driven from its lists with whips and scorpions."

And he could be critical of fellow musicians whom he admired. "Dave was opinionated!" Tom Paxton told me. "He would shoot you down quietly."

As a teenager, Van Ronk's tastes leaned toward ragtime, traditional jazz, and blues but, like so many others, he was drawn into folk music largely through the Sunday afternoon gatherings in Washington Square Park. And he didn't abandon those multiple genres he loved, instead weaving them into signature arrangements, musicianship, and vocal phrasings that were filled with whispers, outbursts, and silences.

For all his adeptness at transposing piano rags to guitar, perhaps Van Ronk's most endearing and enduring appeal laid in the rapport he had with his audiences, in animated live performances, most famously at the Gaslight Poetry Café. The former coal cellar–turned–gay speakeasy–turned–coffeehouse for Beat poets had opened at 116 MacDougal Street in 1958. Allen Ginsberg (fresh from the national publicity of his obscenity trial), Jack Kerouac (who had recently published *On the Road*), LeRoi Jones (later Amiri Baraka), Gregory Corso, Bob Kaufman, Hugh Romney, and Diane di Prima were among those who read for an often-packed house. Folksingers performed in-between sets, almost as an afterthought. Eventually, the music would win out. But the Beats' presence at the Gaslight, the center of the MacDougal Street/Bleecker Street axis, was like the first footprints on the moon. Van Ronk would have a peculiar and characteristic love/hate relationship with the venue, but it was to become his home base of operations for several years.

In his memoir, Van Ronk reminds us that "'folk' describes a process, not a style," and requires an almost academic study of the music. As such, Van Ronk was a great researcher of songs. In 1953, he, along with other aspirants, discovered a gold mine in experimental filmmaker Harry Smith's eighty-four-song, three-volume, *Anthology of American Folk Music*, on the Folkways label. This collection, unlike the rawer Lomax field recordings, was comprised entirely of commercially released records from Smith's personal collection. They had been recorded from 1926 to 1933 for major and independent labels by artists that included the Carter Family, Blind Lemon Jefferson, and the beloved Mississippi John Hurt, along with lesser-known names. Because the tracks on the three-volume album had been marketed, produced records, they were concisely arranged, edited, and ready to serve. The *Anthology* provided a kind of megastore for folk and blues singers' repertoires; a holy grail that helped fuel the folk revival's revival. Its influence, through word of mouth and live performances of the songs by Village musicians, is inestimable, even if the album didn't sell in huge quantities. Musicians who were there at the time still talk about the Harry Smith *Anthology* as hallowed vinyl, a kind of sacred scripture. Dave Van Ronk, for one, memorized all eighty-four songs in the collection.

One of the strengths of the Sunday gatherings in Washington Square Park was the sheer diversity of folk music that was being played there: bluegrass led by Roger Sprung in one corner, ballads and blues being sung in another. The Tarriers were there, and by 1959, the northern bluegrass group called the Greenbriar Boys would join Sprung's bluegrass circle. There were flamenco guitarists and Irish musicians. It was an egalitarian affair, hard to imagine today, in which professional musicians played music beside amateurs in a public space. During this period, young musicians seemed less restricted by genre, and for many, Van Ronk included, distinctions were blurred and blurry. Is this song folk or blues? Bluegrass or country? And so forth. Most musicians just wanted to play it, not categorize it. On those Sundays, it must have been nearly impossible not to have been influenced by all the different sounds being made in such close proximity around the Washington Square fountain; musical styles, and people, were bound to mix, mingle, and clash. Here Van Ronk encountered guitarist Tom Paley, whose finger-style picking caught Van Ronk's ear and who graciously taught it to him on the spot. As time went on and the gatherings became larger and larger, some residents and certain New York City public officials became irritated—with the music and with the influx of the participants themselves, whom the residents referred to as "beatniks" (ahead of which they added a string of pejoratives). Perhaps residents were opposed to the incessant, out-of-time bongo playing in the park. Or perhaps they resented that the whole thing was rather interracial. Or maybe it was the congregation of gay men that would gather on the west side of the Square in a section known as the "meat rack." Even though Greenwich Village was one of the first neighborhoods in New York that accepted interracial couples and would gradually come to accept a gay and lesbian presence, this was still the 1950s. Regardless, the Sundays in the Square continued to grow. It was all going on at once and, frankly, it must have been a blast.

In 1957, Van Ronk, then twenty-one, met five-foot, eleven-inch, eighteen-year-old, also Brooklyn-born college student Terri Thal, who fell for his "funny, smart, witty, brilliant charm." He in turn was smitten with Thal's unabashed sexiness and outspoken smarts. The two would form a remarkable team, both romantically and professionally. A natural-born organizer with opinions as strong as Dave's, Terri helped him navigate his business matters and would become manager and supporter for Dave and other acts that were beginning to come into the picture. With Dave, Thal was instrumental in talking with owners of so-called basket houses, venues that passed a basket for tips, about formally paying artists. A petition they initiated even made it to the musicians' union, the AF of M, Local 802. The result, however, was unsatisfactory. "Local 802 officials wouldn't even speak with us. They did not consider folksingers musicians and weren't interested in helping us organize the basket houses," Thal recollected.

In 1961, Thal and Van Ronk would move to an apartment at 190 Waverly Place, between West Tenth and Charles Streets, that would become *the* hangout, where musicians would crash on the couch after late-night guitar and banjo jams. As the scene grew, different factions and cliques were formed, but when it started, it was made up of a tight circle of friends.

The title of his third album, *Folksinger*, notwithstanding, Van Ronk considered himself a New York cabaret artist, not a "folksinger." Yet, in 1957–1958 he cofounded, in lieu of Local 802 support, the Folksingers Guild, as a kind of union specifically for folksingers, to protect against unscrupulous club owners. The Guild also served as concert producers, a way to book more folk shows with some of the younger acts on the scene. Even though a few more venues for folk music were beginning to pop up around Greenwich Village, when the Guild began, there were very few *unscrupulous* employers because there were very few employers at all. The Guild arrived to the party just a little too early. The folk boom was yet to happen and, by 1958, soon after Van Ronk's return from a trip gigging in California, the Guild petered out.

Although things were about to change, the scarcity of actual folk venues was the reason Van Ronk was gigging in California. By "actual," I mean places where musicians *actually* got paid *actual* money. As much as this scene was not about making money, folks did need to make at least some. Van Ronk had previously hitchhiked to Chicago in a failed attempt to perform at the Gate of Horn, a one-hundred-seat venue in the basement of the Rice Hotel, where he experienced a deflating audition for co-owner and artist manager Albert Grossman. "Cryptic, arrogant, condescending, shrewd, underhanded, cutthroat, even diabolical to some people" is how author Bob Spitz describes Grossman in his 1989 book *Dylan: A Biography*. Obviously, with credentials like that, Grossman was to become one of the most powerful players on the scene.

Chicago, Cambridge, and San Francisco
The Gate of Horn had opened in 1956 and quickly became Chicago's premier folk palace. So much so that when Odetta released her second album for the Clancy Brothers' Tradition label in 1957, she named it *At the Gate of Horn* even though it was not even recorded there. Odetta was, however, a regular performer at the venue and was one of the artists managed by Grossman. As was folksinging,

twelve-string guitarist and banjo player Bob Gibson, who had been inspired by Pete Seeger and would, in turn, influence Phil Ochs, Bob Dylan, and Peter, Paul and Mary, among others, with his songwriting and presentation.

Bob Gibson was another artist whose career had been severely damaged by the House Un-American Activities Committee (HUAC). As a former member of American Youth for Democracy, he was called in for questioning and, although he was not cited for contempt as Seeger was, he was restricted from appearing on television and radio, and his records received virtually no airplay. Gibson was relegated to performing in smaller clubs and subsequently avoided political material. Regardless, his influence on other musicians was substantial. "Gibson had a particular talent for boiling down multi-versed folk songs into more concise, three-minute pieces and, like Seeger, a knack for getting the audiences to sing along," Gibson friend and fan John Heller told me. While firmly rooted in the folk vein, Gibson's own songs made use of unusual chord progressions and modulations that allowed for atypical melody structures. According to Heller, "his use of diminished major ninth and other jazz chords were unheard of in folk." This aspect in particular, of a more sophisticated songwriting style, would inspire Phil Ochs, who later cowrote with Gibson. More ostentatious than others on the folk scene, with a tendency toward the kind of showmanship that might have peeved purists, his musicianship was undeniable and admired, and his humorous material, often cowritten by poet and *Playboy* magazine cartoonist Shel Silverstein, put him in his own unique category. With Silverstein alone, he would cowrite over two hundred songs. Gibson's early albums are intriguing for their mix of traditional folk songs juxtaposed with his own quirky compositions. This was at a time when folksingers writing their own songs was still largely a rarity, although in a few years it would become the norm. In Greenwich Village, when Tarriers manager Art D'Lugoff opened the Village Gate at the corner of Bleecker and Thompson Streets in 1958, Bob Gibson and his performing partner Hamilton Camp became regulars there.

A folk scene was also growing in Cambridge, Massachusetts's Harvard Square, centered around Club 47, a jazz venue which opened in 1958. Seventeen-year-old Boston University student Joan Baez, knowing full well it was a long shot for a *folksinger* to get a gig in a jazz club, auditioned and was booked for a Sunday night. According to Baez's autobiography, on that first night, she performed for an audience of eight: her parents, her sister Mimi, her boyfriend, and a few friends. Regardless, the venue took a risk and began booking folk music once a week, and it became the focal point of the Harvard Square folk scene. It is still operating today, as Club Passim, and still a favorite.

Out of the box, Baez was a gifted vocalist with the facility to sing with restraint while embracing each syllable with profound power, sensitivity, and emotional weight, as if the sound was being emitted from her very soul itself. When she arrived on the scene, her voice sounded almost inevitable, a kind of culmination, containing within it echoes of her influences, combining elements of Cynthia Gooding, Carolyn Hester, and Odetta. It was a sound ringing with the kind of sincerity that young people were looking for; one that mirrored their own feelings. Early black-and-white photos of Baez in Harvard Square show her strumming her guitar, barefoot, with long hair, bangs, and a beatific smile, flanked by two male, guitar-wielding comrades. But the image she projected on stage and that was soon to be projected around the world was of the singular, serious, almost saintly, and beautiful young woman standing alone at the microphone, straight dark hair hanging down, and accompanying herself on guitar, as if in prayer. The sanctified image would not have been alien to Baez. Her grandfather was a Methodist minister in Mexico and had founded the First Spanish Methodist Church in New York. Her father, a physicist and inventor of the X-ray reflection microscope who later worked for the United Nations, and mother, the daughter of an Episcopalian priest, had become Quakers. Baez was raised in a household of pacifism and humanitarianism.

This was an era when a female performer was expected to conform to a kind of sexualized stereotype that Baez resisted. Yet both men and women found her appealing. Her star was to rise quickly. In May 1959, her first album was recorded, a trio project entitled *Folksingers 'Round Harvard Square*. Then, on July 11, 1959, Bob Gibson would help give Joan Baez her first national exposure when he introduced her onstage during his set at the very first Newport Folk Festival, produced by jazz pianist and impresario George Wein, founder of the Jazz Festival in Newport, who brought Albert Grossman on board to help book the talent. Pete Seeger was also recruited to advise for the festival.

In San Francisco's North Beach area, there were two roughly eighty-seat basement clubs, the Purple Onion and the hungry i, where the newly formed Kingston Trio held court. The group's name was a reference to Kingston, Jamaica, inspired by the recent calypso craze, although they were clearly not Jamaican. Influenced by the Weavers but with a far more pop sensibility and collegiate appearance, the Kingston Trio were topping the national charts in November 1958 with their acoustic hit "Tom Dooley." They would be credited, at least by their record label, Capitol Records, with starting the new folk craze. Truth is, the widespread commercial exposure and the Kingston Trio's breezy harmonies and song choices did serve for many as an easy entrée into folk music. Bruce Eder, writing in *AllMusic Guide*, asserts, "On a purely commercial level, from 1957 until 1963, the Kingston Trio were the most vital and popular folk group in the world, and folk music was sufficiently popular as to make that a significant statement." One major aspect of their debut album that stood out was that, unlike the Weavers, whose songs and arrangements they covered, on the Kingston Trio's hits, their basic acoustic sound was not embellished by secondary orchestral arrangements and was therefore closer to the sound of their live performances.

Like the Weavers, Belafonte, Bob Gibson, and the Tarriers, the Kingston Trio covered traditional and calypso-flavored folk songs. However, in folk circles, especially in the Village, they were roundly condemned for their frivolous approach to performing the songs in a way that was seen, by some, as disrespectful. The originator of the arrangement they used for "Tom Dooley," Appalachian banjoist Frank Proffitt, claims he was literally *sickened* when seeing the Trio perform the song on television. "I began to feel sorty sick," he wrote, "like I'd lost a loved one." But that reaction was a bit excessive. Today, viewing the 1958 footage of the Kingston Trio on the *Milton Berle Show* reveals a rather subtle performance. About the only thing you could really fault them for is their having worn matching striped shirts better suited for the Beach Boys who, as Kingston Trio fans, would co-opt the look a few years later. But back then, Seeger ally Irwin Silber, editor of *People's Songs* and *Sing Out!*, referred to the trio's "sallow slickness" in his editorials. With their frat boy crew cuts, those shirts, and their shamelessly commercial appeal, they represented the exact opposite of Dave Van Ronk's dictum for folksingers. And they were widely discredited by the folk community in Greenwich Village, Van Ronk included, for not fully crediting their sources. This transgression would land them in court more than once. Still, the list of major folk, rock, and pop artists who cite the Kingston Trio as an influence is nothing short of impressive. Even Bob Dylan gives them high marks in *Chronicles*, writing, "I liked the Kingston Trio. Even though their style was polished and collegiate, I liked most of their stuff anyway." Selling tons of records, they were, in retrospect, a kind of self-contained, three-man folk revival in themselves. Another trio, the Limeliters, formed by Lou Gottlieb, an arranger for the Kingston Trio, also had commercial success. Literally. They appeared in commercials for Coca-Cola and, in a move reminiscent of the reason Pete Seeger had quit the Weavers, L&M cigarettes.

Folklore versus Fakelore

At the same time in 1958, in the Village, a group formed that might be seen as the anti–Kingston Trio. The New Lost City Ramblers were a trio of folk purists that included Tom Paley, the guitarist who had impressed and taught Van Ronk in Washington Square, along with John Cohen and Mike Seeger, Pete's younger half brother. The New Lost City Ramblers specialized in performing songs from the 1920s and '30s that they learned from old 78 rpm records, the Harry Smith *Anthology* set, and Alan Lomax's Library of Congress recordings, to which Mike Seeger had unique access via his parents. Perhaps more than the others on the scene, the Ramblers were absolutely dedicated not only to performing and recording faithful renditions of these songs but also to teaching about the music, crediting the songwriters, and collaborating with the original artists themselves in concert, such as Mother Maybelle Carter, of the Carter Family, and Elizabeth Cotten, the composer of the classic "Freight Train." Cotten had actually worked as a domestic for the Seegers. "Michael and (sister) Peggy would say, 'You sit here and play "Freight Train," and we'll do your work!'" recounted Cotten in a Ramblers documentary. The New Lost City Ramblers were inarguably devoted pupils and eager educators of folklore.

Additionally, it almost appears as if the Ramblers made a conscious effort to avoid the pitfalls that had spoiled things for the Weavers, in particular for Mike Seeger's older brother. The group focused on the purity of the music, not the passion of the politics, and they seemed to lack any obvious commercial aspirations whatsoever. When they went on the road, they toured in a Volkswagen Beetle, all three members of the group crammed in with their instruments and a battery-operated, reel-to-reel tape machine to listen to recordings and study the music they loved as they traveled.

But for all their earnest, good intentions, the New Lost City Ramblers' authenticity was not immune to scrutiny in folklore circles either. For some, there was a fine line between folklore and *fakelore*. All three founders of the Ramblers were born in New York City and had little if any real contact with the southern rural communities whose music they played, so their propensity for singing with affected southern accents could be considered slightly disingenuous by some. Ed Cray, writing in the journal *Western Folklore*, said he was "perplexed as to how folklorists would characterize this group of 'citybillies,' who play primarily 'hillbilly music' whose origins are most clearly 'folk.'" But he added, "Whatever they may be, they remain good copies of a vigorous tradition." According to author Ray Allen in his 2010 book *In Pursuit of Authenticity: The New Lost City Ramblers and the Postwar Folk Music Revival*, during the height of the commercial folk boom, the Ramblers were kept at arm's length by professional folklorists, even though they were at the forefront of the "purist" or "ethnic" strain of the revival. Some folklore scholars considered the Ramblers to be "imitators," though others, as in a 1971 *Journal of American Folklore* article, credited them in retrospect with being "the first performing group in the urban folk scene to specialize in the material of traditional rural origins."

One could say that what the Ramblers were presenting was a reenactment of the music, accents included, of a rural South that was all but gone and, at the time they arrived on the scene, they were widely loved and appreciated in the Village for keeping it real. Or at least close to real. Their albums on the Folkways label made their way to Dylan, who would write in *Chronicles*, "Everything about them appealed to me—their style, their singing, their sound." And at that first Newport Folk Festival, the New Lost City Ramblers were on the bill, too . . . along with the Kingston Trio.

The last year of the 1950s was as much a year of beginnings as it was an ending. With the inclusion of Alaska and Hawaii, 1959 was the first year that the United States incorporated fifty states. Throughout the year, numerous rocket launches, a lunar probe, Explorer satellites, two monkeys shot into space, and NASA's announcement of the first human astronauts, the Mercury 7, meant the space race was in full effect. And the Cuban Revolution, spearheaded by young activist/lawyer Fidel Castro in 1953, ended on New Year's Day of 1959 when it ultimately overthrew the US-supported Cuban dictator Batista. As Castro, a socialist Marxist-Leninist, aligned himself more and more with the Communist Party and the Soviet Union, the Cold War would escalate to precarious heights, sparking renewed fears of communism and giving the next US president an early and nearly heart-stopping test of leadership.

Meanwhile, the popularity of folk music continued to grow. It was still mostly traditional folk music being played by musicians to small audiences in coffeehouses, with maybe an occasional original song thrown in to test the waters. But the novelty of the music's antiquity couldn't last. Soon, new songs with new messages would be needed. When Pete Seeger was asked what had motivated him to write songs, he replied, "There were things that needed to be said, and I couldn't find a song that said them."

More music venues had begun to open in the Village. By the late 1950s, the midnight folk concerts at the Cherry Lane Theatre, which were put together by labor organizer Lou Gordon, moved to Circle in the Square at 5 Sheridan Square and featured musicians like Jean Ritchie, Oscar Brand, Cynthia Gooding, Sonny Terry, Brownie McGhee, Theo Bikel, Ed McCurdy, Leon Bibb, various Clancy brothers, and Reverend Gary Davis. Midnight concerts were also staged at the Actor's Playhouse on Seventh Avenue at Sheridan Square. But mostly, venues centered around the tiny MacDougal Street/Bleecker Street axis. At the Gaslight, the preferred venue at the time, clapping after a performance had been modified to finger-snapping, to avoid complaints from upstairs tenants to whose apartments the noise would travel via the air shaft. The snapping would be caricatured as a "beatnik thing," but it was actually born of necessity, to prevent eviction. Across the street from the Gaslight were the Commons and Café Wha?, two more coffeehouses. Liquor licenses were expensive and hard to come by unless you had "connections," so coffee was the only game in town. And, apparently, it was not very good. Dave Van Ronk, in his book, refers to the coffee being sold at the venues as "slop" and the Gaslight's as "the worst coffee I have ever encountered." Around the corner, on Third Street, was the Café Bizarre, which had opened in 1957 and was the very first Village coffeehouse to present folk music properly, that is, with a suitable stage, sound system, and lights. Odetta had performed there on opening night, with Dave Van Ronk, Luke Faust, and other folk artists on the bill. But its cheesy, pre-Goth, haunted house decor and theatrics, and sawdust-covered floors were a turnoff to some. The larger, 450-seat Village Gate, where Pete Seeger performed on opening night and where he would record his first post-Weavers live solo album for Columbia Records, was just a couple of blocks away, with ground floor and basement spaces at 160 Bleecker, though it was primarily a jazz room where Miles Davis, Charles Mingus, Nina Simone, and countless others would play legendary sets. Café Bohemia, at 15 Barrow Street, was another mythmaking room for jazz in the Village, but it lasted only from 1955 to 1960. No folk music to be heard there.

In the middle of MacDougal Street, Izzy Young's Folklore Center was a hangout by day or evening, filled with books, records, and musicians. Carolyn Hester, Jean Ritchie, Cynthia Gooding, and Happy Traum were all in attendance at the Folklore Center's gala grand opening in 1957. It was just a tiny shop on a densely packed block, with narrow buildings and businesses stacked one atop the other. Yet it's nearly impossible to overstate the crucial role that Young and the Folklore Center would play in the evolution of the second wave of the folk revival. In his book *Chronicles, Volume One*, Bob Dylan would refer to the Folklore Center as "the citadel of Americana folk music." Folks would learn and play songs there, meet there, and perform in the back room. Happy Traum would write, "Izzy kept voluminous journals in his small, cramped handwriting, which kept track of all the goings-on of our little community: Which musician is recording for which label; where he or she is touring; who's getting married or having children; who has 'sold out' and went commercial; whether or not he liked a given recording, performance, or personality. Minutia in the minuscule world of folk music in New York City at that period of time." Izzy provided such a home for musicians that, according to Dave Van Ronk's memoir, some even had their mail delivered there.

There were a bunch of small, underground cafés sprinkled around and, of course, Washington Square in the center of everything. Then as now, the numerous Italian restaurants and cafés in the Village—such as Café Reggio where the first cappuccino in America was served, Le Figaro Café, and the more recent La Lanterna—along with the Romanesque architecture with mosaic-tiled lobbies—were all reminders of the Village's predominantly Italian heritage. Over in the West Village, the White Horse Tavern, which opened in 1880 at 567 Hudson Street, a former Irish longshoremen's bar—turned—literary hangout, was, and still is, a favorite destination. It's where Welsh poet and writer Dylan Thomas was said to have drunk himself to death in 1953. In the late fifties and early sixties, the Clancy Brothers and Tommy Makem were known to perform rousing Irish rebel and drinking songs there. A visit to the back room at the White Horse today, with its wood-paneled walls, tin ceiling, and old photographs, brings it all back home. Near the center of the Village—on Sixth Avenue at the intersection of Greenwich Avenue and West Tenth Street, adjacent to the old Jefferson Market Courthouse, with its iconic, Victorian Gothic clock tower, and a few steps from the old Almanac House—was the massive art deco structure of the New York Women's House of Detention. Until it was finally demolished in 1973 to make way for the current, formal Jefferson Market Garden, the prison was apparently a rowdy scene. "The women would stand at the windows, and their boyfriends on the sidewalk down below would yell up to them," Carolyn Hester recalled. Shouts of "Honey, bring me some cigarettes!" and catcalls to passersby were common sounds on the block in the 1960s. The Courthouse itself would be repurposed as a branch of the New York Public Library in 1967. These venues and locations, streets, and buildings were just as much characters in the unfolding drama as the people who performed, mingled, worked, and lived within them.

Before long, this bohemian theme park would begin to draw larger numbers of young people, crowding the sidewalks and spilling over into MacDougal Street itself. The term "folknik" began popping up in the press. Already people had started walking around with guitars, rarely in cases, ready to play and sing at any given moment. Some might be rowdy; some might be high. Everywhere, there was music, floating like fine, melodious mists out of every open window and every open door. A number of residents, mostly Italian immigrants who had gotten used to the less-diverse, pre-folknik Village that was reminiscent of their families' villages in the old country, were quick to voice their disapproval, in Italian and Sicilian.

And yet, "it truly was a Village. Everybody knew everybody," recalled Anthony DeCurtis, who grew up there in the four-story, red-brick building at 347 Bleecker Street, on the corner of Bleecker and West Tenth Streets. And for the most part, all coexisted more or less peacefully. While not always embraced, the music scene that was beginning to invade the neighborhood was, at the very least, tolerated. But there was also the shadow of the Mob, which had a grip on many of the businesses, and corrupt cops who benefited from organized crime. And the occasional roving, thuggish street gang, exuding a territorial threat of violence. After all, even though the Village had been proclaimed a "free and independent republic" by Duchamp and those drunken Dadaists in 1917, it was still part of the same New York City where *West Side Story* was set. There were some city officials who wanted to suppress the Sunday gatherings in Washington Square and others who wanted to simply obliterate the Village altogether. Those were just two of the battles to be fought in the new decade. In the meantime, newcomers brandishing guitars continued to arrive in ever greater numbers, stages were prepared, and the 1950s were nearing their end.

Chapter Three

19

> *Freedom to think. Freedom to express yourself.*
> *That was the general idea: "No one's gonna tell me what to do."*
> — **Happy Traum**

MUSIC+REVOLUTION • PAGE 61

Gerde's was one of the dozens of Italian restaurants in the Village,

housed in a slightly sooty six-story brownstone built in 1889 on the northeast corner of West Fourth and Mercer Streets, with neon beer signs in the windows. It was owned by Mike Porco, a jovial immigrant from sunny Calabria (at the southernmost tip of Italy), along with his brother John and cousin Joe Bastone. The Porcos and Bastone had purchased Gerde's Italian Restaurant in 1952 but were forced to relocate a few years later from its original location on West Third Street. The block was scheduled for demolition to make room for one of power-crazed New York City planning commissioner Robert Moses's high-rise, Title 1 housing projects; a building complex that is now part of the NYU campus known as University Village and Silver Towers. Foreshadowing the devastation his construction of the Cross Bronx Expressway would cause to a large swath of the Bronx a few years later, Moses's destruction of those blocks to the southeast of Washington Square displaced scores of families and businesses, including many faithful customers of Gerde's. The disruption was severe. It is a testament to the willpower of Greenwich Village residents that further attempts to scar the neighborhood were to be met with fierce resistance.

Although lunchtime at the new location still drew NYU college students and workers from the nearly three hundred hat-making loft factories that were then operating in the Village, such as the Ackerman Cap Company on Waverly Place, business was down at the new location of Gerde's. Looking for ways to build it back up and to bring in a dinner crowd, Porco would occasionally hire an ambient pianist or roving musician to add atmosphere. But as there was no stage or sound system, and with the constant, friendly chatter of patrons, it was far from a serious listening room. Even so, Tom Prendergast, a Gerde's regular who worked in advertising, apparently thought it would be a good venue for folk music. He talked to his friend Izzy Young at the Folklore Center, who agreed it sounded like a good idea.

Nothing about this plan would have been out of the ordinary for Izzy Young, who had witnessed the folk scene having to find or create its own venues for the past two decades, from square dances in high schools to the hootenannies in the Almanac House basement to the impromptu performances in the back room of his own Folklore Center. A neighborhood Italian bar/restaurant on

West Fourth Street? Why not? Young had long wanted a proper showcase for folk music in the Village, especially now with all the new talent that was continually arriving, and this could be it.

When Young and Prendergast arrived at Gerde's to present the idea to Mike Porco on that November afternoon, Porco greeted them in his usual friendly manner. Over a bottle of beer (yes, Gerde's had a liquor license, making it the first folk venue to serve alcohol in the Village), they asked if Porco would be interested in presenting folk music at Gerde's, essentially remaking it into a folk club. Hmmm. Porco asked them to first tell him what they meant by "folk music." Descriptions followed, but he wasn't getting it. When Young and Prendergast invoked the names of Pete Seeger and Burl Ives, Porco finally understood. "Oh," he replied, "those are people . . . who try to deliver messages through their songs." Bingo.

The deal was simple: Prendergast and Young would be responsible for publicity and would pay the musicians from the money collected at the door. Porco would keep all his proceeds from the sale of food and drinks. That was it. No contract, no written agreement of any kind. And just like that, right after Thanksgiving Day 1959, with only a handshake, Gerde's Folk City was born.

Well, not *exactly* Folk City. The name first chosen for the venue was the Fifth Peg, a reference to the lone tuning peg on the neck of a five-string banjo, a name suggested to Young by the Tarriers' and the Weavers' banjo player, Erik Darling. Compared to the other four pegs grouped at the top in the headpiece of the instrument, the fifth peg is the odd one out, a little bit out of the way, doing its own thing. The shorter, fifth string that it tunes is what makes the banjo unique, giving it its signature drone. And the fifth peg, protruding from the left side of the neck, is the instrument's only asymmetrical element. For these reasons, it's a rather logical name for the new venue: slightly apart from the MacDougal Street/Bleecker Street axis, unique, and decidedly to the left of center. Whether Young and Prendergast considered this interpretation of the name is not known. In fact, the name may have already existed elsewhere. What is for sure is that the following year, it was co-opted by a coffeehouse in the growing folk community of Yorkville in Toronto, Canada, followed by another one in Chicago's Lincoln Park. The Fifth Peg at Gerde's was to only last roughly five months before the name would be superseded by the venue's more familiar moniker. During December '59, to prepare for its official opening, a simple sound system and lights were installed, and a tiny stage was built that could hold maybe three musicians.

Although Porco seemingly needed a crash course in what folk music was, he was unquestionably more familiar with jazz and gospel artists. "Joe Bastone's father owned the Club 845 Dance Hall at 845 Prospect Avenue in the Bronx," Porco's grandson Bob Porco told me. "Jazz artists like Dizzy Gillespie, Louis Armstrong, and Nancy Wilson performed there, and Mike met Mahalia Jackson and others who performed or came to shows there. Because he would hang out at Club 845, Mike knew jazz."

Opening night of the Fifth Peg was on January 26, 1960, and featured Brother John Sellers, a dynamic, soulful performer and Mahalia Jackson protégé who combined gospel, jazz, and blues. Sharing the bill was the popular singer-songwriter Ed McCurdy, who had made his mark as a folk-singer at the Village Vanguard in 1950. McCurdy had written the anti-war folk standard "Last Night I Had the Strangest Dream" that was immediately covered by the Weavers and has been covered by numerous others since. The evening was an unqualified success.

The Fifth Peg provided the first rumblings of a seismic shift that the Greenwich Village folk scene had been waiting for. Izzy Young booked all the A-list performers: Brownie McGhee and Sonny Terry, Tommy Makem and the Clancy Brothers, Reverend Gary Davis and Cisco Houston, the Tarriers, Dave Van Ronk, and Ramblin' Jack Elliot, among others. Business was brisk, if inconsistent, and if the slow nights were worrisome, the nights with packed houses provided further evidence that folk music was, potentially, a commercial force to be reckoned with. By February 1960, Mike Porco decided to turn his traditionally slow Monday nights, on which they had not been booking music at all, into "amateur nights." According to his 1986 book *No Direction Home*, it was *New York Times* music critic Robert Shelton, a regular on the Village scene and friendly with the musicians, who suggested Porco more appropriately call the evenings "hootenannies." Though it started slowly, within a few weeks the Monday night "hoots" were a massive success, and the format became an instant favorite of musicians and fans. Established artists would use the three-song, on-and-off sets to try out new material, and newcomers would use the platform to be seen, perhaps for the first time. All performed for free. Hovering around in the venue would be record label scouts and booking agents, looking for new talent to sign. And, of course, journalists like Shelton would be there, pen in hand, ready to write about a star in the making. Soon, nearly all of the Village venues would have hootenanny nights.

But as the Monday nights were free events with no cover charge, their success excluded Izzy Young and Tom Prendergast entirely. Porco, of course, was still raking it in at the bar nightly, so for him it was a win-win. For Young, who had barely been able to pay musicians at the modest admission charge of $1.50, the whole enterprise was beginning to be a lose-lose. Izzy asked for a bigger cut. That's when tensions began to mount, culminating in Mike Porco asking Young and Prendergast to take a leave of absence. On May 1, 1960, they decided to pull out completely.

For the month of May 1960, there were no shows advertised at Gerde's, except for one booked by Porco that featured singer Vince Martin, famous for his 1956 hit recorded with the Tarriers, "Cindy, Oh Cindy." Martin, an Italian American with matinee idol looks and a bona fide pop hit under his belt, was not considered a folksinger but was one of the early artists to explore the possibilities of merging folk and rock. He would later collaborate with Fred Neil, one of the linchpins of the MacDougal Street circuit.

Taking the reins, Porco hired aspiring manager Charlie Rothschild to handle talent booking, and the two began making plans to rebrand and officially reopen Gerde's. Suffice to say, the split with Young was not amicable and, according to Shelton, on his next visit to the Folklore Center for a chat, Rothschild unceremoniously received a punch in the face from the bespectacled Izzy Young. On May 12, 1960, Young took out an ad in the Village Voice to announce his departure from the Fifth Peg. "I FEEL BAD," he wrote, declaring, "everything I do turns out to be successful—artistically only. Now THE FIFTH PEG is added to the list." In the neighborhood, sides were taken as Van Ronk and others loyal to Young and grateful for the Folklore Center briefly kept their distance from Gerde's. Cracks were beginning to show in the heretofore harmonious folk brotherhood of Greenwich Village.

The evening of June 1, 1960, was the highly anticipated launch of the newly renamed Gerde's Folk City, a name that seemed to hit the nail on the head. The opening night show featured Carolyn Hester and was emceed by folksinger-poet Logan English, who had recorded albums for the Folkways and Riverside labels. Originally from Kentucky and with a master's degree from the Yale School of Drama, English, like Hester, the Clancy Brothers, Odetta, and others, had been pursuing an acting career when he began singing folk songs in Greenwich Village clubs. English was to become one of the regular emcees at Folk City. The evening was a triumph, and Gerde's Folk City rose to become the preeminent folk venue in the country.

Carolyn Hester, then twenty-three, had been continually building a reputation—not just in the Village but in Washington, DC, and in Cambridge, Massachusetts, where Joan Baez had gone to see her perform at Club 57. Hester was now well established on the scene, preparing to sign with the Clancy Brothers' Tradition label. While her first album had a formal charm reminiscent of Cynthia Gooding, her second album, for Tradition, would capture a more unrestrained and free-sounding performance on which she starkly and effectively accompanied herself on guitar. Hearing her sing at Gerde's, Dave Van Ronk wrote in his memoir that he considered Hester "electrifying" and was knocked out by her "set of pipes,"

adding, "Beauty, talent, charm—she had it all." Van Ronk's coauthor Elijah Wald told me, "Carolyn Hester was the first person who sailed into the Greenwich Village scene who was noticeably better than the rest." Robert Shelton also took notice, writing in the *New York Times* that "her voice's range and power are astounding." Shelton was so roused that he asked Hester out, ostensibly to talk about her music career. After dinner, they walked over to the White Horse Tavern, where Paddy Clancy and others were holding court, singing Irish rebel songs at the bar. Alongside Clancy was a striking, dark-haired, young man of Irish-Cuban descent whom Shelton would introduce as Richard Fariña, an aspiring young writer. Fariña's personal magnetism captivated Hester. "I was immediately drawn to him," she recounted. "He said he would come see me the next time I was singing in town." And, sure enough, Fariña was there on that opening night of Folk City and was as mesmerized by Carolyn—and the effect she had on the audience—as she had been charmed by his wit and intelligence at their first meeting at the White Horse. Fariña asked Hester out for dinner, where he further dazzled her with his intensity and romantic overtures. Moving even quicker than Buddy Holly and María Elena, they were married eighteen days later and celebrated with a reception at Robert Shelton's apartment on Waverly Place in the Village. They were a power couple: Hester as the most promising folksinging star and Fariña as . . . well, a brilliant hustler, bursting with ideas. But it would be a rocky road.

For all the sobriety of its nineteenth-century exterior, once inside, Gerde's Folk City was a festive affair, the walls decorated with recent LP album jackets of the folk and blues artists who performed there, with more festooning the ceiling like clotheslines of album covers, and there were garlands around the stage area. On the tables were the familiar, standard-issue red-and-white-checked tablecloths of all Italian restaurants, and from high in the wall to the left of the bar stared the blank, gray screen of a midcentury, black-and-white television set. Photos from the era show an interesting mix of audience members: students in casual attire, men in suits and ties—some with dark glasses—some couples on dates, all in a wide range of ages. There was a dividing wall or partition, about four to four and a half feet high, that separated the bar area from the tables, where people were seated around the low stage for performances. People standing in the bar area could lean on the partition and get a good view of the performers over the seated audience's heads. There was a stairway that led down to the basement, where musicians would practice, jam, or socialize, waiting to go on. Others would watch, listen, drink, and schmooze at the bar, where they would sometimes get loud, much to the annoyance of the performers on stage. "It could be horrendous," folksinger Tom Paxton would later say. "On something like a hoot night, when there were a lot of people in there and the bar part was crowded, the people at the bar to some extent felt removed from the performing space. They would talk and carry on, kind of oblivious to what was happening on the stage. This could be really hard for a performer. A lot of distracting noise going on."

As Gerde's became more and more popular, even the loading dock by its side entrance on Mercer Street became a hangout for socializing and impromptu jam sessions. The venue's legal capacity was exactly the same as the Gaslight's, at 110 people, both venues pushing it to 130 at times. Just large enough to create the feeling of an "event" and small enough to provide the intimacy that was a hallmark of the Village coffeehouse scene. But at Gerde's, unlike at the basket houses, actual fees were paid to performers, and the venue was not in a basement or a grimy, former coal cellar. It's as if folk music had finally emerged from the underground. Gerde's Folk City gave Greenwich Village the proper venue it had been waiting for and, even though he was no longer directly involved with the venue, Izzy Young's mission to have a showplace for folk music in the Village had been accomplished.

Through 1961, Dave Van Ronk—having reconciled with Porco—along with Terri Thal, Logan English, and Robert Shelton would come to serve as an unofficial brain trust for Mike Porco, guiding and influencing his bookings at Gerde's. By 1962, Mike would be booking on his own. Robert Shelton, in his book, was sometimes hard on Porco, going so far as to write, probably accurately, that Porco "barely knew a ballad song from a bologna sausage," and ridiculing Porco's thick Italian accent and poor use of the English language. But it is to Mike Porco's enduring credit that he was able to keep his business not only going but flourishing, serving the folk music community in New York through the next two decades, long after the folk boom had faded like the end of a scratchy side two of a Folkways album. To this day, artists who played at Gerde's always seem to have good things to say about Mike Porco. And although the erudite *New York Times* folk critic and the humble Calabrian immigrant may have had very little in common, their names appear in all the history books about the era, side by side.

I wasn't there, but in my mind's eye, I picture the Greenwich Village of 1960 in black-and-white. The brick buildings, the sidewalks, the cobblestone streets—all monochromatic. I imagine MacDougal Street at night resembling a Polaroid picture in motion: stark, grainy, high-contrast, like a scene in a film noir movie, filled with reflections and long shadows and the muted echoes of finger-style acoustic guitar picking as its soundtrack. The truth is, of course, not so black-and-white. Then as now, the Village was messy, more than a bit cacophonous, vivid with color, with garish neon and painted signs on glass storefronts. There were smells—beer, cappuccino, occasional whiffs of marijuana. And there were characters, with personalities just as colorful as the streets and storefronts. And some were just as smelly. Then as now, against the backdrop of old buildings was a beautiful, young population of inhabitants and frequenters who gathered in coffeehouses, cramped apartments, bars, the streets, and Washington Square Park. For them, the Village was novel in its own antiquity; far from the freshly mowed suburbias many had left behind—an escape from predictability and modern mediocrity. The Village was . . . authentic. Its oldness was new. For all its history, the Village was new with life and new with thought and new with passions of all varieties. And now, with more folk venues, it's no surprise that young musicians would be drawn to it.

The Enigma of Paul Clayton

Paul Clayton was the archetypal, scholarly folksinger—on steroids. One of the earlier arrivals, he was originally from the whaling town of New Bedford, Massachusetts, and his first musical interests of traditional seafaring and whaling songs would provide the themes of his early albums. Singing without accompaniment led to his developing a conversational phrasing style, unbound by strict rhythm patterns, that would later prove to be significantly influential. Clayton was a folk prodigy. While still in high school, he hosted a weekly folk show on New Bedford radio stations WFMR and WBSM, expanding from a fifteen-minute to a one-hour show per week. In 1950, he picked up the Appalachian dulcimer, playing in a gentle, contemplative style influenced by Jean Ritchie. He landed in the Village in 1953, age twenty-two and fresh-faced, after receiving a master's degree in English and American folklore at the University of Virginia. There he had made field recordings during extensive excursions in the Appalachian Mountains, staying in a primitive log cabin, without electricity or running water. Soon he would explore numerous folk styles and create unique concept albums, some of a macabre nature, such as *Bloody Ballads: British and American Murder Ballads* and *Wanted for Murder: Songs of Outlaws and Desperados*. Other motifs—often of manly preoccupations—followed, such as *Timber-r-r! Lumberjack Folksongs and Ballads*, a title ripe for a Monty Python parody. Between the years of 1954 and 1965, Clayton claimed to be, and was, one of the most recorded young folksingers, releasing twenty albums, six in 1956 alone, and miscellaneous singles, for Folkways, Tradition, Elektra, and other labels. These included a 1959 collaboration with his close friend, Dave Van Ronk, that comprised a rowdy collection of drunken sailor sea shanties, and in 1960, Clayton recorded the first version of Woody Guthrie's "This Land Is Your Land" that made it to the pop music charts.

Visually, Clayton's appearance evolved from the conservative look of his first days in the Village. By the later 1950s and early '60s, he came to define the bohemian image of "Greenwich

Village folksinger" with his longish swept-back hair, a beatnikish chin-strap beard, and a propensity for sometimes wearing outrageous outfits or all black and, as an eccentric touch, sometimes carrying an ornate walking stick. But for all the drama of Clayton's appearance and in the songs he so carefully researched and discovered, his singing itself was rather restrained and mannered. Some say that Clayton, who sang in a rich midbaritone with a reverence, clarity, and enunciation reminiscent of Pete Seeger, lacked the showmanship of others on the scene like, for instance, Bob Gibson or Ed McCurdy, who were able to more fully excite their audiences. Still, Clayton's knowledge and sincerity were engaging, and with his credentials and string of albums, he was a good draw on the club circuit and for Folksingers Guild concerts.

Clayton's deep knowledge of folk songs led him to an easy adaptation of the folk process—rewriting, combining segments of traditional, public domain song fragments he had discovered, and adding to or replacing lyrics with his own words to create new songs. It was hard to tell where the song interpretation ended and his own words began, even to a close friend like Van Ronk. A perfect example is Clayton's adaptation of "Gotta Travel On," originally based on the 1891 song "Yonder Comes the High Sheriff." It was a hit for country singer Billy Grammer and was sung by Buddy Holly as the opening song on his fateful 1959 Winter Dance Party tour. Clayton took bits and pieces from various versions of the song and added lyrics of his own:

> *I've laid around and played around this old town too long*
> *And I feel like I've gotta travel on*

Paul Clayton was at the cusp, at that crucial moment when folksingers were about to begin focusing on writing and not just on interpreting and preserving old songs. It must be remembered that, all along, folk songs had always been recycled—melodies and chords were used and reused with different lyrics all the time. Folk songs were still seen as being owned by everyone at that point. Songs were traded, adapted, and rewritten freely. That would soon change, as blurry music publishing and copyright realities came into focus.

Because a new generation was emerging, according to Terri Thal, "being even a few years older meant a lot in those days." At five years his senior, and with all those recordings under his belt, Van Ronk and the others looked up to Clayton. They learned from him, were drawn to him, and were fascinated by him. "Paul was an enigma. We were in awe of him," Thal told me.

One reason Paul Clayton was such an enigma was, perhaps, because of his personal life.

Clayton had discovered while attending his mostly male university that he was gay, and he became active in underground gay culture beginning in college. In public, this was a closely guarded secret.

It must not have been easy to be a gay male folksinger in the fifties and sixties. For all its musical sensitivity, the folk world, like the rest of society, was a male-dominated, heterocentric, macho one. Remaining closeted was Clayton's only option if he was to survive, professionally and personally. "It was a secret. Only a few of us knew he was gay," Terri Thal told me. And even those few, at times, could be knowingly or unknowingly cruel. Looking back at his recorded legacy now, it seems that some of the folk songs he chose to sing gave hints of his sexuality—some with humor, like "Stay Away from the Girls," and others with the heartbreakingly sad loneliness of isolation. On his 1962 Folkways album *Dulcimer Songs and Solos*, accompanied only by his gently strummed dulcimer, Clayton achingly sang:

> *I'm troubled, I'm troubled, I'm troubled in my mind*
> *Oh, if trouble don't kill me, I'll live a long time*

It wasn't all tears, of course. On *Bobby Burns' Merry Muses of Caledonia* (1958), Clayton sang the naughty, bawdy poems of eighteenth-century Scottish bard Robert Burns, such as the rather X-rated "Nine Inch Will Please a Lady":

> *Come lowse & lug your batterin ram,*
> *An thrash him at my gyvel!*

Paul Clayton's unmistakable influence would have an impact on many of the artists and recordings that came from the Greenwich Village scene in the early part of the new decade, including those folksingers who were soon to be crowned its kings and queens. In some ways, without even trying, he was the archetype they strove to be.

Cynthia Gooding

Born in Minnesota and raised in Illinois, Cynthia Gooding moved to Mexico City as a teen, where she picked up a love and talent for playing and singing folk music. Having arrived in New York in 1947, she was encouraged by none other than Josh White himself to perform in the Village. Gooding was now, though still only in her thirties, one of the elders on the scene, certainly in the eyes of the newcomers.

Nearly six feet tall (even Terri Thal had to look up to her, literally), she commanded the stage with tradi-tional Spanish, Mexican, Italian, and Turkish folk songs, sung with a full, throaty tone in an articulated, cabaret style that was assertive and theatrical. But she was also able to convey a deep sensitivity and melancholy, as in her rendition of "All My Trials," sung with emphasis on her lower register and with a haunting vibrato.

It was rare in the 1940s to see a woman standing alone on the stage accompanying herself. "She opened the door for the solo woman onstage with a guitar," Gooding's daughter, Leyla Spencer, told me. "Later, in the sixties as a little girl, I'd be carrying that guitar for her on tour. It was heavier than it looked!" Leyla added. As such, Gooding initiated a new prototype—one that helped to inspire a generation of female folksingers. In some photos of the younger Gooding, when she's dressed simply with a black turtleneck and long hair combed down, you can blur your eyes and see the future Joan Baez, and imagine Baez singing "All My Trials," as she later did, voiced an octave higher than Gooding. Other times, you can see the young Judy Collins or Carolyn Hester. Building up a following in the Village club scene, she was one of the first artists signed by founder Jac Holzman to Elektra Records in the early 1950s, where she helped establish the label as a go-to for world folk music. An archivist herself, she often carried her tape recorder around to capture music and ambient sounds as she traveled, making recordings of Josh White, Reverend Gary Davis, John Lee Hooker, and Ramblin' Jack Elliot. She performed several duets with actor/folksinger Theodore Bikel, including the album *Young Man and a Maid Sing Love Songs of Many Lands* for Elektra in 1958. In 1959, she performed at that first Newport Folk Festival, stunning in a green gossamer gown, and recorded for Vanguard Records' three-volume *Folk Festival at Newport* set, on which she sings two songs in Spanish. According to Dave Van Ronk, for all the formality of her performance style, offstage she was funny and sociable. Snapshots of Gooding at Village parties, often at her apartment on Bleecker Street, confirm this, usually showing her playing her guitar and singing, sometimes with Carolyn Hester, Jean Ritchie, and Logan English, among others. "Oh yeah, she had a lot of parties," Leyla confirms. Circa 1960, Gooding would begin hosting her popular radio show *Folksinger's Choice* on New York's premier noncommercial, listener-supported radio station WBAI, where she would present many of the next generation's folksingers.

While the first-wave folk artists who remained were mostly regarded with a haloed rever-ence, it was the newcomers who were now dominating the landscape. Besides the charming vibe of the Village, the ease of getting around by walking or public transportation, and the lower rents of the neighborhood, by living here they were in New York City—the center of the entertainment universe at that time—so the reasons to be here were manifold. Record label headquarters were here, the venues were here, the song factories and recording studios were here—but also Broadway, comedy clubs, and modeling agencies. As Elijah Wald puts it, "Some who arrived were just coming to be in the big city. Some drifted into the folk scene and stayed if they happened to get lucky. Others, if they hadn't made it by the time they were twenty-three, were gone."

Keep On Keepin' On

One of the new arrivals, classically trained Len Chandler, had played oboe in the Akron Symphony Orchestra before moving to New York to receive his master's degree from Columbia University. Living in Harlem, he began heading downtown to check out the folk scene in the Village where, in the Folklore Center, he met Izzy Young. "And guess who was sitting down playing guitar with hair hanging in his face? Dave Van Ronk! Dave Van Ronk was fingerpicking guitar and I had never, ever seen anybody use their fingers on a guitar, you know, like that," recalled Chandler in an interview for *Activist Video Archive*. At the time, Chandler was working at St. Barnabas School, teaching abused and neglected children, whom he would sing for and take to Washington Square Park to roller skate on Sundays. "In the park, there would be singers. I'd turn the kids a'loose roller skating and then I would borrow somebody's guitar, with my vocabulary of three or four or six chords maybe. . . . But then when I started singing, I would sit there to sing, and a big crowd would gather around me." It was poet Hugh Romney, later reinvented as Wavy Gravy, who saw Chandler singing in the park and invited him to perform at the Gaslight, where Romney was reading poetry. Performing numerous sets of folk songs between the readings, Chandler increased his repertoire considerably. His own writing would flourish until he would become one of the most prolific on the scene, writing topical songs taken directly from events from that morning's papers. Besides the musical invention afforded by his musical training, his reportage lyric style was to be a major influence on some of the Village's new arrivals. Chandler became one of the regulars at the Gaslight, performing most weekends. As it was a basket house, money was collected after each set. Years later, Romney told this story in *Parabola*: "We would jump on [Chandler's] motor scooter at the end of the evening and drive down into the Bowery and find somebody passed out on the sidewalk. We'd stuff his pockets with money and drive off and find somebody else until we'd given away at least half of what we'd made in the course of the evening. It was a lot of fun."

With racial tensions mounting in the South, Chandler, one of the few young African American folksingers on the scene, became an ardent activist, under the mentorship of young singer/activist Cordell Reagon, founding member of the Freedom Singers and the Student Nonviolent Coordinating Committee (SNCC). Chandler traveled, marched, performed his songs, was arrested a number of times at civil rights demonstrations, and even wrote songs while in prison. More and more, his songs were topical, related to the movement. The humorous message song "Beans in My Ears" was covered by the Serendipity Singers as well as Pete Seeger, and "Keep On Keepin' On" was quoted by Dr. Martin Luther King in a speech.

But there's a mountain in the bottom of that sea we flounder in
If we find that mountaintop we wouldn't need to swim

While some of the older, influential African American bluesmen like Mississippi John Hurt, John Lee Hooker, Muddy Waters, and Reverend Gary Davis were performing in the Village clubs, younger Black folk or blues artists on the Village scene were scarce. And for all the diversity of the Village, the folk scene was unquestionably, predominantly white. One night, according to Van Ronk, Len Chandler was jumped outside of the Gaslight by a gang of young Italian thugs who were attempting to "clean up the neighborhood." Whether or not this incident was racially motivated, one thing was for sure: there was a turf war going on, the neighborhood was changing, and some people did not like it. And to say racism didn't exist—even in the idyllic Village—would be naïve.

Tom Paxton

In the spring of 1960, young Tom Paxton was stationed at Fort Dix Army Base near Trenton, New Jersey, when he started taking the NJ Transit bus to the Port Authority, New York City, and heading down to Greenwich Village. "It was a cheap bus ride," Paxton told me, adding that, contrary to his fictionalized depiction in the Coen Brothers' 2013 film *Inside Llewyn Davis*, "I never would have hitchhiked! And, I certainly would never have *dreamed* of wearing my uniform in the Village!" The boyish twenty-three-year-old made his MacDougal Street debut at the Commons. There he met and became fast friends with Dave Van Ronk, who was booking the venue and on whose couch at 190 Waverly Place he would crash on those weekends away from the base. Paxton had first started listening to folk music while in high school, particularly the records of Burl Ives. "It was not what teenagers were listening to," Paxton recalled. "Radio was dominated by R&B, rock and roll . . . teen idol shit." Paxton was instead learning songs from Burl Ives's songbook, thinking of them not as folk songs, but simply as "special songs." "Now you would call them 'quaint,'" he proffered. The Weavers' 1955 Carnegie Hall concert album was also a major inspiration. "Without Pete [Seeger] I wouldn't be here." The influence of Burl Ives and Pete Seeger could be heard clearly in Paxton's song choices and vocal delivery, but being emitted from such a fresh-faced, clean-cut, sturdy, young folksinger, at the beginning of the new decade, it was something new again. Like so many of the others on the scene, Tom Paxton had been a drama student and acted in summer stock theater. But when I asked if this training had been useful to him as a folksinger, he claimed it wasn't. To Paxton, acting and performing music are antithetical. "In acting you have to subsume your entire identity. As a music performer, your whole purpose is to present an edited, but true, representation of yourself." Regardless of his stage experience, he was nervous performing in the Village. "I was shaking in my boots up there," he admits. "Folk audiences were demanding!" When I asked who his favorite performer was, Paxton didn't hesitate: "Van Ronk."

Like Van Ronk, Paxton was soon playing at the Gaslight. "When I arrived in the spring, they still had poets, with folk music in between. By the fall, it was all folk music," he recalled. Paxton's repertoire consisted of traditional folk ballads, performed with a precise, tempered fingerpicking style on a Martin D-28 guitar he purchased the day he got out of the army, an accompaniment that fully complemented his warm vocal tone. Martin guitars had long been Paxton's guitars of choice: Burl Ives had mentioned Martins in his autobiography *Wayfaring Stranger* (1948), and the instruments had also caught Paxton's eye on Kingston Trio album covers. It was Van Ronk who taught Paxton the three-finger picking technique, in a grueling, four-hour session that wore him out. "I had a show at the Gaslight later that night, and my hand gave out while playing Woody's 'The Golden Vanity,'" Paxton admitted. Soon, Paxton's interest in singing only traditional songs began to shift. Like two of his inspirations, Guthrie and Seeger, Tom Paxton wanted to write his own songs as well as play the time-honored ones. "I wanted to contribute to the song bag. I wanted a seat on the bus," he told me. "I wanted to write songs that stood alongside classical music." He started testing out his songs at shows, slyly sneaking them into his sets at the Gaslight. Before long, half his set would be new, original songs. According to Van Ronk, in his memoir, Paxton's originals were getting more attention than the traditional songs, and he began to write a new song each day. This would make him the first of his generation, besides Len Chandler, to write so prolifically, and it undoubtedly helped to kick-start the new song movement.

> And I can't help but wonder where I'm bound, where I'm bound
> And I can't help but wonder where I'm bound

Tom Paxton was the first songwriter signed to Cherry Lane Music Publishing, the Greenwich Village–based publishing company with offices in an apartment above the Cherry Lane Theatre, headed by Milt Okun. Okun had been Harry Belafonte's pianist, arranger, and conductor and had gone on to produce and arrange for the Chad Mitchell Trio, a polished folk trio with a penchant for satirical folk ditties with increasingly political lyrics and anti-racism, anti-war themes. At the height of the Cold War with the Soviet Union, the Chad Mitchell Trio released a version of "Moscow Nights" sung entirely in Russian. You would never know from looking at these three guys with collegiate smiles, dressed neatly in suits and narrow ties, that they were impassioned social activists, banned from radio stations for singing racially charged songs satirizing the KKK and the John Birch Society and for calling out segregationist governors. Their trick, which allowed them to be hired to perform on mainstream, national, network television variety shows, was to mix it up with innocuous, nontopical songs and comedy. When one of the members of the Trio, Mike Pugh, left to return to college, Tom Paxton auditioned to replace him. Though the vocal blend didn't work, the Chad Mitchell Trio would go on to record several Paxton compositions including "The Marvelous Toy" and "I Can't Help But Wonder Where I'm Bound."

It was like Pete Seeger had once remarked, about writing songs because "there were things that needed to be said." Folksingers were running out of traditional songs to perform and needed new material. Before long, the Kingston Trio, Johnny Cash, and even the Weavers (on their 1963 reunion album) would record Tom Paxton's songs. It helped to have a good music publisher, like Milt Okun and Cherry Lane, on your side. But, besides Okun's formidable work as a song publisher for Paxton and others, his inestimable production and arrangement skills would soon play a major role in one of the biggest commercial success stories of Greenwich Village.

A true local music scene, even one that was about to become more than local, is not made by its "stars." It is made by real people whose names you may have never heard, and nowhere was this truer than in 1960s Greenwich Village. By its very definition, folk is the "people's music" anyway. At its purest, especially during the first wave and through the year 1960, it didn't belong to the stars. The folk movement mostly eschewed the star system so prevalent in modern popular culture, even if some names were more widely known than others. In the folk world, modesty could be seen as the distinction of a true star. Pete Seeger was ninety-one years old and had been the recipient of dozens of honors when I first worked with him in 2010, on a live recording. He couldn't have been more humble. "Richard, when you mix it, make sure the audience's singing is as loud as mine," he demanded.

The musicians who strummed and picked, the singers who sang for sometimes sparse audiences or those who accompanied and sang harmonies for others, even the concert attendees and club goers who filled the seats at the Gaslight, the Commons, and Gerde's Folk City—those were the stars just as much as anyone in the spotlight. There were some musicians that, though never to be widely known outside of the folk music community, would nonetheless have a profound impact on the music that was to come, simply by their presence, devotion, and musicianship. Without them, the music and artists we know so well that emerged from Greenwich Village in the early 1960s simply would not exist in quite the same way.

My Lunch with Barry Kornfeld

It was one of the first warm days of spring when Barry and I met for lunch at the Washington Square Hotel, on the north side of the Square. The hotel, lovely now, was known as the Earle in the 1960s and through the years has been home to musicians aplenty. In 1975, referring to the hotel's shabbier days, Joan Baez would sing about it, in her song "Diamonds and Rust," as "that crummy hotel over Washington Square."

Barry Kornfeld's first visit to the Square for the Sunday folk gathering was in 1952, and before long he became part of the regular crowd, playing guitar and banjo. As we sat down for lunch, Barry brought out his worn copy of the red-covered program guide for the 1959 Newport Folk Festival to show me. In it, Kornfeld is pictured, impossibly young, playing a banjo, with a caption stating he spent "a lot of time hitching across the country, and spending much of this time in the South," and that he played "most of the fretted instruments." As if those folk credentials weren't enough for a college student at the time of Newport, New Yorker Kornfeld was set to graduate as "Queens College's only folk music major." As his résumé grew, Kornfeld became one of the most in-demand musicians on the scene. A musician's musician, quite literally. In his memoir, Dave Van Ronk, who met Kornfeld on one of those Sundays in Washington Square, described Kornfeld as "one of the best guitar players I've ever known." Kornfeld performed often with Van Ronk, including playing banjo on the particularly unrestrained and rollicking 1964 album *Dave Van Ronk and the Ragtime Jug Stompers* on Mercury Records, along with Danny Kalb, later of the Blues Project. He also had an ongoing musical partnership with guitar virtuoso Reverend Gary Davis, Davis playing his jumbo Gibson J-200 and Kornfeld on banjo. He would also act as Davis's "lead boy," guiding the blind musician. Kornfeld played on Tom Paxton's Elektra albums; with Liam Clancy, of the Clancy Brothers; at the Gate of Horn, with the dynamic African American folk duo Inman & Ira (Leroy Inman and Ira Rogers); and with Bob Dylan and many more. Kornfeld, like Van Ronk and so many others, had been inspired by the guitar stylings and vocals of Josh White. "I learned some of his guitar licks note for note," he told me over lunch. All these years later, Kornfeld stills speaks with reverence of Josh White's "immaculate technique and sublime vibrato."

Though a real estate agent who happened to be a music fan, Barry Kornfeld was the first of the musicians to move into what was to become a folk music nerve center, the apartment building at 190 Waverly Place. In 1961, Kornfeld brought in Van Ronk and Terri Thal and, before you knew it, the building was crawling with folksingers. Singers like Patrick Sky, who would go on to create some of the most outrageous songs of any era on his controversial album *Songs That Made America Famous* (1971), and Alix Dobkin, who would marry Sam Hood, manager of the Gaslight, but would later come out as a lesbian feminist activist. Not to mention all the ones who would crash on Dave and Terri's couch, like Tom Paxton, Bob Dylan, and others who would drop by at any hour of the day or night, like Paul Clayton, Karen Dalton, or Peter Stampfel, a member of the Holy Modal Rounders.

As it was such a nice day, Kornfeld and I walked the few blocks together toward his subway stop on Seventh Avenue, passing right in front of 190 Waverly Place. We stood in front of the building together for a moment and he looked it over, up and down. Julius's gay bar is still there, right next door, on the corner of West Tenth Street, like it was back then. People were out in the street hanging out—there's rarely much traffic on the tiny block. I asked him if the building had changed much. It had, with its modern security door, renovated facade, and not a note of music to be heard. And Barry, too, had changed. He rarely picks up a guitar these days. Sixty years have passed. We took a selfie on my iPhone and texted it to Tom Paxton, who had spent many nights there. Barry looked at me. "There was no other era like the sixties," he told me, to make sure I understood. I was beginning to.

The Ballad of Happy Traum

Happy Traum's involvement in the Greenwich Village folk community was practically preordained. He was part of the Bronx contingent that included Barry Kornfeld and had been a regular at the Sunday gatherings in the Square since first attending in 1954 at age sixteen. He was in the audience when the Weavers performed at Carnegie Hall on that historic Christmas Eve of 1955. Traum, whose real name is Harry but I have never heard anyone call him that, first learned of the Village scene through three of his classmates at the High School of Music & Art—all of whom were to become major players on the scene: banjoist Eric Weissberg (the Tarriers and countless others), Peter Yarrow (Peter, Paul and Mary), and songwriter/ producer Felix Pappalardi who was to form the Original Rag Quartet, produce the Youngbloods and Cream, and by decade's end, form the influential rock band Mountain. Of his first visit, Traum wrote, "We pulled into the Village at 10:30 or 11:00 p.m., parked the car and ambled through the quiet streets. We ordered cappuccinos (my first) at Cafe Rienzi on MacDougal near Bleecker, peered into the darkened shop windows and breathed the fresh air of bohemia. Around midnight, we wandered into a near-deserted Washington Square." There he witnessed two folk song enthusiasts, who he later learned were Raphael (Ray) Boguslav and Dick Greenhaus, fingerpicking classical acoustic guitars, their harmonies echoing through the empty park. Traum was transfixed. Later, his role in the New World Singers would earn Happy a special place in Greenwich Village history, but even that was just a beginning for him. A highly regarded guitarist, vocalist, five-string banjo picker, and all-round good guy, he was inextricably weaving himself into the tapestry being created. To this day, he is a sought-after musician and teacher of folk music, and his son Adam carries on in the family tradition.

After rejecting an offer from Columbia Records, Joan Baez released her eponymous solo debut on the independent Vanguard label in October 1960. Baez's decision to sign with Vanguard, with its modest headquarters located on West Fourteenth Street as opposed to Columbia's midtown citadel, mirrors an attitude that would also be prevalent in the early 1980s, when the indie-rock scene that continues today was unfolding. In both examples, big labels were sometimes mistrusted and viewed as the enemy, while indies gave the artist a greater sense of creative freedom and control. Baez sensed this. But even with Vanguard's meager promotion budget, her album, a collection of traditional songs—a few which included Fred Hellerman of the Weavers on guitar—was a hit that received near-unanimous critical praise while furthering the commercial folk boom, as the Kingston Trio had done. Bruce Eder, writing in *All Music*, describes Baez's as "a voice from heaven, a soprano so pure and beguiling that the mere act of listening to her—forget what she was singing—was a pleasure." Having lost Baez to Vanguard, Columbia would soon be anxious to sign some folk acts, opening the door for signing Carolyn Hester and, through her introduction to them, Bob Dylan.

1960 was a presidential election year and the growing population of young people in the country had a particular interest in its outcome. The median age of the population in America that year was 29.5 and would drop throughout the decade, compared to 38.5 in 2021. For the first time, both candidates had been born in the twentieth century and one of them, if successful, would be the youngest American president ever elected.

Democratic senator John F. Kennedy's campaign was one that exuded a kind of youthful vitality and change. A World War II hero who had received two medals of honor, Kennedy seemed to be imbued with an appealing joie de vivre and a winning, life-affirming smile, projected via a carefully crafted public image. Some voters, however, were skeptical of his qualifications and claimed to be wary of his Catholicism. Kennedy's opponent, Richard M. Nixon, the former House Un-American Activities Committee member and then-current vice president under Dwight D. Eisenhower, was by far the more familiar of the two. Though Nixon was a symbol of the decade that was ending, his anti-communist views were still held by many Americans at the time. The launch of the orbiting Soviet Sputnik satellite in 1957 was seen as a threatening sign of Russian technological superiority, and the Cuban Revolution was in full force, with leader Fidel Castro supporting communist insurgencies in other developing countries. Four televised presidential face-offs were held—the first in history—changing the political landscape forever by giving viewers an up-close opportunity to form opinions about the candidates based on their appearance and demeanor as well as by their viewpoints. When the dust settled, November 1960 had brought one of the tightest presidential elections in American history. It was with JFK's victory that the sixties era began.

As my lunch with Barry Kornfeld was ending, he pointed to the massive English elm located at the northwest entrance to Washington Square Park. "That's 'the hanging tree,'" he told me in a grim voice, referring to the urban legend of lynchings from that particular tree in the Square. I checked, and no public records exist of actual hangings from that or any tree in Washington Square Park, though hangings did occur, from gallows by the arch, until 1819. But, according to the NYC Department of Parks and Recreation, that tree is well over 340 years old, making it one of the oldest trees in New York City—surviving all those leafless winters, growing luxuriant in summers, and witnessing everything.

Chapter Four

the b

eatnik
riot

Dave Van Ronk, performing at the Newport Folk Festival in 1963.

New York Times *said it was the coldest winter in seventeen years*
I didn't feel so cold then.
—Bob Dylan, "Talkin' New York"

In New York City, the winter of 1960–1961

was one of the harshest on record—a record snowfall and a record cold wave that resulted in a record sixteen consecutive days with temperatures below freezing. MacDougal Street was blanketed in over a foot of snow. It was a transitional scene, a fade-to-white dissolve into the near future. When the snow melted away, so did more of the lingering vestiges of the 1950s. People in the Village were glued to their television screens to watch the inauguration of the new president on January 20, 1961, as JFK delivered a speech that was, for many, a galvanizing and global call-to-arms. Looking directly into the lens, Kennedy was speaking to the young in particular when he said, "The torch has been passed to a new generation of Americans." The famous soundbite bite was "And so, my fellow Americans: ask not what your country can do for you—ask what you can do for your country," but it was followed with "My fellow citizens of the world: ask not what America will do for you, but what together we can do for the freedom of man." Within two months Kennedy had established, by executive order, the Peace Corps, a volunteer organization meant to "make a contribution to world peace" by aiding countries abroad. But around the same time, Kennedy also had a major embarrassment, with the disastrous, failed attempt to overthrow Castro's revolutionary regime in Cuba in a CIA plot he had inherited from the prior administration. This debacle, at the Bay of Pigs on the south coast of Cuba, was to strain Kennedy's relationship with the CIA for the remainder of his presidency and increase tensions between the United States and Cuba.

Meanwhile, stoked by the growing folk craze, folksingers continued to arrive in the Village from all over the country with guitars and banjos. Those who were already established on the MacDougal Street circuit would now be faced with the unexpected dynamic of being outnumbered—and sometimes outshone—by the constant flow of new arrivals.

A Semispiritual Phenomenon

Karen Dalton who, like Woody Guthrie, had lived through the hardship of the Dust Bowl, blew into town from Oklahoma at age twenty-three. With an idiosyncratic, delicately scorched-earth vocal sound and an emotional, sad vibrato, Dalton wrapped folk songs in a bluesy embrace, reminiscent of Bessie Smith and the phrasing of Billie Holiday. With her long, dark hair, missing teeth (she got mixed up in a conflict between two boys fighting over her), and two divorces already under her belt, Dalton possessed a unique beauty and a voice that resonated with experience. She charmed audiences and would become an oft-mentioned favorite among favorites. Palpably shy, Dalton sang traditional songs as did the others, but her interpretations were often revelatory: both the song's lyrics and Dalton's own demons were laid beguilingly bare. Listening to Karen Dalton in the 2020s, she sounds contemporary, recalling more recent vocal stylists such as Antony Hegarty (now known as Anohni), or even Amy Winehouse. One of her admirers at the time, Peter Stampfel of the off-center Holy Modal Rounders and later the Fugs, claimed that Dalton was the only truly authentic folksinger he ever met on the scene.

When Stampfel speaks of "the scene," the implication is cinematic and theatrical, with himself a participant of the drama. He often refers to the Village as "the set," and to its appropriately "old-timey look." I found his way of thinking to be so similar to my own. Peter is one of the most eccentric and indefinable artists to emerge from Greenwich Village, a knee-slapping, immensely entertaining performer with a keen knowledge of twentieth-century popular music. Like Van Ronk, John Sebastian, and so many others, Stampfel has a particular appreciation if not downright devotion to Harry Smith's *Anthology of American Folk Music*. "Harry Smith *intended* it to be as transformational as it actually was," he explains. Stampfel had arrived in 1959 from Wisconsin by way of San Francisco, where he had "met a girl from New York" who led him here. Landing in the Village, his eccentricities, drug experimentation, sly sense of humor, and spontaneous approach to music were to have a major impact on the style and substance that were afoot.

"Music is a semispiritual phenomenon," Stampfel told me. Projecting the trajectory of the decade, he and the Holy Modal Rounders would be the first to use the word "psychedelic" in a popular song. It is an appropriate distinction. I have performed and sung with Peter Stampfel numerous times, beginning in the mid-1990s, and it's fascinating to hear him channel the 1920s and '30s country blues spirit of the Harry Smith *Anthology* while flying off into the cosmos. With his ebullient spirit and keen, in-the-moment musical curiosity, he is still a vital artist whom I admire greatly.

Fred Neil was born in Ohio, grew up in St. Petersburg, Florida, and did a stint in the navy before landing a job writing pop songs at the Brill Building, the legendary song factory in Times Square where he had written tunes for Buddy Holly and Roy Orbison, among others. With his deep baritone voice and twelve-string guitar, he found a home at the newly opened, suitably subterranean Café Wha? at 115 MacDougal Street, across the street from the Gaslight, where he held court. The Wha? had been opened by Manny Roth, who was the uncle of 1980s rock star David Lee Roth, lead singer of Van Halen. Peter Stampfel calls the Café Wha? "the first sell-out, phony venue" and Van Ronk called it "a tourist trap."

Regardless, it was where many of the heroes of this story got their starts, and it is still open to this day.

In February 1961, "Freddy" Neil started hosting afternoon hootenannies that, forty-three years later in *Chronicles*, Bob Dylan would refer to as "an extravagant patchwork [that] featured anybody and anything." "He was the emperor of the place. . . . Everything revolved around him," Dylan wrote of Neil. Indeed, he was the ringmaster of the Café Wha?'s daytime circus that featured more than its share of spur-of-the-moment collaborations. Karen Dalton was a regular, sometimes with Dylan on harmonica, at the afternoon shows, as was one of the most colorful characters on the scene: Tiny Tim. A falsetto-voiced, ukulele-strumming crooner and aficionado of songs from the early acoustic era (1878–1930s), Tiny Tim would miraculously, by the end of the 1960s and for a brief time, become a household name. A decade and a half later, when I was a teenager in Tampa, Florida, and after his fame had subsided, Tiny Tim would become one of my first mentors, the person who first taught me about Greenwich Village. "They walked the streets!" Tiny exclaimed, describing the folksingers of the era as if they were the deities of Mount Olympus. "Mr. Sebastian (referring to John Sebastian), Mr. Dylan, all of them! That's where you should live, Mr. Barone!" Needless to say, I was sold.

In the evenings, established acts would perform at the Wha?, like stand-up comic Noel Stookey, "The Toilet Man," from Michigan, who would do his famous impersonation of a toilet flushing. Stookey's roommate was Tom Paxton. "We laughed our asses off!" Paxton told me. By the following year, Stookey would be rechristened as "Paul" in Peter, Paul and Mary.

Though only twenty-five, Fred Neil seemed slightly older than others on the scene and sounded a bit jaded and world-weary. Some of his songs made reference to wanting to get out of town—to leave the unpredictable and bereft life of a folksinger in the Village behind and to get back to his beloved, sunny Florida. In "The Other Side to This Life" Neil wrote,

> *Well I don't know what I'm doing for half the time,*
> *I don't know where I'm going*
> *I think I'll get me a sailing boat and sail the Gulf of Mexico*

Like Tom Paxton, Fred Neil was part of a trend that was breaking away from the tradition of singing traditional songs by writing and performing new ones, expressing specific, personal statements. No doubt this inspired others to do so as well. The definition of "folk music" was evolving quickly, and the concept of singer-songwriter was coming into play. After a debut LP with Vince Martin in 1964, Neil's solo album *Bleecker & MacDougal* (Elektra Records) featured an album cover that positively fetishized the Greenwich Village folk scene. It depicted Neil standing with authority in the center of the eponymous intersection holding his guitar case, with MacDougal Street, now referred to as simply "the Street" appearing behind him, as glamorous as the Las Vegas strip. The album also yielded songs that would be covered by a diverse range of recording artists on both coasts, making Neil one of the most successful songwriters on the scene.

Red Diaper Baby

Seventeen-year-old Suze Rotolo, after being drawn into the scene via the Sunday gatherings in the Square, was frequenting the folk clubs of the Village, and she wrote in her charming 2008 memoir, *A Freewheelin' Time*, "It was to Greenwich Village where people like me went—people who knew in their souls that they didn't belong where they came from." A lovely, long-haired, creative, and rebellious Sicilian American, Rotolo had come from Queens, just a few subway stops away from the Village on the 7 train, but a world apart. Born in Brooklyn to communist parents—her father a union organizer, her mother the editor of an Italian communist newspaper—she was a so-called red diaper baby, growing up surrounded by leftist politics, activism, and social causes. While in high school, Rotolo had become active with the Congress of Racial Equality (CORE), the organization that would soon put the Freedom Rides in motion, and joined the Youth March for Integrated Schools in Washington, DC. Later, when travel to Cuba was severely restricted, she would make a perilous journey there to meet and interact with Cuban revolutionaries. As much as or more than the others, Suze Rotolo would come to exemplify the quintessential Greenwich Villager of the 1960s, standing with as much authority as Freddy Neil at her own intersection—of music + revolution.

Good-time Music

John Sebastian didn't even need to hop on a subway to get the Village. He was born and grew up there, living with his parents and brother Mark on the perimeter of Washington Square Park, in the stately landmark apartment building at 29 Washington Square West, the northern extension of MacDougal Street. His father, John Sebastian Pugliese was a classical harmonica player signed to RCA Records, and his mother, Jane Bishir, was a radio actress and scriptwriter. Vivian Vance, the actress who played "Ethel" on *I Love Lucy*, was a close family friend and John's godmother. Other family friends included Burl Ives, Josh White, and Woody Guthrie. Across the hall lived former first lady Eleanor Roosevelt, who is now honored with a plaque outside the building. Like Rotolo, Sebastian, also of Italian heritage and also seventeen, had, in his own words, been immersing himself in the "folk scene, the doo-wop scene, the beatnik scene, the blues scene." Soon he would be equally immersed in the jug band scene with the Even Dozen Jug Band. Playing the harmonica—not in the classical style of his father but in a superb and distinctive blues style—he would become a virtuoso in his own right. Sebastian also played guitar and, occasionally, autoharp, soaking in influences like Mississippi John Hurt, Son House, and Doc Watson while listening to the Harry Smith *Anthology*. "Every guitar player should be discouraged after seeing Doc Watson," Sebastian told the *New York Times* in 2013. John Sebastian was and is a consummate musician, who would collaborate with Fred Neil, the Doors, Tim Hardin, Crosby, Stills & Nash, and countless others but would become best known as the affable frontman of the Lovin' Spoonful. While some others on the scene often conveyed introversion, anger, or sadness in their music, Sebastian and the Spoonful could be relied on to bring the exuberance, smiles, and joy that were equally major components of being young in Greenwich Village in the 1960s; they were a bright musical antidote to all manner of darkness that was always lurking just around the corner.

With the demand for folk venues growing at a rapid clip, storefronts and cellars in the Village that had been vacant or underutilized were suddenly made into coffeehouses. The Third Side, Why Not?, Café Id, and the Bitter End (formerly the Cock 'n Bull) were recent additions. Crowds would gather inside and outside the packed venues like never before. On the weekends, the coffeehouses would go on all night, as they did not have the curfew restrictions of venues that served alcohol. Folk music was so prevalent in the Village at this time that tourists could get confused. Will Friedwald, author of *Jazz Singing: America's Great Voices from Bessie Smith to Bebop and Beyond* (1992) among other books, recounted a story to me that the very un-folky Barbra Streisand told onstage. "Barbra was performing at the Village Vanguard in 1961, opening for Miles Davis. After a set of jazz standards, she went to the ladies' room, where she overheard two women talking. 'So,' one woman asked the other as she checked her makeup in the mirror, 'what do you *think* of this *verkakte* folksinger?'" *Verkakte* is the Yiddish word for "crappy." Eighteen-year-old Barbra had previously been performing at the Bon Soir, a basement cabaret at 40 West Eighth Street near Sixth Avenue and, before that, at an upscale gay bar called the Lion, at 62 West Ninth Street, where she competed in a talent contest with Tiny Tim. Every spare square foot of real estate in the Village was occupied by music.

An Actor Prepares

It was onto this perfect set, in this perfect moment in January 1961, with all the actors and audience in place, and a follow-spot ready to track his every move, that a scruffy, nineteen-year-old Minnesotan full of nervous energy who called himself Bob Dylan stepped into the story.

How many times had he watched and studied James Dean—aloof, intense, and inscrutable—in *East of Eden* and *Rebel Without a Cause*? How many times had he stared at the cover illustration of Woody Guthrie's *Bound for Glory* LP—a sketch of Guthrie from behind, with a corduroy cap and guitar, that could easily be Dylan—and imagined himself? How many times had he read Kerouac's *On the Road* and Guthrie's partially fictionalized 1943 autobiography *Bound for Glory*, the tales of boxcars and hobo jungles and life during the Great Depression that had led to some of the greatest songs of the folk revival's first wave? And how many times had he listened to Ramblin' Jack Elliot's renditions of Guthrie songs?

The answers, like pages of the *New York Times* strewn on MacDougal Street, my friend, are blowin' in the wind.

Before Dylan, Jack Elliot was *the* master interpreter of Woody Guthrie. So much so that Guthrie famously said that Elliot "sounds more like me than I do." About nine years older than Dylan—born in 1931 in Brooklyn as Elliot Adnopoz—Ramblin' Jack was the son of a prominent doctor, and his Jewish parents would have liked him to follow in his father's footsteps. Instead, he joined the rodeo, moved out West and created a full-blown cowboy persona and folk song repertoire that was renowned in folk circles. He traveled with Guthrie, learning directly from the master. Then Elliot traveled through Europe with banjo man Derroll Adams—later a mentor and inspiration to Scottish folksinger Donovan—and had therefore been rarely seen around Greenwich Village. His wanderin' ways notwithstanding, the "Ramblin'" part of his name, it was said, referred more to his endless onstage storytelling than to his travels. Dylan writes about listening to Elliot's records in *Chronicles, Vol. 1*, describing Elliot's voice as "sharp, focused and piercing," and writes effusively about Elliot's "explosive" performance style, something Dylan felt was lacking in most folk musicians. By 1961, Elliot had released no fewer than eight albums, beginning in 1956 with *Woody Guthrie's Blues*. Dylan, like Elliot before him, was a superb student. And soon, Elliot would be covering Bob Dylan songs and calling Dylan his "son."

"Everybody will help you, some people are very kind," Dylan would later write in his song "I'll Keep It with Mine." And help, he got. For instance, from Dave Van Ronk and Terri Thal. According to Dylan's soon-to-be girlfriend Suze Rotolo, it was Van Ronk who advised him to cultivate an image "to present to the outside world." And he did so with a vengeance, creating a persona that, arguably, outdid and outlasted them all. His was an image that was too good to be true, because it wasn't.

He took his cues from Jack Elliot, Guthrie, and basically everyone around him in the Village. Like the method actors he admired, he used his knowledge of popular culture and his own experiences to *become* the character he was creating. Like Elliot, he would dress the part, speak the part, and sing the part. The outfits and cap were pure, vintage Guthrie, disheveled for that fresh-off-the-freight-train look and with hair to match. Unlike those who donned a folk persona onstage using phony southern accents only when they sang, à la the New Lost City Ramblers, Dylan was always in character, like Ramblin' Jack, with his affected Okie accent and dropping the final "g" in "-ing" words. In his *singin'*, he developed one of the most singularly distinctive vocal sounds, well, ever: whiny to the point of caricature and with a spectacular, medium-course sandpaper finish. It was to become one of the most recognizable and celebrated irritant factors in the pantheon of popular music. To complete the picture, he would weave outrageously tall tales about his past.

Though you'd have never known from hearing him tell it, he was born Robert "Bobby" Zimmerman in Duluth and later moved to Hibbing, Minnesota. His parents were part of a small Jewish community, and by high school he was playing in a rock and roll band, covering the songs of Elvis and Little Richard. Bobby had been in the audience at the Winter Dance Party show in Duluth, Minnesota, on January 31, 1959, when Buddy Holly took the stage solo with his electric guitar to sing Paul Clayton's "Gotta Travel On," three days before Buddy's plane crashed. "He looked me right straight dead in the eye," Dylan wrote in his Nobel Prize acceptance speech in 2017, "and he transmitted something. Something I didn't know what. And it gave me the chills." It was in college that Dylan discovered folk music. He played around with a name change, first trying "Eston Gunn" on for size when he played piano for teen idol Bobby Vee, before settling on Bob Dylan, a tip of the hat to poet Dylan Thomas and, he claims, a play on his own middle name, Allen. Since he was now Dylan and no longer Zimmerman, it was easy to make up stories about his past as he went along. Orphan, runaway, circus boy, hobo, carnival ride operator. . . . And, anyway, mystery was an important ingredient. As Dave Van Ronk put it, "Personal reinvention was the order of the day." As Barry Kornfeld reminded me, "Never let the facts get in the way of a good story." "Except . . . ," Suze Rotolo elaborated, "some of the tales he wove were out of sync with a previously woven one."

Regardless, the result, as history has proven, was perfect. He had stormed into town during that icy winter, halfway through shedding his baby fat and, with the stealth of a burglar, had cased the place out. It didn't take long to figure out how easy it would be to stand out. He knew exactly what he needed to do. Recordings made by Terri Thal at the Gaslight in 1961 reveal a fully formed Bob Dylan, performing an excellent repertoire with ease to the tiny crowd and to modest applause.

One of the first songs he would write and perform at the Gaslight would be "Song to Woody," a tribute that he sang for Guthrie in person and that name-checked three other heroes from the previous generation: Cisco Houston, Sonny Terry, and Lead Belly:

Hey, hey Woody Guthrie, I wrote you a song, bout a funny ol' world that's a-comin' along . . .
Here's to Cisco and Sonny and Lead Belly too, an' to all the good people that traveled with you

A decade later, in 1971, fellow master shape-shifter David Bowie would echo the thought in his "Song for Bob Dylan":

Oh, hear this Robert Zimmerman, I wrote a song for you
About a strange young man called Dylan with a voice like sand and glue

It goes without saying that there was more than just image that was at play here. Dylan had done his homework; he seemed to know folk music as well as rock and roll, blues, R & B, and all manner of popular music. What the boy didn't know, he learned fast. Some found him annoying—like Erik Darling who, according to author Bob Spitz in his 1989 book, *Dylan: A Biography*, "refused to remain in the same room as Dylan"—while others, like Paxton and Van Ronk, were impressed with his deep-cut song choices, performance style, and vocal phrasing. From the start, his very presence could be divisive.

For now, Bob Dylan seemed mostly intent on visiting his hero Woody Guthrie. Woody had been confined in Greystone Park State Hospital in Morris Plains, New Jersey, frail and trembling, suffering from the rare, degenerative nerve disorder Huntington's chorea. To learn what he could from the ailing master the way Ramblin' Jack Elliot had done, Dylan visited Guthrie regularly, once asking Barry Kornfeld for a ride. By that time, Guthrie had been moved to Brooklyn State Hospital. "I had a car," Kornfeld told me, "and I was happy to do it, of course, to be in Woody's presence. But, he (Guthrie) couldn't really speak." By all accounts, Guthrie was pleased and impressed with Dylan, who would sing Guthrie's songs for him, as well as his own new compositions. That February, barely in town a few weeks, Dylan made his Village debut at the Café Wha?, with guitarist and friend Mark Spoelstra, and played harmonica, in his unconventional style that didn't seem to rely on clichéd riffing, for Freddy Neil.

There were more and more places to be seen and heard and to hang out in the Village. In addition to the Square, there were the venues on MacDougal, West Third Street, and Bleecker, the Kettle of Fish, the Caricature, the Folklore Center, the Music Inn instrument and record shop at 169 West Fourth Street, the White Horse on Hudson Street, and various apartments like Dave and Terri's and Cynthia Gooding's. One place in particular that now seems unlikely yet was a favorite haunt was Allan Block's Sandal Shop at 171 West Fourth Street, next to the Music Inn. The shop was opened in 1950 by its classically trained violinist-turned-folk-fiddler namesake, Allan Block, who made excellent, custom sandals that became de rigueur footwear for men and women in the Village scene. Block had a penchant for putting down his leather crafting tools, picking up his fiddle, and instigating impromptu—or scheduled—hoots. Evenings and weekends, particularly on Saturdays, the joint was jumping. Photos from the era show Ramblin' Jack Elliot and regulars the New Lost City Ramblers hanging out. Terri Thal, Happy Traum, Suze Rotolo, and Bob Dylan were often in the house, and jam sessions could include Cisco Houston, the Weavers' Lee Hays, and Mike Seeger, not to mention Dave Van Ronk. Young John Sebastian saw and heard his heroes Mississippi John Hurt and Doc Watson perform there for the first time. It's a miracle that any sandals were made at all, but apparently, they were a quality product. Legend has it that folks who purchased a pair back then are still wearing them today. Allan's daughter Rory Block became a popular country blues guitarist and singer in her own right, leaving home at age fifteen to travel and hone her craft.

But for all the good vibes and acoustic electricity being generated in the Village, it appeared that the folk scene and all that surrounded it had more than its share of enemies. City planners, many of whom considered the predominantly Italian South Village a slum—or what the *New York Times* regarded as a "blighted area"—were still intent on curtailing the musical and social network that was continuing to flourish in, around, and south of Washington Square. NYU—though it added to the cultural vigor of the Village and provided an unparalleled campus environment for students—was, unfortunately, a more-than-willing participant in the destruction and reappropriating of Village properties for its own use, as it helped further its master plan of becoming a major residential university. And the longtime residents continued to resent the crowds of young newcomers and weekend revelers. Locals were often at odds with the offbeat beatniks, gays, and racial diversity that they viewed as an invasion of their territory.

It should be emphasized that New York City during this period was a city of distinct neighborhoods and districts that, for the most part, are not quite as clearly defined today. It was a grid-within-a-grid that had been established over time, especially as different immigrant communities arrived. Little Italy and Chinatown downtown, Germantown on the Upper East Side, and Harlem further uptown are just a few examples. They were worlds unto themselves. And then there were the wholesale and retail business districts—the meatpacking district in the far West Village, the flower district in Chelsea, the fashion district along Seventh Avenue, the musical instrument shops on Music Row on West Forty-Eighth Street, the Financial District near the southernmost tip of Manhattan. Within them there were subdistricts, like the songwriting district, housed in the Brill Building and 1650 Broadway in midtown, the remnants of Tin Pan Alley. In later decades and certainly in the twenty-first century, business models changed, cultures assimilated, and lines blurred some of these districts into nonexistence. But in the 1960s, NYC was territorial.

The Village could be viewed as the *anything goes* district, and social conservatives apparently felt it must be stopped, controlled, renovated, and more efficiently restructured. The second half of the 1950s had seen an effort by immensely powerful Parks commissioner Robert Moses to construct a roadway smack dab though the center of Washington Square Park. Moses's efforts failed. But the battle did not end there. As the new decade began, a new Parks commissioner, New York City aristocrat Newbold Morris, with narrow views on what culture was and what kind of music had value and rumored to be under the thumb of Robert Moses, seemed especially intent on closing down or minimizing the Square by limiting permission to perform folk music there. In an internal memo, after declaring support for "wonderful symphony concerts, bands, quartets, or chamber music" in Washington Square Park, Morris wrote, "What I am against is these fellows that come from miles away to display the most terrible costumes, haircuts, etc. and who play bongo drums and other weird instruments attracting a weird public." Later in the memorandum, he refers to "these freaks."

The media (who often conflated "folksingers" and "beatniks"), NYU, real estate developers, and longtime residents who opposed the cultural diversity and rebellious spirit in the air seemed to be in unanimous support of the ban on folk music in the Park. It was promptly announced in the *New York Times*. Izzy Young of the Folklore Center then requested a permit for folksinging every Sunday in April, and his request was immediately denied. This, of course, was after seventeen years of peaceful folksinging in the Square every Sunday. Always up for defending folk *anything*, Izzy Young helped organize a protest. What happened on the following Sunday, April 9, 1961, was a clash which, looking at it sixty years later, can be seen as emblematic of the generational and cultural rift that would come to define the decade. Catchily misnamed by the media as the "Beatnik Riot," it was the first major protest of the 1960s in the Village. And, luckily, it was all captured artfully on film by eighteen-year-old filmmaker Dan Drasin—an employee of prominent documentarians D. A. Pennebaker, Albert Maysles, and Richard Leacock—who just happened to live upstairs from the Folklore Center.

The seventeen-minute, black-and-white, 16mm film *Sunday* portrays the protest in its entirety, first setting the scene with little kids playing in the park, interracial couples hanging out on a Sunday morning, and people walking their dogs. Panned shots show police and paddy wagons standing at the ready. Then some views of the Folklore Center, showing the hand-painted sign in the window:

PROTEST RALLY

AT THE

FOUNTAIN

IN

WASHINGTON SQUARE

THIS SUNDAY AT 2PM

In the park, the trees are still without leaves. No doubt, after the long winter, the folksinging regulars were anticipating those Sundays in the Square when spring finally came. And the spring may have brought with it a fighting spirit. Soon, the first arrivals appear with guitars and banjos strapped to their backs or held over the shoulder, like weapons for battle; some are carrying instruments in cases, and some people are raising handwritten protest signs. Happy Traum is there in the crowd and can be seen in four or five scenes. Tom Paxton was there. "I was ready to be arrested," he told me. The music playing is "This Land Is Your Land." When Izzy Young enters the throng and tries to communicate with the police, they might as well have been representatives from two alien races landed in the Park for a summit of two different planets. Especially when Young tells a cop, "We feel the police are illegal in their actions," and "This is our God-given right, to sing folk songs." The crowd becomes more and more dense and more intense; they sing defiantly. The police look confused. Then they start roughing some people up—a bespectacled youth gently singing and strumming an autoharp is grabbed by the collar and pushed to a police car by no less than five officers. They ask him for ID and he shows them his draft card. They say they need more. He is arrested and driven off with the five cops, siren blaring. More cops, more arrests, more songs. "The Battle Hymn of the Republic." "The Star-Spangled Banner." A lot of pushing and shoving by the police. A young girl is grabbed by cops and screams, and then a well-dressed youth in a tie and glasses is pushed and falls hard to the ground. Shouts of "Heil, Hitler!" and "I think the police should sing a song for *us* now: 'Deutschland Uber Alles!'" Then, quiet. The film goes silent as the cops stand around randomly in the center of the Square, now cleared except for a couple of small kids in hooded parkas, one with a sign on their back proclaiming "I Want to Sing Too!"

When it was all said and done, ten people had been arrested, and twenty were injured, including three members of the NYPD. Nearly one hundred participants claimed they had witnessed police brutality. In those pre-bodycam days, Dan Drasin's film captured what actually happened and did so with such style that *Sunday* is part of the permanent film collection at New York's Museum of Modern Art. *Village Voice* film critic Jonas Mekas praised its "authenticity and aliveness" in his May 25,

1961, "Film Journal" column. Speaking in an interview with Boston NPR affiliate WBUR on the event's fiftieth anniversary in 2011, Drasin said, "It was a chaotic day, without a whole lot of rhyme and reason. But it was certainly representative of the era to come, when the people confronted established authority and started holding them accountable. It would've been unthinkable in the 1950s. But this was the beginning of the 1960s."

The episode was far from over. The next day the media, still supporting the ban on folk-singing in the Square, ran biased articles defending the police and praising Commissioner Morris. "FOLK SINGERS RIOT IN WASHINGTON SQ.," blared the *New York Times* and "3000 BEATNIKS RIOT IN VILLAGE," screamed the now long defunct *New York Mirror*. Izzy Young wasted no time. He joined forces with Reverend Howard Moody of Judson Memorial Church, the progressive church located on Washington Square South, Art D'Lugoff of the Village Gate, Oscar Brand, and others to form the Right to Sing Committee. A rally was held simultaneously at Judson Church and the Village Gate on the afternoon of April 16, featuring performances by the Clancy Brothers and Tommy Makem, Erik Darling, Cynthia Gooding, Logan English, Alan Lomax, Ed McGurdy, the Shanty Boys, and of course, Dave Van Ronk. The Village Independent Democrats, led by future NYC mayor Ed Koch, supported their efforts, as did community organizer and author Jane Jacobs. More rallies, more debating, and more petitions followed. It wasn't easy. But finally, in July 1961, a decision in the State Supreme Court of New York ordered the Parks commissioner to once again accept applications for Sunday singing in Washington Square. It was a hard-won victory. But it was more than that, gaining national and international attention for the Greenwich Village folk scene. If they could win this battle, against all odds, over the right to sing in the little patch of land in the middle of the Village, what else might they accomplish?

Bob Dylan asked Terri Thal to help him get gigs, and she became his first manager/booking agent. After a few failed attempts, and after others in Dylan's circle had been badgering him, Thal was able to convince Mike Porco to book Dylan into Gerde's Folk City. It was Dylan's first real gig in the Village, a two-week run of shows opening for blues legend John Lee Hooker, beginning on April 11, 1961, just two days after the Washington Square protest. At nineteen, Dylan was too young to obtain the necessary NYC cabaret license and join the Musicians' Union Local 802 without parental consent, and too poor to pay for it. Porco would sign on as Dylan's legal guardian and front the necessary ninety dollars. Dylan would later call Porco "the Sicilian father I never knew I had." According to Porco's grandson, Bob

Porco, Dylan had actually been "hired for one week, but was held over for a second." "Hooker stayed at the Broadway Central Hotel, as did most of the blues guys, for three dollars per night," Bob Porco added. The Broadway Central Hotel had opened in 1870 as a four-hundred-room, glitzy palace but, in one of New York's most spectacular riches-to-rags stories, had fallen to decline. In fact, it finally, literally, collapsed, killing four and injuring many more, in 1973. Mark Spoelstra told author Bob Spitz that Dylan felt he didn't have anything appropriate to wear for his Folk City debut and went to visit Hooker at his modest room at the Broadway Central to borrow some trousers. Spoelstra loaned him a brown jacket, and Dylan's trademark corduroy cap completed the ensemble.

The Folk City shows were a success, with all the regulars coming out to support him. He had only been in New York for six weeks.

On July 29, soon after the State Supreme Court decision to allow folksinging in the Square, Izzy Young, along with Bob Yellin of bluegrass group the Greenbriar Boys, hosted a twelve-hour folk marathon at Riverside Church in Morningside Heights in Harlem, near Columbia University, that was broadcast live on WRVR-FM, Riverside Radio. Among the over fifty folk and blues acts on the bill were Reverend Gary Davis, blues singer-songwriter Victoria Spivey, Cynthia Gooding, John Cohen, Marshall Brickman (banjoist with the Tarriers and later a successful screenwriter and director who collaborated with Woody Allen and wrote *Jersey Boys*), Roger Sprung, and Ramblin' Jack Elliot. Recordings of the concert reveal an awkward, downer set from Dylan, opening with a false start, fumbling with his tuning, and interminably fidgeting with his broken coat hanger harmonica holder. One song just peters out completely as the holder fails yet again. As this is on live radio, there are minutes of dead airtime as he asks the audience for a knife to fix his coat hanger. He only catches fire when guitarist Danny Kalb joins him for the last song in the set, on which Kalb sings and Dylan lets loose on his signature harmonica playing. Here he comes to life. Dylan returns at the very end of the concert, joined by Ramblin' Jack Elliot, to improvise a bizarre doo-wop song about having acne at the senior prom. Sounds to me like somebody backstage was passing around a bottle of red wine, the alcoholic beverage of choice at the time.

Ever the champion of the Greenwich Village folk scene, Robert Shelton reviewed the concert favorably and insightfully in the *New York Times*, listing among the highlights "Logan English's tart topical song about the Washington Square ruckus." Shelton noted among the "newer promising talents deserving mention . . . Tom Paxton, a Western singer with an obvious potential as a songwriter" and "a 20-year-old latter day Guthrie disciple named Bob Dylan, with a curiously arresting mumbling, country-steeped manner." According to Suze Rotolo, even though they had seen each other before, at

Gerde's with Mark Spoelstra, it was at the Riverside Church event that she and Dylan really met for the first time, and as Rotolo describes the scene in her memoir, the two flirted with each other backstage all day during the marathon concert. Before long, they were a *thing*. According to Happy Traum, Dylan was ubiquitous on the scene at this time. Rotolo, too, seemed to pop up everywhere. Both were living nomadically, Dylan on friends' couches—such as the Van Ronks', or at Miki Isaacson's apartment, a well-known "crash pad for folksingers," on the fourth floor of One Sheridan Square—and Rotolo apartment-sitting for friends on Waverly Place, staying at her sister Carla's, or with her mom just one flight below Miki Isaacson at One Sheridan Square.

Suze Rotolo began working for the New York City office of CORE, the civil rights organization she had volunteered with a couple of years prior while in high school. 1961 was the year of the Freedom Rides, organized by activist Bayard Rustin, in which Black and white activists would defiantly sit together in interstate Greyhound and Trailways buses riding into segregated southern states, challenging those states' failure to observe multiple Supreme Court rulings that segregated public buses were unconstitutional. Future congressman John Lewis was one of the original thirteen Freedom Riders, on the first CORE Freedom Ride from May 4 to 17. They were met with KKK violence, humiliation, and angry white mobs. Many Riders were arrested, including Bayard Rustin himself, who spent twenty-two days on a chain gang for violating segregated seating laws. The rides continued through the summer, and the campaign expanded to include other examples of racial discrimination, such as segregation in restaurants and hotels. All told, there were over four hundred Freedom Riders who traveled throughout the South over seven months. Over the next few years, CORE and the Student Nonviolent Coordinating Committee (SNCC) would find support and forge alliances with the Greenwich Village folk scene and the Newport Folk Festival, especially in the period leading up to Dr. King's monumental March on Washington in August 1963. In 1964, Carolyn Hester and Gil Turner would participate in Freedom Summer, in which hundreds of white volunteers joined African Americans to fight against voter intimidation and discrimination in Mississippi.

Dave Van Ronk and Terri Thal made it official and got married on August 4, 1961. "It was a hot day," Terri told me. And, apparently, the day wasn't all that was hot. Sixteen-year-old Steve Katz was taking guitar lessons from Van Ronk. "Dave and Terri made love constantly," he wrote in his excellent 2015 memoir, *Blood, Sweat, and My Rock 'n' Roll Years*, as he describes them slipping into the bedroom while he waited in the small living room for his lesson to begin. Meanwhile, their apartment on Waverly Place continued to resemble a folk equivalent of Grand Central Station. "We eventually had to lay down ground rules so we could screw without having to worry about people barging in," Van Ronk revealed in *The Mayor of MacDougal Street*. Sexual appetites and bedroom breaks aside, no two people were more active or more important on the Greenwich Village music scene than these two. "I wanted them to be my parents," Steve Katz recalled. "Dave and Terri opened a world for me that I never wanted to leave."

After the Washington Square protest and the "Right to Sing" rallies, the pace seemed to pick up for more public demonstrations, challenging a variety of issues, and musicians in the folk community were particularly active. Even Happy Traum, one of the least outwardly political folksingers on the scene, was arrested and spent the entire week of his twenty-third birthday incarcerated at Hart's Island correctional facility in the Bronx for his involvement in a City Hall Park rally protesting the mandatory civil defense drills, in which all citizens were required to take shelter—ducking into subway stations or other dubious shelters—in preparation for a nuclear attack from the Soviet Union. The Cold War had everyone on edge, and it was only getting worse. The drills, which famously included instructing elementary school students to hide under their desks, seemed, to some anyway, just as ludicrous then as they do now.

Save the Village

Another threat was more local. Former New York City Parks commissioner Robert Moses, who was then chairman of the Triborough Bridge and Tunnel Authority, pushed forward two federal plans. One would wipe out a massive hunk of Lower Manhattan—from Chinatown, through SoHo, and through the center of Greenwich Village—to build the elevated, eight-lane Lower Manhattan Expressway (LOMEX), cutting across the city from the East River to the Hudson, destroying thousands of historic buildings and potentially displacing ten thousand residents and workers. "We simply repeat," the automobile-obsessed but nondriving Moses intoned, "that cities are created by and for *traffic*." Condemning the West Village as a slum, a second plan would demolish fourteen entire blocks of Hudson Street, including, incidentally, the White Horse Tavern on Hudson Street at West Eleventh, as well as the home of author and activist Jane Jacobs on that same block, at 555 Hudson Street. That very year, forty-five-year-old Jacobs had published her book *The Death and Life of Great American Cities*, a landmark study and critique of 1950s urban planning that promoted the sanctity of neighborhoods and communities. Speaking in Ric Burns's masterful *New York: A Documentary Film* (1999) about Jacobs's book, urbanist Marshall Berman said, "[Jacobs] created, maybe without intending to do it, a kind of empathy, and opened up possibilities for empathy as a political force in the sixties."

Moses had further planned to build similar multilane highways across Midtown at Thirtieth Street and uptown in Harlem. But the Village was having none of it and once again came together. They chose as their leader the diminutive, bespectacled Jane Jacobs. What followed was a massive David-and-Goliath fight against hulking Robert Moses. Moses, however, was not prepared for the battle. His previous construction projects that required the destruction of neighborhoods, like the Cross Bronx Expressway, had not met with the kind of fierce resistance he met in Greenwich Village. Echoing the opposition to the New York City grid plan of exactly 150 years earlier, Villagers organized and formed multiethnic coalitions, spoke to the media, and held large rallies. They attended public meetings en masse. The fight was brutal, and Moses used every trick and tactic at his disposal, using intimidation and sexist, strident condescension against Jacobs. She was arrested, charged with rioting, inciting to riot, criminal mischief, and obstructing public administration. But support for Jacobs and the Village coalition continued to grow. Over a year later, in December 1962, Jacobs and her allies emerged from the decisive City Hall hearing victorious. The Village was saved. Three years later, the Landmarks Preservation Commission was established, saving historic buildings throughout New York City.

John Hammond, Carolyn Hester, and Bob Dylan

Charlie Rothschild had been managing Carolyn Hester since soon after her Gerde's debut. "But he was about to be drafted," Hester told me, "and he asked Albert Grossman to look after the artists he had." Hester and Richard Fariña had been living in Charlottesville, Virginia, at the time when, one evening in the late summer of 1961, Rothschild phoned. "Listen," Rothschild told Hester, "word is that John Hammond is looking for folksingers to sign. I want you to get back to New York as soon as you can, by tomorrow night if you can. I'm gonna want you to audition for him. So bring your guitar." Hester made the trip and headed up to Columbia Records to meet with Hammond. "He only heard me do *one song*," she told me, still incredulous. "'Okay, I'm gonna sign you up,'" he told me, "'and I'm gonna figure out with Charlie and Al what is best for you.'" As planning for an album quickly began, Hester told Hammond that she would like as accompanists Bruce Langhorne, a guitarist she adored, and Bill Lee on bass, whom she knew from his work with Odetta. Recording would begin in thirty days or so.

After her first "homegrown" album, recorded back in Clovis with Norman Petty at the controls and her father on harmonica, and her second one for the Clancy Brothers' tiny Tradition label, this was a big deal. Columbia was huge. And she would be working with the legendary John Hammond himself. Hester began choosing songs and thinking about arrangements. But first, she was scheduled to perform at Gerde's. "It was late at night," she told me, describing the evening. "I had already done two sets and was about to do my third, so there were fewer people in there by this time. I started my set with 'Lonesome Tears,' the Buddy Holly song that I've done forever because I credit him for me doing *anything*. So, after I finish 'Lonesome Tears,' this young guy with a cap on pulls his chair halfway across the room, to the stage, beside me. Now I'm looking at him, getting ready for the next song. And he starts *talking* to me. Nobody seems to mind. And he says, 'Did you really know Buddy Holly?' and I said, 'Yeah,' and he said, 'That's . . . a *god*.'" After the set, Hester was in the kitchen of Gerde's packing up her guitar when the young guy came in and introduced himself. "'I'm Bob Dylan. I'm friends with Dave Van Ronk and Terri and they've been trying to get me gigs and all that, but it's slow-goin',' he said. 'So sometime maybe we can play songs together and stuff?' And I said, 'Well, okay.'"

A couple of weeks later, Hester was booked to perform in Boston. "And lo and behold, he's opening the set for me," Hester told me. "Dylan had hitchhiked to Boston and talked Paula Kelly, the booker of Club 47, into letting him open a show for me. Now, at Club 47, there was hardly ever an opening act. But I thought he was terrific. Not only that, but the next day I see him again. He was staying with [Cambridge folkie] Eric Von Schmidt, and Eric wanted us all to go to the beach. So we're all at the beach, Dylan, me, Richard, the Van Ronks, Eric and his wife, and their little girl." This was at Revere Beach, near Boston. On the beach, Hester let Dylan know that she had enjoyed his set the night before and, delighted, he offered to open more shows for her. Both Hester and Fariña were fascinated, if not smitten, by Dylan's quirkiness. "It was magnetism," she told the *Los Angeles Times* in 1989. "He hadn't written 'Blowin' in the Wind' or much of anything yet, but he was filled with magnetism." She told Dylan that she wouldn't be gigging immediately because she had just been signed by Columbia and was getting ready to record an album. "Is there any way I can help you?" Dylan immediately asked. "Well, I've already got a fabulous guitar player, and Bill Lee on bass, but you know what? My dad played harmonica for me on my first record . . . would . . . you be interested in that, maybe on several songs? And he said, 'Here's my phone number. I'll be there. And he was. He was!'" For her album, Hester chose a bouncy blues, "Come Back, Baby," written by Walter Davis in 1940, that Dylan would play on. Back in the Village, they got together for a casual run-through in an apartment at One Sheridan Square, upstairs in the same building that had once housed Café Society in its basement, where John Hammond had held court and booked his star discovery Billie Holiday, where she had debuted "Strange Fruit," and where his artist Josh White had become a star. If only Hammond had shown up there, he would have met Bob Dylan for the first time at that same, historic address. But that would have been too perfect.

Before the recording sessions, Hammond requested a full rehearsal to hear the whole band together. Carolyn and Richard were apartment-sitting in the Village for a friend on West Tenth Street, near Sixth Avenue, and she suggested they rehearse there. In the kitchen was a picnic table that the band sat around. Hester described the scene for me: "Bob was across from me, and Bill was at the end of the table with his stand-up bass, and Bruce was sitting next to me, and Richard was kind of . . . wandering around; sometimes he'd sit down. The main thing was that we really *hit it*. I mean, to me, that is one of the outstanding times I've had in the studio. And, that's how it ended up that Dylan met Hammond: I introduced them in a kitchen on Tenth Street in the Village." Before he left, Hammond asked if Dylan was currently signed to a record label. "I shook my head . . . and that was that," wrote Dylan in *Chronicles*.

A matter of days later, Dylan returned to perform at Gerde's Folk City, opening for the Greenbriar Boys. By this time, he had graduated from couch-surfing all over the Village and was renting his own, top-floor apartment at 161 West Fourth Street, a few doors down from Allan Block's Sandal Shop and the Music Inn, for sixty bucks a month. In November, when she turned eighteen, Suze Rotolo would move in with him there.

It was in the aftermath of those shows at Gerde's, from September 26 through October 8, 1961, that things really took off for Dylan and, arguably, for the Village scene itself. The boy was on fire on that stage. Just as importantly, Robert Shelton's *New York Times* review, published on September 29, basically caused a seismic shift or, to put it in *Star Wars* lingo, a disturbance in the Force, that is still being felt to this day. In terms of music journalism, it is a Magna Carta. Beautifully written, it made Bob Dylan a star: "A bright new face in folk music" . . . "resembling a cross between a choir boy and a beatnik" . . . "Mr. Dylan is both comedian and tragedian" . . . "elasticized phrases are drawn out until you think they may snap." And finally, "Mr. Dylan is vague about his antecedents and birthplace, but it matters less where he has been than where he is going, and that would seem to be straight up."

The timing for the *Times* review could not have been better if it had been scripted. The review was to appear the very same day John Hammond was scheduled to produce the session for Carolyn Hester's album at Columbia Studios; Mr. Hammond would be sure to see it.

Chapter Five

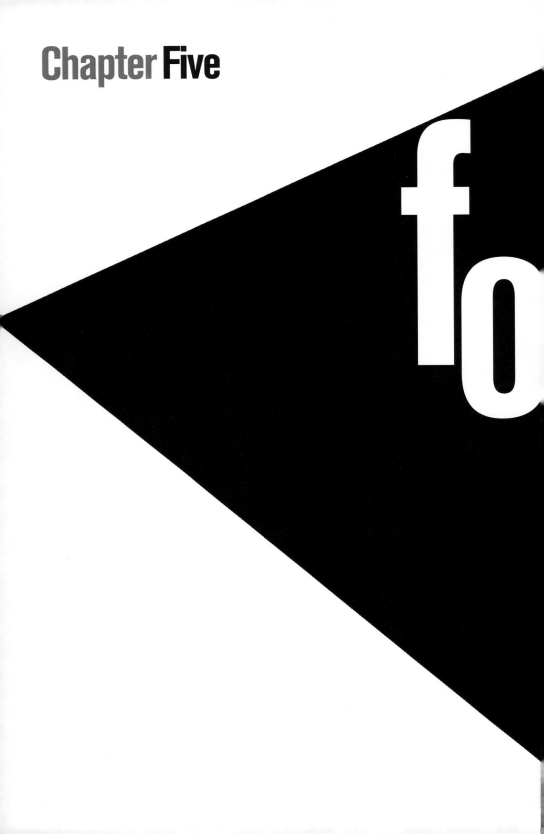

ik
m messiah

Bob Dylan and manager Albert Grossman, backstage at the Newport Folk Festival, 1965, conspiring their full-scale electric assault for Dylan's evening show.

*Everybody was traveling to the same place
but taking different roads.*
— Anthony DeCurtis

Carolyn Hester's first sessions for Columbia

came at a moment when something was about to give. Listening now, you can almost feel the pull of traditional folk music in one direction and sense a contemporary energy hinting at new possibilities in the other. At times, Hester's voice, fulfilling her avian designation as "Texas Songbird," indeed takes flight, not only with the high, sweet trills of a bird's song but also with a vibrato like the delicate fast-fluttering of birds' wings. The opening song for the album, appropriately, is "I'll Fly Away," a southern gospel jam written by Albert E. Brumley in 1932, with an upbeat, bluegrass-like tempo and inflection that underscores her love of country music. "My grandparents were folksingers and they still sing a lot of old songs. Then I heard a lot of country music in Dallas—and my father adored the Grand Ole Opry,"

Hester wrote in the album's liner notes. What follows are more spiritually themed songs, a couple of tunes in Spanish, some blues, and Celtic folk songs. Throughout, Hester's voice is pure and engaging with extraordinary warmth, alternately reverent and playful. She sounds more mature than on her Tradition LP of the previous year, singing in a voice that betrays more life experience, and is more willing to use her lower range and chest voice, which Robert Shelton had praised in the review of her opening night performance at Folk City.

On these sessions, Bruce Langhorne, making his recorded debut although he was already an in-demand guitarist on the scene in live shows and concerts, accompanied Hester on guitar and fiddle. Langhorne had started out playing with Brother John Sellers in the Village, then with the Clancy Brothers and Tommy Makem, and with Odetta. He would go on to be a major component in the evolution of the folk sound through the 1960s. Having three missing fingers on his right hand—lost in a fireworks accident as a child—was said to contribute to his unique playing style. Langhorne's delicate, harmonics-only, performance on "Dear Companion" is positively haunting. On bass for the sessions was Bill Lee, father of film director Spike Lee, who had been the "house bassist" at the Gate of Horn in Chicago and who began performing with Odetta as a duo in the late 1950s. Both African Americans, Lee and Langhorne had each become go-to musicians on the folk scene and, with their knowledge and musicality were, well, instrumental in keeping things interesting. On this album, Lee's jazz sensibility is an attractive contrast to Hester's traditional folk and country instincts, simultaneously propelling and anchoring the songs. The wild card is Bob Dylan's harmonica, inventively busy and chugging, improvising with unusual stretches and bends, and surprising the listener with bold, one-note sustains that cross over chord changes. His soulful, single-note solo on "Come Back, Baby" is particularly effective. It is that song on which Hester is also at her most playful vocally. "He couldn't have suspected what lay ahead of him," Hester told me, "but he was really in the moment."

Carolyn Hester was merging styles here, presaging by a couple of decades the "folkabilly" of her dear friend and fellow Texan Nanci Griffith, mixing elegant acoustic folk with country blues. "I'm really proud of that album," Carolyn told me. "I loved the opportunity of making those albums, because I wanted to do a different feel every time. And, I think that's what Dylan really liked about what we were doing. That I was a gambler." But equally as fascinating is Hester's role as a conduit between two decades, spiritually linking her friend Buddy Holly, whose final session she had attended as the '50s were ending, with Bob Dylan, as his career and the 1960s were just beginning. In *Chronicles*, Dylan wrote of Hester, "That she had known and worked with Buddy Holly made no small impression on me and I liked being around her. Buddy was royalty, and I felt she was my connection to it, the rock-and-roll music that I'd played earlier, to that spirit."

Like others who had fallen under his spell, producer John Hammond had his eye on Dylan throughout the session on September 29. Having just read the *New York Times* review and then seeing the boy in action, freestyling on harmonica in the studio, he was impressed enough to ask Dylan to stay after the session and meet him in the control room. It was then and there, as the others were packing up to leave, that Hammond offered Dylan a contract with Columbia Records. Hammond hadn't heard Dylan sing even one note, other than perhaps some loose harmonies with Carolyn Hester at the apartment rehearsal. Yet as if Billie Holiday, Count Basie, Benny Goodman, and even Pete Seeger weren't enough, John Hammond was about to add Bob Dylan to his list of discoveries, and Dylan was about to step into a realm few would enter. But there was still a ways to go before you could say a star was born. That fact was confirmed on November 4, 1961, when Izzy Young produced a concert by Dylan at Carnegie Hall's smaller, fifth-floor Chapter Hall, promoted with an appearance on Oscar Brand's *Folksong Festival* radio show on WNYC. Only fifty-three people showed up.

Once the contract with Columbia was signed and with the ink partially dried, recording sessions for Bob Dylan's debut album were scheduled for November 20 and 22. There would be three brief afternoon sessions. Dave Van Ronk and Tom Paxton congratulated Dylan, wishing him well. To collect the songs for the album, he visited friends and listened to everything he could get his hands on, all manner of folk and blues records. Suze's sister, Carla Rotolo, who at the time was working as assistant to Alan Lomax, had an especially fine collection of folk recordings at her apartment on Perry Street, and Bob spent hours there, sitting on the floor going through albums, revisiting the Harry Smith *Anthology of American Folk Music*, and choosing songs that were, for the most part, not in his current live set. There would be two originals ("Talkin' New York," and "Song to Woody") and "Baby Let Me Follow You Down," borrowing the arrangement from Eric Von Schmidt and name-checking him on the recording. But perhaps the most famous story of borrowing on this album involves his choice of the song "House of the Rising Sun."

To be fair, "House of the Rising Sun" had already been recorded and performed countless times; it was covered regularly by basically every folksinger on the planet and had been for years. Since first recorded by Clarence "Tom" Ashley and Gwen Foster in 1933, it was recorded by Lead Belly, Woody Guthrie, Pete Seeger, the Almanac Singers, the Weavers, Joan Baez, Carolyn Hester, Josh White . . . you name 'em. They all did it. But Dave Van Ronk's arrangement was different. Van Ronk had devised a particular, defining melody with a clear, trademark, ascending bass line, rising in half steps, that has since become the most familiar, popular form of the song. While clearly, it is strongly inspired by the 1941 version by Van Ronk's hero Josh White—which appeared on White's 1944 album *Strange Fruit*—it does not follow White's chord progression; it changes the rhythm and redefines the melody. Later versions almost invariably use Van Ronk's chords, in various strumming patterns. Van Ronk's own guitar accompaniment is a bed of quick rhythmic strums, almost bolero-like, on which floats his singular, strained, bluesy voice, reciting the words with all the playful seriousness of a Shakespeare soliloquy, phrasing in unexpected ways, stretching words and squeezing every syllable until the note runs dry. In other words, it is unique. So much so, that it became a signature showpiece in Van Ronk's live shows. Hearing the hulking, masculine Van Ronk sing this song from the point of view of a young woman—"It's been the ruin of many a poor girl, and me, oh God, I'm one"—made it sublimely compelling. The right recording of Van Ronk performing "House of the Rising Sun" in his unique vocal style might have been just the thing to make Van Ronk the star he should have been—or at least given him a major boost.

That's why it was so devastating when Dylan came up to him at the Kettle of Fish just after the Columbia sessions and asked Dave if it would, um, be okay for him to record his arrangement of the song. Dave cringed and said no, he'd rather he didn't, because he was planning to record it himself for *his* new album in a couple of weeks. Dylan replied with an "uh-oh." When Van Ronk asked what that meant, Dylan admitted that he had already recorded it. Van Ronk was furious, walked out of the Kettle of Fish, and wouldn't speak to Dylan for two months. Terri Thal tells how, every night, Dylan would beg to talk with Dave, tearfully calling at the same apartment where he had been welcomed and slept on the couch so many times when he first arrived in the Village earlier that same year, without a place to stay. And every night she had to tell him, "Dave won't talk to you." Eventually, Van Ronk buried the hatchet. But neither he nor Terri ever really fully trusted Dylan again.

Since Dylan had already done it, Van Ronk did not record "House of the Rising Sun" for his next album. He would not do so until 1964, in the midst of the "British Invasion." By that time, however, the UK group the Animals had already ridden the song—using Dave's arrangement, which they considered to be Dylan's, and flipping the gender to masculine—to the top of the US singles chart, giving the arranging credit on the label not to Bob or Dave but to the group's organist, Alan Price. Van Ronk's version was released two months later. In a final irony, soon Dylan himself would stop performing the song, as the perception was that he was covering the Animals' hit.

Terri Thal would also feel a personal betrayal when "Bobby" took on Albert Grossman to be his manager and told her of his decision not before but *after* the word was out. Thal had been looking after Dylan's bookings and business affairs basically since he had arrived in the Village, including recording his shows at the Gaslight and trying to get him a record deal. In her heart, she knew she couldn't compete with the Svengali-like Grossman, a managerial messiah who also represented Odetta, Bob Gibson, John Lee Hooker, Peter, Paul and Mary, and Ian & Sylvia, as well as looking after Carolyn Hester and others for Charlie Rothschild . . . and not to mention had helped book the 1959 Newport Folk Festival and had the experience of co-owning the Gate of Horn in Chicago. His tentacles reached throughout the folk world. But like Dave, Terri had reservations about Grossman. "He was scary. If he came into a room, I froze. If I was talking, I would shut up." Describing the scene at her and Dave's apartment at 190 Waverly Place, Thal recalls, "Folk music people sitting around playing guitars, socialists . . . it was like a hotel. But I always walked around the apartment in just my panties and a bra. Not really sexy ones, just ones my mother had sent me. But when Albert Grossman came over, I would always run into the bedroom and put on a slip, which to me was like getting fully dressed. He was creepy."

Peter, Paul and Mary
Ever since the success of the Kingston Trio, the idea of forming and managing a hipper folk trio had

been on Albert Grossman's mind and, in 1961, he started scouting in the Village, vetting possible members. Peter Yarrow, who had melted Grossman's heart with his moving rendition of "Buddy, Can You Spare a Dime?" and was already managed by Grossman as a solo artist, was a logical starting point. As the group was to be mixed gender, the search for the right woman was on. How about Carolyn Hester? Hester was asked by Grossman but, of course, she turned down the offer—she was happy doing her own thing. Climbing up the narrow stairs on MacDougal Street, Yarrow and Grossman stopped into the Folklore Center as everyone did at the time, especially when looking for musicians. As recounted by Mary Travers in Jim Brown's documentary *50 Years with Peter, Paul and Mary* (2014), "On the walls were pictures of anybody who had ever sung a note of folk music." Apparently, one such photo stood out to Yarrow. "She's interesting-looking," Yarrow said to Grossman, pointing to a picture of a lovely, blond, female folksinger that caught his eye. "Oh, that's Mary Travers," Grossman replied. "She'd be good, if you can get her to work." "Well, it wouldn't be hard to locate her," Izzy mentioned, pointing out that Travers was living right there on MacDougal, across the street.

It would be hard to think of a more perfect choice for this role than Mary Travers. Though born in Louisville, Kentucky, Travers had grown up, like John Sebastian, in Greenwich Village, around Washington Square, and had attended the progressive Little Red School House and Elisabeth Irwin High School, where she saw, heard, and met Pete Seeger, Paul Robeson, Theodore Bikel, and other folk musicians, actors, and activists who encouraged her to sing. Joining the folk group the Song Swappers in high school, she had sung background vocals on four Pete Seeger albums in the 1950s. Yarrow and Grossman called on Travers, telling her of their plans to form a new trio. She and Peter sang a little together in her apartment, it sounded good, and they invited her on board. "Yes," she replied. She was in. Now the search for the third. Grossman approached Dave Van Ronk who thought about it for a few days, discussing it with wife Terri. But ultimately, he turned down the offer. Van Ronk was a beautiful, creative (read: stubborn, idiosyncratic) solo artist in his own right and, as he put it in his memoir, would have "stuck out like a sore thumb" in every way as part of that trio. His and Terri's instincts were correct, even if the decision was to be parodied in the Coen Brothers' film *Inside Llewyn Davis,* over fifty years later. Okay then, so if not Van Ronk, who will it be? Please don't tell me they will ask "the toilet man," the stand-up comedian, singer, Hitler impersonator, and some-times host at the Gaslight, Noel Stookey? You can't be serious. You're kidding, right? Well, actually no. Not kidding. The story goes that Mary Travers recommended Stookey, whom she knew from the scene, and that Grossman approached Stookey after an especially uproarious routine at the Gaslight, convincing him to join the group. Using his middle name, Paul, the trio became Peter, Paul and Mary, and they would soon blow things wide open.

And, Grossman saw that it was good. The names, Peter, Paul and Mary, combined, sounded biblical, communicating a kind of antiquity, sanctity, and inevitability that was ideal for folk music. There was a reason for that. In actuality, the group's name was inspired by the lyrics of a traditional, humorous song first recorded in the 1920s, "I Was Born Ten Thousand Years Ago," that Peter Yarrow was singing in his act:

> *Saw Peter, Paul and Moses playing ring around the roses*
> *I'll lick the guy that says it isn't so*

Which explains why Noel became Paul. Anyway, the combination of personalities and vocal blend—the earnestness of tenor Yarrow; the pure, sincere, soulfulness; and power of contralto Travers's sound; and the easygoing charm of baritone "Paul" Stookey—would prove irresistible.

Their repertoire was carefully curated. They would choose the best possible songs: some from the traditional canon, some they would write themselves, and many from the amazing new writers that were emerging right there in the Village. From the very start, the message and mission of Peter, Paul and Mary were an intentional continuation, picking up where Pete Seeger and the Weavers had left off but targeted to baby boomers. The fastidious planning, the respect they showed for the folk tradition, the quality and purity of their polished presentation would, for the most part, help prevent the criticisms from folk purists that befell the Kingston Trio. They certainly weren't frat boys. Even if some accused them as being "slick," it had to be admitted that they were not phonies. They could not fail.

Peter, Paul and Mary made their debut at the Bitter End on Bleecker Street, right around the same time of Dylan's run at Gerde's and Robert Shelton's *New York Times* review. The trio was booked for a few weeks and, while the first two went okay, it was the third week—after a series of hyperbole-loaded advertisements in the *New York Times*—that they packed the joint. It was then that Warner Bros. Records made an offer. The shows launched not only Peter, Paul and Mary but helped establish the Bitter End as one of the most popular venues in the Village.

Where Have All the Flowers Gone?

The Kingston Trio happened to catch an early Peter, Paul and Mary show at George Wein's Storyville nightclub in Boston and were especially taken by one of the songs they sang, "Where Have All the Flowers Gone?" written by Pete Seeger and released by Seeger on his Folkways album *Rainbow Quest* in

1960. The Kingston Trio rushed into the studio and recorded the song themselves almost immediately; legend has it that they did so the very next day. They released it in December 1961—five months before Peter, Paul and Mary's album was released in May 1962. The Kingston Trio's recording is one of their most effective. The brisk tempo, light guitar strumming, soft vocals, and close harmonies suit the song and place it among the most familiar renditions of Seeger's classic. It was a top-40 hit, reaching 21 on the pop chart and 4 on the easy listening chart, continuing the Kingston Trio's winning streak. Once again, however, there was an irregularity with the song credit. According to David King Dunaway, in his book *How Can I Keep from Singing? The Ballad of Pete Seeger* (2008), and as Pete once told me, the Kingston Trio originally claimed authorship, apparently thinking "Where Have All the Flowers Gone?" was a traditional, public domain folk song. It must be admitted, it certainly sounds like one. But luckily, Seeger, through his publisher, got wind of their mistake before the record was pressed by Capitol, so on every copy I have ever seen, the song is correctly credited to Pete Seeger.

To give full credit where credit is due, the final two verses of "Where Have All the Flowers Gone?" had actually been added by a summer camp counselor who had been singing the song to the kids. "The counselor added two actual verses: 'Where have all the soldiers gone? / Gone to graveyards every one' and 'Where have all the graveyards gone? / Covered with flowers every one.' Joe Hickerson is his name, and I give him 20 percent of the royalties. That song still brings in thousands of dollars from all around the world," Seeger told *Performing Songwriter* magazine in the May 2013 issue.

Also performing the song during that time, but with far more gravitas, was actress and singer Marlene Dietrich, who was concurrently starring in the film *Judgment at Nuremberg* (1961), directed by Stanley Kramer, which centered around the trial of four judges for crimes against humanity in Nazi Germany. Dietrich performed "Where Have All the Flowers Gone?" in concert, singing in German, French, and English, arranged by Burt Bacharach, and always name-checking Seeger as she introduced it. "Here's a song by Pete Seeger, a song that I love very much," she would say, singing the song in a glittering, skintight evening gown. Dietrich would perform the song in German on tour in Israel, where it was warmly received, breaking an unofficial ban on using the German language that had been in place in that country since World War II. In 1963, she would perform Seeger's "Turn! Turn! Turn!" in German as "Glaub, Glaub, Glaub."

While his songs were being sung around the world, 1961 was also the year that Pete Seeger faced sentencing by the House Un-American Activities Committee. It was in 1957 that he had been indicted on ten counts of contempt of Congress for refusing to answer questions about his affiliations and political beliefs. At the 1961 jury trial, Seeger contested his indictment but was found guilty and sentenced to one year in prison (the sentence was actually ten one-year terms, to be served simultaneously). He had brought his banjo to court, echoing his mentor Lead Belly, who successfully sang for his release from prison all those years ago, but Seeger's request to sing for the jury was denied. Though the sentence was overturned a little over a year later, the blacklist remained in effect, especially with regard to major concert venues and national television. While other folk artists took the spotlight, Pete would be relegated to the sidelines until 1968—when folksinging comedians and Seeger fans the Smothers Brothers were hosting their own, popular CBS television show and invited Seeger to perform. Regardless, Seeger was active in peace marches, in movements against American Cold War policy, and at anti–nuclear testing rallies. He performed benefit concerts at the Village Gate and participated in a major Ban the Bomb march that culminated in a massive gathering at United Nations Plaza. Then, in the fall of 1961, he embarked on a tour of England with Ramblin' Jack Elliot. There was no stopping Pete.

The Singing Socialist

Phil Ochs was studying journalism at Ohio State University, in Columbus. Shy and introverted, he had experienced a troubled and unstable early life with a remote, aloof, and manic-depressive father, a doctor, whose work caused him to regularly transfer the family to different towns. His mother could be equally distant. Phil retreated by going to the movies any chance he got, and was especially fond of those starring Marlon Brando or James Dean. In high school, he turned to music and became an accomplished clarinetist, playing in the orchestra. By fifteen, he was accepted in the Capital University Conservatory of Music, and by sixteen, he was leading soloist. Then, enrolling at Staunton Military Academy, he continued in the marching band. At Ohio State, Ochs met Jim Glover, a student and folksinger who would quickly become his best friend and roommate and who would teach him about leftist politics. Ochs wrote radical articles for the college newspaper and played the Kay acoustic guitar he had won from Glover in a bet over who would win the 1960 presidential election. Ochs was sure it would be Kennedy, while Glover was convinced Nixon, with his experience and name recognition, was a cinch to win. Ochs, who would come to be known as the most politically driven of all the folksingers of the era, was outspoken and informed and, at the time of the early 1960s, had a particular interest in the Cuban Revolution. Yet he had grown up in a household that was apolitical. "There were no politics whatsoever," recalled sister Sonny Ochs. It was Jim Glover, whose father was an open Marxist and with whom Ochs would discuss the issues of the day, who not only taught him guitar basics but turned him on to Woody Guthrie, the Weavers, and Pete Seeger. "I kinda introduced him to the left-wing music, you know, the people's music," Glover told me. With the encouragement of Glover, Ochs organized protests of the Reserve Officers' Training Corps (ROTC), an organization which was compulsory for all male students at Ohio State. He would soon organize protests at numerous other colleges and universities.

Before discovering folk music—and politics—through Glover, it was *rock and roll*, and particularly Elvis, along with country singers Hank Williams, Lefty Frizzell, Johnny Cash, Faron Young, and Webb Pierce—some of the same musicians who had also influenced Bob Dylan—that had interested Ochs. Ochs, with his lyrical talent and drive, and Glover, with his pop star good looks, formed a folk duo, the Sundowners, named after the 1960 western starring Robert Mitchum. As Marc Eliot wrote in his Phil Ochs biography *Death of a Rebel* (1979), Ochs also referred to the duo as "The Singing Socialists," although the name never caught on. Right out of the gate, Ochs was writing topical songs, and one of his very first was an enraged tirade about the recent, disastrous Bay of Pigs invasion in Cuba. Due to a personal squabble over Glover's relaxed attitude about rehearsing (Glover didn't want to), the duo never made it to their first professional gig, and the Sundowners, or Singing Socialists, unceremoniously disbanded. Venturing out on his own as a solo act, Ochs combined his now-feverish interest in politics with his new enthusiasm for folk music, writing more topical, political songs drawn directly from the news headlines. That summer, while opening for Bob Gibson at Faragher's, a venue in Cleveland Heights, he was mentored and encouraged by Gibson. The two collaborated on writing songs, Ochs overflowing with words and Gibson an endless source of melodies. "It was like Bob collaborating with his political self, and Phil collaborating with his nonpolitical self. It was perfect," Dave Van Ronk was later to say of the two, insightfully as ever.

Meanwhile Ochs's former bandmate Jim Glover, pursuing his career as a folksinger, had arrived at Greenwich Village, met up with drama student Jean Ray on his second day in town, moved in with her that night, and formed the folk duo Jim & Jean. They were performing at the tiny Café Raffio on Bleecker Street—a café described by Robert Shelton as "probably the dingiest in the Village"—where Jean worked. It was only a matter of time before Ochs would also find his way to the Village. At this point, the Village had the gravitational pull of a small planet, drawing in young people of a certain age and sensibility from all over the country with remarkable, irresistible force.

August 1961 had seen the beginning of construction of the Berlin Wall, a concrete symbol of the Cold War and a literal chunk of the Iron Curtain. After World War II, Germany was divided into two zones:

the Soviet Union now occupied East Germany and imposed a rigidly controlled communist state, while the Allies—the United States, Great Britain, and France—occupied West Germany, rebuilding the western part of the country as a capitalist democracy. The city of Berlin, two hundred miles into East Germany, was also divided. A mass exodus had been occurring, as over four million East Germans, unsatisfied with life under communist rule, fled to the West. The Wall was to stand for decades, dividing Berlin, until it would finally come down in 1989. Tensions with the USSR were to become a defining battle of the Kennedy administration. JFK's relationship with Soviet leader Nikita Khrushchev started off badly at a summit in Vienna in the summer of 1961. According to records in the JFK Presidential Library, "Though Kennedy chose not to challenge directly the Soviet Union's building of the Berlin Wall, he reluctantly resumed testing nuclear weapons in early 1962, following the lead of the Soviet Union." With the competitive "space race" between the United States and the USSR also in full effect, a sense of one-upmanship between the two countries was escalating. And with nuclear weapons now in the mix, this was not a pleasant situation for the citizenry of either country. Or the world, for that matter. There was a feeling of instability and insanity that would be portrayed with comedy in Stanley Kubrick's brilliant 1964 film *Dr. Strangelove*, a few years later. Antinuke rallies were more and more prevalent, and it wasn't long before the sense of foreboding found its way into songs coming out of Greenwich Village.

Twenty-year-old Canadian folksinger Bonnie Dobson had just watched the Stanley Kramer film *On the Beach* (1959), about the aftermath of a nuclear apocalypse that takes place in 1964, a few years in the future. In the film, the Northern Hemisphere has been devastated, nuclear fallout having killed all human life. Especially haunting are scenes of San Francisco's barren streets and waterfront, completely devoid of people. The film's jarring plausibility inspired Dobson to sit and write her very first song, "Morning Dew." "Everybody was very worried about the bomb and whether we were going to get through the next ten years," Dobson would say in a 1993 interview for the early website *Roots of the Grateful Dead*.

In 1961, Dobson had been on tour, opening for Sonny Terry and Brownie McGhee when she arrived in Greenwich Village to perform for three nights at Gerde's. There she performed "Morning Dew"—with lyrics conveying a conversation between the last two survivors of nuclear annihilation—in a show that was recorded for her debut album, *Bonnie Dobson at Folk City*, released in 1962 on Prestige Records. On the album, Dobson introduced it by saying, "This is a song about morning dew. And I hope that it never falls on us." In a high, pure, sincere voice reminiscent of Joan Baez's, and with a charming Canadian accent, Dobson sang:

Won't you tell me where have all the people gone?
Don't you worry about the people anymore.

What Dobson wrote was a gorgeous song in the folk style, profound in its simplicity, that sounded simultaneously new and old, and with words that were understood with minimal detail. Even though the song uses all major chords, they create a compelling, melancholic, and evocative wistfulness when combined with the melody and lyrics. Structurally, the song is based on two modulated three-chord progressions, one for each of the two characters. The words of each character are sung over their respective progression—a simple but effective technique.

Sometimes called "(Walk Me Out in the) Morning Dew," it was immediately covered by Fred Neil and Vince Martin and eventually by a long list of rock and pop artists, including the Grateful Dead, Lulu, Robert Plant, the Jeff Beck Group, and even DEVO. An unfortunate episode involving a successful 1967 cover version of "Morning Dew" by rock artist Tim Rose, another artist with strong Village connections, in which he claimed a writer's share, was thought by Dobson to be finally resolved decades later. But his name still appears on the publishing data. Like a land grab, some artists and songwriters seemed to feel free to stake their claim on every song they heard or sang, exploiting the legitimate utilization of the so-called folk process—in which music is transformed and adapted in the process of its transmission from person to person and from generation to generation—by infringing on copyright laws and the rights of current, living writers who were the known composers.

But, no matter. More and more, folksingers were writing their own songs. It's almost as if interpreting traditional folk songs of the past was suddenly not *enough* or that the canon had just been exhausted. "What they were thinking was 'How do we take a big idea of the heart and mind and make it into a song?'" Columbia Records producer Steve Berkowitz told me as we discussed the burgeoning topical song movement. Years before, when asked, Pete Seeger said he wrote songs when there was something he wanted to say. Now it seemed like there was a hell of a lot to say. Happy Traum, a fan of Bonnie Dobson's, described this particular period, when 1961 was ending and 1962 beginning, as "the roots of self-expression in songwriting." Some, like Terri Thal, didn't like every new song that was being written in the Village. "I wasn't always interested in what was going on inside their heads," she told me.

To support and give a forum to these new songs and songwriters, a new publication would be required. *Broadside* magazine was founded in 1962 by Agnes "Sis" Cunningham and husband Gordon Friesen, both leftist activists originally from Oklahoma and members of the Almanac Singers and alumni of Seeger et al.'s *People's Songs. Broadside*, its name referring to early one-page printed sheet music for ballads and, often, news in the 1500s and 1600s, would prove to be not only influential but motivational, fanning the flames for a true revolution in songwriting. It can be seen as a complementary publication to Irwin Silber's *Sing Out!* but with more emphasis on new, topical songs and on being a resource for activists. Its mission statement, from issue #1, published in February 1962, stated in part:

> **Broadside** *may never publish a song that could be called a "folk song." But let us remember that many of our best folk songs were topical songs at their inception. Few would deny the beauty and lasting value of some of Woody Guthrie's songs. Old or new, "a good song can only do good."*

And songwriters in the Village rose to the occasion. To this day, they credit *Broadside* for the exposure they received. Tom Paxton, Phil Ochs, Janis Ian, Buffy Sainte-Marie, and others say they owe the start of their careers to that little hand-drawn, handwritten, and crudely typed fanzine printed using a mimeograph machine (that had been thrown out by the American Labor Party) and sold for 35 cents a copy. And you can add Bob Dylan to the list. He appeared in the very first issue, with his typewritten lyrics for "Talking John Birch" (later titled "Talkin' John Birch Paranoid Blues"), a satirical song about the Far Right, anti-communist extremist group.

But *Broadside* was more than just a publication. There were also at least twenty-five *Broadside* albums showcasing the songs and artists, and a large number of individual tracks, all still available as of this writing at the Smithsonian/Folkways Recordings website. The proceeds from album sales were meant to benefit and support the publication, and many artists contributed songs to be included. But besides a magazine and a series of albums, concerts, and radio shows, *Broadside* was a *sensibility*, a political-musical forum that inspired competition as well as camaraderie and unity among the Village songwriters. *Broadside* was in the right place at the right time, because it had helped create it.

Angelic Intervention

In the fall of 1961, Perry Miller, who, like Phil Ochs and Jim Glover, was another Ohio State student, arrived in the Village and enrolled at NYU. Miller had been kicked out of the prestigious Phillips Academy in Andover, Massachusetts, for incessantly playing guitar and singing Everly Brothers songs with his roommate. And writing songs. Having had watched Stanley Kramer's biker-gang drama *The Wild One* (1953), starring Marlon Brando, at least ten times since age ten had probably prepped Miller better than anything he learned in Andover anyway. That was the film that contained the famous exchange: "What are you rebelling against, Johnny?" to which Brando answered, "Whaddaya got?" And it was also that film that inspired Miller to get a Triumph motorcycle, like Brando's character's, a bike he'd soon be parking on the streets of the Village. "I was living behind a record store while attending Ohio State," Miller recalled. "That store provided me with a musical education; I was picking up albums by Mississippi John Hurt, Lightning Hopkins, T-Bone Walker, and Pete Seeger."

"It was angelic intervention that caused me to end up at NYU," he told me. "In the middle of the Village, within a block or two of MacDougal Street, and with Washington Square Park, filled with folksingers and acoustic guitars, as the University's front lawn." It must also have been angelic intervention that he would happen to arrive at the very moment that one of the greatest music scenes in American history was exploding before his very eyes. "I started to notice students in the halls and stairwells with guitars and would ask them about the basket houses on MacDougal and Bleecker, if they played there," he told me. He wanted to perform in them and, before long, he would. But first, he needed to do something about his name. "'Perry' sounded like Perry Como to me," he said, referring to the popular singer from his parents' generation, and not exactly the hippest one at that. "The name needed to be an outlaw name, a cowboy name." Getting down to work, Miller mashed up the names of two outlaws, Jesse James and Cole Younger of the James-Younger Gang, and in the middle, he added Formula One race car designer and driver Colin Chapman. Done. Living off campus and moving to a few different East Village apartments, including one on St. Mark's Place across the street from the legendary Five Spot Café jazz club, with his Triumph motorcycle parked outside on the street, and with B & H Dairy Kosher Restaurant on the corner to sustain him, it truly was angelic intervention. Now he could play the basket houses, as Jesse Colin Young.

Four months after it was recorded, and without too much fanfare, Bob Dylan's debut album was released by Columbia on March 19, 1962. Comprised mostly of traditional songs, borrowed arrangements, and only two originals, the album gives but the slightest hint of the songwriter that was emerging. Still, it was an auspicious debut for sure, one that captured a remarkably uninhibited performance. Listening to it now is fascinating. Yes, you can hear the heavy influence of Woody Guthrie, of course, along with all the various folk, blues, rock and roll, and rhythm and blues he had absorbed, and you can sense the out-on-a-limb spontaneity of Dave Van Ronk's influence. At times, Dylan sounds almost like a punk rock singer, jittery, exploding with energy and unafraid to contort his voice, laughing, screaming, and attacking the guitar strings with such force that his playing pops off the grooves. On "Freight Train Blues," he has the audacity to hold a high, screeching, scratchy falsetto note for nearly fifteen seconds. He makes his voice grindingly nasal, he mimics Elvis, he lays it all out on the table. In the liner notes for his 1985 box set, *Biograph*, Dylan would say, "Actually, attitude had a lot more to do with it than technical ability and that's what the folk movement lacked. In other words, I played the folk songs with a rock n' roll attitude." The harmonica playing is as jumpy and chattery as he indicated it would be on the Carolyn Hester sessions and in all his live gigs. John Hammond's minimal production seems primarily to have been to keep Dylan on mic as much as possible. It is in-your-face, bare bones with barely the *slightest* hint of sonic ambience in the recording. Of course, this would be due partially to the limited studio time and budget. Hammond was later to joke, or not, that the budget was a whopping $402.

Some stories claim that, within the ranks of Columbia Records, there was resistance to releasing the album at all—that it had few fans at the company besides Hammond himself and that it was referred to as "Hammond's Folly." Certainly, it was not the kind of release Columbia was used to; there were no hit singles, and the exceptionally scruffy artist was far from nationally known. Everyone knew it would not be an easy sell. And it wasn't. In fact, commercially, the album was a total flop. Besides its inherent limitations, by the time it was released, Dylan's repertoire and much of the scene had changed dramatically. "Dylan, when he finds his own style, could win a big following," said *Billboard* on April 14, 1962. But it was the sound of something happening. For those who were listening, Dylan wrenched the folk idiom from all restraint, from its past custodians, and handed it, on a black vinyl platter, to a new generation.

Erik Jacobsen was banjo picker for the young bluegrass band Knob Lick Upper 10,000, another act managed by Albert Grossman. "I was in the office when Bob saw his first album cover," recalls Jacobsen. "His comment? 'They cleaned my fingernails!'"

Chapter Six

two bea
prOph
blonde-a

rded
ets and a
nd-a-half

Peter, Paul and Mary, performing at the Newport Folk Festival, 1963.

Greenwich Village offers a shelter within which identities may be tried and discarded. In a world of rapidly changing values there are few places left where confused young people can go to find, or lose, themselves.
— **Cosmopolitan**, May 1963

Up until the spring of 1962, the folk

music scene in Greenwich Village had not been about making money. Not because musicians didn't want it but because it just didn't seem to be there to be made. The offertory baskets passed around at the coffeehouses were like those passed around in a church—it was hit or miss. But, then again, expenses for musicians living in the Village were low. "Our rent at 139 Thompson Street was sixty dollars a month," Jim Glover of Jim & Jean told me. "We could make that in one night in a basket house—on a *good* night." For folk artists who had been lucky enough to make an album, expectations for making a serious dent in the marketplace were, expectedly, low. Sure, there had been breakthroughs, like the Weavers twelve years prior, Harry Belafonte five years prior, and more recently the Kingston Trio and Joan Baez, but, realistically, folk music was—by definition—not commercial. And the albums were usually released on record labels that were just trying to break even, not trying to break new artists. All of that changed in May 1962. What happened when Peter, Paul and Mary released their first, self-named album, guided by Albert Grossman, was nothing short of a phenomenon. A success story of biblical proportions led by "two bearded prophets" who were "in league with a bright, young blonde-and-a-half," according to the liner notes.

Musically, the album didn't break much new ground: There were two Pete Seeger songs, a Reverend Gary Davis song ("He was *God*," Terri Thal always reminds me), a lovely rendition of "500 Miles" by Hedy West, some originals by Peter Yarrow and Noel Stookey, and even a song written by Dave Van Ronk. They played a couple of acoustic guitars, there are uncredited sidemen on upright bass—primarily everyone's bassist-of-choice Bill Lee—and three human voices are harmonizing. Nothing out of the ordinary for a folk album. So what made it such a big deal in 1962? Well . . .

After discussions with Atlantic Records and Columbia, Albert Grossman had made a landmark record deal with Warner Bros. Records, then only a few years old and whose biggest pop success was with the Everly Brothers. The label had been set up initially to market the soundtracks of the venerable Warner Bros. movie division but had decided to go great guns into the record business only a year before, in 1961. They were the youngest and hungriest of the major record labels. Beating out Columbia and Atlantic, Warner Bros. offered Peter, Paul and Mary a $30,000 advance, not bad for the time, especially for a new act, plus complete creative control. This clause would come in handy, as they could choose not only their repertoire but also their all-important imaging and packaging.

To create their album cover, they chose one of the greatest graphic designers of all time, Milton Glaser and his Push Pin Studios. Glaser, a folk music fan and champion of Tiny Tim, would go on to design such iconic logos and designs as the famous "I (Heart) NY," DC Comics, the 1966 psychedelic Dylan profile poster, and the Brooklyn Brewery beer logo, and he was a cofounder of *New York* magazine. The first PP&M album cover photograph, by Bernard Cole, portrayed our heroes leaning against the bare red brick wall of the Bitter End stage—Peter and Paul in suits and narrow ties like members of their soon-to-be labelmates, the Modern Folk Quartet, and with their guitars at rest. On the wall, just above Mary Travers's head, is a chalk-drawn yellow heart with "PP&M" written inside (hints of Glaser's famous NY logo to come?). The title lettering was in a sharp, fresh-looking, ready-for-the-1960s bold, cursive script, with each name in its own color. It was to become the group's logo, with different colorations, for the duration of their long career. The logo served the purpose of conveying, in one quick glance, the message that this was a young, modern act, even if their style of music was rooted in the old school. On the back cover, in all-caps, boldface type: "ROUSING . . . AND REAL," and in the liner notes, phrases like "strong with the perfume of sincerity," "No gimmicks," and "Honesty is back. Tell your neighbor."

Perhaps more important than the visual imagery and the promises set forth in the liner notes, was the presence of another Milton, Milton Okun—producer and arranger of the Chad Mitchell Trio, arranger and pianist for Harry Belafonte, and publisher of Tom Paxton's songs—as musical director. They could not have asked for a better musical partner. The sound of the LP, engineered by Bill Schwartau, was, in terms of audio quality, a cut above other folk records of the time. From the start, the three voices complemented each other as if they were born to sing together, and Travers's in particular had an uncommon emotional power. But equally significant was the way they were recorded and mixed. On this album, the vocals were not as dry and in-your-face as most folk recordings of the day favored. Through the judicious use of limiting and compression, the blend with the instruments was more rounded and balanced. Unlike Dylan's release of two months prior, stark and unembellished, here was the careful use of chamber reverb, and the recording can be described as very full-range high fidelity, even with the minimal instrumentation. Audio quality was one of the marketing points of Warner Bros. Records, who issued the album in both mono and stereo versions with the word "Vitaphonic" emblazoned on the label and album jacket as a wave to audiophiles and a nod to the company's history. It was a reference to Vitaphone, an old Warner Bros. film sound system using synchronized discs for audio in early sound films, beginning in 1926, that was considered at the time far superior to the sound-on-film method of film audio. The stereo version of PP&M's album separated the vocals and instruments far left and right, sometimes with Travers's beautiful, yearning contralto in the center, creating a "wide-screen," almost cinematic listening experience unusual in folk records at the time. In fact, where I grew up, Peter, Paul and Mary albums were often used in stores as test records for customers purchasing hi-fi sound equipment. The whole thing worked. The sound, the visuals, the story.

The album would go to up to number one on the *Billboard* 200 chart and stay there for seven weeks. It stayed in the top ten for *ten months* and stayed on the chart for an incredible 185 weeks. That's *three and a half years*. Which meant a lot of people were now listening to Peter, Paul and Mary's variety of folk music, on the radio, on television, and on their stereos. And buying it. According to Terri Thal, the inclusion of Dave Van Ronk's song garnered him a $16,000 payday, one of his biggest. And Reverend Gary Davis's royalties enabled him to buy his house. Folk music was suddenly making money. And it was suddenly for the masses, for real, no longer just for the small folk community. As Van Ronk puts it, after PP&M's album hit, "the Great Folk Scare was upon us."

Phil Ochs decided not to finish his last semester at Ohio State and had arrived into town with the intention, according to his brother Michael Ochs in the 2010 documentary *Phil Ochs: There But for Fortune*, of being "the best songwriter in the country." After safely landing at Jim Glover's doorstep, Ochs moved in with Jim and Jean in their tiny, cramped, Greenwich Village apartment at 139 Thompson Street. Writing feverishly, he tried his best to talk them into including him in their act. It was not gonna happen. Neither Jim nor Jean could be swayed. "Phil could be a little bit bossy," Jim Glover recalled, undoubtedly remembering Ochs's controlling ways in college as a Singing Socialist. "So when Phil showed up, he wanted us to be a trio. Phil, Jim, and Jean? Not for me. Phil was disappointed. What could he say, except he might have mentioned Dylan's manager as an incentive? He was always afraid and in awe of Al Grossman." Ochs frequented all the Village clubs, voraciously checking out sets by all the other performers on the scene and feeling confident he could make it. Armed with his new songs, Phil embarked on performing at the basket houses, landing a gig at the Third Side—on West Third between MacDougal and Sullivan Streets, across from the Café Bizarre—where he styled himself as the "singing *journalist*." "The owner would guarantee him twenty dollars," Ochs's sister

Sonny told me, "so at least he'd get *something*." Onstage and off, his appearance was handsome but perpetually unkempt and disheveled, resembling a young reporter storming into the newsroom with a scoop on a story.

One day, Pete Seeger invited both Phil Ochs and Bob Dylan uptown to join him on a visit to Sis Cunningham and Gordon Friesen's Upper West Side apartment, headquarters of *Broadside*. "I sat back listening to song after song that they'd just written within the last few weeks," Seeger was to say in the 2010 Ochs documentary. "Here I am, with two of the greatest songwriters in the world, and someday they'll be famous. Right now, nobody is printing them except this little mimeographed magazine." Ochs befriended Cunningham and Friesen and would often drop in on them at their apartment, bringing them new songs. According to Michael Schumacher, in his book *There But for Fortune: The Life of Phil Ochs* (1996), on one occasion Ochs arrived with seven new songs he had written on the subway ride uptown. "When I asked where he got the idea for the lyrics, he would respond, 'From *Newsweek*, of course,' and hold up a copy of the latest issue," Friesen told Schumacher. The melodies, Ochs added half-kiddingly, came "from Mozart." His work would first appear in *Broadside* #13, and he would go on to have sixty-nine songs printed in the publication, more than any other songwriter. "*Broadside* was the hub," Sonny Ochs told me. "And they loved Phil." *Broadside* #36 would feature a photo of Ochs on its front cover—the quintessential young folksinger, clear-eyed, idealistic, and filled with hope for the world he was confident he could help to change for the better.

In some ways, Phil Ochs was the opposite of Bob Dylan, yet they were to become friends, and Ochs intensely admired Dylan's writing. They shared musical and cultural commonalities, but Ochs was an open book, sincere and immediate, while Dylan was evasive and secretive. "Phil was very real. Genuine. He really, *really* cared," Sonny told me. "Dylan knew how to get his name out there, and he couldn't stand competition." Ochs eschewed creating a stage name or imposing a faux persona when he became a performer, instead building on and amplifying his own personality and allowing his beliefs and emotions to write the script. Revealing himself so completely would ultimately leave Ochs unshielded and vulnerable to external and internal enemies, however, while Dylan was protected—by the image he had created and by constantly changing his narrative. Upon meeting Dylan and hearing his songs, Ochs revised his goal. It was now, he would say, to be "the *second-best* songwriter in the country." But, while Dylan once admitted it was hard keeping up with him, he was never to give Ochs the positive support and encouragement that Ochs so badly wanted and needed from Dylan.

Protest against War, and the War against Protesters

Phil Ochs was one of the first songwriters to write about and talk about the United States' involvement in the Vietnam War, the conflict in the Southeast Asian nation—between the communist North and the politically unstable South—that had been going on since 1954 but had intensified as a result of the Cold War. By 1962, about nine thousand American troops were stationed in South Vietnam, and the numbers would keep climbing. Though the United States never formally declared war on communist North Vietnam, over 2.2 million American men over the age of eighteen were drafted and sent there from 1964 to 1973. Ochs, the irony of his ROTC and military academy background intact, would stand on the front lines of the war resistance movement with his acoustic guitar, singing his anthems for peace. In 1964, he would release one of his signature songs, "I Ain't Marching Any More," written from the point of view of a person who had, himself, marched:

> *It's always the old to lead us to the wars*
> *Always the young to fall*

Another singer-songwriter who was quick to address the Vietnam War in her songwriting was Buffy Sainte-Marie. A strikingly beautiful native Canadian with long, straight, black hair and a strong Indigenous identity, Sainte-Marie had been performing in the coffeehouses of Toronto, where in 1963 she would write "Universal Soldier."

> *And he knows he shouldn't kill, and he knows he always will*
> *Kill you for me my friend and me for you*

"'Universal Soldier' was not about 'Where Have All the Flowers Gone?,' and I didn't believe for a minute that 'the answer was blowing in the wind.' My song 'Universal Soldier' was about individual responsibility for the world we're building right now, and it nailed the issue differently," Sainte-Marie told me. The song would be covered by numerous artists, including and especially Donovan, who would have a hit with it in 1965. But when Sainte-Marie performed that and other original compositions at the Gaslight, the Village scene was still made up of folksingers singing traditional songs. "I came to Greenwich Village straight from college. Here I was in New York City for the first time, and I was a songwriter. But you weren't supposed to be one yet, and the 'folk police' could get after you," she told hip-hop producer Rick Rubin in a 2020 interview for his podcast *Broken Record*. Signed to

Vanguard Records, Sainte-Marie would become one of the most familiar faces on the scene and one of its most familiar voices. But with her outspoken advocacy of Native American rights as well as the anti–Vietnam War protests, her voice was known for more than just singing and would be met with opposition from other authorities besides just the folk police.

Also from the Toronto coffeehouse scene and signed to Vanguard was the folk duo Ian & Sylvia. Ian Tyson had been an amateur rodeo rider and, unlike the faux cowboys on the folk scene, he was a real one: you can actually find photos of Ian Tyson riding. Singing partner Sylvia Fricker had come from a musical household in Chatham, Ontario, where her mother was a classically trained pianist and church organist. By 1959, Sylvia had left home and was frequenting the coffeehouses of the budding Toronto scene, where she met Tyson. They began performing together and moved to Greenwich Village in 1961, developing a rhythmic, country-tinged sound with unusually tight harmony vocals—Tyson with his deep chest voice and Fricker with her sweet, throaty highs. Together, more than most duos outside of the Everly Brothers, they seemed to sing with one voice. Onstage, looking intently at each other when they sang, the couple had an obvious personal chemistry. So obvious, in fact, that in 1964, Ian & Sylvia would marry. Meeting them soon after they arrived, Albert Grossman negotiated their Vanguard Records deal and then one with ITA, International Talent Associates, who also represented Peter, Paul and Mary, the Kingston Trio, and Bob Dylan. They slowly built up a strong following on the college concert circuit and in the Village, and as the shift away from traditional songs continued, they became prolific songwriters.

As had happened for Bonnie Dobson, the very first song ever written by Sylvia and the first song written by Ian were each to become their most successful. In 1961, "You Were on My Mind" was famously written by Sylvia in the bathtub of their suite at the Hotel Earle, the current Washington Square Hotel. It was to become one of the catchiest and most successful tunes to come out of the Village scene at the time. A cover version by the California pop vocal group We Five would reach number three on the *Billboard* chart in 1965 and become one of the biggest-selling records of that year. Ian's first crack at songwriting resulted in "Four Strong Winds." In a 2018 interview with Toronto newspaper *The Globe and Mail*, Tyson said, "We were palling around with Dylan a bit. He influenced me to write. I wrote that little ditty that's still around today." The little ditty was inspired in particular by "Blowin' in the Wind," which Tyson said Dylan played for him one night at the Kettle of Fish.

Written in Albert Grossman's Village apartment, though presumedly not in the bathtub, "Four Strong Winds" would become the title song of Ian & Sylvia's second Vanguard album. The song would go on to become a number three country hit for Bobby Bare in 1965 and was covered by the Journeymen, the Chad Mitchell Trio, the Brothers Four, Waylon Jennings, Harry Belafonte, the Carter Family, the Searchers, Neil Young, the Kingston Trio, Dave Van Ronk, and even Bonnie Dobson. It might have also been a partial inspiration for director Christopher Guest's brutally funny mockumentary *A Mighty Wind* (2003), which parodies the early 1960s folk scene and includes an Ian & Sylvia–like couple, played by Eugene Levy and Catherine O'Hara. But there was more to the story. Ian & Sylvia presaged the country rock movement by bringing their unabashedly country influences to the Village in the early days and then by their 1969 Vanguard album *Nashville*—released five months before the Byrds' *Sweetheart of the Rodeo* and nearly one year before Dylan's *Nashville Skyline*.

Folksinger's Choice

Listening to Bob Dylan's March 11, 1962, radio interview on Cynthia Gooding's WBAI radio show *Folksinger's Choice*, while knowing his actual backstory and penchant for embellishment, is itself like listening to the soundtrack of a mockumentary. Dylan just keeps spinning and fabricating a past that at times seems to make Gooding want to laugh. Even though the show was called *Folksinger's Choice* and that Gooding was known to be a folk traditionalist from the early days of the revival, Dylan makes a point to separate himself from the folk scene whenever possible. Referring to Dylan's successes so far, barely a year in the Village, Gooding begins by observing, "This is one of the quickest rises in folk music, wouldn't you say?" Dylan replies, "Yeah, but I don't really think of myself as in a folk, you know folk, folksinger thing . . . I'm not on a circuit like those other folksingers." Asked about his past, Dylan answers, "I used to travel with the carnival." Gooding seems surprised. "How long were you with the carnival?" "Oh, I was with the carnival, off and on . . . six years?" Remember, he was just twenty years old at this time. "Wha' . . . what were you doing?" she seems concerned. "Oh, just about everything. Uh, I was the clean-up boy. I used to . . . uh . . . I dunno . . . be on the mainline, on the Ferris wheel. Used to just run rides. Used to do all kinda stuff like that." Gooding tries to bring it back to music. "At the carnival did you . . . did you learn songs?" "No, I learned how to sing, though. That's more important." "Yeah," she sighs. When I was discussing this interview with folk historian Stephen Petrus, he offered, "Ironically, with these stories, Dylan was trying to create a kind of authenticity."

Dylan contrasts the stilted interview segments with typically energetic and unrestrained performances, more off-the-cuff than on his appearance on Oscar Brand's radio show. Here, he covers Hank Williams, Bukka White, Howlin' Wolf, and Woody Guthrie, and he borrows an arrangement of "Makes a Long Time Man Feel Bad" from Ian & Sylvia, who happened to be performing at the Bitter End that week and to get a gracious plug from Gooding. Amusingly, after talking about lifting songs from Len Chandler, Ralph Rinzler of the Greenbriar Boys, and Ian & Sylvia, he performs an animated performance of "Stealin', Stealin'" by the Memphis Jug Band. "That's called 'Stealin'," he offers at the end. "I figured!" laughs Gooding.

But about twenty-three minutes into the program, Dylan provides a clue as to why people were so willing to put up with his, well, bullshit. He performs a breathtaking rendition of "The Death of Emmett Till," his own composition, telling of the fourteen-year-old boy brutally murdered in the Jim Crow South in 1955, a horrific event that helped kick-start the civil rights movement. It was a story that had been relayed to him by Suze Rotolo, one she would have surely known from her work at CORE and SNCC. Rotolo's muse-like influence was beginning to be heard in Dylan's songwriting more and more. "She'll tell you how many nights I stayed up and wrote songs and showed them to her and asked her, 'Is this right?'" Dylan told Robert Shelton in the *New York Times*. Based on a chord structure he borrowed from Len Chandler, whom he credits on the air, the one-week-old song is the showstopper. The lyric ends with a breaking of the fourth wall, the songwriter talking directly to the listener, like Kennedy in his inaugural speech:

> *But if all of us folks that thinks alike, if we'd give all we could give,*
> *We could make this great land of ours a greater place to live*

As soon as it is over, an anxious Dylan quickly asks Gooding, "You like that one?" She nearly gasps. "That's one of the greatest contemporary ballads I've ever heard. It's TREMENDOUS!" she replies. "Do you think so?" Dylan asks, almost bashfully. "OH YES! It's got some lines in it that just . . . make you . . . stop *breathing*. It's great."

In some ways, by approving of his songwriting so strongly, Cynthia Gooding was, literally, broadcasting an endorsement not only of Dylan but of the new song movement itself. And it was coming directly from one of the stalwarts of the old guard who had spent a career singing *traditional* folk songs. There would be no looking back. The interview closes with this exchange:

> *"When you're rich and famous, are you gonna wear the hat too?"*
> *"Uh, oh, I'm never gonna become rich and famous."*

"And you're never gonna take off the hat, either?"
"No."

The previous year, at the suggestion of Noel "Paul" Stookey who handed him a newspaper clipping at the Gaslight, Dylan wrote his first topical song, the humorous "Talkin' Bear Mountain Picnic Massacre Blues," a tale of greed and too many forged tickets that had spoiled a festive, chartered boat ride up the Hudson River to Bear Mountain National Park. The song, its story exaggerated, of course, was written and performed in the deadpan talking blues style that had been popularized in the 1920s by singer Chris Bouchillon from South Carolina, who had been a major influence on Woody Guthrie. It is said that Bouchillon developed the style as a way around his horrible singing voice. Listening to Bouchillon's 1926 track "Talking Blues" on Columbia Records now is like finding the missing link. It's all there. Since then, having written "The Death of Emmett Till," Dylan began to show his range as a writer. He was gathering a body of songs that could shift an audience's emotions from laughter to anger in a matter of seconds, like changing channels on a black-and-white television set. And one of his next songs would, arguably, change everything.

Meanwhile, Phil Ochs had been introduced by Jim & Jean to their downstairs neighbor, Alice Skinner, long-haired acting student, excellent photographer, and waitress at the Café Raffio. "So Jean let him stay for a while. He was going to *Broadside* meetings. Jean wanted him to leave, so she fixed him up with Alice downstairs. What a setup. Thank God!" Jim Glover told me. Ochs and Skinner began seeing each other, fell in love, and before long, Skinner found herself pregnant. Phil and Alice were married in a private, City Hall ceremony on May 16, 1963, with Jim & Jean as their best man and maid of honor. The happy couple reportedly giggled throughout. Soon the Ochses moved into an apartment at 178 Bleecker Street that was to become another folksinger hangout, rivaling the Van Ronks' at 190 Waverly Place. With neither of them being really prepared for married life, and with Phil's narrow focus on his career, it would not be easy for them. Especially now, as his career—through the sheer power of his will, constant songwriting, and impassioned performing—was just beginning to pick up steam.

And it wasn't just Ochs's career that was picking up steam. By this time, the Village was heading toward a peak. On weekends, the coffeehouses and all the music venues were packed. The sidewalks of MacDougal, Bleecker, and West Third, filled with celebrity-seeking fans, were getting too crowded to walk on, so the streets became unofficial pedestrian walkways, with frustrated drivers honking their horns. With successful acts, in particular Peter, Paul and Mary, recording new, folk-flavored songs by Village writers, the neighborhood was becoming a song factory that, over the next few years, would rival the Brill Building. Artists, record label executives, and producers went to the Village to find new songs to record as well as acts to sign, and the sense of competition among songwriters began intensifying and widening. Especially, as supported and encouraged by *Broadside*, when it came to topical songs.

Persuasion, Propaganda, and Protest

What are generally referred to as "topical" or "protest" songs actually fall into separate types and categories, and a more correct overarching term might be "sociopolitical" songs. Based on concepts presented by R. Serge Denisoff, in his 1972 book *Sing a Song of Social Significance*, Benjamin Scott Holbrook, in his 2017 master's thesis for the School of Music, Jordan College of Fine Arts at Butler University in Indianapolis, Indiana, proposed three categories—persuasion songs, propaganda songs, and protest songs. I came across Holbrook's thesis because, in it, he analyzes one of my own songs, written in 2012, "Hey, Can I Sleep on Your Futon?," written for the Occupy Wall Street movement with my musical partner Matthew Billy. The following chart is from Holbrook's thesis:

Persuasion Song	Solicits and arouses outside support and sympathy Reinforces the value structure of individuals who are active supporters Creates and promotes cohesion, solidarity, and high morals Attempts to recruit individuals
Propaganda Song	Points to some problem or discontent in the society, usually in emotional terms
Protest Song	Invokes solutions to real or imagined social phenomena in terms of action to acheive a desired goal

While the songs coming out of Greenwich Village during this time would cover lots of subjects, some of the most famous were to fall into one of these three categories. They would come to define the place and the era. It was as if the world was waiting for someone to stand up and say something. Before long, Pete Seeger's notion of the "power of song" would be magnified into a movement that, using the media, modern songwriting and performance styles, and the inestimable energy of youth, would become a dominant force in popular music.

But it wasn't just popular music that was going through a transformation during these early years of the 1960s. A movement of change was taking place in all the arts. *To Kill a Mockingbird* by Harper Lee, published as the decade began, was a novel that starkly addressed racial inequality yet made its way into mainstream American consciousness. Other authors, like Tom Wolfe, Ken Kesey, Truman Capote, Joan Didion, and, later, Hunter S. Thompson developed a style of creative, novelesque, nonfiction known as "new journalism." According to the *New York Times*, Betty Friedan's *The Feminine Mystique* (1963) "ignited the contemporary women's movement." And in 1965, Malcolm X and Alex Haley's *The Autobiography of Malcolm X* was one of the most powerful calls to political awareness and action in history. Meanwhile, in the off-Broadway houses of the Village, avant-garde and experimental theater companies were producing groundbreaking works at the Cherry Lane Theatre (with Milton Okun's Cherry Lane music publishing offices upstairs); La MaMa Experimental Theatre Club; the Living Theatre, on Fourteenth Street; and even at Judson Memorial Church, on Washington Square.

Experimental music and performance art, as practiced by composer John Cage, who was teaching his legendary composition class at the New School in 1960; LaMonte Young; and young Japanese artist Yoko Ono, who would stage avant-garde concerts in her Chambers Street loft and made her own Carnegie Hall debut two weeks after Dylan's, on November 24, 1961, were expanding the definitions of "music" and "art" in the same way that Marcel Duchamp and the Dadaists had done fifty years prior.

European cinema, too, was evolving and finding an American audience—especially among students. "I think everybody loved Visconti's *The Damned* (1969) with Dirk Bogarde—one of my top five favorites," singer-songwriter Eric Andersen told me. "Truffaut's *400 Blows* (1959) and *Jules and Jim* (1962). All of Bergman's barren, bleak dramas, and most especially Fellini's Circus-Tivoli Parade takes on life and films. Seeing his film *La Dolce Vita* (1960) in college was the game changer for me and sent me down the wrong, risk-filled path to enroll in a lifetime mission of seeking art and music—and making art and music for myself."

In the early 1960s, painting and graphic art were also transforming. The phrase "pop art" was first used in 1958 to describe the work of Jasper Johns and Robert Rauschenberg. Roy Lichtenstein followed, painting comic-strip images. Then in 1961, Andy Warhol painted thirty-two, nearly identical Campbell's Soup cans, each of a different variety. After years of creating commercial art illustrations for clients like Bloomingdale's, and record covers for RCA, Columbia, and Prestige Records, Warhol was suddenly an overnight sensation. He began a series of paintings and then silk screens that were, perhaps, the most intentionally superficial art ever created. The work appears cold, emotionless, with a look of being manufactured. The media were fascinated, and Warhol himself, who loved "stars," himself became a celebrity. Upon Warhol's death in 1987, Jesse Kornbluth wrote in *New York* magazine, "Warhol created art that defines the glossy superficiality, manic denial of feelings and process, and underlying violence of the sixties."

In 1963, Warhol's recently relocated studio in Midtown was an abandoned factory on East Forty-Seventh Street and Third Avenue. Later, in 1968, Warhol would move his operation to Union Square, closer to the downtown music community. Hated by some, adored by others, Warhol and his entourage became newsmakers who would influence the fashions, films, and attitudes of the decade more than could possibly have been predicted. "You couldn't open a newspaper and *not* see a story on Warhol," Anthony DeCurtis told me.

Consciously or unconsciously, all of this ended up as sources of inspiration and influence for the songwriters in Greenwich Village. And many of these progressive movements in the arts can be seen to have been influenced by the Beats. The very ethos of "life as art" that Kerouac, Burroughs, Ginsberg, and the others had established in the 1950s had spawned a generation that celebrated nonconformity, creativity, free love and sexual expression, and an almost fetishized appreciation for all the arts. While, arguably, the Beat movement's most obvious influence may be seen in literature and poetry, that is really only the tip of an iceberg that includes screen and theatrical writing, performance art, and songwriting. The songwriting that would soon be coming out of Greenwich Village, especially from Dylan, Richard Fariña, and even Paul Simon, would directly reflect their influence. The attire of the Warhol crowd, with the perpetual wearing of dark Ray-Ban sunglasses, black jeans, boots, turtle-necks—all so very Beat—matched the musicians playing in the coffeehouses. Need I mention Dave Van Ronk's and Paul Clayton's carefully curated facial hair? They might have been folksingers, but they sure did look like beatniks. No wonder the media got confused.

In *Aftermath: The Philosophy of the Beat Generation*, Jack Kerouac wrote, "The Beat Generation, that was a vision that we had . . . of a generation of crazy, illuminated hipsters suddenly rising and roaming America, serious, bumming and hitchhiking everywhere, ragged, *beat*ific, beautiful in an ugly graceful new way—a vision gleaned from the way we had heard the word 'beat' spoken on street corners on Times Square and in the Village, in other cities in the downtown city night of postwar

America—beat, meaning down and out but full of intense conviction." Their vision, in all its ragged, beatific, and beautiful glory, came true in the 1960s.

Talking Cuban Crisis

The Cuban Missile Crisis, perhaps the tensest thirteen-day stretch in modern history, had all of humanity on edge from October 16 to 28, 1962. The failed attempt to overthrow Castro at the Bay of Pigs in 1961 had led the communist leader to asking the USSR for protection. Russian leader Nikita Khrushchev was more than willing to oblige, secretly supplying Cuba with nuclear missiles aimed at the United States. This strategic move was not only to protect Cuba but also to counterbalance the threat posed by US missiles in Turkey and Italy, aimed at Russia. Though US military advisors pushed for an all-out invasion of Cuba, President Kennedy opted to implement a naval blockade instead, to stop missile shipments to the island. The Soviets considered the blockade an act of war. This led to a six-day standoff: the United States demanding the removal of missiles and Russia contending it was only protecting the island. A US spy plane was shot down over Cuba, and a Soviet submarine was hit by the United States, causing a nuclear torpedo to nearly be launched, as the Soviets assumed from their hit that the war had begun. The launch was stopped just in the nick of time. Things couldn't have gotten any more intense. Still, the crisis was not over. The US military was set at DEFCON 2, meaning that the world was one step away from nuclear war.

Attorney General Robert Kennedy, JFK's brother, then met secretly with the Russian ambassador in Washington. After a heated negotiation, they reached a proposal that the United States, promising never to invade Cuba, would remove its missiles from Turkey and Italy. In exchange, Russia would withdraw from Cuba and comply with United Nations inspections. At 9:00 a.m. the next morning, the missiles were removed from Cuba, and the missile crisis was over. But not the crisis of fear and distrust. The Cuban Missile Crisis was a study on the meanings and levels of "power": political power and nuclear power. After the deal was struck, some Americans said Kennedy was weak on communism, and Russians criticized Khrushchev for bargaining with the enemy. Regardless, it was ballet of diplomacy that, at least, did not end up in total annihilation, as witnessed by the fact that I am able to sit here and type the story for you now, between strumming on my guitar the chords to Bonnie Dobson's "Morning Dew."

Phil Ochs, ever the singing journalist and using the talking blues template, set the entire affair to eight verses of words and music in "Talking Cuban Crisis," including:

Well, the deadline was set for ten o'clock
For a cold war it was a-gettin' hot

Pete Seeger responded to the Cuban Missile Crisis by immediately performing and recording a version of "Guantanamera," Cuba's most famous and beloved patriotic song with lyrics by exiled Cuban poet and independence hero José Martí. First, Seeger sang it with the Weavers at their May 2 and 3, 1963, Carnegie Hall concerts, which were released as a live album for Vanguard. Then to make sure his message was received, he recorded the song again the following month, on June 8, at his solo Carnegie concert. That performance was also released as a live album, *We Shall Overcome*, on Columbia, and is considered to be the definitive version of the song. Telling the story of Martí and the meaning of the lyrics as the music played, Seeger had audiences simultaneously captivated and singing along with him in Spanish as a symbol of unity between the Americans and Cubans. A few years later, the California folk-pop singing group, the Sandpipers, would have a top-ten hit with the song, using Seeger's arrangement and including the spoken passage. So even with the media blacklist still in effect, Pete's message was getting on the airwaves. The power of song.

Just Another Song

"Blowin' in the Wind," Bob Dylan says, was written in a café on MacDougal Street, across from the Gaslight. According to his friend, folksinger David Blue, it was at the Fat Black Pussycat, on the afternoon of April 16, 1962. Blue said that, over coffee, Dylan handed Blue his guitar and asked him to strum the chords to the somber "No More Auction Block for Me," a post–Civil War, freed slave song that most folksingers knew, as Dylan furiously wrote the rhymes down. It's easy to picture it. Some people say that it was a song written by the times, the era, or that the song wrote itself. But someone had to *actually do it*. A quick look of the viewer comments on YouTube, below Dylan's own version of his song, reveal that it is still, even after sixty years, inscrutable, enigmatic, and yet as absolutely understandable . . . as a Rorschach test.

The title phrase, the refrain of "Blowin' in the Wind," might have come from Woody Guthrie's book *Bound for Glory*, a passage likening the author's political beliefs to pages from newspapers blowing through the streets and alleys of New York City. The context in Dylan's song may be different, but the meaning is equally elusive. "Wind" and "blowin'" appear repeatedly in Guthrie's book as well:

Bound for glory? This train? Ha!
I wonder just where in hell we're bound.
Rain on, little rain, rain on!
Blow on, little wind, keep blowin'!

If the verses of Dylan's song seem biblical to you, there may be a reason for it. British author Michael Gray, in his exhaustive *The Bob Dylan Encyclopedia* (2006), cites references to Jewish prophets Ezekiel and Isaiah in the Old Testament and a rhetorical style that is repeated in the New Testament:

> **Son of Man, you dwell in the midst of the rebellious house, who have eyes to see but do not see, who have ears to hear but do not hear, for they are a rebellious house.**
> (Ezekiel 12:1–2)

Dylan writes:

Yes, 'n' how many times can a man turn his head, and pretend that he just doesn't see

and

Yes 'n' how many ears must one man have, until he can hear people cry?

The music of "Blowin' in the Wind" also has deep spiritual roots, which of course, Dylan knew, though maybe not fully at the time. The melody is most associated with "No More Auction Block for Me (Many Thousand Gone)"—first published in *Slave Songs of the United States* in 1867—the song that Dylan apparently had David Blue strum the chords to as he wrote at the Fat Black Pussycat. That song had recently been recorded by Odetta on her 1960 album *Odetta at Carnegie Hall* (Vanguard) and by Paul Robeson in 1947 for Columbia; locally, Delores "Dee" Dixon—a SNCC planning member and civil rights activist who would borrow her Harlem church's Volkswagen mini-bus and park it outside the venue on West Fourth Street—sang it regularly at Folk City, often at the end of the evening. Dylan himself recorded "No More Auction Block" live at the Gaslight in 1962 and released it in the 1991 box set *The Bootleg Series 1–3* (Columbia). The music of the "modern," familiar form of

"We Shall Overcome" as popularized by Pete Seeger—a gospel song first published in 1901—was also based on "No More Auction Block." But it all goes back even further. The melody of all three songs can be found in the first movement of the "Sicilian Mariner's Hymn" or "O Sanctissima," a solemn Roman Catholic hymn that was first published in *The European Magazine and London Review*, back in 1792. Adapted by Reverend Charles Tindley in 1901 as "I'll Overcome Some Day," the song evolved over time in a sanctified version of the folk process. These elements, combined with Bob Dylan's Guthrie-esque strumming and articulation, created a new kind of folk song, one with a kind of contemporary antiquity.

Later that night, Dylan showed up for the Monday night hootenanny at Folk City. Gil Turner, who besides being the emcee at Gerde's was editor at *Broadside* magazine and a member of the New World Singers, was hosting. Dylan told Turner that he had just written a song that Turner should hear. Dylan played it for Turner downstairs in Gerde's basement and showed him the chords. When Turner went upstairs for his next set, using Dylan's rough, two-verse manuscript, he announced to the audience, "I'd like to sing a new song by one of our great songwriters. It's hot off the pencil and here it goes. . . ." Turner proceeded to perform "Blowin' in the Wind" in public for the first time. According to David Blue, it was a hit that night at Gerde's. Later that evening, Dylan returned to stage to perform the two-verse version of the song himself—a recording of which was released by Columbia in July 2018 on the album *Live 1962–1966: Rare Performances from the Copyright Collections* (Columbia Records). In May 1962, *Broadside* #6 put the song on its front cover, now complete, with all three verses. When I spoke with music historian Elijah Wald, he said, "Post–'Blowin' in the Wind,' the world shifts. Everything can be said to be 'before and after.'" Happy Traum told me, "We knew it was a song for the ages. It was unlike any song you had ever heard." But Bob Dylan said, in the liner notes of 1985's *Biograph*, "It was just another song I wrote."

The New World Singers, which included Turner, Happy Traum, Bob Cohen, and Delores Dixon, were the first to record and release the song on record, on *Broadside Ballads, Vol. 1*, the first album in the *Broadside* series. They delivered a fully fleshed-out, traditional guitar-banjo-vocal arrangement that included dense, four-part harmonies and featured vocalist Delores Dixon breaking out solo for each chorus refrain. All of the artists on the album were recorded on the same day in the small, uptown studio of Folkways Records, and in the room as they recorded were also Pete Seeger, Phil Ochs, Peter LaFarge, Mark Spoelstra, the Freedom Singers, and Bob Dylan. A peculiarity of this performance is Dixon's smooth enunciation of the word "blowin'" which sounds like "blown." "The answer, my friend, is *blown* in the wind, the answer is *blown* in the wind." Dylan, standing in the studio facing the group as it all went down, didn't seem to mind at all. "He *really* liked Delores," Traum told me. Indeed, the *New York Times* was not the only publication to refer to Dixon as Dylan's "sometime girlfriend."

When I spoke with Dixon and referred to "Blowin' in the Wind" as Dylan's song, she corrected me. "That's our song," Dixon explained, "it's my song, too. We were having dinner at my apartment on St. Nicholas Avenue in Harlem." Dixon's mother lived down the hall and brought dinner over to Dee's six-room apartment. "He loved my mother's cooking, and she loved cooking for him. She always had a big spread out." Regardless of later refinements made in the Fat Black Pussycat or elsewhere with David Blue, it was there—according to Dixon—that Dylan started writing the song. "He had been, you know, imbibing, and was a little tipsy, knocking over some plates and dishes," she said of Dylan. "I sang 'No More Auction Block' while we sat around the same grand piano I have now. We talked about it, I sang a bit of it, then he said 'Wait, wait, wait.' He pulled out one of those black composition books, loaded with lyrics, and started writing. It didn't take him long. Especially when the food came. That was the end of that!" Of the lyrics, Dixon said, "He was inspired [by "No More Auction Block"] to come up with the updated, modern verses. His verses explained what I was singing in the song, in that Negro spiritual."

The first commercial recording of "Blowin' in the Wind" was by the Chad Mitchell Trio, produced and arranged by Milt Okun. With a bright, steady tempo and a guitar, banjo, and thumping upright bass accompaniment, the trio sounds as if they might have just been listening to Paul Clayton's album of lumberjack songs. Yet it is a straight reading that further showcases the song in a kind of traditional, folk format. Unknowing, casual listeners might have thought that "Blowin' in the Wind" was a recently discovered long-lost gem from the first wave of the folk revival. The Chad Mitchell Trio had wanted to release the song as a single and make it the title track for their next album. However, the label, Kapp Records, opposing, for commercial reasons, the use of the word "death" in the lyrics, rejected the idea and delayed its release. It *was* included on their album, however, released in January 1963 with the less-memorable title *The Chad Mitchell Trio in Action*.

The next release of "Blowin' in the Wind" would be on Dylan's own next album, *The Freewheelin' Bob Dylan*, performed in his typical, off-the-cuff, casual style but sung with atypical restraint. Even *he* knew this song was different. When Peter, Paul and Mary's single of "Blowin' in the Wind" was released three weeks later, in June 1963, they, Dylan, and the song itself would all become household names.

Chapter Seven

an arti
rev

stiC
olutiOn

Buffy Sainte-Marie backstage at the Newport Folk Festival in 1966.

Sharp social commentary and songs of resistance

were not the only sounds heard emanating through the doors of venues and onto MacDougal Street on Saturday nights in 1963. The old-timey, ragtime-era, jug band music that Dave Van Ronk, John Sebastian, and others on the scene were so fond of was enjoying a brief but meaningful resurgence at this time as well. In fact, Van Ronk had tested these waters himself as early as 1958.

The skiffle fad had started in the UK a few years prior, when Lonnie Donegan had his hit with Lead Belly's "Rock Island Line" played in jug band style. That success inspired the Lyrichord label, a company specializing in classical music and field recordings, to make a record that was to be Dave Van Ronk's first recorded appearance on an album. A band was assembled by Van Ronk and influential blues historian Samuel Charters, adding some friends and calling themselves "The Orange Blossom Jug Five with Dave Van Ronk." Picking up on the new stereo technology that had just been released to consumers for the first time that year, and riding the British skiffle craze with hopes it would take off in the States, Lyrichord called the album *Skiffle in Stereo*. The problem was not in the quality of musicianship or the enthusiasm of the band members or the songs but in the primitive recording technique used to achieve the stereo effect, which required each musician to be in a separate, isolated room in the studio—without proper monitoring of the others. They simply couldn't hear each other to keep in time. Though *Skiffle in Stereo* is an absolutely joyful and entertaining mess, Van Ronk was to say in his memoir that the album "included some of the most appalling moments I have ever heard on record."

Four years later, in 1962, Erik Darling was listening to Samuel Charters's seminal, 1959 blues anthology *The Country Blues* (Folkways), the companion album to Charters's book of the same name, and one track jumped out at him. On side 1, track 3, was a catchy 1929 jug band tune credited to Cannon's Jug Stompers, "Walk Right In," recorded for Victor Records. Knowing somehow that the old song could be a contemporary hit, Darling gathered two friends, guitarist Bill Svanoe and jazz singer Lynne Taylor to form the Rooftop Singers, for the sole purpose of recording it. Having already experienced chart success in the mid-1950s with the Tarriers, making a hit record was not new to Darling. He knew what was needed. The Rooftop Singers (1) took Cannon's song and wisely folked it up sixties style, using twin Gibson twelve-string acoustic guitars (a rare, left-handed one for Svanoe had to be special-ordered and took several months) that created a massive rhythm guitar sound and provided for some distinctive soloing in the middle of the tune; (2) replaced the jug with an upright bass for a more precise rendering; (3) added drums playing a subtle, skiffle-like beat that suggested rock and roll; (4) worked out a tight, three-part harmony arrangement; (5) dumped the wild, cocaine-fueled harmonica and kazoo of the original 1929 version; and (6) added some contemporary lyrics for the second verse: "Walk right in, set right down, *baby let your hair hang down*."

In the days before multicolored hair, facial piercings, and full-body tattoos, simply letting one's hair hang down was a blatant gesture of rebellion. Anyway, all these elements came together to indeed give the Rooftop Singers a hit and Vanguard Records its biggest-selling single ever. The rather lame, homemade-looking, black-and-white 45 rpm single sleeve proudly proclaimed:

VANGUARD
From the Company That Gave You Joan Baez
A New Folk Group Destined to Go to the Top of the Ladder
THE ROOFTOP SINGERS
Singing "Walk Right In" b/w "Cool Water"

Well, if the ladder Vanguard was referring to was the *Billboard* Hot 100 singles chart, their prediction was absolutely correct. The song went to number one in January 1963 and stayed there for two weeks. The whole country was singing, "Walk right in, set right down. . . ." It's an undeniable treat to listen to, even now. One strange thing, though. For the songwriting credits, instead of correctly listing the song's actual songwriter Gus Cannon, the label of the record was printed with the names of Rooftop Singers Erik Darling and Willard Svanoe. That was just wrong.

Gus Cannon was born in Memphis in 1883, the son of slaves. Before forming the Jug Stompers in the late 1920s, he had traveled on the medicine show circuit as Banjo Joe with his guitar-playing partner Hosea Woods. Cannon made his own first banjo using an old guitar neck, "a bread pan my mama used to bake biscuits in," and a raccoon-skin head. In 1963, Cannon was alive and not well, then seventy-nine years old, and living in poverty in Memphis, Tennessee, having not recorded since the Great Depression wiped him out in the 1930s. The previous winter he had to pawn his banjo, according to his Stax Records bio, "to buy coal for his stove." If the Rooftop Singers had learned "Walk Right In" from Sam Charters's *Country Blues* collection, as they claimed, they would have known it was written by Cannon. In filmmaker Todd Kwait's 2007 documentary *Chasin' Gus' Ghost*, Erik Darling incorrectly states that on the Charters album there is only a small fragment of the song. "On this record was 'Walk Right In.' And it was just a little, teeny . . . it was just a snippet on there," claims Darling. But that is simply untrue. The entire 2:57 version of Gus Cannon's circa 1929 recording of "Walk Right In" is on that album, and it is longer, in fact, than Darling's 1963 version with the Rooftop Singers, which clocks in at 2:35. I asked John Sebastian about Darling's apparent indiscretion, and John replied, "Well, I can't say anything about that. I did it too. We all did. It seemed like music from the ancient past."

According to the Cannon documentary, it was Samuel Charters who pointed out to Vanguard Records' Maynard and Seymour Solomon that Gus Cannon was the songwriter and was still alive. The song had been published in 1929 by Ralph Peer's Southern Music publishing company and co-credited to his guitar-playing partner and fellow Jug Stomper Hosea Woods. Charters and Solomon located Cannon in Memphis, and a mechanical license was issued for him to receive royalties. Cannon then signed a record deal himself with Stax Records in Memphis, and made a new album at age eighty. According to Dom Flemons of the Carolina Chocolate Drops in his 2013 profile on Cannon for the *Oxford American,* Cannon's was one of the first releases on the Stax label. Even with the renewed attention, Cannon still lived in poverty. Yet the jug band, good time, country blues, old-timey sound his Jug Stompers and the Memphis Jug Band across town had created in the 1920s was now a sudden craze in the Greenwich Village and Cambridge, Massachusetts, coffeehouses.

In Cambridge, Jim Kweskin had just formed his Jug Band, bringing back all the wild-card elements that the Rooftop Singers had edited out, the things that had made the original recordings of this music so appealing in the first place. Kweskin and his group, and similarly Dave Van Ronk, made the music fun, funny, wild, and unrestrained within the parameters of their excellent musicianship. In the Kweskin band, the harmonica, kazoos, washboard percussion, and, of course, the *jug*, played by Fritz Richmond, who also played washtub bass, were irresistible. Devotees of Gus Cannon's Jug Stompers and the Memphis Jug Band, they managed to make '20s music sound perfectly relevant, cool, in the moment, and alive. Geoff Muldaur's beautiful vocals juxtaposed with wild kazoo outbursts kept things from ever getting too serious. But it was always clear that these guys were true aficionados and could really play. In his *AllMusic* review of their Vanguard debut, *Unblushing Brassiness*, music critic Ronnie D. Lankford Jr. would later write, "The band's wide arsenal of unusual instruments, humorous material, and professional approach represented a quantum leap for folk music in 1963."

Back in the Village, the Even Dozen Jug Band was forming in the late spring of that same year by a bunch of college kids hanging out with their instruments in Washington Square Park. Steve Katz, a Van Ronk guitar student, was one of them. "We were New York's adolescent answer to the older, more experienced Kweskin Jug Band. We idolized Cannon's Jug Stompers and the Memphis Jug Band. We subsisted on 78 rpm records that were discovered in the shacks and hovels of the rural South by collectors like Harry Smith, Nick Perls, and Alan Lomax," Katz wrote in his memoir. "We would rehearse any place we can find," he told me. "We were the generation after the old-timey, blues people. We were just picking some songs we liked, hanging out at Gerde's, and jamming downstairs in the basement." Besides Katz, who would go on to form two more seminal bands born out of the Greenwich Village scene, the Even Dozen Jug Band also included the ubiquitous John Sebastian, Stefan Grossman, and David Grisman. The legendary 1920s blues singer Victoria Spivey had moved to Greenwich Village and made a comeback during the folk revival. Spivey had taken an interest in the group but told the boys they needed to add some "sex appeal." She recommended adding Greenwich Village native Maria D'Amato, a cute and talented young singer on the folk scene with undeniable charm and charisma whom, it seemed, everyone on MacDougal Street wanted to date. D'Amato joined the band, mentored by Spivey who taught her blues songs from the 1920s and '30s and gave her performance tips. Maria explained, "She'd say, 'Now, baby girl, when you get up there, it ain't enough to *sound* good, you've got to look good too. You need to get up there and strut your stuff, and make all eyes be on you.' Then she looked at me, very meaningfully, right in the eye, and said, 'That's what they call—*stage presence*.'" Maria took Spivey's words to heart.

The business-savvy Spivey let them rehearse at her place and signed them to her own Spivey Records, one of the first artist-owned labels and one of the first to record Bob Dylan, who had added harmonica accompaniment for Delta blues guitarist Big Joe Willams on a 1962 Spivey release. But Jac Holzman, bitten by the jug bug, bought the Even Dozen Jug Band out of their Spivey deal and signed them to his own Elektra label. "He thought we would be the next big thing," Katz told me. Robert Shelton, describing the group in *Hootenanny*, a magazine he edited, wrote, "For sheer joy of making music, one must search widely to find the equal of this aggregation, whose average age is 18." Going the Rooftop Singers one better, the Even Dozen Jug Band posed for their first, and only, album cover on an actual New York City rooftop, amid two of the City's iconic, rusted water towers. The group would go on to be featured on major network television shows like the *Tonight Show with Johnny Carson*, with Carson himself joining the band on comb (yes, a hair comb is a jug band instrument—just add waxed paper), and they would perform on a bill at Carnegie Hall with Nina Simone in "The Folk & Jazz Wing Ding—Presented by Ford CARavan of Music." Not bad for a bunch of rowdy teenagers with jugs and washboards.

In that same December 1963 *Hootenanny* article "A New Trend in Folk Music," Robert Shelton wrote, "All the makings of a major new trend among city folk musicians are becoming visible this fall. No one can predict when it will develop, but interest in the new ragtime jug bands is running high. The music is fun, infectious, bouncy and exuberant. The instruments are colorful and odd. The link with the past is strong. The adaptability of the new jug bands to ragtime, jazz, blues, stomps and skiffle music promises diversity."

Dave Van Ronk himself gave jug band music another shot with his group the Ragtime Jug Stompers, recording an album for Mercury later in 1963 that was released in January of the next year. The group was formed as a result of a suggestion from Shelton, after receiving a call from Village Vanguard owner Max Gordon. Gordon was inquiring about jug bands in New York after seeing the long lines outside a Kweskin Jug Band show at Club 47 in Cambridge. Suddenly everyone wanted to be in on the jug band action. Always up for a challenge, and a gig, Van Ronk recruited Barry Kornfeld on banjo, Danny Kalb (another of Van Ronk's students) on guitar, and Artie Rose on mandolin. Samuel Charters returned on jug, washtub, and vocals. Van Ronk was especially suited to this music, and he delighted in working out arrangements for the larger band. But he was as pragmatic as ever, having no illusions of jug band music becoming the next big thing that labels and others were banking on. And he was right. A month after the Stompers' album came out, the Beatles performed on the *Ed Sullivan Show*, and jug band music was soon all but forgotten. Regardless, Van Ronk considered the resulting album, *Ragtime Jug Stompers* (Verve Records), among his *best* work—which must be seen as a vast improvement over his opinion of his first effort.

The Even Dozen Jug Band were also not to not see it through 1964. In what Steve Katz calls "a small bout of jug band crossbreeding," Maria D'Amato met Geoff Muldaur of the Kweskin band while on a date with John Sebastian. After a nice dinner at an Italian restaurant, Sebastian took Maria to check out "the competition," the Kweskin band, who were performing at the Bitter End. Unfortunately for Sebastian, Maria couldn't take her eyes off Geoff Muldaur, while Sebastian couldn't keep *his* eyes off *her*. "He sounds like a white Mose Allison," Maria thought about Geoff, she told me, not realizing at the time that Mose Allison was actually white. Then according to Katz, the two met again at a party that Elektra Records threw for the Even Dozen Jug Band at the group's funky rehearsal loft next to the Chelsea Hotel on Twenty-Third Street, where "Maria got plastered and threw up all over Geoff." "It's true," confirms Maria. "I wasn't feeling well and started drinking sherry, my grandma's remedy, early in the day. And popping Excedrins. They were a new thing. I was high as a kite by the time I got there. Everyone was jamming, and I started singing a blues, making up rhymes about Geoff. Then I sort of passed out on him, on his leg as he played guitar. Suddenly he yelled out, 'Hey, this chick just barfed all over me!'" Later, Maria encountered Geoff again at Izzy Young's Folklore Center. Embarrassed, she tried to hide, but a confrontation was unavoidable. She told him how sorry she was for her breach of etiquette. Geoff replied, "No need to apologize. It was an honor." "They were engaged not long after, and she became Maria Muldaur," said Katz. Maria left the Even Dozen Jug Band, moved to Cambridge with Geoff, and joined the Kweskin band.

Still with high hopes for the ragtime jug craze, Elektra wanted the Even Dozen Jug Band to tour and compete with other top folk acts like the New Christy Minstrels. "We really need you to quit school and get on the road," Jac Holtzman told the group. Except for John Sebastian, who was not in school and was a member of the musicians' union, all the remaining members thought it would be foolish to quit college, and they instead voted to end the group.

But jug music itself did not die. With Maria Muldaur on board and soon adding banjo picker, harmonica master, and future sixties cult leader Mel Lyman, the Kweskin Jug Band would continue to tour and record throughout the decade. In California, the Grateful Dead would get its start from the remnants of Mother McCree's Uptown Jug Champions, from Palo Alto. And in the Village, the jug band spirit and attitude would be put to good use in new bands that were soon to be born. Especially one that would be formed by John Sebastian.

Freewheelin'

The recording of Bob Dylan's second album, released on May 27, 1963, had been a very different process than the slap-dash couple of afternoon sessions at Columbia Studio A that had resulted in his first one. This time the sessions covered a period of an entire, eventful year—from April 24, 1962, to April 24, 1963—and two different producers—John Hammond and Tom Wilson—over eight sessions. It was a year that also saw Dylan walk off the *Ed Sullivan Show* when censors decided to cut one of his songs, "Talkin' John Birch Society Blues" (as it was then titled), asking him replace it with another song. He refused. Sullivan himself, it seems, liked it, but CBS execs considered the song defamatory to the Far Right organization and its followers. Though it is now owned by Sony Music Entertainment, Columbia Records at the time was owned by CBS and, before you could say "freedom of speech," Dylan was asked to replace the song on his forthcoming album as well. He was in no position to refuse after the poor showing of his debut. The happy ending, besides the good publicity the episode garnered, was that, since he had been recording the album over such a long period of time, he now had newer and stronger compositions that could replace the older ones, making it a better album than it would have been initially. Rare early copies of the original sequence were pressed and then recalled; only a handful survive.

The difference between Dylan's first two albums was not so much in the audio quality, although the mix of the second is far more listenable, but in his more-tempered, thoughtful vocal performances and, most obviously, in the material itself. This time, except for two, the songs were his own compositions, and credited to Bob Dylan. That is not to say there was not a lot of musical borrowing going on, for which payments and settlements were made. And over the year, at least one young heart was broken, if not two. Or three.

Suze Rotolo had been living with Dylan on West Fourth Street for months when her mother, who never really approved of Dylan, invited her on a trip to Europe and to attend art school in Perugia, Italy. This was a trip that had been planned for the previous, pre-Dylan year. But that first attempt had ended in a disastrous car accident before it began. Now, over a year later and in a relationship, Rotolo agonized over whether she should go. After discussing it with friends Terri Thal and Sylvia Tyson, who both convinced her that a trip to Europe to study art was too good an offer to refuse, Rotolo decided to go for it. The SS *Rotterdam* disembarked from the Holland America Lines dock in Hoboken, New Jersey—directly across the Hudson River from the Village—on June 9, 1962. Dylan was there to see her off, and the two joked as they said their good-byes. But the long separation would prove especially difficult for Dylan.

While Rotolo soaked in European art and culture, Dylan sulked in the Village, kvetching to friends incessantly about how Rotolo had abandoned him. But he also wrote songs. A lot of them. Good ones. On the resulting album, *The Freewheelin' Bob Dylan*, Rotolo's presence and absence can be heard and felt throughout. The writing laid bare his pining away for her in detail, revealing his pain but also reversing or manipulating the story and, in the case of "Don't Think Twice, It's All Right," demonstrating how quickly love can turn into a kind of bitchy spite, as in the lines "I gave her my heart but she wanted my soul" and "You just kinda wasted my precious time." The truth is, the wisps of male privilege and possessiveness—typical of the time—that come through might have been the very things Rotolo, at nineteen years old, was trying to escape from. When she returned to the Village over six months later, she wrote in her memoir, she felt "unwelcome" by friends who accused her of deserting Dylan "when he needed her most." She was uncomfortable with the way her personal life had been bandied about in Dylan's songs and conversations. "The gossipy insinuations by the folkies around the Village hit hard," Rotolo wrote. "I began to feel that people knew more about my life than I did." Dylan seems to point to Rotolo and their life together in subtle and obvious ways throughout the album, making a personal reference to the rooster they could hear from their West Fourth Street bedroom crowing "at the break of dawn," echoing through the Village streets from the chicken coops in the Italian meat market on nearby Thompson Street. And going so far as to specifically report that Rotolo has left him, by ship, and gone to Italy:

The ocean took my baby, my baby took my heart from me
She packed it all up in a suitcase, Lord, she took it away to Italy, Italy.

Dave Van Ronk would refer to these songs as "self-pitying . . . self-pitying, but brilliant." But the album, of course, was more than just those songs. Opening with "Blowin' in the Wind," sung to great effect in a world-weary voice that belied Dylan's twenty-one years, the album goes on to debut the stunning "A Hard Rain's A-Gonna Fall" and the brutal "Masters of War"—all three undisputed masterpieces of protest music. These, too, show Rotolo's influence, as she had acquainted Dylan with issues of civil rights and political activism, an influence he often admitted. "Suze was so far ahead of the rest of us when it came to social issues," Maria Muldaur reaffirmed. That's why Rotolo's appearance on the album cover art for *Freewheelin'* is so fitting: Dylan and Rotolo strolling just outside their West Fourth Street apartment, huddling on a snow-covered Jones Street on a cold February day, framed by the Village itself as the third character in the drama. It was beautifully and simply shot by Columbia staff photographer Don Hunstein. Some misinterpret the image as portraying Rotolo as the subordinate, clinging girlfriend on his arm—his "chick," as Rotolo hated to be called—and Dylan as the sensitive male artist lost in thought. But Rotolo can also be seen as supporting and guiding him, mature with her own wisdom and convictions, through streets she knew better than he did, that they are learning to navigate together. "People say I was an influence on him, but we influenced each other," she was later to express. Regardless, by the time *Freewheelin'* came out, Dylan was having a fling with Joan Baez, making its title all the more appropriate.

While some of the lyrics on *Freewheelin'* were groundbreaking, the accompaniment was still traditional blues and ballads. The music of "Masters of War" had been based on Jean Ritchie's dulcimer arrangement of "Nottamun Town," a song that had been sung in her family for generations. According to Howard Soule's book *Down the Highway: The Life of Bob Dylan* (2001), Ritchie was okay with the appropriation, saying, "A lot of people do that . . . I don't think he was out to try and rob anybody." It wasn't Ritchie's first time at this rodeo—she had been through all it before with the Kingston Trio. But she *did* request acknowledgment on the song credit that the arrangement Dylan had used was hers. Instead, Dylan's attorneys paid her a flat $5,000 settlement in return for waiving her rights to make any further claim. While "Girl from the North Country" was based on the English folk tune "Scarborough Fair," "A Hard Rain's A-Gonna Fall" was born, without legal conflict, out of "Lord Randall," another Scottish-English ballad that had recently been recorded by Jean Ritchie on her 1961 Folkways album *Ballads from Her Appalachian Family Tradition:*

Oh, where have you been, Lord Randall my son?
Oh, where have you been, my handsome young one?

Jean Ritchie, apparently, provided one-stop shopping for new songwriters. It is not for nothing that she is still referred to as the "Mother of Folk."

An Artistic Revolution

Of course, it's the words that Dylan brought to this music and structure—fusing imagist beat poetry with traditional folk music—that made "A Hard Rain's A-Gonna Fall" mind-blowing. "Hard Rain" may or may not have referred to nuclear fallout—the song's author himself has alternately claimed both interpretations. But if it did, it predicted a far more violent form of radioactive precipitation than Bonnie Dobson had forecasted in "Morning Dew." Dylan performed the song at a Carnegie Hall hootenanny presented by *Sing Out!* magazine on September 22, 1962, one month before the Cuban Missile Crisis, after reportedly debuting it to a Gaslight crowd that was left speechless. Pete Seeger was on the bill at Carnegie Hall that night and soon began performing the song himself. Dave Van Ronk was likely voicing the reaction of all the folkies along MacDougal Street when he perceived the song as "the beginning of an artistic revolution."

Phil Ochs, always one of Dylan's most ardent supporters, wrote an article for *Modern Hi-Fi & Stereo Guide* entitled "Topical Songs—History on the Spot" in which he opined, "The major writer today is 22-year-old Bob Dylan, who brought topical songs to a new height with the quality of his poetry." Ochs goes on to compare Dylan to one of his heroes. "The contrast between Dylan and James Dean illustrates the difference between the two decades. Dean was the rebel without a cause in the '50s; Dylan maintains the rebel image while speaking out on the basic moral issues of our day."

Dylan's friend, folksinger Paul Clayton, had recently given Dylan his twenty-first birthday party in Charlottesville, Virginia, during a car trip to the South they took together along with Suze Rotolo. Ever the folklorist and having recorded numerous albums, Clayton had discovered, rewritten, and arranged the tune "Who's Gonna Buy You Ribbons?" based on a traditional song and played on dulcimer in the style of Jean Ritchie. Clayton's song has the same wistful melody and the same lyrical hook as "Don't Think Twice," along with other lyrics and themes in common.

It ain't no use to sit and wonder why, darlin'
Just wonder who's gonna buy you ribbons when I'm gone

Barry Kornfeld recalled, "I was with Paul one day, and Dylan wanders by and says, 'Hey, man, that's a great song. I'm going to use that song.'" And of course, he did. Again, there was an out-of-court settlement and no hard feelings, but many on the scene's inner circle, such as Van Ronk, who mentions the episode in his memoir, thought it would have been only fair for Dylan to at least cut his friend in for the publishing—even just a little. Clayton, like so many musicians then and now, struggled to survive while others benefited from their vision and labor. Everyone in the Village knew of Clayton's money problems and Dylan would have been especially aware. Van Ronk said, "You could see the soles of Clayton's feet through his worn-out shoes." When I spoke with Barry Kornfeld, though, he reminded me of something Paul Clayton himself would jokingly say: "If you can't write, *rewrite*; and if you can't rewrite, *copyright*." Those words must have haunted him, though, when, just a couple of months later in October, Peter, Paul and Mary released the song on their third blockbuster Warner Bros. album, and as a hit single. Clayton would have heard his melody and words, for which he held a copyright, playing out of every car radio that passed, every record shop he entered or walked by, and, of course, it was being credited 100 percent to Bob Dylan. Although the two would remain friends, and would even take a cross-country trip together in 1964, for Clayton this episode was a personal disappointment—one more thorn in the side of his already troubled psyche. Especially since, by that time, he had fallen in love. "Paul was *horribly* in love with Dylan," Kornfeld, one of Clayton's closest friends, told me. "That's why he let things play out the way that he did."

Newport '63

On July 26, 1963, the Newport Folk Festival returned after a two-year absence. George Wein, who also produced the Newport *Jazz* Festival, explained to me what had happened: "There was a riot in Newport during the Jazz Festival in 1960. The town had become an oasis for all-night drinking, and thousands of people descended on the city with the festival in mind. The festival was sold out, and the town became a drunken mess, with people throwing beer bottles at the police. The riot was not at the festival itself, but the police asked that we keep the festival going until 2:00 a.m. so they could clean up what was going on downtown."

"The nonprofit foundation that was the original Newport Jazz presenter was finished—bankrupt," Wein continued. "Some city businessmen tried to put on a festival in 1961, but it was a total failure. I decided to go back in 1962 and put on the *Jazz* Festival by myself, and it was a success. So in 1963, I revived the Folk Festival with Pete Seeger. It was a huge victory. All the artists performed for a fifty-dollar fee plus expenses. It shook the world—Joan Baez, Bob Dylan, Pete Seeger, Peter, Paul and Mary."

Murray Lerner's 1967 documentary *Festival!*, filmed over the course of three Newport Folk Festivals (1963–1965), is cinematic proof that they indeed shook the world.

So much of our story comes together, and was elevated, at the 1963 Newport Folk Festival. According to the *New York Times*, there were thirty-eight thousand people in attendance, giving the Greenwich Village folksingers—and the nascent topical song movement—their largest platform and most national recognition to date. And because this was the first Newport Folk Festival since 1960, there was a lot of new talent. Besides the names George Wein mentioned when we spoke, the stunning lineup in 1963 included a strong showing from the MacDougal Street mob and their favorites: Phil Ochs, Paul Clayton, Dave Van Ronk, Reverend Gary Davis, Jean Ritchie, the Tarriers, Ian & Sylvia, Ramblin' Jack Elliott, John Lee Hooker, Doc Watson, Mississippi John Hurt, the Rooftop Singers, Brownie McGhee and Sonny Terry, Theodore Bikel, Eric Weissberg, Dock Boggs, Judy Collins, the Freedom Singers—they were all there. Watching *Festival!* now, there are sometimes unexpected moments of silliness and humor among the folk artists in their stage banter and with their audience. It's a reminder that, for all their seriousness, they were mostly all under the age of twenty-five and, as Judy Henske said in the Phil Ochs documentary *There But for Fortune*, they were all "really there to have a good time." Pete Seeger can so clearly be seen as a father figure, savoring his role a bridge between the generations and keeping an eye on things. With the blacklist still in effect and without mainstream media exposure, the festival provided him, and all of the Greenwich Village artists, a massive audience.

"It seems like my mission in life was to create the stage upon which the most important jazz and folk artists could perform," George Wein told me. "I was aware of the popularity of the Greenwich Village artists and knew that they could reach a larger audience if presented outside of the little clubs and bistros in Harvard Square and Greenwich Village." It was through Wein that I first met Pete Seeger—and many other folk and jazz artists in the mid-2000s. I worked with Wein and his Festival Productions, producing three major concerts with him, and I am forever grateful for his mentorship. Our interviews for this book were among his last.

The 1963 Newport Folk Festival also was the unofficial coronation of Bob Dylan and Joan Baez as the new king and queen of folk music. Baez at this time was at the pinnacle of her success, having been featured, in a bizarre, barefoot portrait by Russell Hoban, on the cover of *Time* magazine on November 23, 1962. Yet she generously promoted Dylan in her sets and in interviews, inviting him up onstage to join her and performing his songs, much like Bob Gibson had propelled Baez's own early career. But there was more to the story. Two months prior, at the Monterey Folk Festival in May, Dylan and Baez had begun an affair. It was supposed to be a secret but would have been hard to miss, onstage or off.

And it must have been difficult for Suze Rotolo, at nineteen, to deal with it. She would later say that Dylan was "the elephant in the room of her life," and the affair was the elephant in the room of the Festival. Even George Wein, in his excellent 2003 memoir *Myself Among Others: A Life in Music*, wrote that he noticed how Dylan and Baez "disappeared into a room by themselves. So much was happening that no one noted their absence." Wein stuck his head in the room and saw they were trading songs. But that was not all that was happening. Having performed at the very first Festival in 1959, for Baez this was a triumphant return. As for Dylan, he had arrived at his first Newport Festival to become its star. And he did. Among many highlights, his evening performance of "Only a Pawn in Their Game," a song about the assassination of Medgar Evers, was delivered in a brilliant blaze of irony and chilling fire.

Phil Ochs was invited to perform in one of the daytime workshops in Newport's Freebody Park but, according to Michael Schumacher in *There But for Fortune*, it was not so easy for him. Ochs was suffering from a severe headache and had to be rushed to the hospital—twice—the beginning of what appeared to be severe performance anxiety. It was something that was to plague him throughout his short life, though he would never miss a show as a result of the illness. Ochs was medicated at the hospital and advised not to perform. But, of course, he did. And, Ochs won the crowd over, with a song he had written with Bob Gibson that was, like Dylan's "Only a Pawn in Their Game," about the recent killing of Medgar Evers. Evers was a civil rights activist who had worked to end segregation and enforce voting rights in Mississippi. He was assassinated in front of his home by a member of the White Citizen's Council, an organization that opposed racial integration. Phil started shakily at first but gained confidence as he sang.

His name was Medgar Evers and he walked his road alone
Like Emmett Till and thousands more whose names we'll never know

Ochs's sincerity shined through his anxiety, and the song was well received. He followed with "Talking Birmingham Blues," another forceful attack on segregation in the South told in a particularly sarcastic way that was simultaneously humorous and brutally biting. By this point, he showed no sign of his illness and, at the end of his set, Ochs received a standing ovation. "Emotionally spent," Schumacher wrote, "Phil left the stage and collapsed under a tree." Although it was iffy at first, Ochs was a hit at his first Newport Festival, and would return in 1964 and '66.

Dave Van Ronk, Judy Collins, Paul Clayton, Tom Paxton, and many others made their Newport debuts in 1963. "The experience was like going to Oz!" Paxton told me. But it was the surprise appearance of beloved bluesman Mississippi John Hurt—heretofore known only by his Okeh recordings from the 1920s on Harry Smith's *Anthology of American Folk Music* and assumed to have died—that was, as George Wein puts it, "a folklorist's fairytale." People who were there still talk about Hurt's magnetic performances that year with reverence and awe of his subtle vocal nuances and distinctive guitar playing. He was the real deal. The Festival gave Hurt a renewed career. At age seventy-one, he was soon performing on the college, concert hall, and coffeehouse circuit as well as appearing on the *Tonight Show,* and he made several albums, including three for Vanguard, produced by Patrick Sky. Sadly, Hurt would pass away only three years later, in 1966. But his smiling, beneficent manner and supreme musicianship endure through the musicians who adored him, then and now.

Peter, Paul and Mary had already achieved superstar status. At Newport, their star was raised even higher. And they, along with Seeger and Theo Bikel, shined further starlight on Dylan, singing his praises as well as his songs. In a further star-making move, Albert Grossman insisted that Wein schedule the lesser-known Dylan to close Friday night's program instead of the act that Wein expected would close the show, P, P & M. But then Dylan brought Peter, Paul and Mary back onstage, along with Baez, Seeger, and the Freedom Singers, for an encore of "Blowin' in the Wind" that brought down the house. Then, according to Wein in his memoir, amid a roar of applause, they all returned to the stage, along with Theo Bikel, and sang "We Shall Overcome." "The unaccompanied blend of voices onstage gave heft to the song's plaintive chorus—as did the fifteen thousand voices beyond the stage. To me it was a moment never to be forgotten. I still get emotional when I think of it," wrote Wein.

March on Washington

Just a month after Newport, on August 28, the March on Washington for Jobs and Freedom—a push for comprehensive civil rights—took place under blue skies in the nation's capital. It was at that march that, not far from where John F. Kennedy had given his inaugural address, Martin Luther King Jr. delivered his "I Have a Dream" speech. The march was itself the dream of labor and civil rights leader A. Philip Randolph, who had aspired to it for decades. When it finally came together, it did so quickly. The event was organized by openly gay civil rights activist Bayard Rustin, who had also organized 1961's Freedom Rides in the South. Rustin began his career as a singer and had performed on Broadway first with Paul Robeson, in the musical *John Henry*, and then with Josh White. Beginning in the late 1930s, Rustin performed regularly at Café Society in the Village, where he had been invited by White to join his group Josh White and the Carolinians, and it became a steady gig. In 1940, he sang first tenor on White's landmark concept album *Chain Gang* (Columbia), produced by John Hammond, foreshadowing the actual chain gang he would be sentenced to during the Freedom Rides. The racially diverse, intellectual, and openly gay scene of the

Village, especially surrounding Café Society, appealed to Rustin. But more and more, he became drawn to social activism by the labor movement and the American Communist Party, which he had joined during the Great Depression and soon quit. Discovering and being inspired by Indian ethicist Mahatma Gandhi, leader of the nationalist movement against British rule in India, whose methods were in consort with his own Quaker upbringing, Rustin became a believer and proponent of nonviolence and peaceful protest to bring about social change; theories that were to be similarly adopted by Dr. King. The plan for the March in 1963, with its focus on jobs and economic justice was, according to Rustin, to be "intensely nonviolent."

It was a beautiful summer day in Washington as buses began arriving, and the crowd grew to over 250,000 people, far greater than the anticipated 90,000. It is still listed as one of the largest protests in American history. Besides the speeches, given by labor leaders, activist leaders such as John Lewis of SNCC and representatives from the NAACP, CORE, and the National Urban League, there was a concert on the National Mall at the end of the march, at the steps of the Lincoln Memorial, with performers lined up by Harry Belafonte. Belafonte chose not to put the spotlight on himself and sang only in the group sing-alongs that day. Instead, he brought on board Mahalia Jackson, Marian Anderson, and Odetta to perform, as well as Josh White—in a day that had been organized by White's former singing partner of twenty years earlier, Bayard Rustin—singing "Freedom Road" with lyrics by Langston Hughes and music by Emerson Harper.

> That's why I'm marching, yes, I'm marching
> Marching down Freedom's Road
> Ain't nobody gonna stop me, nobody gonna keep me
> From marching down Freedom's Road

But, intimately familiar with the Greenwich Village scene, he also included white folksingers Joan Baez, Peter, Paul and Mary, and Bob Dylan. "Nothing that made up the American mosaic was not represented," said Belafonte to the *LA Times* in 2013. "Looking out at that sea of humanity . . . we were looking at what Dr. King was describing as 'the dream.'"

After Mahalia Jackson and Marian Anderson performed, Joan Baez led the crowd singing "We Shall Overcome" and performed the post–Civil War song "Oh, Freedom" that had previously been recorded by Odetta—Baez's voice soaring over the crowd in defiance of earthbound restraints. Dylan, joined by Baez, sang his freshly written "When the Ship Comes In," followed by "Only a Pawn in Their Game," which would have seemed to have been a good choice. But with a crowd of that size, it would have been nearly impossible to convey the nuanced irony that had come across so well to the audience at Newport a month earlier. The words of the song seem to imply that the blame for killing Medgar Evers did not lie with the murderer but with race-baiting white politicians, and they could be read literally:

Two eyes took the aim, behind a man's brain
But he can't be blamed, he's only a pawn in their game

Watching the footage of the performance now, it feels awkward. With the murder itself having happened only a couple of months earlier and still fresh in people's minds, the crowd looks increasingly restless and uncomfortable as he sings verse after verse. Quick to pick up on the reaction, Dylan appears ill at ease and out of his element. At the end, he walks off to polite applause. However, regarding the song itself, civil rights activist Bernice Johnson Reagon was to later say to Robert Shelton that "'Pawn' was the very first song that showed the poor white was as victimized by discrimination as the poor Black." Odetta, accompanied by Bruce Langhorne, sang a rousing, celebratory, call-and-response "I'm On My Way," a traditional gospel song that she had recorded in a suite with "Oh, Freedom" on her first album in 1957.

"Odetta's great, full-throated voice carried almost to Capitol Hill," the *New York Times* said at the time. Indeed, her voice was like thunder on a clear day. Odetta's was a special gift that could bring great joy and deep gravitas together—the sound of hope and optimism ringing out through the struggle. It was church.

At that moment, Peter, Paul and Mary were the most popular singing group in the United States. On August 28, 1963, their single of "Blowin' in the Wind" was sitting at number five on the *Billboard* 200, its tenth week on the chart. Their latest album, *Moving*, had just been certified gold the day before and was at number four on the album chart. Their first album, after seventy-one weeks, was still in the top ten, at number seven, and was also certified gold. But, with all their commercial success, what they projected seemed to be fulfilling their promise, singing with a kind of dignity, sincerity, and purpose that was, and is even more so now, rare on the pop charts. Peter, Paul and Mary delivered memorable and heartfelt performances of "The Hammer Song" and "Blowin' in the Wind" on that day. Belafonte and Seeger, who had laid the groundwork in the previous decade or two, must have been pleased to see their message of freedom carried on through young artists in such a big way.

The March on Washington was unquestionably a turning point in the civil rights movement. A whole lotta white folks watched Dr. King's speech on every television network along with a lot of Black folks. There was some criticism by some of the March's participants—including by comedian/activist Dick Gregory—for the large number of white performers on the stage that day. But I think Harry Belafonte and Bayard Rustin knew exactly what they were doing. Recalling Congressman John Lewis's call for "good trouble," Rustin himself said, "We need, in every community, a group of angelic troublemakers." The folksingers were up to the task.

When the musicians returned home to the Village after making national headlines at high-pro-file events, they found even more newcomers had arrived. Guitar sales nationally were skyrocketing—more than doubling between 1960 and 1965, according to *Business Week*—and the media had picked up on folk music for exploitation and parody. Warner Bros. Records released comic Allan Sherman's *My Son, the Folk Singer* on which he satirized revered folk songs, rewriting them with humorous, Jewish-themed lyrics. The African American traditional song "Water Boy," for instance, became "Seltzer Boy." The album was a smash hit, nominated for Best Album of the Year at the 1963 Grammy Awards. Folk music was not-so-suddenly everywhere. But alongside its star-making benefits, the harsh glare of media attention could also bring unwelcome scrutiny. A November 4, 1963, exposé in *Newsweek* by E. Coleman revealed Dylan's real name and conventional upbringing, interviewed his parents and kid brother, and criticized his image and songwriting. According to Robert Shelton, Dylan "exploded with anger."

Debates continued in *Sing Out!* and in the coffeehouses about the validity of commercial folk music. Traditional folklorists saw the new song movement, and the new folksingers in general, as a reflection of the "instant culture" of the 1960s. In the past, folk songs developed over decades and centuries. They had been sung by workers in the fields and handed down for generations with history and meaning; they evolved as a link to the past. Nowadays, someone could write seven songs on the subway ride uptown to visit the editors of *Broadside* and land on its front cover, not to mention the cover of *Time*. Folksingers, in the opinion of traditionalists, should be academics, scholars—like Paul Clayton—who studied, researched, and made field recordings. Or singing labor activists, adapting traditional songs for rallies, like Woody Guthrie and the Almanac Singers. Or singing archivists and internationalists like the Weavers, who were sharing folk music from around the world and encouraging unity. Regardless of such controversies, the musicians kept coming to the Village. A seventeen-year-old, blind Puerto Rican boy named José Feliciano played the basket houses in an attempt to help support his family in Spanish Harlem and wound up signed to RCA Records. Childhood friends Paul Simon and Art Garfunkel had enjoyed some pop success performing as Tom & Jerry in high school with an Everly Brothers–type act but now wanted to try their hand at folk music. They came to the Village and got signed to Columbia. All eyes of the enter-tainment industry were fixed on Greenwich Village.

But then, someone flicked a switch.

John F. Kennedy had been a popular, but controversial president, and there had been backlash to his handling of the situation in Cuba, the war in Vietnam, and civil rights. After the March on Washington on August 28, he welcomed the dignified leaders of the March, including Dr. King, to the White House for a meeting, certainly irritating segregationists in the South and in conservative states in general, like Texas. On June 10, Kennedy gave his forcefully antinuclear "Peace Speech" at American University, in Washington, DC, where, when speaking about the Soviet Union, he said, "Peace need not be impractical, and war need not be inevitable" and "For in the final analysis, our most basic common link is that we all inhabit this small planet, we all breathe the same air, we all cherish our children's futures, and we are all mortal."

In November 1963, to help shore up his base for his reelection the following year, and to mend political fences, the president took a trip to Texas on the gleaming new Boeing 707, *Air Force One*. He was to speak in San Antonio, Houston, Fort Worth, Dallas . . . that's as far as he got. On Friday, November 22, arriving at Dallas Love Field airport at 11:37 a.m., the First Lady, Jacqueline, wearing a pink Chanel suit and squinting in the sun, was handed a dozen red roses. It was in the broad, bright daylight of midday when the motorcade slowed down to a near stop as they drove through Dealey Plaza in Dallas. The big, digital, Hertz Rent-A-Car clock atop the Texas School Book Depository struck 12:30 p.m. as Kennedy, in the long, dark metallic blue Lincoln Continental presidential convertible, waved to admirers. Suddenly, multiple loud shots rang out. The president, shot in the head, slumped toward his wife. On television, bulletins interrupted regularly scheduled programs. At 1:00 p.m., President Kennedy was pronounced dead.

Six decades later, the shots fired that day are still ringing out. In early 2020, Bob Dylan would describe the events in a seventeen-minute opus, "Murder Most Foul":

> *President Kennedy was a-ridin' high*
> *Good day to be livin' and a good day to die*

For the rest of the unspeakable day, the thirty-four-year-old First Lady continued to wear the pink Chanel suit, now splattered with her husband's blood the color of the red roses she had carried, their petals now strewn on the limousine's floor. She even wore it when standing next to the new president as he took the oath of office, his right hand on the Bible. "I want them to see what they have done to Jack," she told the new first lady, Mrs. Lyndon B. Johnson.

In America, little kids were sent home from school, watching the horrific story unfold in real time on television with a feeling of dread and confusion. On Sunday, November 24, the accused assassin Lee Harvey Oswald was himself shot and killed on live national television, in the basement of Dallas Police headquarters as he was being transferred to the county jail. "I'm just a patsy!" he had shouted to reporters, words that echoed like the shots. Minutes later, the caisson bearing President Kennedy's casket left the White House for the US Capitol, where Kennedy would lie in state. The next day, November 25, the young president was laid to rest following a somber procession. It was all televised to a dumbstruck nation.

In 1966, Phil Ochs wrote in "Crucifixion,"

Planets are paralyzed; the mountains are amazed,
but they all glow brighter from the brilliance of the blaze
With the speed of insanity, then he dies

The whole world held its breath, wondering what would happen next. For a moment, everything was put on pause.

power an

d the glory

Richie Havens, backstage at the Woody Guthrie
Memorial Concert, Carnegie Hall, January 20, 1968.

Many of us felt the protective shadow living under Kennedy's wings during his too brief span in flight. It was a shadow of light that provided safety for all the positive social changes happening in America. He gave people hope.

—Eric Andersen

The decade was shaping up to be a head-spinning spectacle of sorrows and promises. At the same time that the nation was mourning its fallen president, the folk boom that had been promised, twice, was reaching its highest peak of popularity. In such an unstable world, could folk music, with its links to a simpler past, hold some answers? One thing was for sure, the spotlight on Greenwich Village was brighter than ever before. Besides the music, the beatnik lingo, and the manner of dress, the attitudes of the Village folk scene were now seen regularly on mainstream, prime-time television and heard on the newly expanded reach of FM radio. American car manufacturers had begun installing FM car radios in 1963, and by 1964, the FCC ordered that FM stations stop simulcasting AM signals, freeing them to break away from the top-forty format. The songwriters on MacDougal Street were busier than

ever cranking out songs, and labels couldn't seem to print up recording contracts fast enough. It was a quantum leap for the folk revival. In November 1963, the number two record in the country was "Washington Square," a banjo instrumental by the Village Stompers. Folk music was poised to dominate the entertainment market once and for all. What could possibly go wrong this time?

In the spring of 1963, the ABC television network had launched the live TV concert series *Hootenanny*, featuring primarily pop-oriented folk acts like the Chad Mitchell Trio, the Limeliters, the Journeymen, Ian & Sylvia, Judy Collins, the Tarriers, Bob Gibson—alongside some names that are less known today, such as Jo Mapes and the wonderful folksinger/ activist Leon Bibb, father of blues singer-songwriter Eric Bibb. The concerts were filmed live on college campuses, in-the-round, with the performers surrounded by the student audience. The show took off and later that year was the second-highest-rated show on the ABC network. Two different magazines with the *Hootenanny* title (one edited by Robert Shelton, another branded as *ABC-TV Hootenanny*) appeared on newsstands, and nearly every major and independent record label released a folk compilation with the word "hootenanny" in the title. There were *Hootenanny* beach towels, and in August 1963, MGM Pictures released the feature film *Hootenanny Hoot*, starring Johnny Cash, Judy Henske, and the Brothers Four, among others. Meanwhile the television series itself was picked up for a second season.

You would think, considering he was, at least partially, the source of the show's name (along with Woody Guthrie) and since he was seen by many as the father of the folk revival, that Pete Seeger would have been invited to appear on *Hootenanny*, alongside all of the artists he inspired, right? Nope.

By March 1963, it was revealed that the producers of the show would not allow Seeger or the Weavers to appear due to their past political affiliations. When word got out of this latest incident of blacklisting, *Variety* magazine reported that Joan Baez refused to appear on the show. And Baez wasn't the only one. Carolyn Hester, Tom Paxton, Ramblin' Jack Elliot, singer/activist Barbara Dane, and the Greenbriar Boys also refused to appear, citing the banning of Seeger. The list of boycotting folksingers grew, embarrassing the network. ABC then made an offer to Seeger but required that he furnish "an affidavit as to his past and present affiliations, if any, with the Communist Party, and/or with the Communist front organizations." Of course, Pete refused. When the story of ABC's request was disclosed by Seeger's manager Harold Leventhal to the *New York Times*, more artists refused to appear. Pete did not encourage the boycott, however, as he saw the show as an opportunity for folk musicians to be seen and heard. It was an uncomfortable situation all around. None of it was to matter by the next season, however. The show would be unceremoniously cancelled in the fall of 1964 because of sinking ratings, perhaps due to an unforeseen invasion of an entirely different type than the one ABC so feared when they banned Seeger.

On January 14, 1964, Peter, Paul and Mary made an impressive debut on the popular *Jack Benny Program* on CBS Television. Benny, who had a created a caricatured persona as a cheapskate and minimally talented musician, was a mainstay on American radio beginning in the 1930s. Unlike some others in the medium, Benny made an easy transition to television with his absurdist show-within-a-show format, in which much of the action happened in behind-the-scenes skits. The fact that Benny was more associated with their parents' generation might suggest that Peter, Paul and Mary's appearance on this show would have spelled d-i-s-a-s-t-e-r. Instead, the resulting appearance is charming, even today. After Benny's opening monologue about his difficulties with topical humor, a clever bridge to help the audience understand the nature of topical songs, he announces the trio, who perform a spellbinding, beautifully paced rendition of "Blowin' in the Wind." It is staged in a simply lit, backstage set revealing the lighting rigs, ladders, wires, and equipment that are normally hidden from an audience's view. As the show continues, the group shines with their surprisingly effective comic timing. Noel "Paul" Stookey, of course, was a comedian himself, but all three rise to the occasion. With the nation still in a state of shock induced by the Kennedy assassination, the comedy segments—juxtaposed with the somber sincerity of the group's musical performance—must have been comforting. Folk music had proven it could command the attention of prime-time audiences and help in the healing process. Bookings for folk artists on television shows increased further. But no one could have predicted what was to shake things up just about three weeks later.

The British Invasion

That little skiffle group from Liverpool, England, the Quarrymen—the ones who had been inspired by Lonnie Donegan's cover of the Lead Belly song "Rock Island Line" and Elizabeth Cotten's "Freight Train" in 1956—had evolved into a tight rock and roll combo, especially after some extended engagements in the sleazy Reeperbahn district of Hamburg, Germany. There, in black leather outfits, they had been required to play for four or five hours a night to drunken shouts of "Mach schau!" ("Make show!"). Back home in Liverpool's thriving Merseybeat music scene, they began focusing on their own inventive songwriting. Now known as the Beatles, the group had a lunchtime residency at a local basement club, the Cavern. There they were approached in the venue's scant dressing room by twenty-seven-year-old entrepreneur Brian Epstein, then in charge of the record department in his parents' music store. Sensing the group's potential, he convinced them to let him be their manager, signing them to a contract in January 1962. Like a mega, real-life episode of *Queer Eye*, the somewhat discreetly gay Epstein polished up the band's rough image by dressing them in tailored, Pierre Cardin suits and Italian boots and giving them stage tips he had recently learned as a student of the Royal Academy of Dramatic Art. Trying to acquire the group a record deal, he was turned down by four major labels. Undeterred, he finally convinced the small Parlophone division of EMI Records to sign the band. They built a loyal local, then national, following. After a string of hit singles and a couple of LPs in England, Epstein was intent on breaking the group in America, a difficult endeavor as so few British musical acts had ever succeeded in the States. But he managed to land them a string of three consecutive Sundays on the weekly *Ed Sullivan Show*. The first of these occurred on February 9, 1964. An estimated seventy-three million viewers tuned in to see these four British guys playing electric guitars, a bass, and drums on the live broadcast from CBS-TV Studio 50, at 1697 Broadway in Midtown Manhattan. The audience's unified response from the second they were introduced, a continuous shriek of unbridled joy sounding more like the four engines of a Boeing 747 than anything human, was a primal scream, a nuclear release of pent-up teenage emotion and repressed sexual energy that tore through the night. It ripped through the television speakers into homes as families watched together and broke through the dark clouds of grief that had been hanging over the country. "I Want to Hold Your Hand" was just what we needed someone to say to us at that moment.

Overnight, there seemed to be Beatles records and merchandise everywhere—not only beach towels and magazines. Entire departments in stores were stocked with all manner of Beatles-branded products, especially wigs that mimicked the band's mop-top haircuts. My mother brought home for me a small, plush Beatle holding a yellow plastic acoustic guitar with rubber bands for strings and, later in the year, I myself would be transformed into a small, plush Beatle for Halloween. On April 4,

1964, the Beatles outdid everyone by occupying, for the first and only time, *all* of the top five positions on the *Billboard* 100, with a total of twelve records on the chart at the same time. The slew of British acts that followed the Beatles on the American charts—the Dave Clark Five, Gerry and the Pacemakers, and countless others—was quickly dubbed the British Invasion.

Even if some staunch folk purists were initially immune to the Beatles' charms, the musical and cultural shift the Fab Four heralded was unavoidable. For musicians, alarm bells rang out with the Beatles' chiming electric guitars. Dave Van Ronk and Terri Thal were tuned in to CBS that night at 190 Waverly Place. "Dave and I watched them on the *Ed Sullivan Show* just as millions of other Americans did. We thought they were wonderful. I still have four of their LPs that we bought back then," Thal told me. As John Sebastian explained it, for the younger musicians, like himself, the Beatles were a blast of new energy. "It affected *us* heavily. By *us*, I mean my specific generation. All of us were immediately struck by things like 'hey, that's like Travis picking that the guy was doing,'" Sebastian told me, referring to George Harrison's guitar playing. Sebastian watched on a black-and-white TV set in the Village with his friend Cass Elliot, of the folk trio the Big 3, and his new friend, Toronto-born guitarist Zal Yanovsky, who had been playing with the Halifax Three. Already ideas were forming.

1964 was a banner year for albums from Greenwich Village, beginning on January 13 with the release of Dylan's *The Times They Are a-Changin'*. Political and biting, often grim and pessimistic, the album's overall mood represents possibly the most obvious example of Dylan tapping into and expressing the zeitgeist of the moment. In the title song, he addresses the widening generation gap head-on by proclaiming to parents: "Your sons and your daughters are beyond your command." That song, and the moving "The Lonesome Death of Hattie Carroll," were again based on Irish-Scottish folk songs. "With God on Our Side" took the borrowing a step further, appropriating the theme and melodic phrasing, and parodying the first verses, of Irish songwriter/poet/playwright Dominic Behan's "The Patriot Game," a rebel song that Dylan had heard performed by the Clancy Brothers at the White Horse and was on the recent Kingston Trio album, released a month earlier. As with "Don't Think Twice, It's All Right," and "Who's Gonna Buy You Ribbons?," playing the two songs back-to-back is a bit of a shock. Unlike Paul Clayton, however, Dominic Behan was by no means in love with Dylan and called him out on the matter. According to Mike Evans in his book *Fighting Talk* (2014), legend has it that when Dylan suggested that "my lawyers can speak with your lawyers," Behan replied, "I've got two lawyers, and they're on the end of my wrists." At the Newport Folk Festival in 1963, Dylan performed "With God on Our Side," nervously announcing, "Yeah. You know, Jean Redpath sang a song here a while ago which I heard Liam Clancy sing about two years ago and, I was listening to her sing it and I thought that I never . . . I thought I wrote this song called 'With God on Your Side' [sic]. And it must have somewhere stayed in the back of my mind hearing Liam Clancy sing 'The Patriot Game.'" In spite of any confusion, "With God on Our Side" cannot be denied its own power, especially when performed live during that time. Such as the scorching rendition at the Town Hall concert on April 12, 1963, displaying Dylan's command as a live performer. He had taken an Irish rebel song and turned it into a universal statement. Balancing the topical songs with romantic ballads and more references to Suze Rotolo, the album also was his first to be produced entirely by Tom Wilson. This time out, Wilson devised a clever and subtle use of chamber echo, mixed just under Dylan's voice. The trick is that his voice is still extremely present and intimate with just a suggestion of the reverb underneath. Even though Wilson's background was recording larger, jazz ensembles, he always seemed to find ways to make the most of minimal instrumentation.

It's Her Way

Released in April 1964, Buffy Sainte-Marie's *It's My Way!* (Vanguard Records) was one of the most auspicious debuts of any artist on the folk scene of any year. She lays it on the line from the very first song, a metaphorical allegory in three-four time about cultural extinction, the systematic mistreatment of Native Americans, and the confiscation of Indian lands. "'Now that the Buffalo's Gone' addressed the breaking of America's oldest treaty in order to make a dam—and a fortune—that flooded the Seneca reservation in upper New York State and evicted the Senecas, right under the noses of the Eastern establishment, who were singing 'Goodnight, Irene' and 'Tom Dooley,'" Buffy told me.

"Since I didn't think I was going to last anyway, maybe never even get to make a record, I used every opportunity on stage to give audiences—mostly my youth peers—the content that only I could give them. I wanted them to know so they could maybe help fix it, and many of them did. I wanted to cover the bases that other writers were not. I wasn't trying to be original. It was just what was true in my own life that I thought others wouldn't hear anywhere else."

On the album, besides the writing, Sainte-Marie's was a beautiful and unique vocal sound, with its signature tremolo that was at times reminiscent of Edith Piaf and other times echoed her own Indigenous heritage, always with tremendous power. Hers was, in some ways, the antithesis of the polite vocal approaches of Cynthia Gooding or Joan Baez, styles that had been generally associated with female folk singers. Sainte-Marie, especially on songs like "Ananais" and "Cod'ine," breaks through gender-based expectations with a new kind of feminine aggression, similar to what Patti Smith will do for female rock singers in the following decade. Both "Universal Soldier" and "Cod'ine" were widely covered. "Cod'ine was about opiate addiction and overprescribing doctors, which would not become important to most people for another fifty years; but it was already true in my life, so I wrote it," Buffy told me. And, predating Lady Gaga's "Born This Way" by nearly five decades, the title song, "It's My Way!" was a virtual manifesto—not just for herself but for the burgeoning singer-songwriter movement:

> *I've got my own stakes, in my own game*
> *I've got my own name, and it's my way*

I spoke to Buffy Sainte-Marie in 2021, after a triumphant outdoor concert in Brooklyn's Prospect Park, and asked for her impressions on first arriving in Greenwich Village, circa 1962. "I found the music scene to be very tricky," she told me. "I was an amateur from seriously outside. Compare my background to those of Paul Simon, Bob Dylan, Judy Collins, Joan Baez, and other sixties singers. My family were not businesspeople, musicians, college teachers, or lawyers, and there was a lot I didn't know about show business. Folk music in the early sixties was a rather preppy, very vanilla glee club and barbershop quartet harmonies, white boys singing 'Negro spirituals.' And then there was Woody Guthrie and Pete Seeger and their families, fans, and friends, who were far more progressive, using songs as vehicles of information regarding unions, in championing equality, pointing out systemic injustices.

"And all of those people were as blatantly ignorant as their audiences about Indigenous *everything*. Pete Seeger's team couldn't understand my reluctance to stand on a stage holding hands with a bunch of white people singing, 'This land is your land, this land is my land.' Actually, it used to be my land. Years later, Pete finally got it and apologized, but I mention it because it explains—even among the 'good guys'—the state of consciousness about Indigenous people in the 1960s. Hell, American Indians only got freedom of religion in 1974! That was the atmosphere I walked into."

Sainte-Marie's passion and self-awareness were equally apparent in her musical accompaniment. Like Phil Ochs, her refreshingly original melodies also set her apart, especially when shadows of Native American musical references peek through. On "He Lived Alone in Town," Sainte-Marie is joined by friend Patrick Sky, the politically radical singer-songwriter and producer, himself of half-Native descent, whom she had met while on tour in Florida and brought back to the Village. Sky added a lovely fingerpicking guitar accompaniment. Peter LaFarge was another on the Village scene who sang of Native American themes on his Folkways albums. I asked Happy Traum about how these artists were accepted in the Village. "We were largely white kids on the scene," Traum told me. "It was important for us to have Native Americans as part of it." Describing the impact of hearing Sainte-Marie's unique music, Traum said, "Buffy Sainte-Marie was more musically sophisticated than the others. And very political, along with

Ochs and Paxton." When reviewing Buffy's debut album for *Broadside of Boston* on April 15, 1964, Ochs himself wrote, "It is one of the most striking and original albums to be released in a long time." And in *Broadside* #39, "She could be the most exciting new talent since Bob Dylan." But when I spoke with her, Buffy wasn't aware that Phil had lavished such praise on her work. "No, I didn't know that Phil was a fan. Thanks for telling me. It's really nice to hear that he liked my songs. I liked his, too, and he was the one who I thought was the best of us all. 'There But for Fortune' and 'I Ain't Marching Anymore' are both brilliant, and the latter is even funny, which is a triumph. Tom Paxton wrote some great songs, too, and he and Phil seemed to write topical songs about whatever was in the headlines, kind of a scattergun approach."

Both Ochs and Paxton would also have their debut albums released in 1964. Tom Paxton's debut for Elektra, *Ramblin' Boy*, was actually his second release—the first being a limited-distribution LP recorded live at the Gaslight for the short-lived Gaslight label. *Ramblin' Boy* found Paxton walking the fine line between traditional-style folksinger—with a vocal approach and formality that echoed Burl Ives and Pete Seeger—and the modern singer-songwriter, with songs like "Daily News" and his classic "The Last Thing on My Mind." In "Daily News," he treated the topic of manipulation in the media not with anger, but with humor:

> We've got to bomb Castro, bomb him flat
> He's too damn successful, and we can't risk that

One of Paxton's trademarks is the personal authenticity of his singing. He didn't attempt to sound older, world-weary, southern, or of another ethnicity. He sounded like a young white guy who loved folk music. This avoidance of affectation made his music all the more believable and has served him well over the past seven decades. The album, produced by Paul Rothchild, was recorded in an especially crisp style that gave his acoustic guitar an appealing fullness, even when playing simple or familiar chord patterns. And Paxton's guest musicians, the omnipresent Barry Kornfeld on banjo and guitar and Felix Pappalardi on guitarrón—the Mexican mariachi bass resembling a large guitar—were put to exceptionally good use. It sounds like friends playing music together; something that should but does not always happen in the recording studio. Kornfeld added melodic and expressive picking throughout, and Pappalardi's snappy attack on the guitarrón make it an appropriate counterpart to the acoustic guitars. In a few years, Pappalardi would emerge as one of the top producers of 1960s folk and rock. The album's truly lovely title song, on which Paxton sounds almost like a young Pete Seeger (and indeed Pete performed this song beautifully by himself and with the Weavers), is timeless, and the entire generous fifteen-song album was a remarkable introduction to one of the most enduring singer-songwriters of his generation.

Along with Paxton and Dave Van Ronk, Phil Ochs was now part of the overlapping inner circles of the MacDougal Street crowd. As Paxton describes it, "We had a rolling scene that was based either in the Gaslight, the room upstairs over the Gaslight that had a permanent penny-ante poker game going, or the Kettle of Fish bar next to the Gaslight at street level. We had a table in the front which was kinda permanently occupied by Bob Dylan. Phil Ochs and Dylan would be going back and forth. You know, Dylan was always giving Phil a terrible time."

Like Paxton, Ochs had also recorded an album prior to his Elektra debut, but his name appeared nowhere on it, and it was only discovered by Ochs fans in 2000. It was supposed to be a secret. Little did Ochs know in 1962 or 1963 that we would have something called the internet, with which you can find *any-thing*. With baby boomers being sent to summer camps in record numbers, the Cameo-Parkway label thought it might be good idea to release an album of campfire favorites. And did precisely that, calling it *Campfire Favorites*. Phil Ochs, new to the Village and needing money, was recruited to be the lead vocalist, surrounded by an unnamed female singer and a whole bunch of unnamed kids, all singing a whole bunch of innocuous, traditional campfire songs like "Polly Wolly Doodle." Oh, and "A Thousand Years Ago," with that line about Peter, Paul, and Moses. Throughout, Ochs's voice can be clearly heard above the others, often sounding slightly sardonic. For Ochs, his participation was contingent on his anonymity. In fact, there are no credits on the album for anyone except for banjoist Dick Weissman, of the Journeymen. But, as amusing as it is, that release doesn't count as his first album. Especially since he would have preferred for it to remain hidden.

Phil Ochs's *official* debut, released in 1964, was the aptly titled *All the News That's Fit to Sing*, a play on the famous *New York Times* motto, "All the News That's Fit to Print." I always found it interesting that, coincidentally, the name of the publisher who purchased the *Times* in 1896 and made it the successful paper of record was also Ochs: Adolph S. Ochs. But, alas, no relation. Inside a sleeve that showed the young Phil Ochs sitting on his guitar case reading a newspaper was a recording of songs written from those very articles. But there was more, and the album was to be one of the most fascinating debuts in a year that was filled with fascinating recordings.

Listening now, Ochs sounds like a man in a hurry. There's no time to lose as he rushes in to share the news with energized strumming—tempos as quick as a teletype machine of the Associated Press wire service transmitting a hot story. As breathless as a current-day cable news reporter, he shares breaking news from Vietnam and reports on American journalist and foreign correspondent William Worthy, who was denied reentry into the United States after visiting Cuba.

William Worthy isn't worthy to enter our door
Went down to Cuba, he's not American anymore

There's other news, but there is also a manic reading of the Edgar Allan Poe poem "The Bells," put to music; two talking blues; a stately tribute to Woody Guthrie, "Bound for Glory," that features John Sebastian on harmonica; and his own Guthrie-inspired anthem, the patriotic but aspirational "Power and the Glory":

Oh her power shall rest on the strength of her freedom
Her glory shall rest on us all, on us all

The song was covered widely, including by two of the Weavers, Theo Bikel, and the US Army Soldiers' Chorus. Throughout the album, the influence of Bob Gibson can be heard in the melodies and chords. "I was a real mentor to Phil Ochs, musically," said Gibson in his autobiography. What Gibson instilled in Ochs was the idea that the melody and musical foundation of the song needed to be as strong as the words, for the song to have any real impact. "Bob Gibson brought in the harmonies," Barry Kornfeld told me. This was sometimes missing from the early singer-songwriters, who were inclined to simply write new words over an old song or to use the simplest three major-chord progressions or to regurgitate tried-and-true blues progressions. Like Buffy Sainte-Marie, Ochs was, in a sense, working without a net. Gibson was to co-write two songs on Ochs's debut, including the album's anti-war opener, "One More Parade," and the powerful "Too Many Martyrs," their song about Medgar Evers. Carrying the Village endorsement of liner notes by *Broadside* founders Sis Cunningham and Gordon Friesen, second guitar accompaniment by Van Ronk associate Danny Kalb, and production by Jac Holzman and Paul Rothchild, this album arrived with the full folksinger's stamp of approval. But perhaps the most important hallmark of *All the News That's Fit to Sing* is its signature urgency. At times, Ochs seems so invested in the news he is delivering that he steps beyond his role as singing journalist and into the role of singing politician—the songs become like speeches on the stump. And though the album could be said to be flawed by his reckless performance style and heart-pounding tempos, and though it was not a commercial smash, with its release Phil was now poised to compete one-on-one with his best frenemy, Bob Dylan.

The Life I'm Living

On May 30, 1964, Carolyn Hester landed on the cover of the weekly newsmagazine the *Saturday Evening Post*, the illustrated, general-interest glossy that had been in publication since 1821 and was famous for its covers painted by Norman Rockwell—often depicting American archetypes. On this one, photographed by John Launois, Hester appeared as the archetypal folksinger, strumming her guitar in mid-song, under the heading "Folk-Music Fad." Everything in the 1960s, it seems, was considered to be a fad. The previous year had seen the release of Hester's second album for Columbia, *The Life I'm Living*. Its traditional songs showcased every bit of the exquisite, true beauty of Hester's voice. Her guitar accompaniment, augmented once again by Bruce Langhorne, was flawless, and the album was again produced by John Hammond, this time with musical direction by Milt Okun—hot off his successes with Peter, Paul and Mary and the Chad Mitchell Trio.

But since her first Columbia album, the times had a-changed, and some of it had been Hester's own doing. After all, it was she who had introduced John Hammond to scruffy Bobby Dylan, helping facilitate a chain reaction that had shifted the spotlight away from traditional folksingers. Regardless, staying with her original vision, Carolyn Hester was able to renew the traditional not by changing it but by instilling it with her own truth, soul, and experience. No matter that now all eyes seemed to be on the new breed, and especially on Hester's own ex–harmonica player.

And there was another ex in the picture too. Hester had divorced Richard Fariña in early 1963. And it had been a rough ride. By 1962, Fariña had found ways to insinuate himself into Carolyn's act. First, he appointed himself as her agent. Then he began joining her onstage—singing songs and playing the dulcimer she had given him as a wedding present and taught him to play. And that was only the beginning. "The thing about Richard is that he was not a folksinger. He wormed his way into it. It was just sad. I mean, in other words, he didn't come to the Village and do the hootenanny nights and all that and then have people say, 'Oh you're so good' and 'Let me book you somewhere,' you know what I mean? He didn't do that. He tried to zoom to the top. He would have me let him sing a few songs and stuff like that. It made me very uncomfortable, but, okay." And that was only part of the problem. Richard claimed, though it's difficult to substantiate, to have had worked with members of the Irish Republican Army and to have visited with Fidel Castro in the mountains of Cuba before and during the Revolution, events that required him to continually carry a firearm for protection. When traveling through Europe, Fariña convinced Carolyn to carry the concealed weapon through airport customs and security. "Richard was carrying a gun with him, but he was having *me* smuggle it. He strapped it to my back. I was just not able to take it anymore," Carolyn explained. "I knew early on that I was in trouble," the woman whom Dylan would describe in *Chronicles* as "double-barrel beautiful" said in 2005 to the *Washington Post*, "and, I cried every day."

The couple took a trip to London in the spring of 1962, Richard arriving first alone, with Carolyn fulfilling concert commitments in the States and then meeting up with her husband. Once there, they proceeded to perform at the handful of clubs that constituted London's folk circuit. But, with worsening tensions between them, Richard felt a break was needed and suggested a trip to France. It was there, at an intimate picnic on the French countryside outside of Paris, that Richard first met sixteen-year-old Mimi Baez, Joan's younger sister. Mimi was living in Paris, where her father's United Nations UNESCO job had relocated him. Also at the picnic were Mimi's mother, known as "Big Joan," and sister Joan Baez, who was visiting, along with Scottish folksinger Alex Campbell and John Cooke, of the Charles River Valley Boys bluegrass group, who happened to be performing in town. At the picnic, in an idyllic setting with the kind of scattered sunlight that so inspired the Impressionist painters, there was unmistakable flirting going on between Richard and Mimi. It did not go unnoticed by Carolyn.

"But I was sort of like, 'ho-hum.' It all just was so . . . *crass*. Because I knew Mimi and, I mean, who *wouldn't* love Mimi?" Carolyn told me. "I had already been trying to get a divorce from Richard for two years. And in the last year, I was waving legal papers. But one of the reasons I didn't leave him earlier was that he was dependent on me. It's complicated. He would not get a job. He just wanted to write his novel. I typed the first ninety pages of it, in England, just before I split." When the picnic ended, they all drove back to Paris. The next day Richard and Carolyn went out to dinner, and matters got worse. "We had a situation where we had an argument in the restaurant. And so, this time, I just got up and walked out. It was the only time I'd ever done anything like that, but I was worn out of it. I mean, I couldn't handle it anymore. So I just walked back to the hotel. He walked in a few minutes later, still being his negative self. And so I opened the drawer of the dresser, and I took out the pistol. I held it in my hand, I looked down at it, and then I held it toward him. And he said, 'Oh . . . Don't do that. This is a very old building, and there's a lot of people in it. You might miss me, and you might get somebody else.' That was good, that was very, very good he said that, because it brought me to my senses. But then I said to him, 'I'm holding this gun here, and I mean it. LEAVE ME ALONE NOW. We have one more show. You'll get some money for it, and then I'll be gone.' And he said, 'Okay.'"

After that show, Hester got on the next flight to Austin and, when she arrived, she was honored with a festive celebration, *Carolyn Hester Day*, on May 8, 1962, kicking off two days of concerts. Then in September, scheduled to appear at the Edinburgh Folk Festival in Scotland, Carolyn flew back to the UK, where she performed with Richard. Mimi was also at the Festival. Throughout, Fariña remained persistent. "I got fifty letters from Richard," Carolyn told me. "In one of the letters, he was begging me to come back to England because the McEwen Brothers (Scottish folksingers Rory and Alex McEwen), who were just so important in all of the things I did in England, had in mind to do a tour of Russia, and Richard wanted me to come back because he wanted to go on the tour. If I was going to be breaking up with Richard, he was not gonna be on that tour. I told him there was not going to be a tour of Russia, and there wasn't. That's when he goes down to France and gets with Mimi."

When Hester returned to Texas, she made a quick trip to Mexico and filed for divorce. Richard was still in France. "My lawyer sent him the divorce papers. By time he received them, he said, 'Oh, man. I've been a divorced man for two weeks, and I didn't even know it!'" Back in New York, she performed at Village Vanguard owner Max Gordon's posh uptown supper club, the Blue Angel, where the Weavers had played. "Boy, it's with a heavy heart when you're depressed over a nasty divorce. It's really hard to get up on that stage and do it. But that helped me get my mind out of it." During her residency, in the daytime, she began apartment hunting in the Village. An apartment in the commanding building at 225 West Twelfth Street was one of the first ones she looked at, and she took it. It was across the street, at the time, from the Greenwich Theater—a wonderful art-house cinema that had once staged folk concerts—and just around the corner from Susan Reed's antique shop. "All those years after learning about her in the seventh grade . . . it just blows my mind. And then I found out that Liam Clancy lived in the same building. All these ties and connections with the Village. It's so important." Carolyn was happy to be home.

To Carolyn Hester's everlasting credit, she is astonishingly philosophical about the whole thing with Richard Fariña. "That was my turn to live with the whirlwind," she told the *Washington Post*. "I wouldn't trade it." By April 1963, Richard, twenty-six, and Mimi, seventeen, were married. The Baez family embraced Fariña. "And they were happy to have him," Carolyn told me. "My mother asked, 'What's gonna happen with Richard? What's he going to do?' And I answered, 'Well, I think that's Joan's problem now.'"

Simon & Garfunkel

One of the more confounding debuts of 1964 was *Wednesday Morning, 3 A.M.*, with its front-cover promise of "Exciting New Sounds in the Folk Tradition," by Simon & Garfunkel. And that tagline was exactly what made it confounding. While new and, yes, at times exciting, it also had some elements that drew heavily from folk's recent past and contained only five original songs at a time when listeners were hungry for songwriters of their generation to talk to them directly. A new kind of communication was emerging between the audiences and artists that was unprecedented in popular music. Paul Simon's originals here were part of that conversation. But first, the duo needed to get people to listen.

Paul Simon and Art Garfunkel had grown up together in the predominantly Jewish neighborhood of Kew Gardens Hills, Queens, and had recorded their first single, "Hey School Girl," as Tom & Jerry, by the time they were juniors in high school. It was 1957. "We met when we were eleven years old, started to sing when we were thirteen, we started to argue when we were fourteen, made our first record at sixteen," said Simon, while introducing the song in concert in 2003. Tom & Jerry's single made the *Billboard* charts, hitting number forty-nine and selling one hundred thousand copies, a stunning achievement. But the duo's early success was fleeting and hard to replicate. They went back to high school, and then Simon went to Queens College and Garfunkel to Columbia University. But Simon stayed close to the music industry, learning the business and landing writing and singing gigs at the Brill Building and 1650 Broadway. As the attention of the music industry started shifting away from the Midtown song factories and looking toward MacDougal Street and West Fourth, Simon was on it. He reunited with his high school singing partner—both now living again in Kew Gardens, both having discovered Bob Dylan and the Greenwich Village scene, and according to Marc Eliot in his 2010 biography *Paul Simon: A Life*, both having had discovered *weed*. And the new duo, now calling themselves Kane & Garr, began performing in the Village. Dave Van Ronk, in his memoir, recalls "hearing them down at the Gaslight, and nobody would listen. I thought they were damn good, but people who wanted to hear Mississippi John Hurt and Dock Boggs wanted no part of Simon & Garfunkel."

Things began to look up for the duo at a Monday night hootenanny at Gerde's Folk City. That was in the fall of 1963. Their relatively clean-cut, collegiate appearance and wildly differing heights (Simon is five-two and Garfunkel five-ten) when standing together on the tiny Folk City stage might not have projected quite the ideal image, and their voices might have lacked the grittiness and intensity that was currently in vogue, but their harmonies must have rung true. Because in the audience that night was sitting Columbia Records and Dylan producer Tom Wilson, scouting for the label, and Wilson was impressed. Particularly when, during their three-song set, they sang "He Was My Brother," a powerfully moving song about the Freedom Rides. It was the very song that Wilson wanted for a British act he had signed, the Pilgrims, considered now to be the first Christian rock group. According to Simon biographer Eliot, Simon refused to sell the song and, in a bid to get the group a deal with Columbia, convinced Wilson to audition the duo instead. By March 10, 1964, they had signed the deal and started recording their first album.

"He Was My Brother," depicting a fictionalized tragedy of the civil rights struggle, was sadly prophetic. It would later be dedicated to Simon's friend and Queens College classmate, twenty-year-old Andrew Goodman, a white Jewish volunteer who was part of the Freedom Summer campaign in Mississippi. Goodman was killed along with two other young volunteers on June 21, 1964, a few months after the recording session on March 17. Goodman was attempting to help register African Americans to vote when he, James Chaney, and Michael Schwerner were abducted and murdered by the KKK, a killing that was aided by the local sheriff's office and police. The horrific story shook the country.

> *Freedom Rider, they cursed my brother to his face*
> *Go home outsider, this town's gonna be your buryin' place*

At Gerde's, they also sang "The Sounds of Silence," a Dylanesque song (yes, now there were Dylanesque songs) that was to become a kind of anti-anthem for alienated youth. In the album's sweet liner notes, framed as a letter to Simon, Art Garfunkel writes, "Its meaning is man's inability to communicate with man." When Van Ronk first heard the song, he was less than impressed, writing in his memoir that it "actually became a running joke: for a while there, it was only necessary to sing 'Hello darkness, my old friend,' and everybody would crack up." But this unfortunate assessment is unfair and may have been a reaction to the personal nature of the lyrics—a hallmark of the singer-songwriter movement itself. Of the new songs coming out of the scene, Van Ronk's wife, Terri Thal, said to me, "I didn't think many were that good." And she added, after a pause, "I didn't want to know the insides of their heads."

Opening side 1 of the record is Bob Gibson and Bob Camp's arrangement of the traditional gospel song "You Can Tell the World," on which Paul and Art's harmonies and acoustic guitar strumming recall their early heroes, the Everly Brothers. It sets the tone for an album that rings out under an unexpected halo of spirituality. At first it sounds like the Pilgrims had found their way into Simon's songbook after all. But it is a spirituality that is contrasted and opposed throughout by harsh realities and crass secularism—messages of prophets scrawled on subway walls and stabbing flashes of neon lights. Like Phil Ochs and other songwriters influenced by Bob Gibson, the melodies and chords are adventurous—the original songs here are not rewrites of old folk songs. Enhancing the spiritual themes, the music is often hymnlike and, without question, the purity of Art Garfunkel's voice is indeed very close to the sound of a Catholic choirboy—the antithesis of what most on the scene were going for.

Besides Simon originals "He Was My Brother" and "The Sounds of Silence," the album was rounded out by several religious, Christian-themed songs including one, "Benedictus," adapted from a

Renaissance-era Roman Catholic mass, delivered in its full solemnity, and another traditional African American Christian spiritual, "Go Tell It on the Mountain." It would not have been your first guess that these guys were two Jewish kids from Kew Gardens, Queens. In a chipper rendition, they covered "The Times They Are a-Changin'" and Ed McCurdy's folk standard "Last Night I Had the Strangest Dream"— all with references to prayer and biblical passages. The theme continues on two other Simon originals, "Sparrow" and the beautiful paean to the Village, "Bleecker Street." The latter, with its particularly ecclesiastical melody, contained an Old Testament reference invoking the biblical region of Canaan, a nod to Allen Ginsberg's *Howl*, and a comment on the current rent prices in the Village:

> *A poet reads his crooked rhyme, Holy, holy is his sacrament*
> *Thirty dollars pays your rent on Bleecker Street*

Not to nitpick, but I checked, and according to the average rents on Bleecker Street in 1964, you would have needed a roommate or two for your rent to be $30. Another anomaly of "Bleecker Street" is that its songwriting credit was "Jerry Landis"—actually Paul Simon—a holdover from their Tom & Jerry days; Landis was an ex-girlfriend's surname. Garfunkel had been "Tom Graph," a reference to his mathematics studies. Winding down, the album ends with the disconcerting title song, which climaxes with a robbery of "a hard liquor store." In the liner notes, Garfunkel avoids analyzing that one, instead simply offering that it "sets a mood, sketches some details and quietly concludes."

The location chosen for the album's cover was far uptown from Bleecker Street. Photographed by Henry Parker, it was actually the lower subway platform of the outbound E and F trains at Fifth Avenue and Fifty-Third Street—a stop that the boys would have known from their subway rides in and out of Manhattan from Queens. They look positively angelic on the underground platform in their clean suits as a train whooshes past. Contrastingly, as the story goes, many of the photos from this shoot had to be scrapped because of a certain four-letter-word scrawled on the wall behind them—echoing the lyric in "The Sounds of Silence" that proclaims, "the words of the prophets are written on the subway walls," and leading to Simon's future composition, "A Poem on the Underground Wall."

The additional musicians on *Wednesday Morning, 3 A.M.* were Barry Kornfeld on guitar and banjo and Bill Lee on bass, both bringing tremendous musicality to Simon's own guitar accompaniment. Barry Kornfeld, Bill Lee, Bruce Langhorne, Danny Kalb . . . these names and others that appear on so many albums from this era represent the New York folk music equivalent of LA's Wrecking Crew, the gang of studio musicians who played on countless, eternal, West Coast pop hits. Kornfeld, in particular, became close friends with Paul Simon—who began to hang out with the crowd at 190 Waverly Place. In fact, Simon and Kornfeld were to become partners in publishing Simon's songs, including "The Sounds of Silence"—Kornfeld probably having learned a thing or two about copyrights from his close friend Paul Clayton. Kornfeld, a consummate musician, considered Simon's songwriting to be "even better than Dylan's." "That's how I saw it," he told me.

One issue that came up during the sessions was the little matter of the name of the act; Garfunkel's name in particular. To some at Columbia, it sounded too "ethnic"—meaning: too *Jewish*. "Even Dylan changed his name," they reminded the duo. While Marc Eliot in *Paul Simon: A Life* claims that Simon insisted that they use their real names, Barry Kornfeld remembers it differently. "Paul wanted Artie to use a pseudonym," Kornfeld told me. "And Artie thought that would be a sellout." Both Kornfeld and biographer Eliot agree that it was Tom Wilson who stepped in, defending Garfunkel's wishes to use his own name and not another phony stage name. At a meeting with Columbia executives, Wilson declared, "It's 1964!" meaning, correctly or not, that in the modern world artists needn't conceal their ethnic identities. The company agreed. No more Tom & Jerry. No more Kane & Garr. That was that. It was going to be Simon & Garfunkel.

And, unfortunately, it was going to be a depressing flop. When released, the album sold only about three thousand copies, even less than Dylan's debut, which was considered a disaster. So Garfunkel went from Columbia Records back to Columbia University, and Simon went to London to pursue a solo career.

The Song Poet

In 1963, nineteen-year-old Eric Andersen had left college and hitchhiked to San Francisco with his notebook and guitar, in search of the Beat poets he idolized. There, he first heard Allen Ginsberg, Lawrence Ferlinghetti, Neal Cassady, and Michael McClure. "They taught me new ways to see, and a new way to live. Their words have freed and inspired my own writing with as much intensity as any reality that surrounds me," Andersen said in Paul LaMont's riveting 2021 documentary, *The Songpoet*. I asked Eric what that intensity meant. "It meant jumping out of the windows of books into life itself and becoming a free spirit learning to become a writer using real vernacular American speech patterns, and sleeping with people without having to get married," Andersen told me. "Of course, Kerouac was the main line. And Ginsberg. Corso, and especially Burroughs came later. I had come from a world of Rimbaud, Baudelaire, and Russian writers, in particular." Of all the songwriters in Greenwich Village inspired by the Beats, by imagist poetry and visionary literature, Eric Andersen was arguably the most adept at translating those influences into song form—with a beauty and a subtle, internal fire that was uniquely his own. With his movie-star good looks and stylishly long hair, Andersen stood out visually among folksingers as well. And he did so without the usual affectations associated with trying to stand out.

In Berkeley, Andersen met folksinger Debbie Green, who had previously inspired and taught guitar to young Joan Baez back in Cambridge, where Green had also been one of the first folk performers at Club 47. She would play guitar with Andersen, sharing folk fingerpicking styles and, before long, the two fell in love. Green had moved to Berkeley in 1960 and owned a coffeehouse there, where Andersen performed. He and Debbie met Ginsberg and Ferlinghetti at the City Lights bookstore in San Francisco and, on November 22, 1963, the evening of the Kennedy assassination, Andersen heard them recite poetry for the first time in Haight-Ashbury. Later that night, he met Cassady and McClure at Ferlinghetti's house. Around the same time, Tom Paxton was performing in Los Angeles and, by an invitation from Debbie Green, had traveled up to Berkeley and stopped in to play at Green's coffeehouse. "My future wife Debbie Green brought Paxton over the bridge from Berkeley to North Beach to hear me play at the Coffee Gallery," Anderson recalled. There, Paxton met Andersen for the first time, and the two became fast friends. "If you ever get back to New York, look us up," Paxton told him as he was leaving. By early 1964, Eric was on a Greyhound bus traveling cross-country to New York City and ringing Paxton's doorbell at 49 Morton Street in the West Village.

The tempo of Eric Andersen's progress in New York was at first as rapid as Dylan's. "He slept on our sofa for a couple of nights," Paxton recalled in *The Songpoet*. "He was, immediately, one of the gang." As was Dylan's three years earlier, Andersen's debut at Gerde's Folk City was also a slot opening for John Lee Hooker. Under a headline that read, "This Long-Haired Singer Is No Beatle" Robert Shelton reviewed him favorably in the *New York Times*. Shelton called Eric an "antidote to the Beatles: a sensitive, very musical 20 year old with long hair and a lean and esthetic face who is quietly making his New York nightclub debut," going on to say Eric possessed "that magical element called star quality." Robert Shelton went one step further and introduced Andersen to Maynard Solomon, who signed Eric to Vanguard Records. This was only February 12, 1964. Andersen had only been in the Village a few weeks. Oh, and he already had a publishing deal too. If luck is needed in show business (it is), luck was on Eric's side. "People were very welcoming and friendly to Debbie and me. I was treated very well and regarded as an important songwriter right off the bat and brought into that circle. But remember, I was lucky. I was introduced to people by Phil Ochs, Robert Shelton of the *New York Times*, and Tom Paxton. So through them, I met the likes of people like Pete Seeger, Sis Cunningham and Gordon Friesen of *Broadside* magazine, Dave Van Ronk, Patrick Sky, Fred Neil, Tim Hardin, Buffy Sainte-Marie, Richie Havens, and Bob

Dylan, who had met Woody Guthrie. Later I met Son House, Mississippi John Hurt, Lightnin' Hopkins, and the blues greats playing the Gaslight," Andersen told me.

"I didn't have a TV, so I would go over to Phil and Alice Ochs's place to watch the news once in a while and check up on the Vietnam War and events in the civil rights movement," Eric continued. "Phil and I would often walk the streets to take subways, and we'd sing songs to each other traipsing along on the sidewalks. I sang him 'Thirsty Boots' and 'Violets of Dawn,' a cappella. He was actually the first person to hear them as works in progress. He told me 'Violets' was 'too short.' So I slept in the Hotel Earle one night and dreamed up the fifth verse."

When I asked Eric about the jazz he listened to in the Village, he told me, "I knew the club owners, so when I wasn't listening to blues artists at their weeklong engagements at the Gaslight and Gerde's, I haunted the Village Gate and Village Vanguard to hear Mingus, Jimmy Smith, Miles, Bill Evans, and countless others. This was my graduate school. Though I didn't write or record blues or jazz myself, it taught me how to hear, appreciate space and time in music, and how to become a better singer and get people to listen. I learned guitar on rockabilly records and preferred this kind of music to folk music. But folk music taught me the beauty of narratives, words, and story-telling."

It was an education that provided another part of the equation he was attempting to solve, to achieve his obsession of expressing poetry and literature through his songs. Hootenannies with Phil Ochs, Paxton, Peter LaFarge, and Pete Seeger followed—suddenly he was everywhere. Eric found special support from *Broadside*. He would stay at Cunningham and Friesen's apartment, and they would publish his songs in the magazine. Ochs would write in *Broadside* #39 that Andersen "is especially adept at poetic love songs, and his singing can best be described as the logical musical extension of Elvis Presley." That summer, Andersen, Paxton, and Ochs would travel to the Newport Folk Festival of 1964, where Ochs invited Andersen onstage. Together, they performed a rousing version of the Beatles' "I Should Have Known Better." The folk audience was thrown for a moment, but the performance was infectious and filled with good humor. The crowd loved it. With Eric standing with him, Phil praised the Beatles, telling the audience, "Musically, I think the Beatles are the most exciting thing, really, going on." Maybe Eric Andersen was a bit of a Beatle after all. Robert Shelton failed to mention the duet in his daily reports from the Festival in the *Times*.

The Blue Ford Station Wagon
On February 2, 1964, Dylan had embarked on a twenty-day, cross-country drive in a blue Ford station wagon with Paul Clayton, *New York Daily Mirror* writer Pete Karmon, and friend, driver, confidante Victor

Maymudes. It was a decampment away from the Village to experience the real America and possibly inspire songs for his follow-up to *The Times They Are a-Changin'*. They stopped at random bars along the way, talked with locals, visited poet Carl Sandburg, gave some concerts, and went to New Orleans for Mardi Gras. It was in the station wagon that Dylan first heard "I Want to Hold Your Hand" blasting on the radio and was blown away.

The resulting songs were a marked change—moving away from the political, topical songs and toward something introspective. But at times, compared to some of his past writing, the shift was from virtuous to vitriol. Listening now, I'm reminded of Terri Thal's comment about not wanting to know "the insides of their heads," because that's exactly what the aptly titled *Another Side of Bob Dylan* revealed. The songs are about breaking bonds—with protest music, with traditional folk, with idealized romance—and expressed at a new level of poetic freedom inspired by French symbolist poet Arthur Rimbaud, the Beats, and everything else he had absorbed. The wordplay throughout, at times enunciated like a recitation, was captivating. Again produced by Tom Wilson and recorded in just a single session on June 9, 1964, the album included soon-to-be classics "Chimes of Freedom," "My Back Pages," "It Ain't Me Babe," "All I Really Want to Do," and a song parodying the 1960 Alfred Hitchcock film *Psycho,* "Motorpsycho Nitemare." But the real nightmare played out in the eight minutes and seventeen seconds of "Ballad in Plain D," a brutal reality show depicting, in alarming detail, the breakup of Bob Dylan and Suze Rotolo, told in thirteen agonizing verses. Here Dylan blames older sister Carla, of whom he writes, "For her parasite sister, I had no respect."

> *Beneath a bare light bulb the plaster did pound*
> *Her sister and I in a screaming battleground*

As she wrote in her memoir, no longer able to cope with the "pressure, gossip, truth, and lies that living with Bob entailed," Suze had moved out of the West Fourth Street apartment she shared with Dylan in August 1963 and moved into an apartment with Carla. It was a floor-through railroad-style apartment on Avenue B at the corner of East Seventh Street, across from Tompkins Square Park. Soon, according to her memoir, Suze discovered she was pregnant. The decision to have an abortion was an agonizing one. And, as it was illegal and often administered by questionable practitioners, a potentially dangerous one. The procedure left Suze depressed and withdrawn. "The way I saw it, Bobby and Carla had some kind of rivalry for controlling interest in me," the nineteen-year-old Rotolo wrote about the tensions between her boyfriend and her family. I spoke to their close friend Barry Kornfeld. "It was an uncomfortable scene," Kornfeld told me. "Carla was very protective of Suze. One night, late, Carla called Paul Clayton and me. We raced over to their apartment on Avenue B and found them in desperate straits. They were screaming. Carla had kicked Dylan out. Paul grabbed Suze, and I grabbed Carla. We tried to calm them down."

To make matters worse, now Carla had fallen in love with Paul Clayton, who was gay and in love with Dylan. Dylan still loved Suze, and Suze was having difficulty breaking ties completely with Dylan. "Carla wanted to *marry* Paul," Terri Thal told me, "and was telling people that they were engaged." It was a bizarre love rectangle. When you include Joan Baez in the mix, it gets even more complicated. Barry Kornfeld summed it up: "It was such a small scene," he sighed.

At the Newport Folk Festival that year in July, Dylan was introduced onstage by Ronnie Gilbert of the Weavers. The words she said that day would rattle him for decades. After a long lead-up describing Dylan as a hero who "grew out of a need," she wraps it up with "I don't have to tell you . . . you know him . . . he's yours, *Bob Dylan*." It may have seemed innocent enough at the time, but those words were to put a wedge between Bob Dylan and the folk community. You can read it on his face in the Newport film footage. Forty years later, in *Chronicles, Vol. One*, he was still angry and wrote, "What a crazy thing to say! Screw that. As far as I knew, I didn't belong to anybody, then or now." Besides the audiences, the folk movement's inner circles had expectations of Dylan also, Joan Baez included. "I wanted him to be a political spokesperson. I wanted him to be, you know, out in public, and to be on our team," she said in the 2009 documentary *Joan Baez . . . How Sweet the Sound* for the BBC arts series *Imagine*, adding, "That was *my* hang-up." For many, Dylan was seen as a kind of leader, a savior, a role he can't be blamed for rejecting. Everyone knows what happens to messiahs.

The month after Newport, on August 28, Dylan was introduced to the Beatles by their mutual friend, rock journalist Al Aronowitz, at the Hotel Delmonico at 502 Park Avenue and Fifty-Ninth Street. Outside the hotel, scores of teenagers had gathered, screaming for the Beatles and waving hand-painted banners. In the next room, there was a separate reception for guests where Peter, Paul and Mary, the Kingston Trio, and other celebrities were waiting to meet the group. After having picked up the *Freewheelin'* album on tour, all four Beatles, especially John Lennon, were keen on meeting Dylan, so he was quickly whisked into the inner sanctum by the group's road manager, Neil Aspinall. It was at that meeting that Dylan turned the group on to marijuana, Aronowitz claiming in his journals that it was from his stash. Actually, the Beatles later admitted that they had previously tried it in Hamburg but to little effect. This time, Aronowitz apparently provided a stronger, more potent strain. According to Beatles' associate Peter Brown in his 1983 book *The Love You Make*, the Beatles were apprehensive. Brian Epstein, not knowing they had, told Dylan that the band hadn't smoked before. Dylan seemed dumbfounded. Looking back to the Beatles, he asked, "But what about your song? The one about getting high?" They all looked at each other, confused. What was he talking about? Then, Dylan proceeded to reference the bridge of "I Want to Hold Your Hand." "You know," he said and then sang, "'And when I touch you . . . I get high . . . I get high.'" The words hung in the air for a moment. Finally, an embarrassed Lennon corrected Dylan. "Those aren't the words. The words are, 'I can't hide, I can't hide.'" Regardless, after precautions were taken to conceal the smoke, a splendid time was had by all. When recalling the evening on Conan O'Brien's *Late Night* TV show in 2012, Ringo Starr summed it up: "We got high and laughed our asses off." For the Beatles, as Brown wrote, "the evening was the start of a long, albeit intermittent, friendship with Dylan." Oh, by the way, and also with pot.

In spite of—or as a result of—the British Invasion, the momentum in the Village only picked up. I found an article in the April 25, 1964, issue of *Billboard* in which poet-songwriter Rod McKuen credits the Beatles with saving folk music by weeding out phonies. "McKuen feels that the johnny-come-latelies are now out of the folk picture and that it will remain a dominant force by those who believe and know what they are doing," the article reports. But the Beatles' success also changed the dynamic in other ways. In *The Songpoet*, John Sebastian remarked, "The British Invasion made us all learn that there was a lot of money to be made." As another autumn befell MacDougal Street, the influx of starry-eyed new arrivals and new bands being formed showed no sign of slowing down.

Chapter Nine

The Lovin' Spoonful, photographed on the streets of the Village in 1966.

*The world was way more strange than I had realized,
and way more vast than I had ever dreamed.*
—Peter Stampfel, The Holy Modal Rounders

Charlie Washburn's Third Side, the basket house

across the street from the Café Bizarre on West Third Street between MacDougal and Sullivan, was one of the most eclectic of the eclectic venues in the Village. John Sebastian, Maria D'Amato, José Feliciano, Richie Havens, fiddler/banjoist Peter Stampfel, and Tiny Tim, along with Phil Ochs, were all regular performers at the ground-floor venue, a storefront where the musicians were situated to be visible through its large plate glass window. As John Sebastian described it for me, "You would perform three feet from the street." For all these musicians, the basket houses were an essential training ground. "You gotta have a place to be bad," Sebastian told me. Pedestrians walking by the Third Side toward MacDougal Street would peer in through the window to see who was playing. One can only imagine the reaction they might have had in viewing Tiny Tim through that window.

The Improbable Saga of Tiny Tim

Seeing Tiny Tim for the first time, at six foot one with his shoulder-length black hair, a nose that *The Guardian* described to be "as big and majestic as the beak of a bald eagle," white face makeup, shopping bag overflowing with old-time sheet music next to him, singing at times in a high, almost ultrasonic falsetto, wearing an ill-fitting suit and playing his dwarfish ukulele, your instinct might have been to either rush inside to see if he was for real or to run for your life. Born Herbert Khuary, from uptown in Washington Heights, Tiny had gone through several name changes before settling, rather randomly, on Tiny Tim—a shortened version of his most recent moniker Sir Timothy Tims. Before that he had been Larry Love, Darry Dover, and had numerous other handles. Through it all, his persona was consistent: obsessively polite and mannered, with an encyclopedic knowledge of recordings of the acoustical era through the 1930s, and a flaming, campy effeminacy. Before landing in the Village coffeehouse circuit, Tiny had performed regularly at Hubert's Museum and Live Flea Circus, a Coney Island–style freak show in Times Square, where he was billed as the "Human Canary." Bob Dylan and Tiny's other future friend Lenny Bruce were among those known to frequent the sleazy Forty-Second Street sideshows at Hubert's. From there, Tiny found his way down to West Third Street, where he was booked at the Café Bizarre, then across the street at the Third Side, then down the block on MacDougal at the Café Wha?— the place where he had scrounged his next meal with Dylan in the kitchen during Fred Neil's afternoon sets. At the Café Wha?

Tiny was fired as the result of a particularly spirit-filled performance of Eden Ahbez's "Nature Boy" during which he proceeded to remove all of his clothing while rolling around on the floor. That was followed by a stint with the Living Theater on Fourteenth Street, where he met avant-garde filmmaker Jonas Mekas, was favorably reviewed by Robert Shelton in the *New York Times*, and was featured in a major piece in the *Village Voice*. Then it was back to MacDougal and the corner of Minetta Street, at the Fat Black Pussycat, before finding a home at the Page Three, a gay bar on Seventh Avenue and West Tenth Street.

It was a decade and a half later, when I was a teenager growing up in Tampa, Florida, that I met and spent time with Tiny Tim. Tiny reveled in telling my friends and me stories, recounting the glory days of Greenwich Village in the 1960s. "Mr. Dylan and Mr. Sebastian . . . they walk the streets!" he proclaimed incredulously, as if speaking about the gods of Mount Olympus. "Oh, Mr. Barone, you should be there." I was wide-eyed, hanging on every word of his "tales of truth" as he called them. The tales of truth were chapters of his own fantastic journey, for which he had kept meticulous diaries.

Tiny was the most complex person I have ever met. His attraction to women was all-consuming, and yet his image was about as flamboyantly campy as you can get. And for all his outrageousness, he could be intensely shy. To add another layer of complexity, Tiny was, incongruously, innately conservative, perhaps a reaction to his leftist parents—a Yiddish-speaking Orthodox Jewish mother and Lebanese Catholic father—who believed in "free love" and didn't believe in marriage. "His entire existence was a reaction to his parents," biographer Justin Martell, author of *Eternal Troubadour: The Improbable Life of Tiny Tim*, proffered to me in a late-night phone call. "He invented a self-styled Christianity with its own, strict moral code. His conservatism was his own form of rebellion."

By the time I met him, where he was performing at the pitiful roadside bar of a third-rate TraveLodge motel, Tiny had performed at major concert venues all over the world, from Royal Albert Hall in London to headlining at Caesar's Palace in Las Vegas. But of all the places he had played, he particularly loved talking about his days in the Village, especially at the Page Three. The venue's mixed but predominantly gay clientele was immediately receptive to Tiny's antics, such as his falsetto rendition of "I Enjoy Being a Girl" by Rodgers and Hammerstein, or the male-female duets with himself. Tiny told me of poet Hugh Romney, later known as Wavy Gravy, who saw him perform at the Page Three, invited Tiny to join him in his sets at the Gaslight, and became just one of the long list of luminaries and showbiz celebrities Tiny met there. But, to Tiny, the real thrill of performing at the Page Three was that he was surrounded by beautiful lesbian women. "The girls liked each other," he said to me and my two female friends from high school, while sitting on the bed in his TraveLodge motel room. "Some of them were my dearest friends. In fact, I loved all of them, they were so wonderful, because they lived in a wonderful, strange world. They were magnificent . . . *magnificent* beauties," Tiny recounted, lowering his voice as if sharing a secret knowledge, "and they have a very fantastic power. I was so thrilled to be in their company. I was one of the few men (giggles) that they allowed to their parties. I was so happy being with them, just talking with them, and praising the good Lord for their *beauty!*" Tiny would write songs and give trophies ("they were gold-plated, with a female symbol of victory") to his favorites, like the tough eighteen-year-old Miss Snooky (yes, everyone was Mr. or Miss) who was "the queen of them all," Greta Garbo–like but with a missing front tooth—the gap of which served as a convenient cigarette holder. Tiny explained to us that to be eligible for a trophy, the requirement was not necessarily the standard conception of physical beauty. "Some glamorous girls never got the trophy because they didn't have . . . my ideal of dreaming."

Interestingly, the songs Tiny Tim performed in his sets in the Village were from the same general period that was popular with the MacDougal crowd—the era of the early Lomax recordings and the Harry Smith *Anthology*. But Tiny's choices came more from the British musical halls, Tin Pan Alley, vaudeville, or the Yiddish theater. He'd mix it all up in a dizzying musical cocktail that included Southern blues or "race" records of the twenties to forties, novelty tunes, and some current hits—all sung in a stylized falsetto or deeper crooner voice with a signature vibrato, while accompanying himself on his trademark ukulele. For all his eccentricities, Tiny Tim was building an influential fan base that now included Hugh Romney, Jonas Mekas, Milton Glaser—the founder of Push Pin Studios and designer of Peter, Paul and Mary's album covers—and record producer Richard Perry. Making the transition from sideshow freak to the darling of New York's art scene intelligentsia, Tiny beat the odds. At the Page Three, as Beatlemania raged in the spring of 1964, Tiny was billed as "Our Answer to the Beatles" and performed falsetto versions of their songs. But for all its charms, the Page Three was not immune to the NYPD vice squad, who especially targeted gay establishments. "Working in that place was a magnificent thrill!" Tiny told us. Then, his voice deflated: "Until, you know, the police closed it down." In those pre-Stonewall days, gay and lesbian bars were routinely raided for any number of reasons. In Page Three's case, it was an undercover sting operation in July 1965, and the charge was prostitution. The venue lost its liquor license and was unable to sustain itself as a coffeehouse.

In April of '64, Tiny Tim opened two shows for the controversial and embattled social critic and satirist Lenny Bruce at the newly opened Café Au Go Go, in the basement of the Garrick Theater at 152 Bleecker Street. Bruce had built a loyal following but was plagued by repeated arrests on obscenity and drug-related charges. The two shows were billed as LENNY BRUCE SPEAKS FOR PROFIT—TINY TIM SINGS FOR LOVE. "I met Mr. Bruce back in '64," Tiny told me. "I was so happily thrilled to be with that wonderful man." At both performances, Bruce was arrested on obscenity charges. He had been arrested on similar charges several times before, including at the Gate of Horn in Chicago. This arrest led to a grueling, six-month trial in New York that was a landmark case for freedom of speech in America and is chronicled in the 1974 film *Lenny*, directed by Bob Fosse and starring Dustin Hoffman as Bruce. During the crushing trial and its aftermath—he was blacklisted from nearly every nightclub in the country, and his life spiraled into drug addiction—Bruce listened repeatedly to the tapes Tiny Tim had given him, particularly to the love songs Tiny wrote and recorded for the young girls he had met at the Page Three. "And Lenny Bruce still has those tapes," Tiny told me. Only symbolically, however. Bruce had passed away a decade prior.

Holy Modal Rounders

I wish I could ask Tiny Tim today what he thought of the Holy Modal Rounders. Peter Stampfel had been performing at the Third Side on a bill with Tiny when, through a mutual friend, he met guitarist Steve Weber. Before long, the two formed a duo that was one of the most irreverent and yet one of the most authentic acts on the scene. What set the Holy Modal Rounders apart from others mining the songs and artists from Harry Smith's *Anthology of American Folk Music* was the duo's impeccably genuine looseness and sly humor—elements that had been a major part of the appeal of those 1920s and '30s recordings in the first place but had often been lost through the ensuing decades as folklorists dissected and, in some cases, mummified the songs, turning them into holy relics. Like Dave Van Ronk, the Rounders raised these songs from the dead. But going further, they took liberties with the lyrics, emphasizing the humor with comic timing and Stampfel's impossibly idiosyncratic singing, and made the songs new again. "They took folk music and stood it on its head," said Terri Thal, who managed the group and still speaks of them with affection. For one thing, they restored the sex, drug, and alcohol references of the 1920s and '30s that were in the original songs but had been whitewashed or downplayed in the 1950s. And they added contemporary references and slang, the way the original artists would have done in *their* time. But it was obvious to all who saw and heard the Holy Modal Rounders that there was more than just the Harry Smith *Anthology* being absorbed by these boys. "They were stoned out of their birds all the time. Everybody knew it. They made no bones about it," said Dave Van Ronk in the 2006 documentary *The Holy Modal Rounders . . . Bound to Lose*. "Yes, they took *everything*," Thal concurs. The Rounders' version of "Hesitation Blues," a jug band and bluegrass standard that can be traced back to 1916, was based on a 1930 recording by Charlie Poole and the North Carolina Ramblers titled "If the River Was Whiskey." They rewrote most of the lyrics with their own hilarious rhymes and famously included in the lyrics the very first use of the word "psychedelic," albeit with a different spelling, in a pop song. The Rounders' joyful experimentation with the surreal made them one of the earliest examples of psychedelic folk.

> *Got my psychodelic feet in my psychodelic shoes*
> *I believe, lordy mama, I got the psychodelic blues*

The duo's eponymous debut album was released on Prestige Records in 1964. "We started recording the day before the Kennedy was shot," Peter Stampfel told me. Listening now, the album still sounds remarkably fresh. In fact, as I write for you, I've had *The Holy Modal Rounders* on repeat-play for three days. I never tire of their giddy interpretations of these songs. The effect of the melancholy blue notes in Stampfel's fiddle playing juxtaposed with their absurd lyrics is positively magnetic. And the unconstrained performances. "How do we end?" Stampfel asks. "Like this," answers Weber, ending their song "Mr. Spaceman." One of the reasons they have held up so well may have to do with the Rounders' studio ethos, as Stampfel explained it to me: "First drafts were good. Rewrites were bad. Overdubs were bad." The result was the same kind of spontaneity that was the hallmark of the original, early recordings, made with minimal technology and very little fuss but with a lot of attitude and vibe.

As you can imagine, the Village crowd loved these guys. Suze Rotolo wrote that Peter Stampfel "sang mostly off-key in a strong nasal tenor voice. I don't know why, but it worked. I thought Peter was terrific," and that "the two of them were a sight to behold. Peter was tall and skinny, but Weber was even taller and skinnier and could carry a tune. It was mutating music—spoken word madness." Speaking in the *Rounders* documentary, Peter Tork, later of the Monkees, said, "Stampfel and Weber were really a whole new level of authenticity . . . they were absolutely hilarious and so far-freakin'-out!" Discussing the folk performers who "knew the Harry Smith *Anthology* inside out," revered music critic Robert Christgau said, "Next to Bob Dylan, Peter Stampfel is the closest thing to a genius that the scene produced."

As for Stampfel himself, speaking to me now of the Harry Smith *Anthology*, he pleaded, "We must not let it die!" In 2021, he released his own mammoth hundred-song collection, *Peter Stampfel's 20th Century* (Louisiana Red Hot Records), for which he recorded a song for each year of the century. But in 1964, the question was, after the Holy Modal Rounders, where could folk music go?

Bringing It All Back Home

Released as 1965 began, the next Bob Dylan album, *Bringing It All Back Home*, was another step away from, well, everything. Like a new Buick, this year's model was built on a brand-new chassis. Divided into two acts, electric on side 1 and acoustic on side 2, he was bringing rock and roll back home to its country of origin after it had been so deftly borrowed by the Brits. But with it, he brought gorgeously surreal images from deep in Rimbaud territory, symbolist poetry swirling psychedelically and mixed up with rock and roll iconography. Folk music, particularly folk music of an overtly political nature, was growing smaller and further away in Mr. Dylan's rearview mirror, along with Suze Rotolo. Old ways rapidly fading. Once so fresh and barely a year old, "The Times They Are a-Changin'" was beginning to sound as old-fashioned as its melody's ancient Irish origins. The protesting now was something personal and open to endless interpretations and speculation. Was "Maggie's Farm" his declaration of independence from the folk scene itself? "I always tried my best/to be just like I am/But everybody wants you/to be just like them/they say 'Sing while you slave' and I just get bored/I ain't gonna work on Maggie's farm no more," he wrote. The talking blues of yore had evolved into upbeat rock and roll repartee. In "Subterranean Homesick Blues," singing to his own generation, he managed to jam their entire lives from birth to young adulthood into thirteen seconds, while earning himself his first top-forty hit in the process:

Twenty years of schoolin'
And they put you on the day shift

"Mr. Tambourine Man" was inspired by guitarist Bruce Langhorne, who, on sessions, sometimes played an oversized Turkish tambourine-like drum with bells. Langhorne added exquisitely picked, almost piano-like single notes on electric guitar to this track. That song plus "Gates of Eden," "It's Alright Ma (I'm Only Bleeding)," and "It's All Over Now, Baby Blue"—all on the acoustic side of the album—served up a smorgasbord for recording artists shopping for new Dylan songs to cover. And they did. "Everybody was scrambling to cover a Dylan song," author Mitchell Cohen told me. Besides being a writer and cognoscente of pop culture, Cohen has been vice president of A&R at Arista, Columbia, and Verve Records.

The album cover of *Bringing It All Back Home* was also revolutionary. The first front cover on Columbia that did not list song titles, the design centered on a carefully staged image shot using an in-camera effect devised by the photographer, Daniel Kramer. Framed in white, the photo depicted the newly minted rock star surrounded by a blurred collage of items—books, record albums, magazines, a fallout shelter sign—artfully strewn about the room at Albert Grossman's Woodstock home. Dylan is in the calm center, cat on his lap, seated on a velvet couch that had been given to Grossman by Mary Travers. Grossman's wife, Sally Grossman, in red, reclines behind Dylan, cigarette raised in the air like the Statue of Liberty's torch or a Virginia Slims ad. The two of them are like a mid-sixties *American Gothic*. Also behind Dylan—actually, metaphorically, and ironically—is a copy of last year's model: his own previous album,

Another Side of Bob Dylan. The back cover was comprised of his now-trademark abstract liner notes and images of Joan Baez, Allen Ginsberg, and eighteen-year-old avant-garde filmmaker and Warhol associate Barbara Rubin, with whom he was said to be having an affair. Front and back, the album is surrounded with intrigue. This would begin a trend in album covers over the next several years: images that would give hints or clues about the artists. It was raised to the level of high art on the 1967 cover of the Beatles *Sgt. Pepper's Lonely Hearts Club Band*. "If you wanted to be cool, you would check out everything he was referencing," Mitchell Cohen told me, regarding the *Bringing It All Back Home* cover. "Everything Dylan did was dissected microscopically." Breaking the top ten for the first time, reaching as high as number six on the *Billboard* album chart, Dylan was indeed bringing it all back home.

Malcolm X

The assassination of Malcolm X on February 21, 1965, was another reminder of the violence always lurking just beneath the surface of American culture. Shots rang out while Malcolm X was addressing an assembly of four hundred people at the Audubon Ballroom in Washington Heights, in a plot purportedly carried out by three members of the Nation of Islam—the organization for which Malcolm X had previously been the most visible spokesman and had left the previous year. But there were questions. When asked if he believed that the convicted gunmen were responsible for the assassination, filmmaker Spike Lee, speaking to Charlie Rose on PBS in 1992 while in postproduction of his film *Malcolm X*, said, "Yes, but I believe the FBI and New York City police and the CIA had their hands on it too." Rose asked, "They knew about it? Or had their hands on it?" "They had their hands on it," Lee replied. Later, it was confirmed that Malcolm X had in fact been under surveillance by J. Edgar Hoover's FBI since 1953. In a 1965 speech, Malcolm X said, "We declare our right on this earth . . . to be respected as a human being, to be given the rights of a human being in this society, on this earth, in this day, which we intend to bring into existence by any means necessary." Even though Malcolm X had been initially critical of the civil rights movement in America and was often at odds with its leadership's adherence to nonviolence and its inclusion of whites in the movement, his views evolved. And there was no more impassioned and articulate advocate for Black empowerment than Malcolm X. "Dr. King wants the same thing I want—freedom!" he was later to say. By the later 1960s and '70s, as more radical activists emerged and the Black Power movement adopted his teachings, Malcolm X's principles of Black pride would become more prevalent. *The Autobiography of Malcolm X* (1965), cowritten by Alex Haley, whose next project was *Roots* (1976), was based on over fifty interviews with Malcolm X conducted at Haley's writer's studio at 92 Grove Street in Greenwich Village. Published eight months after his assassination, it gave a more accurate portrayal of Malcolm X's life than the popular media had given him during his lifetime, provided the basis for Spike Lee's film, and was named one of the ten most influential nonfiction books of the twentieth century by *Time* magazine in 1998.

California Dreamin'

Cass Elliot, who had watched the Beatles' *Ed Sullivan Show* debut flanked on her Village couch by John Sebastian and Zal Yanovsky as they all had their collective minds blown, had first come to New York pursuing a career in musical theater. It didn't quite work out the way she had planned.

If ever there was a star waiting to happen, it was Cass Elliot. Everything about Cass was larger-than-life—her voice, her personality, her body—everything. After touring in a road production of *The Music Man*, and losing a part in the 1962 musical *I Can Get It for You Wholesale* to the more conventionally proportioned Barbra Streisand, Elliot had been singing in the Big 3—a folk trio with banjoist-singer Tim Rose, who had played with the Journeymen, and guitarist-singer Jim Hendricks. The Big 3 had their origins in Georgetown, DC, went on the road, inevitably made their way to the Village coffeehouse circuit, and finally found themselves a gig at the Bitter End on Bleecker Street, where Cass had recently been the coat check girl. Arriving in the lingering afterglow of Peter, Paul and Mary's debut, they performed folk songs, ballads, and originals delivered in punchy, full harmonies—somewhat gutsier and with more of a rock and roll attitude than the other folk trios on the scene. Tim Rose's growl and shout may have been uncommon in folk circles, but it was the sheer power of Cass Elliot's belting voice rising above the men that dominated the group's vocal imprint. "Her voice pushed with such positive energy," John Sebastian told me, comparing her sound to that of Ronnie Gilbert in the Weavers. Even without commercial hits, the Big 3 quickly landed on major television shows including the *Tonight Show with Johnny Carson* and, of course, *Hootenanny*, for a total of twenty-six TV appearances in their short existence. Their rewrite of Stephen Foster's "Oh, Susanna," completely restructured as a driving acoustic folk strumfest with a Peter Gunn–like bass riff and retitled "The Banjo Song," was itself reworked with new lyrics in 1969 by the Dutch rock group Shocking Blue and turned into the number one international hit "Venus." But all their exposure and two albums on the FM label notwithstanding, Tim Rose left the group in 1964 to go solo and later had hit singles with his covers of "Hey Joe," by Billy Roberts, and "Morning Dew," by Bonnie Dobson. For both songs, Rose claimed songwriting credits.

Elliot and Hendricks stayed together. The couple had gotten married in a platonic arrangement to protect Hendricks from being drafted into the military. Oh, yeah. That was a thing. To keep up with the ever-escalating conflict in Vietnam, conscription in the United States had become a threat hanging over the heads of all young males in the draftable age bracket of eighteen to twenty-six. Until midnight on August 27, 1965, married men were exempt. There was a mad dash: long lines of young couples at courthouses and marriage chapels to marry before the midnight deadline.

Nary missing a beat, Cass and Jim joined up with Canadian ex–Halifax Three member Denny Doherty, mutual friend and guitarist Zal Yanovsky, and, yes, John Sebastian, to form the Mugwumps. Even shorter-lived than the Big 3, the Mugwumps dabbled in proto folk-rock and pop with electric instruments and drums. The group would be remembered, though, not because of any particular song or recording but because four of the five members were to become major pop stars by the next year or so. In 1964, the Mugwumps' combination of folk, rock, and pop sounds were a hint of what was to come in 1965. But though the sound they created was prescient, the group fizzled out fast.

Meanwhile, the Journeymen, originally comprised of singer-guitarists John Phillips and Scott McKenzie, along with banjoist Dick Weissman, had found success in the Village following their 1961 debut and five-month residency at Gerde's. With McKenzie's sweet, unforced tenor, the trio's political humor, and Phillips's artful harmony arrangements, they had gone on to record three albums for Capitol. By 1964, however, amid a changing aesthetic and all the other factors that make groups splinter, McKenzie and Weissman departed. Phillips, who had recently married lovely eighteen-year-old West Coast scenester Michelle Gilliam, formed a new group that included her and Marshall Brickman, former banjoist of the Tarriers, calling the group the *New* Journeymen. But that lineup was to be as short-lived as the Mugwumps. Brickman departed to become a highly successful television writer and screenwriter, later known for being Woody Allen's Oscar-winning cowriter of *Annie Hall* (1977) and for the Broadway musical *Jersey Boys* (2005).

With the Mugwumps having split up, John Phillips asked Denny Doherty to join the New Journeymen, replacing Brickman. Although no albums were released by this configuration, a few live clips survive, along with a long-lost promotional film featuring the group that was unearthed in 2020. It was made for a Jewish charity, the Women's Labor Zionist Organization of America Inc., known in 1965 as Pioneer Women, a nonprofit that supported women and children in Israel. Written by Phillips, "Pioneer Women" was to be their last song in the traditional, acoustic folk style. Soon, Doherty would recommend to Phillips that his fellow former Mugwump and best friend Cass Elliot be asked to join the group.

After a trip to St. Thomas in the Virgin Islands to work out the music—and their internal love affairs—the group was reborn in California as the Mamas and the Papas. With them they had brought their seminal song "California Dreamin'," written by John and Michelle Phillips late one night in their room at the Hotel Earle on Washington Square Park.

"If I could tell you how many people have come up to me and said, 'Oh, you're responsible for me being in California, you know,'" John Phillips laughed to Scott McKenzie in a 1995 interview. "I mean, thousands and thousands and thousands, literally, probably three or four today, so far, as a matter of fact. So I should have some kind of recompense for this sort of thing. I'm really a guilty guy," he told McKenzie. He's right. The Mamas and the Papas' folk-rock success at the end of 1965 and early 1966 surely had widespread cultural impact. "California Dreamin'," with its complaints of the brown leaves and gray skies of winters in New York—and their song "Twelve Thirty (Young Girls Are Coming to the Canyon)" that referenced the long-stuck clock atop Jefferson Market Library's tower—were partially responsible for a migration that saw the Laurel Canyon neighborhood in the Hollywood Hills become a center for singer-songwriters. The community of musicians included Roger McGuinn and David Crosby, of the Byrds, and Barry McGuire, of the New Christy Minstrels, whom they had known from the Greenwich Village folk scene. It was a far more temperate, laid-back, and upscale version of Greenwich Village, with rustic homes and the smell of eucalyptus. A Disneyland replication that became real. Of course, without the climate extremes, cultural diversity, and historical layers of the New York City streets to inspire or aggravate, the musical output was bound to be as different as the two coastlines. Sheila Weller, in a 2007 *Vanity Fair* profile of Michelle Phillips wrote, "The Mamas and the Papas were the first rich hippies, stripping folk-rock of its last vestiges of Pete Seeger earnestness and making it ironic and sensual."

The Lovin' Spoonful

At the same time that the New Journeymen were sorting things out, John Sebastian and *his* fellow former Mugwump Zal Yanovsky were looking to form a new group. For this they would be helped by manager Bob Cavallo and producer Erik Jacobsen. A tall, lanky, blond Norwegian, Jacobsen is a fascinating fellow. He played banjo in the curiously named bluegrass trio Knob Lick Upper 10,000, a group he formed after graduating from Oberlin College in Ohio. The trio arrived in the Village in 1962 and, according to Jacobsen, were discovered and signed by Albert Grossman for management while jamming at Washington Square Park. Soon they were booked at the Bitter End and every coffeehouse in the Village before heading out on the folk tour circuit. They made two albums for Mercury Records. But by 1964, with the Beatles dominating the charts, they could not get on the radio. Jacobsen, dropping in some coins and listening to the Fab Four's singles on a jukebox while on tour, understood why. "I asked myself, why not combine a rhythm section like this with folk instrumentation?" he recounted in a biographical video on his website. "I decided then and there to put down the banjo, quit the group, and go back to New York City, try to write songs, and become a record producer." He wrote songs, tried every angle, and ensconced himself in the scene. Sebastian,

Yanovsky, Cass Elliot, Jesse Colin Young, Tim Hardin—practically all of the artists who represented the future core of folk rock in Greenwich Village were in Jacobsen's orbit. Though rarely credited as such he was the missing link.

While living on Prince Street in Little Italy, Jacobsen's next-door neighbor had been John Sebastian, whom he had started to work with on songwriting and production and, according to Jacobsen, "smoking reefer." Now Jacobsen moved to 97 MacDougal Street, the center of the action, and created a business partnership with Bob Cavallo to help Sebastian and Yanovsky form a band. They recruited Steve Boone (from a Long Island group, the Sellouts) on bass and, first Jan Carl but then finally Joe Butler on drums and vocals. With all their collective musical experience, there was a sound there somewhere just waiting to be made. But it was shaky at first. The group's name was recommended by Kweskin Jug Band's jug player, Fritz Richmond, who borrowed it from the lyrics of Mississippi John Hurt's "Coffee Blues." In that song, Hurt extolls the virtues of Maxwell House Coffee, singing that it only takes one "lovin' spoonful" to "make him feel alright." With that good luck charm of a phrase from John Hurt, they called themselves the Lovin' Spoonful. After a week's rehearsal on Long Island, they landed a gig at the Night Owl Cafe, located at 118 West Third Street, a short block west of the Café Bizarre and the Third Side, across MacDougal Street. "You see, we had to *break into* the Night Owl Cafe," Sebastian said to the audience at City Winery, NYC, on November 2, 2018, "because we were a four-piece band. And that was wrong in those days." But the configuration of the band was only part of the problem. They were booked for a week, which Jacobsen said was "shaky." After a particularly rough performance, owner Joe Marra called the band over to talk with him. "He said, 'Guys . . . come here,'" Sebastian recalls, gesturing. "When an Italian man goes, 'Come 'ere' . . . that's not good." The band froze. Still standing on the Night Owl's tiny stage, as Sebastian tells it, Marra told the group in his Italian accent, "So, guys, uh . . . here's the thing. You guys . . . *are no fuckin' good."* That sent the group back to rehearse, this time in the *horrible*, by all accounts, basement of the Hotel Albert at East Tenth Street and University Place. The Albert was an admittedly fleabag joint that was nonetheless a favorite hangout of musicians. The hotel's list of residents and basement-jammers is a virtual who's who of sixties rock. It was in that dump where the Lovin' Spoonful polished up their act considerably. It didn't take long for them to hit their stride. After playing at the Café Bizarre, Marra hired them back at the Night Owl, and this time things were different.

Every time I've spoken with John Sebastian, we talk as much about Eddie Cochran and Little Richard as we do about Mississippi John Hurt. What I mean to say is, although Sebastian had, literally, grown up surrounded by the folk revival right outside his front doorstep on Washington Square Park, he was young enough, like producer Jacobsen and the others in his magic circle, to know and love the power of rock and roll. With Sebastian's jug band experience—and with the help of Jacobsen, who was also working at the same time with Jesse Colin Young and Tim Hardin—the group was able to infuse the kind of zany, good-time aspect that was also embedded in the concurrent British rock and roll via their skiffle influence, and the group would come to inspire the NBC television series *The Monkees*. The Night Owl, Sebastian recalls, was a venue which did not have much in the way of a teenage audience. One night however, in another instance of history writing itself, it all came together. "On this particular night, we looked out in the audience and there was a young girl dancing. And this is in a setting where most of the other people are, pretty much, sort of beatnik types sitting around playing chess. So this really made a difference. It was like seeing the beginning, because we knew, if she was there, she would tell her friends next week. I wrote 'Do You Believe in Magic' the next day."

Jacobsen recorded the song but, at first, he and Cavallo could not land the boys a deal. "We shopped the record to every major label but found no takers. The tape sat unwanted in my apartment," said Jacobsen. It would be through the newly formed entertainment company headed by Charlie Koppelman and Don Rubin that the group got signed to Kama Sutra Records. Released as their first single on July 20, 1965, "Do You Believe in Magic" became a top-ten hit—the first of seven top tens in just over a year. Joe Marra would celebrate by distributing hundreds of helium-filled balloons all over the Village printed with "I Love The Lovin' Spoonful." Although he had written several songs by that time, including his first, "Warm Baby," when he was interviewed by Paul Zollo for *More Songwriters on Songwriting* (2016), Sebastian said, "Do You Believe in Magic" was "the first visible song I ever wrote." Within its lyrics is as good an explanation of what was going on at the time than anything I can write here.

> *I'll tell you about the magic, and it'll free your soul*
> *But it's like trying to tell a stranger 'bout a rock 'n' roll*

Sebastian equates rock and roll with freedom itself, and by the end of the song he turns the question into an invocation: "Yeah, believe in the magic of the young girl's soul, believe in the magic of-a rock 'n' roll, believe in the magic that can set you free." To believers, this would be a rallying cry that would herald the next phase of the revolution. The Lovin' Spoonful's pop hits on the radio brought secondhand attention to the other folkies in the Village who were not getting on the radio, like Phil Ochs, Tom Paxton, and Fred Neil.

The Night Owl was quick to embrace the new sound of the Village. After the Lovin' Spoonful's reign there, the Magicians, a short-lived, psychedelic garage band who made only four singles, became the house band. Two members, Alan Gordon and Garry Bonner, became successful songwriters who wrote "Happy Together" for the Turtles in 1967. In the 2018 short film *Joe Marra: The Night Owl*, made by his nephew, Andre Marcell, and shown at Marra's eighty-fifth birthday party at the Bitter End, Marra talked about the dynamics of the block, the balance of power between the Mafia and the NYPD. "Initially, I had a restaurant. There were eight or nine nightclubs on West Third Street. All these stripper bars. We'd get the beer drinkers and we'd get the johns, we'd get the gangsters and then we'd get the FBI watching the gangsters," he laughed. "One day, a big, six-foot, three-inch Irish policeman, Fitzgerald, came into my business and said he wanted me to give him twenty-five dollars a week." Marra protested the extortion, claiming his business was doing nothing wrong. According to Marra, Joseph "Joe the Wop" Cataldo of the Genovese crime family called him, explaining that all of the mob-owned clubs on West Third were paying Fitzgerald. "That's more money than I pay in rent for my apartment," Marra told the mobster, still refusing to pay. But Fitzgerald kept coming around for payment. Finally, Marra threatened Fitzgerald with a warning. "You know, Fitz, you oughta walk on the other side of the street." "Why is that?" responded the cop. "Well, Fitz, you know, this is an old building. Up on the roof there's a chimney, and all the bricks are loose. And if you walk on this side of the street, it's liable to fall on you." After complaining to Joe the Wop, Fitz left Marra and the Night Owl alone.

"At first, the Mafia was scared of folksingers," Jim Glover told me, "until the money started rolling in." When Joe Marra started booking music at the Night Owl, Fred Neil and Vince Martin were one of the first acts he hired, a scene he described in his interview with Marcell. "Fred would play at two in the morning. You'd look around, and there'd be a hundred people waiting to see Fred Neil play. And there'd be all the heads of the recording companies. They'd be drifting in out of the shadows. There's Clive Davis. There's Ahmet Ertegun. They were all there to see Fred. He was so brilliant. He played a twelve-string, and you'd think he had a harp."

Bleecker & MacDougal

Fred Neil's debut solo album *Bleecker & MacDougal* (Elektra) was released in August 1965. Neil had been one of the most well-loved anchors of MacDougal Street for years and was, in fact, one of the most accomplished, with his history of having written songs for Buddy Holly and Roy Orbison before hosting the afternoons at the Café Wha? Yet except for his duet album with Vince Martin the previous year, his own album was slow in coming. Bob Dylan, a complete unknown when he played harmonica for Neil practically the minute he arrived into town, was already on his sixth album as Neil released his first. But all artists work in their own way, at their own pace, with their own intentions, regardless of public perception.

Bleecker & MacDougal is an attractive period piece that has all the energy of a rock band but is mostly acoustic guitar driven, with no drums. The aforementioned album cover, itself a perfect slice of Village propaganda, promotes an almost idealized view of the MacDougal strip at night, a blaring beacon of light, filled with possibilities, the Empire State Building standing guard in the distance, and a prominent view of the Beat hangout, the San Remo Café, on the corner of Bleecker. The music inside serves to showcase Neil's forceful, rhythmic twelve-string strumming and what *Mojo* magazine in 2001 called his "impossibly resonant baritone" voice, with its unique balance of emotion and detachment—and his highly coverable, inward-looking songs. But what always stands out to me about Fred Neil's songs is that they are often about leaving New York. Even in the opening title song, which you would think would be a paean to the fabulous music center of the universe, the refrain is "I wanna go home! I wanna go home!"—and he means to *Florida*, where he would later settle in Coconut Grove. In "Other Side to This Life," he bemoans the uncertainty of a musician's life and dreams of sailing the Gulf of Mexico; in "Country Boy," he's "got sand all in . . . [his] shoes" but he got "stuck in the big city, gotta sing the big city blues." He wants out, for sure. Another thing that is for sure about this album is the excellent, if not fabulous, musicianship—led by Neil with all the confidence gained from his many Village afternoons and nights on MacDougal Street and featuring, throughout the album, some of John Sebastian's best harmonica work. Sebastian is stunning on "Gone Again" and brilliantly cops John Lennon's lick for the Beatles' "I Should Have Known Better" on Neil's "Mississippi Train." But the song that always gets to me is "A Little Bit of Rain." I can barely type the song's title without feeling the urge to grab my guitar and strum its four melancholy chords: D, D7, G, A7. Within that chord progression dwells a young lifetime of regret.

> *And if you look back, try to forget all the bad times*
> *Lonely blue and sad times, and just a little bit of rain*

Neil's friend and disciple Karen Dalton would record her own version of the song in 1969. By that year, another of Fred Neil's songs would be heard in movie theaters and on radios all over the country. But for now, as far as the national scene, he was still one of the Village's best-kept secrets.

But not all the songwriters of the Village were so inward-looking, and not all of them were creating the good-time sounds of the Lovin' Spoonful. The escalation of troops being sent to Vietnam had personal resonance for US Army vet Tom Paxton, and on his 1965 album *Ain't That News!* (Elektra), he name-checked and called out the sitting, dour-faced president in his song "Lyndon Johnson Told the Nation."

Johnson's presidency was never fully embraced by young Americans. First, because he had attained the office not by election but by assassination. And second, when he actually was elected in 1964, he insisted on digging the country deeper and deeper into the mire of the Vietnam War. LBJ's substantial successes, which included sweeping social programs referred to as the Great Society, and the landmark Civil Rights Act of 1964, passed on June 2 of that year, were overshadowed by the ongoing failures in Vietnam, the sense of hopelessness and loss it fostered, and the unnecessary deaths of so many young men. It was the first time the horror of war could be witnessed in real time, on live network television. The perception was that the president was uncaring and unsympathetic to soldiers, on one hand, and resistant and resentful of legitimate student protesters on the other. For LBJ, it was a lose-lose.

> *Lyndon Johnson told the nation, have no fear of escalation . . .*
> *Though it isn't really war we're sending fifty thousand more*

Paxton performed the song in a bright, fingerpicking folk style, clear-eyed, and clear-voiced, phrasing like the young Pete Seeger. Of all the songwriters on the scene and amid all the musical changes, Tom Paxton was heroically keeping Seeger's sound and spirit alive, while Seeger himself was still limited nationally due to the blacklist.

Frustrated over the network ban (see chapter 8) and taking matters into his own hands, Seeger self-financed his own local, low-budget television show called *Rainbow Quest* beginning in 1965. Broadcast over UHF Channel 47, primarily a Spanish-language channel based in Newark, New Jersey, and directed by wife Toshi, they produced thirty-nine episodes during the 1965–1966 season with an impressive list of folk artists as guests, including Paxton, the Clancy Brothers, Buffy Sainte-Marie, Donovan, Judy Collins, Mississippi John Hurt, and many more. Intimately staged around a kitchen table–like setting, it was the antithesis of shows like *Hootenanny*.

As the escalation in Vietnam continued, the focus of the protest songs coming from the Village shifted from civil rights issues to anti-war themes. But it can be argued that the war was *itself* a civil rights issue. Young men of ages eighteen to twenty-six had little recourse if they were drafted—this at a time when those under twenty-one did not have the right to vote for their elected officials. And, Black Americans were more likely to be drafted than whites were. The Vietnam War witnessed the largest proportion of African American soldiers than any other American conflict.

Also released in 1965, Phil Ochs's "I Ain't Marching Anymore"—the title song for his second Elektra album—addressed head-on what young people were feeling. Written in the first person, "I Ain't Marching Anymore" uses a historical timeline idea similar to Buffy Sainte-Marie's "Universal Soldier." But instead of an international theme, "Marching" tells strictly of American conflicts, beginning with the British-American wars and progressing to Japan and Germany in WWII and the recent tensions with Cuba. For Ochs, it is the military-industrial complex that is the real enemy.

Ochs took unfair criticism from his peers, particularly from Dylan, and from music critics then and now, that his songs were too topical and too specific to have any kind of longevity. I think that was a shortsighted view. How many work songs and folk ballads discovered by Alan Lomax or archived in the Harry Smith collection were songs capturing a particular moment or event of the past? And yet, they were uncovered and performed decades later. "I Ain't Marching Anymore" was arguably the most familiar song sung at anti–Vietnam War rallies in the 1960s—often by Ochs himself. Yet the lyrics never mention Vietnam by name. To me, it has not lost any of its resonance. Sadly, at least somewhere in the world at any given moment, it is as relevant as the day he wrote it.

Call it peace or call it treason, call it love or call it reason
But I ain't marching anymore

Like a Rolling Stone

Released on July 20, 1965, was Bob Dylan's single "Like a Rolling Stone," universally considered to be a revolutionary milestone in popular music. Confrontational, cynical, edgy, aggressive. All cylinders were firing. All stops and no punches were pulled. This was a full-out rock record, without an acoustic guitar to be heard and, as with the songs on *Bringing It All Back Home*, its politics were personal. My favorite thing about the single—recorded over two days, June 15 and 16—is how the band, with Mike Bloomfield on lead guitar, Bruce Langhorne fulfilling his role as the Tambourine Man, Bobby Gregg on drums, Joe Macho Jr. on bass, and Frank Owens on tack piano, sounds at times like it's on the verge of falling apart. And yet it triumphs. Dylan, at the center, keeps it together. Al Kooper appeared on the second day, invited to play guitar on the session by his friend, producer Tom Wilson. But aware of Bloomfield's prowess, he retreated into the control room. Then at one point, as Wilson took a phone call, Kooper wandered into the live room and sat at the Hammond B-3 organ. "What are you doing out there?" Wilson said to him over the talk-back speaker. But he let him stay and, eventually, Kooper hit on one of the most familiar organ hooks in rock. Upon playback, Dylan commanded, "Turn it up louder in the mix!" He loved it. "From the perspective of an engineer, working with recordings and seeing how they did it, you can see that they were not equipped to handle the dynamics that Bob was about to bring to them," producer/engineer Steve Addabbo told me. "There were times when you can see the needles getting slammed, and you can hear it. You can picture the engineer jumping for the knobs. They got their asses kicked! I really felt for them. But it was brand-new territory. I mean, my God, it was a pioneering time in terms of recording engineering. Trying to capture this unlikely artist with this unruly band and not rehearsed and going in there, flying by the seat of their pants, and every once in a while, magic struck. It was incredible." For reasons that have never been fully explained, though Wilson was to cite a disagreement with Al Grossman, "Like a Rolling Stone" was the last Dylan session to be produced by Tom Wilson. Addabbo has been working with Columbia Records' Steve Berkowitz on a meticulous series of box sets, remixing and restoring the original Dylan session tapes. In 2016, the two won Grammys (for Best Historical Album) for *The Cutting Edge 1965–66: The Bootleg Series Vol. 12*. I visited Addabbo in the studio as he was working on the new mix of "Like a Rolling Stone," and he played session tapes for me that revealed how the arrangement evolved in the studio, changing from three-four waltz time on the first day to four-four on the second. That was the moment when it all gelled. Released on July 20, 1965, the record was a smash. It was everywhere, making it to number two on the *Billboard* Hot 100, and number one on the competing *Cashbox* chart. In 2010, the song ranked number one on *Rolling Stone* magazine's 500 Greatest Songs of All Time, though it slipped to number four in 2021. Andy Warhol, whose Factory Dylan had been frequenting, wrote in his 1980 book *POPism: The Warhol Sixties*, "[Dylan] was out of folk and into rock and he'd switched from social protest songs to personal protest songs, and the more private he got the more popular he got, and it seemed like the more he said 'I'm only me,' the more the kids said 'We're only you, too.'"

Four days after the single was released, Dylan was back performing at the Newport Folk Festival. And this is where things got ugly. Or not, depending on your point of view. On July 24, Dylan performed a three-song solo acoustic set at an afternoon workshop. But sometime on that Saturday, an altercation occurred between Festival board members Alan Lomax and manager Albert Grossman over the young, electrified Paul Butterfield Blues Band. And when I say "altercation," I mean a real *fight*—fisticuffs—over Grossman's disapproval of Lomax's condescending onstage introduction of his soon-to-be clients. According to Robert Shelton in the 2021 edition of his book *No Direction Home*, edited by Elizabeth Thomson, "Invective began to fly, and shortly the giant of folklore and the titan of folk business were wrestling on the ground, before onlookers separated the two hulks." In response to the Festival's apparently dismissive attitude toward electric acts (although Howlin' Wolf had played electrically with no issue), Dylan was even more determined to perform electrically for his set the next evening. Although he had not brought a band, he had brought an electric guitar. He put together a pickup band with members of the Butterfield band, including Mike Bloomfield and Barry Goldberg. Al Kooper was to play organ. Late that night, the group rehearsed in secret in a Bellevue Avenue mansion, arranged by George Wein. On the evening of Sunday the 25th, following the traditional, country folk singer and fiddler Cousin Emmy, Dylan took to the stage wearing a black leather blazer and with his sunburst Fender Stratocaster, fronting a full electric band. In 2013, that guitar would be sold at auction by Christie's for $965,000.

They opened the set with a blazing rendition of "Maggie's Farm," a punishing blues-rock workout—Dylan sounds like he's singing the entire song in capital letters: "I AIN'T GONNA WORK ON MAGGIE'S FARM NO MORE!" The band wails, loud, relentless. He spits out the words, his face deadpan, his tone angry, arrogant, making sure the audience gets his message. What followed the song was a shocking, confused din of boos and scattered cheers. Watching the footage now, in Murray Lerner's brilliant and revealing 2007 film *The Other Side of the Mirror*, it sounds like the crowd not of a folk festival but at a sporting event, cheering and/or booing for opposing teams—a battle royale. According to George Wein, in his memoir, "People began booing; there were cries of 'Sellout!' It goes on for a minute as the band tunes-up and then breaks into 'Like a Rolling Stone.'" "HOW DOES IT FEEL? HOW DOES IT FEEL?" Dylan sneers, squinting the audience down. Richie Havens was there, sitting in the fifth row with Albert Grossman, who was also his manager. "I understood why the audience booed: the music was too loud. I was sitting with Albert and we were, like, 'Wow! Something is really falling here, being misunderstood,'" Havens was quoted as saying in the *Montreal Gazette* in 2013.

"The prevailing feeling among the crowd was a sense that they had been betrayed," George Wein would recall. I wondered if those booing were remembering Ronnie Gilbert's innocent but now-haunting introduction of Dylan a year earlier—"You know him, he's yours." Well, no, he seemed to be answering, you don't know me. And, no, as a matter of fact, I'm *not* yours. Or did they remember Dylan's own words to Cynthia Gooding on her radio show in 1962, when he said, "I don't really think of myself as in a *folksinger* thing." After the band sheepishly left the stage, Peter Yarrow, who was emceeing the show, standing helpless at the mic, called Dylan back. Backstage, George Wein confronted him: "You have to go back. You've got to play something acoustic." According to Wein, he resisted but relented. He had to borrow an acoustic guitar; Wein called for one from the musicians backstage; Yarrow grabbed one, and handed it to Dylan. Returning to the stage to calls of "Mr. Tambourine Man," he obliged, asking the audience for an "E" harmonica (many rained on the stage floor with thuds), and then closed his set, appropriately, with "It's All Over Now, Baby Blue."

Strike another match, go start anew
And it's all over now, Baby Blue

The stage lights faded to black. Dylan would not return to Newport for thirty-seven years.

Dylan headed back to the Chelsea Hotel, where he was living with former model Sara Lownds, whom he would secretly marry in November 1965. Four days later, from July 29 to August 4, Dylan was back in the studio, completing work on his next mold-shattering album, *Highway 61 Revisited,* with his new producer Bob Johnston. Bookended by "Like a Rolling Stone" and the eleven-minute-plus acoustic opus "Desolation Row," the album is often cited as among his best work. A 2016 *Rolling Stone* article by Joe Levy is subtitled "the album that destroyed folk music and set a new standard for Sixties pop." The cover, once again photographed by Daniel Kramer, was appealingly random—Dylan wearing his Triumph motorcycle T-shirt, Bob Neuwirth seen partially behind him in a striped T-shirt with one of Kramer's cameras dangling on a strap—taken on the steps of Albert Grossman's home on Gramercy Park.

But while Dylan was recording in Columbia Records Studio A in New York, the dust had not yet settled on the scene at Newport. Nor would it ever. Describing the audience's reaction from his perspective as production manager of the Festival in his wonderful book *White Bicycles: Making Music in the 1960s* (2007), record producer Joe Boyd wrote, "There were shouts of delight and triumph and also of derision and outrage. The musicians didn't wait to interpret it, they just plunged straight into the second song." While this was going on out front, the drama that was happening *backstage* during Dylan's set has itself sparked more than half a century of rumor and hysteria. It has been said, falsely, that Pete Seeger was so angered by the sound that he grabbed an ax to cut Dylan's cable. While it's true Pete wasn't pleased with the sound—understandably, as the sound system used at Newport was meant for acoustic folk music and was easily overloaded—that is not what happened. Pete *was* known to use an ax at home. In fact, he chopped the wood to build his log cabin house in Beacon, New York. In fact, he was always chopping wood. But that's not what went down at Newport. There are so many differing stories. Writer Elijah Wald, author of *Dylan Goes Electric!*, told me that Peter Yarrow had said to someone looking for Seeger backstage, "Pete's going to get his ax," meaning his banjo, and that the rumor spread from that innocent comment. Indeed, Yarrow said the same line, "Bobby's going to get his ax," onstage to the audience before Dylan returned for his acoustic encore. But that's not right either. As George Wein told it, Pete, after complaining to the production crew, had retreated to a parked car in the field behind the stage where he pleaded to George, "Make it stop. That noise is terrible," and remained there until it was all over. In the 2005 film *No Direction Home*, directed by Martin Scorsese, Seeger recalled complaining about the sound, saying, "Get that distortion out of his voice. . . . . It's terrible. If I had an axe, I'd chop the microphone cable right now." Pete has also said that the loud music was upsetting to his elderly father, Charles Seeger, who was one of the guest speakers at the Festival that year, wore a hearing aid, and was sitting near the stage. In fact, Pete told me that himself on a phone call in 2011, when he invited me to perform at an event honoring George Wein. But I have always suspected that there was something more: that a symbolic ax *did* fall as Dylan seemingly cut his ties with the protest song movement. Forty-six years had passed, and Pete was ninety-two. Since he brought it up, I had to ask. "Pete, you can tell me. Is there more to the story? What really happened that year at Newport? Were you upset with Bob?"

"Richard," Pete sighed. "He was . . . our *voice*."

Chapter Ten

"First Night in the Village"
Havens in the basement
Hands like a Collier
No teeth to speak of
I had to descend

Below the streets
To hear where the song sang
There sat great Richie
Thumb like a Capo

Belting it out
His raw vox of gravel
We palled it up then
He knew that I knew

We were the first wave
Cresting the splendor
Of all that soon will be
A Haven for youth

—Donovan, 2021

xploding,

laStic, and

itable

xploding,

lastic, and

the

itable

Donovan, helping Bob Dylan with harmonica selection, at the Newport Folk Festival, 1965. Photographed on Murray Lerner's production truck. In the background over Donovan's shoulder is Patrick Sky.

Folk-rock officially became a thing
on June 26, 1965, when the Byrds' cover

of Bob Dylan's "Mr. Tambourine Man" hit number one on the US pop charts. While often considered a West Coast phenomenon, a more accurate observation would be to see folk-rock as a combination not just of two genres but also of two coasts. Although they were recorded in Los Angeles with harmonies that, via David Crosby, were influenced by early Beach Boys, the first two number one hits by the Byrds were written by two of Greenwich Village's most prominent figures, and the trio at the nucleus of the group all had folk credentials on the Village coffeehouse circuit. In a 2013 interview with Stuart Rosenberg at Monmouth University, Roger McGuinn (born James Roger McGuinn) explained that, as a high school student, it was the Weavers, and Pete Seeger in

particular, who had inspired him to play music. "He was so engaging. I looked at that and said, 'That's what I wanna do.'" Soon after, a fortuitous meeting with the Limeliters at the Gate of Horn led to his entrée as a professional musician. Within a few weeks of finishing high school, McGuinn was working with the Limeliters in California, playing guitar and banjo on their album *Tonight: In Person*. Inevitably, he made his way to Greenwich Village, where he played the basket houses and provided accompaniment for the Chad Mitchell Trio, Bobby Darin, and Judy Collins. Gene Clark had been in the New Christy Minstrels, and Crosby had

performed in a folk duo with Terry Callier, who introduced him to then Jim McGuinn one night at the Bitter End on Bleecker Street.

A demo of "Mr. Tambourine Man" had been brought to the group by their manager and Greenbriar Boys' producer Jim Dickson prior to Dylan's own release of the song on the acoustic side of *Bringing It All Back Home*. But the group needed to be persuaded to record it. In a 2020 *Songfacts* interview by Roger Catlin, Byrds bassist Chris Hillman remembered, "Bob Dylan had written it in a very countrified groove, a straight two-four time signature, and Roger took the song home and worked with it, put it in four-four time, so you could dance to it. Bob heard us do it and said, 'Man, you could dance to this!' It really knocked him over, and he loved it." It was this endorsement from its composer that convinced the group to record the song. The severely edited arrangement included only one of the song's four verses (the second) and featured McGuinn's jingle-jangling electric twelve-string Rickenbacker model 360-12 guitar, an instrument first introduced by George Harrison on the Beatles' 1964 recording of "I Call Your Name" and, visibly, in the film *A Hard Day's Night* that same year. Produced by Terry Melcher, son of actress-singer Doris Day, the sound of "Mr. Tambourine Man" was inspired by Brian Wilson's reverb-laden, Phil Spector-ish production on "Don't Worry Baby," a hit for Melcher's pals, the Beach Boys, from the previous year. Unsure of the

Byrds' studio proficiency, Melcher brought in the Wrecking Crew studio musicians—including drummer Hal Blaine, pianist Leon Russell, and guitarist Bill Pitman—who had all played on Beach Boys tracks, instead of using Byrds bassist Hillman and drummer Michael Clarke, much to their dismay. The result, however, was a beautifully performed wall of sound. The record would become a kind of fountainhead and template for folk-rock and surely affected Dylan's own decision to plug in. In September, California folk-rock quintet We Five's rousing version of Ian & Sylvia's "You Were on My Mind," the song Sylvia wrote in her bathtub at the Hotel Earle, was chasing "Like a Rolling Stone" up the charts, and LA's the Turtles (originally named the Tyrtles as a mash-up of "Byrds" and "Beatles") were in the top ten with their version of Dylan's "It Ain't Me Babe." On December 4, the Byrds would score their second number one with their electric arrangement of Pete Seeger's "Turn! Turn! Turn!" On this one, the band played on the record themselves, McGuinn masterfully frailing his twelve-string Rickenbacker like Seeger himself, and the Wrecking Crew were not missed. All of these records were bicoastal, written in New York, and recorded in LA. By the time, three months later, that the Mamas and the Papas' "California Dreamin'"—also written at the Hotel Earle—peaked at number four on the charts, on March 4, the flag had been planted in the Hollywood Hills, forever framing folk-rock as a California phenomenon. But back in New York, producer Tom Wilson was not about to be outdone.

The Sound of Silence

Even before the electric side of *Bringing It All Back Home* and "Like a Rolling Stone" were recorded, Wilson had been on a mission to electrify Dylan's recordings, going so far as attempting to overdub electric instruments on the acoustic version of "House of the Rising Sun" from his first album. That experiment failed. However, a track from Simon and Garfunkel's all-but-forgotten 1964 debut album gave Wilson the opportunity for another try, with another Columbia act.

In the spring of 1965, around the release of the Byrds' breakthrough hit, a late-night disc jockey in Boston began spinning the original, acoustic version of "The Sounds of Silence" to strong audience reaction. Then it was picked up by a cluster of stations in Cocoa Beach, Gainesville, and throughout Florida, where college students gathered during spring break. Wilson got wind of the traction the record was getting and sprang into action. For their part, Simon and Garfunkel had ostensibly called it quits—Simon had moved to England and had quickly made a solo album, performing throughout Europe, and Garfunkel had returned to his graduate studies at Columbia. Without their knowledge, Wilson gathered some of the musicians who had played on Dylan's recent electric sessions, bassist Joe Macho (also known as Joe Mack), guitarists Al Gorgoni and Vinnie Bell, and drummer Bobby Gregg—most of whom had played on *Bringing It All Back Home*—and brought them all back home to Columbia Records Studio A to overdub on the original recording of the song.

Now, anyone who has ever tried to overdub a rhythm section on top of a previously recorded acoustic track recorded without a click-track or drums knows that this is not an easy task. Folk musicians tend to speed up or slow down as needed during a song, either for emphasis of certain parts, or simply because they speed up or slow down. The reason is not important here, just the idea that it was hard to stay in time with the original recording. In a 2010 interview with Dave Simmons for *BMI Magazine*, on the forty-fifth anniversary of the session, guitarist Al Gorgoni admitted, "I hate it. I mean, I love the song, but those guitars—they're just *awful*. I really can't listen to it now. I took it out for this occasion just to hear it again, but that was enough. Of course, all the things that are wrong with the recording didn't stop it from becoming a huge success. So there you go." Barry Kornfeld, who played on the original, acoustic track and copublished the song with Paul Simon, had a similar reaction. "You know, Richard, I don't need to tell you. It was done backwards," Kornfeld told me. "Paul was mortified when he heard it." Indeed, the rhythm section audibly struggles through it, trying to keep up or slow down as Simon and Garfunkel go through the song. "I would have made sure the drums and bass were in sync with the voices at the end of the fourth verse," Garfunkel told *Smithsonian* magazine in 2016, "but I was interested in having a hit record." Oh, and they did. After climbing its way up the charts, the song, now titled "The *Sound* of Silence," eventually hit number one on January 1, 1966, just a week after the Byrds' "Turn! Turn! Turn!" vacated the slot. Simon, an avid reader of the trade magazines, watched the climb and headed for home. He reunited with Garfunkel, and they began planning their next album. Folk-rock had its latest signature anthem, and Simon's and Garfunkel's names, for all their ethnicity, were becoming household ones. Regardless of the record's rhythmic anomalies, the record has a unique character that endures—a life of its own. By the time "The Sound of Silence" was used in Mike Nichols's blockbuster film *The Graduate* in 1967, it was permanently embedded in the American zeitgeist. Without Tom Wilson, it wouldn't exist. His vision had also helped turn the tables and made Columbia Records a successful rock label.

Jonas Mekas and the Underground Film Movement

As the musical nexus at the intersection of Bleecker and MacDougal and Folk and Rock was reaching its peak, a revolution in underground cinema, led by Jonas Mekas, was simultaneously taking place a few blocks away. Having fled the Soviet occupation of their Lithuanian village, Jonas and his brother, Adolfas, were exiled in a displaced persons camp near Hamburg, Germany, until the United Nations Refugee Organization released and relocated them to the United States in 1949. They arrived in New York City in October of that year, instantly falling in love with the city. Borrowing money to buy a Bolex 16mm movie camera—the versatile, compact, and affordable camera that made independent cinema possible—Jonas began chronicling his life on film and, in 1954, he and his brother founded *Film Culture* magazine. Four years later, Jonas began writing the influential, and radical, "Movie Journal" column for the *Village Voice*. In 1962, he founded the Film-Makers' Cooperative to distribute independent films and, two years later, the Film-Makers' Cinematheque, a showcase for underground screenings. The Film-Makers' Cooperative operated out of Jonas's loft at 414 Park Avenue South, which quickly became a hangout for experimental filmmakers, artists, and poets—a salon vibe, similar to what Warhol's Factory would soon emulate and magnify. Like musicians sharing their latest songs at the Kettle of Fish or downstairs at Gerde's, filmmakers screened their latest works and compared ideas. It is there that Jonas met Andy Warhol, then working in painting and silk screen, and encouraged him to make films. Jonas was, in fact, the cinematographer for Warhol's landmark avant-garde *Empire* (1964), a single, stationary shot of the Empire State Building as night falls that runs over eight hours. "To see time go by," Warhol explained at the time. Over a decade later, I was the only student in my film class who stayed for the entire film.

Jonas's theories of film and art were inherently musical. In a 2012 video interview for *Frieze*, he compared his style as a filmmaker, a style in which he created most of the effects within the camera itself as he shot, to that of a jazz musician. "You structure the piece that you are making during the actual moment of playing," he explained. "Improvisation has stronger logic than anything you can invent by your mind artificially, because it is out of your control." Himself a poet, Mekas defined underground cinema as "films that explore the poetic, instead of narrative" aspect of the art. Through the efforts and energy of Jonas Mekas and the film community he built, underground film in New York was becoming the height of radical, subversive art in the early 1960s.

Because of our mutual admiration for Tiny Tim and the fact that we had both made recordings of him during different phases of his life and career, Jonas contacted me in 2009 as I was hosting a tribute to Tiny at the Public Theater's music venue, Joe's Pub, on Lafayette Street. We instantly hit it off, and it was a joy and an honor to have Jonas as a friend and mentor until his passing in 2019. During those ten years, Jonas would often tell me about the legend of Barbara Rubin. I can still hear him say her name: Bar-bar-a Ru-bin, each syllable affectionately enunciated in his captivating Lithuanian accent. But who was she?

"She was the one who helped to make the chemistry of that period," said Jonas. "Everybody wanted to talk to her, invite her, to be with her." A red diaper baby born to exceptionally permissive Jewish parents, Rubin had started hanging out on the Village scene by the age of thirteen. At seventeen, deemed to be at risk, she was sent to a drug treatment facility in Connecticut and was allowed to be released only when Jonas Mekas, whom her parents admired, agreed to hire her as a full-time intern at the Film-Makers'

Cooperative. It was the spring of 1963. Instantly, Rubin met and befriended everyone on the scene—poets, musicians, filmmakers, artists—and became one of the most ardent advocates of the experimental film movement. Inspired by Jack Smith's playful, nudity-laced, drag-orgy film *Flaming Creatures* (1963), Rubin made her own underground film, *Christmas on Earth*, taking its title from a line in Arthur Rimbaud's *A Season in Hell*. Rubin's film was one of the most sexually explicit of the era, a milestone of queer and feminist cinema. Rubin sincerely believed that underground cinema, through its unfiltered self-expression, could change the world.

Christmas on Earth's unique multi-image screening technique—using two projectors simultaneously, one image on top of the other, and colored gels in front of the projectors—was a precursor to the trippy, psychedelic, multimedia light shows and happenings that were soon to accompany rock performances. The few who saw the film in 1963 were astounded, whether or not they liked it. In his *Village Voice* column, Jonas himself wrote, "This 18-year-old girl must have no shame. Only angels have no shame. Barbara Rubin . . . is an angel." The film led to Rubin meeting and having a surprising sexual encounter with Allen Ginsberg, who adored the film and, apparently, Barbara. It would be the beginning of a complicated relationship with the loudly gay Ginsberg. At one point, she convinced Ginsberg to reveal his handsome face and cut off his famous beard, an act that he allowed Rubin to do herself, using a pair of Jonas's film-editing scissors. One night circa 2014, over fifty years later, I was visiting Jonas at his Brooklyn loft when he mentioned the beard story to me, offering to prove it. "Jonas, please don't tell me you saved it," I said, already knowing the answer. After disappearing into his archives for a minute, Jonas returned with his famous, sly grin and produced a small, red plastic box labeled "Allen's Beard," which contained a plastic bag filled with Ginsberg's beard hair, along with the scissors that had done the deed.

Like the *Red Channels* blacklist of the 1950s, the shadow of censorship had been a threat looming over the underground film community, as it had for the Beat writers, Lenny Bruce, and others. Chuck Smith, director of the enchanting *Barbara Rubin & The Exploding NY Underground* (Juno Films, 2018), told me that Barbara Rubin was "like a public relations person for fighting censorship." In March 1964, Mekas was arrested on obscenity charges for screening *Flaming Creatures* at the Film-Makers' Cinematheque in the East Village. After the arrest, Mekas defiantly screened Jean Genet's homoerotic, prison love story *Un Chant D'Amour* (1950) to generate financial support for his defense fund but, again, he was arrested. Ginsberg, Susan Sontag, and other filmmakers and historians testified at Jonas's trial. Barbara Rubin was one of the loudest voices in Jonas's defense. "She would stand on cars in the Village with a megaphone yelling, 'Fuck Censorship!' She became a very vocal advocate for free speech," Chuck Smith told me. At the trial, Jonas was convicted but given a suspended sentence, a move that echoed Pete

Seeger's overturned conviction a few years earlier. In a subsequent statement in the winter 1964 edition of *Film Comment*, Mekas wrote, "Our art is for all the people. It must be open and available to anybody who wants to see it. The existing laws are driving art underground."

Dylan Meets Donovan

Barbara Rubin reunited with Bob Dylan on his May 1965 trip to England, staying at the Savoy Hotel and introducing him to Allen Ginsberg. Donovan was in town, too, fresh from the release of his debut album, *What's Bin Did and What's Bin Hid* (Hickory Records). When Dylan arrived in London, Donovan was riding high in the UK charts—and in newspaper headlines—with one of the biggest hits of that year, his lovely folk-style ballad, "Catch the Wind." Dylan's fiercely competitive nature was triggered, especially when the press referred to the handsome eighteen-year-old as "the new Dylan." Truth is, though he admired Dylan, Donovan had been just as heavily inspired by Woody Guthrie as Dylan had, and Donovan had literally studied at the feet of Ramblin' Jack Elliot when Elliot had rambled through the UK folk circuit. Plus, Donovan, a Scotsman, with a father who was a poet, was raised around the Celtic folk music that Dylan had been borrowing for years. So musical comparisons were inevitable. Watching D. A. Pennebaker's spectacular 1967 documentary *Dont Look Back* (punctuation omitted intentionally by the director), and in the raw footage, one can see Dylan and cohort/road manager Bobby Neuwirth plotting to *destroy* the five-years-younger Donovan. "Right away, I hate him!" Dylan says in one scene. Looking at that day's headline, Dylan proclaims, "Donovan! Donovan! Next target! He's the target for tomorrow!" However, when he arrives at the Savoy on May 8—finding Dylan in the middle of an angry, agitated rant in his crowded hotel suite—Donovan is charming, strums his guitar, and disarms the wound-up Dylan with a gentle, comforting folky song, "To Sing for You," from his debut album:

> *Call out to me as I ramble by, I'll sing a song for you*
> *That's what I'm here to do, to sing for you*

Donovan then requests that Dylan sing the song "It's All Over Now, Baby Blue," which he does for all in the room, including a smiling, Jabba the Hutt–like Albert Grossman who is overseeing the circus around his star client. Writers have analyzed the exchange between Dylan and Donovan for decades, but to anyone watching the footage objectively, it is clear that they are simply swapping songs, the way Dylan did at the Kettle of Fish and the way Donovan does with his friends. Soon after filming that scene, Pennebaker created the innovative music video of "Subterranean Homesick Blues" that opens the movie, filmed in the rather New York—looking alley way behind the Savoy Hotel. This is where Barbara Rubin's introduction of Allen Ginsberg to Dylan came into play, as the poet appears throughout the iconic shoot. During the performance, Dylan stands over to one side, holding up handwritten signs based on key words and phrases from the song's lyrics as they are sung. Who hand painted many of these signs? None other than Donovan. In his 2005 autobiography *Hurdy Gurdy Man*, Donovan writes of visiting the Savoy one more time before Dylan headed back to the States, this time finding all four Beatles in the suite, in what sounds like a UK version of the smoky scene at New York's Hotel Delmonico. Throughout the decade, Donovan would forge his own distinctive, evolving sound, adventurously augmenting his formidable acoustic guitar-picking skills with jazz, Indian, psychedelic, reggae, chamber, and orchestral pop flavors that, according to *Billboard*, landed him on the American charts at least twenty times during the 1960s. Pete Seeger loved the gentle Donovan and presented him on his television show, *Rainbow Quest*, in 1966, accompanied by Shawn Phillips on sitar, in an episode that also included Reverend Gary Davis. And Donovan's friendship with the Beatles blossomed. In a few years, he would join them on a spiritual quest to India to study transcendental meditation with Maharishi Mahesh Yogi. Each evening, the ashram became a folk music summer camp, as the musicians brought out their acoustic guitars. There Donovan would teach the Beatles the clawhammer, the Carter Family's fingerpicking style that became a hallmark of the group's "white album" in 1968. Already, the Beatles had shown the influence of Dylan and others from the Greenwich Village scene, especially on their 1965 album *Rubber Soul*. And Paul McCartney admitted to being influenced by the Lovin' Spoonful, whose good time sound would find its way onto the Beatles' next album. The natural blurring of genres and crossing of influences that occurred in the 1960s should be celebrated and emulated but has instead been stifled in subsequent decades by the music media's, record companies', and critics' insistence on labeling and dividing artists, exaggerating rivalries, and amplifying artificial genre wars.

Another of Dylan's and Neuwirth's targets, Joan Baez, fared far worse on that 1965 UK tour. One scene in the Pennebaker film has Neuwirth berating Baez wildly, taking verbal jabs that visibly upset her, while Dylan laughs. "The tour in England was hell. There's not really much else to say. It was just . . . it was just hideous," Baez said in the 2009 BBC documentary, *Joan Baez: How Sweet the Sound*. "Probably because everyone was doing drugs. And I didn't understand that. It was really demoralizing, and I was letting myself be demoralized by him not asking me onstage with him. It was just a very unhappy time." Things would never really be the same between the two, although she *would* join Dylan's *Rolling Thunder Revue* in the 1970s. For Donovan, however, a new friendship formed with Baez, who introduced him to the fifteen-thousand-strong crowd at her headlining performance on the first night of the Newport Folk Festival that year, just as she had done for Dylan in 1963. There are photos of Donovan and Dylan palling around at Newport, and Donovan witnessed, and enjoyed, Dylan's closing-night rock spectacle. Of all the performers at the Festival, Donovan was the only one who addressed the Vietnam War directly, in two of the songs he performed: his rendition of "The War Drags On" by English folksinger Mick Softley, captured in Murray Lerner's Festival film, and his own "The Ballad of a Crystal Man."

Vietnam, your latest game, you're playing with your blackest Queen . . .
For seagull I don't want your wings, I don't want your freedom in a lie.

That year, while in the States, Donovan made the mandatory musical pilgrimage to Greenwich Village where, after hearing a coffeehouse set by Richie Havens, he met and befriended John Sebastian. "Meeting John made my first real experience in Greenwich Village the best possible," he told me. "John's hero Fred Neil had forever immortalized the Village for me, and when I visited those fabled bohemian streets, I made sure to stand for a moment on the corner of Bleecker and MacDougal . . . close my eyes . . . and hear Fred Neil's song of the same name." That first visit to the Village, and seeing and hearing Richie Havens perform at the Why Not?—a tiny underground café opposite the Café Wha?—inspired the poem Donovan wrote specially for the start of this chapter.

"Those folk clubs were so close together," John Sebastian said to the *Southern Illinoisan* in 2009. "You could go to the Bitter End and see somebody like Peter, Paul and Mary or the Kingston Trio; but then if you went over to Gerde's Folk City, the bill was much more likely to have Ralph Rinzler or Victoria Spivey, all these great people. Then there were clubs that were pass-the-basket type houses, with people who were unknown . . . Richie Havens, Roger McGuinn, and myself, we were all playing those clubs as the 'not-quite-big kids.'"

Richie Havens

By 1965, Richie Havens was a favorite on the Village circuit, including at the Night Owl on a bill with Fred Neil and Tim Hardin. "Richie was . . . beautiful," Joe Marra recalled. "Richie was the hardest-working person going. If you had to do an extra show, you'd ask Richie, and he would get up onstage, and he would *push*. Everybody loved him." One of the few young African American singers on the Village scene, Havens developed a singular playing style using his thumb in open-D tuning and strumming in a highly percussive, rhythmic style. According to Havens's 2013 obituary in the *New York Times*, "His hands were very large, which made it difficult to play the guitar. He developed an unorthodox tuning so he could play chord patterns not possible with conventional tunings. The style was picked up by other folk and blues singers." I asked Walter Parks—a brilliant musician in his own right who was Havens's protégé and played guitar on the road with him for nearly ten years in the 2000s—about Havens's guitar technique. He said, "Richie told me that he developed that style because he was a doo-wop singer on the streets, and what he needed to hear [as accompaniment] was for the guitar to be tuned to a major triad. The singers all harmonized with the one, three, and the five. And then he figured out a way to drop the natural third down to a minor third, so then he had half the chords that he could possibly need." That workaround made Havens's sound instantly recognizable. "I learned a lot from him," said session guitarist Elliot Randall, who at sixteen played on a bill with Havens at the Café Bizarre in 1963. "I mean, you talk about a hard-driving rhythm. Holy crap! That guy could do it better than anybody. He was a whole band in himself," Randall recalled in a July 2021 interview for *Produce Like a Pro*. "But what was really interesting about it," Walter Parks told me, "is that Richie had a way of . . . surviving. That was an example of him surviving in a very unschooled way. I think it was a survival technique more than anything." I remember John Sebastian telling me that he never wanted to follow a set by Havens when performing at the basket houses because, by the time Sebastian would come on, the audiences had already emptied their pockets for Havens and had nothing left to give. Richie Havens's rise to fame would be one of the most breathtaking, when he was catapulted to stardom overnight at Woodstock in 1969—by literally making up a song on the spot that he called "Freedom" in front of nearly five hundred thousand people.

In the late 1970s, singer-songwriter Cliff Eberhardt was befriended and mentored by Havens and played guitar for him on the road like Walter Parks would do in the 2000s. "He never talked about his own life. He talked about the *world*," Eberhardt told me. Havens would be picked up for management by Albert Grossman and continued to build a following in the Village. His first official album release, *Mixed Bag* (Verve/Folkways), would be released in December 1966 and contain his moving protest anthem "Handsome Johnny." That song, while echoing the eternal warrior themes of Buffy Sainte-Marie's "Universal Soldier" and Phil Ochs's "I Ain't Marching Anymore," added one more raging battle to the list.

> *Hey, look yonder, tell me what you see, marching to the fields of Birmingham?*
> *It looks like Handsome Johnny with his hand rolled in a fist,*
> *Marching to the Birmingham war.*

"Richie would sit in Washington Square Park with Jimi Hendrix, and they would share songs with each other," Walter Parks told me, "and Richie would use the language 'I gave him a song' or 'he would give me a song.' That is part and parcel of that sixties ideology of 'what's mine is yours.' The sense of proprietary possession of an artistic piece was just not developed at that point. A lot of people were getting together to share ideas, and they all learned from each other. The Village scene of the sixties was a way of life that created a certain kind of music, and it will never happen again. It will never be that way again."

The Velvet Underground

A twenty-six-minute walk and a world apart from Washington Square, at 56 Ludlow Street on the Lower East Side, Lou Reed, John Cale, Sterling Morrison, and enigmatic percussionist Angus MacLise were busy creating music with an entirely different set of objectives that were just as revolutionary as those of any music that emerged during the 1960s. Combining rock with avant-garde musical experimentation, and driven by Lou Reed's idiosyncratic, poetic lyrics often dealing with illicit drug use and sexual realities here-tofore relegated to society's most private realms, the Velvet Underground's sound was shocking, grating, loud, hated, and feared by many, if not most, who heard them. But Reed's songs, though he would never admit it, were a new kind of urban folk music that spoke to and for the disenfranchised, the alienated, misfits, and outcasts. It was music born of the dirt, desperation, and darkest alleyways of New York City. The group's appearance—often wearing all-black, dark glasses, straight-legged skinny jeans, and leather boots—was far from the look of the bluegrass bands on the stage of Gerde's Folk City. Closely associated with, and inspired by, the underground film movement, they performed in mixed-media happenings at Jonas Mekas's Film-Makers' Cinematheque—with film, lights, poetry, and music—often accompanying exper-imental films with a live score, performing behind the screen. They developed a repertoire and reputation that caught the attention and imagination of Barbara Rubin. She then introduced the Velvets to Al Aronowitz, the Dylan and Beatle confidante we met at Hotel Delmonico, who soon became their manager. Aronowitz got the band their first actual concert, which was held on December 11, 1965, at Summit High School in Summit, New Jersey, opening for another of his acts, the Myddle Class, an established garage rock group. Percussionist MacLise refused to be part of such a commercial gig and was replaced by Maureen "Moe" Tucker, the younger sister of a high school friend, whose Bo Diddley–influenced primitive, tribal, tom-tom pounding and androgynous, tomboy appearance completed the picture. From all accounts, the audience reaction appears to have been somewhere between horror and repulsion. Especially by the time the band began playing "Heroin," an elaborately dynamic two-chord recitation that recalled the writing of William Burroughs and simulated the effect of shooting-up through musical crescendo and decrescendo. Oh, and their vivid depiction of S-and-M sex in "Venus in Furs," which featured John Cale's screeching electric viola. According to Anthony DeCurtis's masterful 2017 book *Lou Reed: A Life*, by the time the band ended their three-song set, half of the student audience had run for the door. Among the half who stayed was my own future roommate and bandmate in the Bongos, Rob Norris. "Richard, it was like watching a UFO land," Rob told me. "None of us had ever seen or heard anything like it. It was totally transgressively 'other' and we were mesmerized. And then, like a vision, it was over, and they took off again."

Next, Aronowitz booked the Velvets at the Café Bizarre. It was there, at a sparsely populated performance in that sawdust-floored folk club on West Third Street, just down the block from where the Lovin' Spoonful were being contrastingly tuneful at the Night Owl, that Barbara Rubin and Gerard Melanga introduced the group to Andy Warhol and the Factory entourage. "The Café Bizarre was a place where they could work things out. Like a rehearsal place," DeCurtis told me. Andy invited them to the Factory, where they became the house band. Warhol invested in purchasing proper Vox amps and other gear for the group. Dumping Aronowitz, Warhol took over as manager. Through Jonas Mekas and the Rolling Stones' Brian Jones, Warhol was introduced to the stunningly beautiful German actress and model Nico—who had illuminated the screen in Federico Fellini's *La Dolce Vita* (1960)—and, taken by her now-legendary icy detachment and distinctive vocal style, he suggested to Reed and the others that she join the band. Hesitantly, the band agreed. What followed was an outrageous performance for a convention of psychiatrists at the Hotel Delmonico, at which Barbara Rubin and Jonas Mekas accosted guests guerrilla-style—Jonas with his invasive camera and Rubin with her graphic sexual questions. Soon after, *Andy Warhol Up-Tight*, a mixed-media art happening that included dancers Melanga and Warhol superstar Edie Sedgwick, lights, and films had a weeklong residency at the Cinematheque. Then, renaming the whole affair as the *Exploding Plastic Inevitable*, a phrase concocted from some random words mutated from the back cover liner notes of Dylan's then-current album *Highway 61 Revisited*, Warhol took the sensory overload to St. Mark's Place in the East Village, renting the former Polish National Home for a month and turning it into The Dom (meaning "home" in Polish). According to Jan Błaszczak in his book, *The Dom* (2018), every evening the *Exploding Plastic Inevitable* was presented, the venue was packed. The happenings were merging radical art with rock music and presaging the psychedelic light shows to come.

For anyone familiar with the Velvet Underground's pounding beats, distorted guitars, and droning viola, one of the most shocking things you can hear is their original demo recording that they made on Ludlow Street. On it, the songs, stripped of their electric arrangements, are revealed to be rooted in folk songs. Lou Reed's "Venus in Furs," sung on the demo by John Cale in his lilting Welsh accent, sounds almost like one of the lovely English folk ballads that Cynthia Gooding or Carolyn Hester might have sung—until you listen to the words about flagellation and submission. Even the intensity of "Heroin," which was to become one of Reed's signature songs, started out almost as a kind of talking blues.

> *And all the politicians makin' crazy sounds*
> *And everybody puttin' everybody else down*

To say the Velvet Underground was polarizing is putting it mildly. It was obvious at the first performance at Summit High School and was a kind of power that Lou Reed was to cultivate throughout his long and celebrated career. "We didn't care for them much," John Sebastian whispered to me as we performed together in 2018 in a concert that featured some artists doing Velvets songs. I wasn't surprised. In 2008, I performed a version of Reed's "I'll Be Your Mirror" at Carnegie Hall, and Lou graciously performed a reading of the lyrics for me, which was filmed and projected on the screen behind me as I sang. At the filming, Reed reminded me, "Richard, I wrote that song in 1965," sounding surprised not only of how many years had passed but perhaps that he had composed something so enduring. "You are timeless, Lou," was about all I could muster for a reply as the moment and emotion were sustained in the air like Lou's melody itself.

Warhol managed to get the band a deal with Verve/MGM Records in 1966, where they were signed by Tom Wilson, who had recently left Columbia. Wilson would produce some of the debut album, with Warhol himself rightfully credited as the primary producer. Although Warhol's production credentials were often questioned or misunderstood, it should be said that allowing the group to follow their artistic vision and not succumb to commercial concerns was the best direction a producer could give them. Widely ignored at the time, *The Velvet Underground and Nico* (1967), with its iconic, peelable, Warhol banana painting cover, is now considered one of the most consequential albums of the decade, alongside the Beatles and Dylan. In the 1970s, musician-producer Brian Eno would famously say, "The Velvet Underground didn't sell many records, but everyone who bought one went out and started a band." Rob Norris and I can vouch for that.

Still, for all their influence, the Velvet Underground was never really embraced by the Greenwich Village scene. Steve Katz, who in 1965 had recently joined the Blues Project, said of the two bands, "We were West Village potheads, and they were leather-wearing, East Village speed freaks. I was scared shitless when I met the Velvets." Ironically, by the mid-1970s, Katz would go on to produce three of Lou Reed's best-selling solo recordings, including the savagely majestic live album, *Rock 'n' Roll Animal* (RCA Records, 1974).

And the reception on the West Coast was not so great either. According to Velvets drummer Maureen Tucker, "I hope you fucking *bomb*," is what Bill Graham, who had booked the group to play at his venue The Fillmore in San Francisco, told the band just as they were going onstage.

Many in the Village were not smitten with Warhol and his entourage at all and were suspicious of his intentions. Dave Van Ronk, in his memoir, wrote, "You could tell where things were headed when Andy Warhol and his 'beautiful people' showed up at the Gaslight. That towhead was like a vulture—when he appeared, you knew the fun was over."

Still, many musicians, Dylan and Donovan included, were brought to the Factory by Barbara

Rubin. The Factory became an uptown hangout for some of the Village musicians and their friends, and musicians on tour passing through. Donovan told me that "it was the thing for bands to do, to visit Andy's studio, when working in New York. Silver Pillows floating on the ceiling. I met the Velvets there." He, Dylan, Lou Reed, and nearly five hundred other visitors posed for Warhol's three-minute, black-and-white "screen tests." After Dylan's was filmed, he was given, or by most accounts *took*, one of Warhol's huge, silver, "Double Elvis" paintings. Dylan, with the help of Bobby Neuwirth and Victor Maymudes, tied it to the top of his station wagon and brought it back to his place in Woodstock, where he later traded it——for Albert Grossman's couch. In 2012, a similar Warhol work sold at Sotheby's for $37 million, once again proving Grossman's talent at dealmaking. Eric Andersen also found his way to the Factory, brought by journalist, publicist, and eternal scenester Danny Fields, who chased Andersen down to Le Figaro Café, on the corner of Bleecker and MacDougal, drawn by Andersen's movie star looks. Andy put Eric in the film *Space*, with Edie Sedgwick, for which Eric also provided the music. As for Danny Fields, by the next year or so, he would work with the Doors, Nico and the Velvets, Iggy Pop and the Stooges, and the MC5. And in the 1970s, he would manage the Ramones. Like Barbara Rubin, he seemed to always be at the center of things.

Jonas Mekas captured everything——on film and in his journals. In Todd Haynes's brilliant and beautiful 2021 documentary *The Velvet Underground* (Apple Original Films), a film that is dedicated to Mekas, he declares, in a way that only Jonas could, "We are not part of the counterculture. We are the culture." Speaking at the Cannes press conference, director Haynes described the Velvets and their merging of rock and art as "an absolutely unique artistic moment in New York life."

A Singer's Singer

Between the extremes of the Lovin' Spoonful's good-time music and the Velvet Underground's rock noir, the singer-songwriters continued to establish a style of self-expression that would dominate the music industry into the mid-1970s. Writing much if not all of their own material, they revolutionized the business model, changing the roles of music publishers and A&R departments, and practically put song factories like the Brill Building out of business. In the process, they gave us a cast of heroes and antiheroes. Tim Hardin, influenced by Fred Neil, was one of the most promising.

Tim Hardin slipped into town in 1961, first pursuing a career in acting——attending the American Academy of Dramatic Arts——but then dropping out to focus on his music. Deciding to move to Boston, he was discovered by future Lovin' Spoonful producer Erik Jacobsen while performing on the Cambridge folk scene, and he then returned to Greenwich Village. "His stunning voice and easy way of blending folk, blues and jazz influences steadily earned him a reputation on the folk scene around Boston and, after he returned in 1963, New York," wrote Anthony DeCurtis in the liner notes for the 1994 release *Tim Hardin: Reason to Believe* (*The Best Of*) (Polydor). It's a remarkable collection of songs that defies genre. Besides the elements that DeCurtis lists, there is a dash of country and a songwriting precision that, when combined with the jazz influence and inventive percussion, created something game-changingly undefinable. Hardin's blend of styles would be echoed by Van Morrison (particularly on his *Astral Weeks* album in 1968), Nick Drake, and many others. A startling aspect to Hardin's early songwriting is that the completeness of his melodies and the sharpness of the lyrics make it less noticeable that, often, he has written only two verses and a chorus, simply repeats the first verse for the third, and keeps it all roughly under two and a half minutes. There's a reason for that. After receiving zero interest from record labels for demos of blues covers they recorded, producer Erik Jacobsen suggested to Hardin that he go write some original songs. "I'll give you fifty bucks for every song you write with two verses and a chorus," Jacobsen told him. "He went back to Boston to write some songs." The quality of the results astonished Jacobsen.

Originally from Eugene, Oregon, Hardin had left home at age eighteen to join the US Marine Corps. According to Mark Brend, in his 2001 book *American Troubadours*, it was while he was in the Marines, stationed in Vietnam, that Hardin became addicted to heroin. The addiction and a debilitating stage fright were to plague him for his entire career. Yet he was one of the most gifted musicians to emerge from the Village. Rarely opening his eyes onstage, Tim Hardin playing electric guitar would jam at the Night Owl with Fred Neil on second guitar and John Sebastian on harmonica, and others would join them. Night Owl owner Joe Marra said of Hardin, "People [venues] wouldn't hire Tim. Tim had a drug problem . . . a heroin problem. And heroin was very cheap." But Marra added that, despite his addiction, "musicians would fight to play with him." Phil Ochs, who wrote for several publications, reviewed Hardin's appearance at the Night Owl for *Hit Parader* magazine's January 1966 issue, in an article titled "Tim Hardin: The Singer's Singer." In it, Ochs describes Hardin "holding a number of fellow musicians in awe." He closes the excellent review with "[Hardin] has all the makings of a legend, and when musical historians look back on this period to check the deepest roots and the most important influences and translators, Hardin will have to take his place along with Dylan, the Beatles, and the rest."

Hardin's debut album, *Tim Hardin 1* (Verve Forecast), flawlessly produced by Jacobsen, included Sebastian on harmonica, string arrangements by Artie Butler, and jazz vibraphone played by Gary Burton. Released in 1966, it contained at least three bona fide classics of the era, "Misty Roses," "Reason to Believe," and "Don't Make Promises."

It seems the songs we're singing are all about tomorrow,

Tunes of promises that we can't keep

"Misty Roses," recorded as a vibes and jazz, bass-driven bossa nova, sounds pleasantly meandering and melodically complex with its eight-bar bridge and yet is *under* two minutes. It's that very simplicity and brevity that made his songs so coverable and successful for a wide range of artists, including Bob Dylan who, according to *Rolling Stone*, once called Hardin "the country's greatest living songwriter."

His next album, *Tim Hardin 2*, would bring another cache of songs ready to cover, including "If I Were a Carpenter," "Black Sheep Boy," and "The Lady Came from Baltimore." Later albums showcased Hardin's exquisitely fragile voice and impeccable phrasing, but, as Mitchell Cohen writes in the 2021 book *White Label Promo Preservation Society*, "after those first two Verve Forecast albums, and third one live at Town Hall (1968) it all skidded off the rails, and Hardin never pulled together a consistent album of original songs again." Even Erik Jacobsen, his biggest champion, could no longer work with him. "It was heartbreaking to see such a fabulous talent self-destruct," Jacobsen said.

In spite of mounting health issues and his ongoing dependency, Tim Hardin had performed at the Newport Folk Festival in 1966, sold out Royal Albert Hall in 1968, and performed at Woodstock in 1969. Describing the Woodstock performance, drummer Steve Booker, now known as Muruga, described the scene in *Relix* magazine: "After a while we played and, I must say, not well. To everyone's disappointment, Tim Hardin was more stoned that we would have wanted. Since he was the director and the one we needed to follow, it was rather difficult because he barely wobbled up on stage." Like John Sebastian, Steve Katz was a friend of Hardin's. "Tim wasn't fun to be around. I was young and innocent, I didn't know from heroin," Katz told me, describing Hardin's nodding out before his Newport '65 appearance yet delivering a brilliant performance once onstage. Katz added, "But he was not a bad person." Others were less kind. Including Jacobsen, who told me just the opposite. Ultimately, Hardin's addiction would finally do him in, at age thirty-nine, amid a final comeback attempt in 1980. He exited the scene as quietly as he had entered.

The Blues Project

Since the decade began, Danny Kalb had been one of the most in-demand acoustic guitarists in the Village, performing on sessions and live performances with Phil Ochs, Bob Dylan, Judy Collins, and Pete Seeger. As a protege and student of Dave Van Ronk, he played acoustic guitar in Van Ronk's Ragtime Jug Stompers. But walking into the Night Owl one evening in November 1964 and hearing Tim Hardin's signature mix of blues, country, R & B, and jazz—played on *electric* guitar—switched on his own electrical impulses and sparked a desire to form his own band. Earlier that year, Elektra Records had recruited Kalb and seven other white, twenty-something male artists to contribute tracks to an album called *The Blues Project: A Compendium of the Very Best on the Urban Blues Scene*. It was an appealing and entertaining collection of performances, including some truly excellent takes from Van Ronk and Eric Von Schmidt, some magnificent guitar-picking from Kalb, and two spectacular vocal showcases for Geoff Muldaur. There was more virtuoso harmonica-blowing by John Sebastian, and Bob Dylan even made an anagrammed appearance, as "Bob *Landy*," playing piano for Geoff Muldaur. The album sold over three hundred thousand copies and, for many white kids all over the country, would serve to introduce them to the blues.

But I'm not gonna lie. The extensive back cover and inside-booklet liner notes to this album are filled with some truly questionable assertions, beginning with an opening-line zinger by Barry Hansen, the Los Angeles editor of the *Little Sandy Review*: "It seems inevitable that by 1970 most of the blues worth hearing will be sung by white men." Similar statements follow, written by the *LSR*'s New York editor, Paul Nelson. Inside, within the four pages of additional, often painful-to-read notes, one of the performers, twenty-one-year-old Dave "Snaker" Ray, later of Koerner, Ray & Glover, explained, "As far as white men playing blues, that's all who do play blues . . . the new Negroes are too busy (doing other things)." Reading these notes in 2021 gave me pause again and again. Of course, appropriation and fetishization of Black music and culture were nothing new. But the fact that these notes were written in the middle of the civil rights movement, a struggle that was supported by some of the very same Greenwich Village folk musicians who performed on the album, made it all the more shocking to me.

Greg Tate, writer, musician, producer, and founding member of the Black Rock Coalition, wrote in the introduction of his highly recommended book *Everything but the Burden: What White People Are Taking from Black Culture*, "Readers of Black music history are often struck by the egregious turns of public relations puffery that saw Paul Whiteman crowned the King of Swing in the 1920s, Benny Goodman anointed the King of Jazz in the 1930s, Elvis Presley propped up as the King of Rock and Roll in the 1960s, and Eric Clapton awarded the title of the world's greatest guitar player (ostensibly of the blues) in the 1960s." Not everything had a-changed.

After the release of *The Blues Project* album, Kalb wasted little time in putting together the Danny Kalb Quartet in early 1965. But it was a false start. After a two-week run at the Gaslight, signing with the prestigious William Morris Agency, and then getting booked to open for the Lovin' Spoonful at the Night Owl, Kalb picked up and went to Europe for the summer instead. As did bandmate Artie Traum, Happy's brother. Everyone, it seems, was just so freewheelin' in those days. Kalb returned to New York, but his quartet's rhythm guitarist, Traum, remained in Europe. A replacement was needed, and he began the search.

Fretted Instruments, like Allan Block's Sandal Shop and Izzy Young's Folklore Center, served as a meeting place for musicians. "How did we communicate before cell phones?" Fretted Instruments shop owner Marc Silber posed to me. "These places allowed us to stay in touch. Who's on tour? Who's looking for a guitar player? Who is somebody currently dating? This is how we stayed in touch with each other without phones." Circa 1962, Izzy Young had relocated the Folklore Center from its original address on MacDougal Street to 321 Sixth Avenue. It was right next door to Fretted Instruments, at number 319. Both were on the matching second floors of side-by-side nineteenth-century townhouses, situated at the foot of West Third Street and next to the Waverly Theater. Izzy Young became a partner in the shop with Marc Silber. Himself a blues guitarist and musician's musician who appears multiple times in David Gahr and Robert Shelton's beautiful 1968 photo book, *The Face of Folk Music*, Silber sold high-end Martin and vintage guitars and did custom shop repairs, such as the rather daunting service of converting six-string guitars to twelve-string. John Sebastian was working at the shop at the time and described for me the time he was minding the register one afternoon in 1963 and Bob Dylan came into the shop to purchase the early 1930s Gibson Nick Lucas Special acoustic guitar that he played on his next two albums, *Another Side of Bob Dylan* and *Bringing It All Back Home*. About Fretted Instruments, "It was a *hang*," Sebastian told me. "Everybody ended up there at some point." Along with the venues, cafés, and bars, it was part of the complex social network of the Village.

On a Saturday afternoon, while stopping in at Fretted Instruments on his search for a guitarist, Danny Kalb ran into Steve Katz, whom he knew as a fellow former student of Dave Van Ronk and from the Even Dozen Jug Band. Katz was teaching guitar lessons in the shop. Impulsively, Kalb invited Katz to join his reconstituted combo and, with Katz accepting, they began rehearsing the group in the basement of the Night Owl Café. Later, they moved rehearsals to the grungy Hotel Albert (where else?), where they shared the space with James Taylor and the Flying Machine and Mose Allison. Taking the title of the successful album he had recently been a part of, Kalb named the new band the Blues Project.

Steve Katz had never played electric guitar before and had to adjust, first adding a DeArmond electric pickup to his Gibson J-200 acoustic but eventually settling on a "real" electric guitar, a classic Gibson Les Paul. Bass player and NYU student Andy Kulberg also played flute. Roy Blumenfeld on drums and vocalist Tommy Flanders rounded out the initial lineup. Their first shows were October 7–9 at the Night Owl. That same month, Tom Wilson brought them in for an audition, recording a demo for Columbia

Records. It was then that Wilson recommended Al Kooper to play keyboards on the session. Almost imme-diately following the demo recording date, Kooper was asked to formally join the band. By November, just a month after their debut, the Blues Project was performing at the Café Au Go Go on Bleecker Street, where Lenny Bruce had twice been arrested and where they would soon become the house band. The list—and range—of acts who performed at the Café Au Go Go is staggering. "Café Au Go Go was an amazing venue at an amazing time," Katz recalled. Dylan, who had wanted Al Kooper to join his *own* backing band, would come to the shows and heckle the Blues Project from the audience. "He became really arrogant. He just lost all humility. A brilliant kid, but he was a *putz*," Katz told me. Later that month, having signed to MGM's Verve/Folkways with Tom Wilson, who brought them with him when he migrated from Columbia Records to MGM, they began recording live performances to be included on their debut album, *Live at the Café Au Go Go*, released in March 1966. By the time the album was released, and following a promotional trip to California, vocalist Tommy Flanders had exited the group, which settled into a five-piece, with Kalb, Katz, and Kooper sharing vocal duties.

While the Blues Project *did* play blues, they also played rock and roll, rhythm and blues, rocked-up gospel, and folk-rock—like their electric arrangements of Donovan's "Catch the Wind" and Eric Ander-sen's "Violets of Dawn." The phrase "blues" seemed to now cover a lot more ground than it had even less than a year prior. The Blues Project were a surprising blend of sounds and styles. Listening now, besides sounding quintessentially sixties, because they helped create what we call quintessentially sixties, you can see how they—along with the Paul Butterfield Blues Band—were massively influential in the shaping of late-1960s and '70s rock music. When I spoke with Al Kooper, he spoke about the Blues Project's relation-ship with the Butterfield band. "There was a very strong understanding between the two bands. And there was a week when we played on the same bill, at the Café Au Go Go, that was amazing. I think the people who came to see us immediately understood what the difference was between the two bands, without hav-ing to put it into words: They were exceptionally traditional, and we weren't. We both loved the same sources and understood that, but we were going somewhere else." Kooper also cites bluesman John Hammond Jr. as an inspiration. Hammond, son of producer John Hammond, did not receive professional support from his father yet became a successful, influential interpreter of the blues who has released at least thirty-four albums since first signing with Vanguard in 1962 and is still active today. Simultaneously, England had been experiencing a blues revival of its own, led by Alexis Korner's Blues Incorporated, John Mayall, and Brian Jones and other members of the Rolling Stones, who formed in 1962. With Cream founders Jack Bruce and Ginger Baker, and Clapton, the British blues movement, a primarily electrified adaptation of American blues, was to flourish throughout the decade.

The Blues Project's live shows were positively combustible, with Kalb's superfast electric guitar licks, Kooper's rhythmic, glissing keyboards and organ outbursts, and Katz's solidly anchoring rhythm guitar. There were drum solos. There were *flute* solos (especially in Kooper's instrumental "Flute Thing"), often with long, repeating tape delay effects. Performing at the Avalon Ballroom and the Fillmore, in San Francisco, all of this would be augmented with a psychedelic light show, consisting more of fluid colors than the superimposed images of Warhol's projections on the Velvet Underground. According to Katz, the light show encouraged the group to experiment further. "For the musicians onstage, these light shows were hypnotic and fantastic. While almost begging you to take drugs, the light shows inspired improvisation," Katz wrote in his memoir. Katz's own "Steve's Song" (its actual title, "September Fifth," was misinterpreted by a hasty label employee) was pure psychedelic folk-rock, with an intro that was practically medieval. However they came to be, the Blues Project's improvisations—like Paul Butterfield's—would be the beginnings of "jam bands" and of full-blown, electric, psychedelic blues. Listening to their eleven-plus-minute opus on their first studio album, *Projections* (Verve Folkways, 1966), "Two Trains Running"—Kalb's tribute to Muddy Waters that combined that song with Waters' "Catfish Blues"—you can hear the dynamic template that Led Zeppelin would use in songs like "Dazed and Confused" more than two years later. And you don't need to strain to hear traces of the Blues Project's extended, expanded arrangements in the music of the Grateful Dead and even post–Syd Barrett Pink Floyd. It's all there. But when I asked Katz, he told me, with humility, "I didn't really know what other bands were doing at the time or if we influenced anyone. Muddy was Danny's mentor, but Danny interpreted Muddy's music to fit his own style, which, of course, changed from day to day. That's why our records never came close to matching our live shows. Things were always changing." I asked Arthur Levy, journalist and founder of the 1970s music magazine *Zoo World*, about the Blues Project and their place in rock history, and he told me, "That transitional moment was unique to the rock of the late '60s and '70s, that rootedness in folk and blues and trad-jazz, with their rich traditions of jamming and improvisation. It never happened in the subsequent generation."

Between the Velvets' influence on 1970s glam, punk, and art rock; Tim Hardin, Eric Andersen, and Janis Ian creating the new face of the singer-songwriter; the Lovin' Spoonful's folk-rock; and the Blues Project's psychedelic jamming, the next ten years of popular music were pretty much covered.

There But for Fortune

While sonic possibilities were being explored by the bands in the Village, singer-songwriters were testing their own limits. Phil Ochs's "There But for Fortune" was recorded by Joan Baez and by his former roommates, Jim & Jean, on their debut album in 1965. Like many of Ochs's songs, it was about empathy—an emotion that was apparent not only in the words but in the crafted, somber melody. It's a song that evokes and emits compassion regardless of who is singing it.

> And I'll show you a young man with so many reasons why
> And there but for fortune, may go you or I

In Village circles, it was widely known that Dylan was especially brutal to Phil Ochs. It was a private conflict that was played out in public for all to see and hear. Michael Schumacher's book, *There But for Fortune*, details the scenes. According to Schumacher, as well as to Bob Spitz in his 1989 Dylan biography, and to Ochs himself in a series of *Broadside* interviews, Dylan would taunt not only Phil, but Eric Andersen, Dave Van Ronk, Tom Paxton, and others, an elite group of some of the best songwriters the Village had produced, while holding court at the Kettle of Fish. "He was beautiful then, and he was also super arrogant then," Ochs told Gordon Friesen for *Broadside*, "and he used to walk around and try to categorize all of the other writers in terms of himself. He went through this whole fantastic riff of how we shouldn't really write, and that he was the writer. I would admit it was true, that he was the *best* writer." "Hey, maybe you think you're gonna make it like me? Nobody's gonna make it," Dylan would jeer. Spitz called it "playful," and most of his victims, like Van Ronk, brushed it off. It seemed so long ago that Dylan had said, flatteringly, "I just can't keep up with Phil."

According to Eric Andersen, "There wasn't really a big competition thing going on. The only one you were competing with was yourself." And Tom Paxton contends, "We were rivals, of course, but we were much more than rivals. We were friends and colleagues and supporters." But Phil, who admired Dylan so much, took it all personally. "You ought to find a new line of work, Ochs," Dylan would tell Phil. "You're not doing very much in this one." Writer, DJ, and Sirius XM radio host David Fricke posed this: "Maybe Dylan was especially hard on Phil because he saw how much he actually had, and how much he could give." Others saw it differently. "Dylan was always brutal," Len Chandler weighed in. "It was always competitive between him and Phil." Night Owl owner Joe Marra was more blunt. "Oh, he was a nasty son of a bitch," Marra said of Dylan.

As Phil Ochs told Gordon Friesen on *Broadside Ballads, Vol. 11: Interviews with Phil Ochs*, one day in 1965, at a photoshoot with Jerry Schatzberg, Dylan played for Ochs a new recording he was proud of and planned to release as a single. David Blue was also there. Accounts differ whether the song was "Can You Please Crawl Out Your Window?" or "One of Us Must Know (Sooner or Later)." After playing the song, Dylan asked Ochs what he thought of it. "I said I didn't like it," Ochs recalled to *Broadside*. Instantly angry,

Dylan replied "WHAT? What do you mean you don't like it?" "I told him, 'Well, it's not as good as your old stuff.' And I said, speaking commercially, I said it wouldn't sell. And he got *furious*." Dylan was still fuming when a limo arrived to take the three to an uptown club. As Schumacher wrote, Dylan continued, "You're crazy, man. It's a great song. You only know protest, that's all." Suddenly, while heading up Sixth Avenue, Dylan told the driver to stop the car. Pulling over to the curb, Dylan demanded, twice, that Ochs get out of the car. "Get out, Ochs." "He said to get out of the car. So I got out of the car," recalled Ochs. "And that's the last time I saw Dylan." As he was stepping out, Dylan mocked Phil one more time, hurling, "You're not a folksinger. You're a journalist." The two would not associate with each other again for nearly a decade. At least Phil was able to leave by the door and was not forced to crawl out the limo's window. Imagining it now, knowing Ochs's fragile psyche, the humiliation must have been hard to bear. You can hear it in his stuttering retelling two years later.

Of course, Ochs was correct about Dylan's song, whichever one it was. Neither was a commercial hit: "Can You Please Crawl Out Your Window" peaked at number 58 on the charts, and "One of Us Must Know (Sooner or Later)" fared even more poorly, reaching only 119. But ultimately, these chart positions were of little consequence for Dylan. In 2020, he would sell the publishing rights to his catalog of songs to Universal Music, for an estimated $250 and $300 million, according to the *New York Times*. Then, in January 2022, he would sell the rights for his master recordings to Sony Music, Universal's competitor, for another estimated $200 to $300 million, making these among the largest single-artist deals the music industry has ever seen.

Dylan's next single, "Positively 4th Street," was a hit and was one of the most vindictive, spiteful, vengeful rants ever committed to vinyl. Aimed at doubters and critics, it made "Like a Rolling Stone" seem like the theme to *Mister Rogers' Neighborhood*. The mischievous "king of folk" had transformed into the punishing despot leader of rock, using AM radio as a kind of prehistoric Twitter to crush his perceived enemies. Musically, the song was a repetitive loop, like an endless, circular, one-sided argument. Its lyrics could have referred to any number of people, including those in the folk community who criticized him for abandoning them. Or— doubtfully—he could have been singing about another Fourth Street entirely. Izzy Young, whose Folklore Center had been a second home to the young Dylan, was a suspected target. Speaking about the song to Anthony Scaduto in *Bob Dylan: An Intimate Biography* (1971), Young said, "Dylan comes in and takes from us, uses my resources, then he leaves and he gets bitter. He writes a bitter song. He was the one who left."

You've got a lotta nerve to say you got a helping hand to lend
You just want to be on the side that's winnin'

Yet, for all its anger and derisiveness, the song resonated with listeners and still does. Its brutal, raw lyrics, juxtaposed with a jaunty, tack piano–driven arrangement, opened up more possibilities for singer-songwriters, for example, Joni Mitchell, who has said of the song, "I remember thinking as I heard it for the first time, "I guess we can write about anything now—any feeling." Reaching number seven on *Billboard*, it was one of Dylan's biggest hits. Regardless of Dylan's personal target or gripe, listeners had their own, and he spoke for them. He was Brando as Johnny on his Triumph motorcycle in *The Wild One*, lashing out. "Nobody tells me what to do. You keep needlin' me. If I want to, I'm gonna take this joint apart and you're not gonna know what hit you," says Johnny. Dylan seemed to be speeding on his own slick and slippery road, straddling his own Triumph Tiger motorcycle, wearing his Triumph T-shirt, racing either to or away from something as fast as he could go. It was hard to see where he was headed, but it was easy to see something had to give.

Chapter Eleven

On of the
Witch

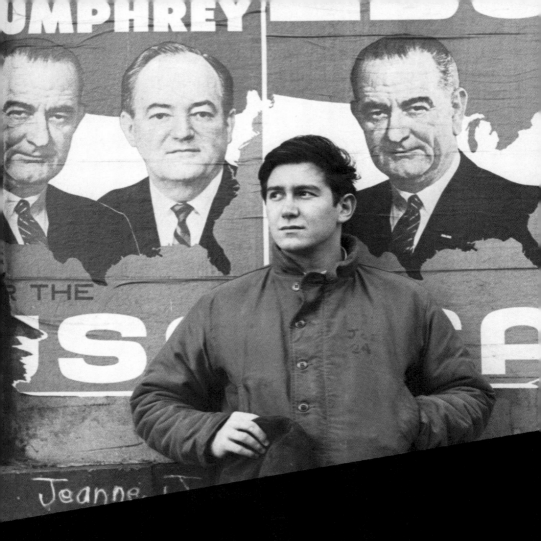

Phil Ochs, photographed on the streets of the Village in 1966

> *A golden carrot of pure wealth was tossed in*
> *front of everybody, literally,*
> *and literally everybody grabbed at it.*
> —Phil Ochs

While the phrase "You're a *journalist!*" may have been hurled as an insult,

it was in fact, accurate. Even Phil's friend, author Marc Eliot, whose first book was his 1979 Ochs biography *Death of a Rebel*, told me, "Phil was basically a journalist. It's really what he was and, if he had lived, he would probably have been a journalist." While studying journalism at Ohio State University, Phil had developed a fresh, satirical style of reviewing music and politics in the college paper, *The Lantern*, and in the campus humor magazine, *The Sundial*. Humor and satire were often missing in folk circles, and Ochs brought them in spades when he arrived to the Village. He began writing reviews and articles for *Broadside* in March 1963 and then for *Modern Hi-Fi & Stereo Review*, the *Village Voice*, *Cavalier*, and other publications. And he did so with a mix of sensitivity and sarcasm that foreshadowed sardonic rock critics like Lester Bangs writing in *Creem* in the 1970s. An impressive collection of Ochs's writings, *I'm Gonna Say It Now: The Writings of Phil Ochs*, edited by David "Lapis" Cohen, was published by Backbeat Books in 2021. But Ochs's unique dual talent of being both an artist and a music journalist might have done more harm than good for him personally, aggravating his already schizophrenic nature and causing him to get hit from all sides. Besides Phil having to endure *Dylan's* barbs, music critics could be especially harsh, perhaps because they knew he was playing their game from the inside and, as both an artist and critic, was able to play both sides of it.

In August 1965, Ochs wrote a stinging letter to the *Village Voice* slamming a critic who had tried to use him as ammunition against Dylan, portraying a fierce rivalry between the two. "It ain't me, babe," Ochs wrote. "I'm only a writer who, in fact, goes out of his way to defend Dylan and his changes." And to be sure, he had done so, many times in *Broadside* and elsewhere, regardless of the friction between the two. But the serious war between factions in the Village folk scene, triggered in part by the success of Dylan and his new song style, was rooted in a problem that was bigger than the both of them. The scene was suffering from the shock treatment of commercial success. "The whole Village thing where guys would trade songs and sit around in circles saying, 'I've got one,' and 'I've got one,' that had gone away. That had turned into 'How do we sell records?' not about 'How good a writer are we?' And that was his downfall. Phil wanted to be a star, but he didn't know how to do it," Marc Eliot explained. David Amram often tells me that, in the sixties, it was considered a mortal sin to have any kind of success "because then you were perceived as 'selling out.' And that was the most horrible sin." But now that some in the Village were attaining it, it was only natural for the others to want it. "God help the troubadour who tries to be a star," Ochs would write in his song "Chords of Fame."

Always the observer as well as a participant in his own competitive UK scene, Donovan wrote, in his 1966 song "Season of the Witch," a track on his influential psychedelic folk album, *Sunshine Superman*,

> *When I look over my shoulder, what do you think I see?*
> *Some other cat lookin' over his shoulder at me*

Richard & Mimi Fariña

Richard and Mimi Fariña had been living in idyllic Carmel Valley, California. There they came up with an appealing acoustic guitar and dulcimer sound that suggested traditional folk but was combined with rhythmic, open-tuning ragas and contemporary rock and roll, at times in equal measures. The breezy sound seemed to have sprung from the Carmel countryside itself, and Richard Fariña's Beat-inspired wordplay was beginning to give Dylan a run for his—now considerable—money. Richard had obviously learned a lot about traditional folk music from his years with Carolyn Hester, as well as from his old friends at the White Horse Tavern, the rowdy rebel-song-singing Clancy Brothers, and he put the knowledge to good use. And his pointed protest songs picked up where Dylan had left off. Harmonizing with Mimi, Richard created delightfully effective, folky grooves that were often danceable and uplifting, especially when augmented by Bruce Langhorne's exceptional electric guitar playing and trademark tambourine accents. Langhorne was yet another important element borrowed from his former wife, whom she had invited to play on her Columbia debut.

Making their professional debut at the first Big Sur Folk Festival in California on June 21, 1964, Richard and Mimi soon began performing on the Cambridge folk scene, where they met up with Eric Andersen, Tom Rush, and others. They spent considerable time with Dylan and Mimi's sister Joan, in Woodstock, New York, and on excursions to the Village. Their repertoire grew quickly, and the duo were signed to Vanguard Records. The title of their debut, *Celebrations for a Grey Day,* became prophetic when they performed at the fateful Newport Folk Festival in 1965. Soon after their set began, the skies opened and, dare I say, a hard rain fell. But instead of stopping the show, as announced by Peter Yarrow from the stage, they continued to defiantly play in the rain, adding musicians and guests including sister Joan, and encouraging the audience to dance in the mud, in what we might look back on now as a mini-Woodstock.

Pete Seeger described the scene in his book, *The Incompleat Folksinger* (1973). "Not a soul scurried for shelter," Seeger wrote. "The music played on, hotter and stronger. Some in the audience started stripping, and dancing in the downpour. Everyone, soaked to the skin, was hollering for more." The duo's appearance on Seeger's *Rainbow Quest* show (episode 17) is a highlight of Pete's television series. Seeger joined in for a few songs and listened intently when they broke into "House Un-American Blues Activity Dream," a song about the recent experiences of an American who went to Cuba and was indicted for breaking the travel ban. It's an acoustic rock and roll song—punctuated with a dash of Elvis Presley in the "uh-huh-huh" refrains at the end of each verse. As Carolyn Hester said, Richard was surely not a real folksinger. But regardless of the genre, watching the footage now, the sound he and Mimi came up with was compelling, and the subject matter surely resonated with Pete, who responded with a hearty "Woo-hoo!"

> *Well, I was lying there unconscious, feeling kind of exempt*
> *When the judge said that silence was a sign of contempt*

On September 15, 1963, one of the most horrific events of the civil rights movement had occurred when four young Black girls, who were attending Sunday school, were killed in a vicious KKK bombing attack on the church where Dr. King and other leaders had launched a campaign to register African American voters. Racist Alabama governor George Wallace had been quoted a week earlier in the *New York Times* saying that, to stop integration, his state needed a few "first-class funerals." He got just that. The level of hate and the deaths of innocents—in a decade that marked the death of innocence itself—shocked and saddened the nation. Richard Fariña was moved to write "Birmingham Sunday," a song that Joan Baez would record on her fifth Vanguard album in 1964. Using the melody of "I Loved a Lass," a traditional folk ballad from the British Isles that Fariña had learned from and performed with Carolyn Hester, he crafted one of the most haunting songs of the civil rights era. Langston Hughes called it a "quiet protest song" in his liner notes for the Baez album. In 2017, contemporary Americana musician Rhiannon Giddens recorded an epic version for her *Freedom Highway* album.

> *On Birmingham Sunday the blood ran like wine*
> *And the choir kept singing of freedom*

Judy Collins was quick to record Fariña's jaunty "Pack Up Your Sorrows" and invited him to play dulcimer and write the liner notes for her *Fifth Album* on Elektra. With songs like "Bold Marauder" and "Hard Lovin' Loser," Richard Fariña was proving himself as a songwriter. Both of his Vanguard albums with Mimi had been positively reviewed. And his novel, the cult classic *Been Down So Long It Looks Like Up to Me*, the one Carolyn Hester had helped type for him back in 1962, was finally published by Random House on April 28, 1966. All the personal intensity that had swept Hester off her feet in 1960 and had charmed Mimi when they met at that picnic in France, all of the alpha-male competitiveness and drive that forced the Greenwich Village scene to take notice—they were all coming to a climax. Fariña was achieving the fame that he had been so ardently seeking.

Saturday, April 30, two days after the official publication of his book, was Mimi's twenty-first birthday. After a midday book-signing party at Thunderbird Bookstore in Carmel Valley, there was a surprise birthday party that Richard had secretly planned for his young wife at the home of her *other* sister, Pauline. One of the guests, William Hinds, had ridden his new, red Harley-Davidson Sportster motorcycle to the party. Richard took notice of the awesome bike parked outside, with its chrome engine and twin chrome tailpipes, and asked Hines for a ride. It was just after 7:00 p.m. when Richard handed his wallet and keys to Mimi to hold until he returned. As Hines started up the Harley, the motor roared with its signature, earth-shaking rumble, and Fariña climbed on back. Heading east toward Cachagua Community Park, they opened it up on the open road through the rolling hills of Carmel, reaching speeds of ninety miles per hour. Fariña probably found it hard to stay firmly planted on the bike as Hines took each winding turn. It was less than fifteen minutes later when Mimi and the others at the party heard sirens in the distance. The guys had lost control and wiped out on Carmel Valley Road, just about a mile from the house. Though driver Hines would survive the crash, Richard had been thrown across two fences and into an embankment and was killed instantly.

Mimi, still holding Richard's wallet and identification, was required to identify the body. She had become a widow on her twenty-first birthday.

Society's Child

How must it have felt for Janis Ian to perform at the Village Gate in 1964—at age thirteen? What must have the audience thought? And, indeed, what must other musicians have thought—seeing such a young girl perform original songs that rivaled their own? Born Janis Fink to liberal, Jewish-born parents in Farmingdale, New Jersey, Janis was drawn to music by age two, learning piano and a variety of instruments, including guitar, by the time she was approaching her teens. Odetta, performing on Harry Belafonte's landmark *Tonight with Belafonte* television special in 1959, Joan Baez, by way of her records, and later, Buffy Sainte-Marie had inspired the young Janis to sing and write her own music. It was in 1963, when Janis Ian was twelve, that she wrote her first song, "Hair of Spun Gold," published in *Broadside* the following year. By that time, she had legally changed her name to Janis Ian—borrowing her brother's middle name—and was booked to perform at a hootenanny that the magazine was sponsoring at the Village Gate. Being on the scene allowed her to meet and connect with other musicians, including Reverend Gary Davis, from whom she hoped to get some tips. Davis was preparing for some shows at the Gaslight Café. "His wife took a liking to me and told the [manager] of the Gaslight, Clarence Hood, that she needed me to open for Reverend Gary," Ian told Carl Wiser for *Songfacts* in 2003. It was at that show, as a result of that gracious favor, that Janis was "discovered" and brought to meet producer George "Shadow" Morton.

At the time, Shadow Morton had been known for his extravagant girl group pop productions like "Remember (Walking in the Sand)" and "Leader of the Pack," both in 1964, for the Shangi-Las; records that contained scripted, spoken-word sections and sound effects (such as a revving motorcycle on "Pack") and were played out as mini teen dramas. Other than his contemporary, the brilliant-but-mad-as-a-hatter Phil Spector, Morton was perhaps the most *unlikely* producer in the music industry to produce an acoustic *folk* artist.

Of the eight songs Janis performed for Morton in his office that day, he gravitated toward one in particular, which he immediately began planning to record and deliver to Atlantic Records as part of a production deal. It was a song that, according to Ian, she had started writing at age thirteen in the guidance counselor's office at her East Orange, New Jersey, school, where she was among only a handful of white students. She continued writing on the bus ride home. "I was seeing it around me when Black parents were worried about their daughters or sons dating white girls or boys." The song, "Baby I've Been Thinking," was eventually retitled "Society's Child."

> *Now I could understand your tears and your shame*
> *She called you "boy" instead of your name*

The production by Morton drew its drama not from special effects but from the music and lyrics, the arrangement—by Janis and Artie Butler—that used perfectly placed tempo and key changes, and an innocent-but-defiant vocal performance from Janis. The record was to be an auspicious but troubled beginning for the fifteen-year-old. Atlantic Records rejected it, returning the master back to Morton, explaining they could not release it due to the song's subject matter. According to Ian in a 2003 interview with *Speaking Freely*, a television program produced by the First Amendment Center in Washington, DC, the record was shopped to labels by Shadow Morton. "We went through twenty-two record companies in the United States, all of whom passed," Janis recalled. It was MGM's Verve/Forecast label that finally took a chance and released the record in 1967. "I honestly think they wanted it as a tax loss," Janis joked on *Speaking Freely*. While getting local radio play from Murray the K in New York City on the recently launched WOR-FM and on radio stations in a few other cities, the record was banned on many radio stations nationally.

Finally, it was Leonard Bernstein, presenting Janis on the primetime CBS television special *Inside Pop: The Rock Revolution*, airing on April 25, 1967, who helped break the ban. Bernstein praised the record's composition, arrangement, and production, noting "its strange use of harpsichord, and that cool, nasty electric organ; there are astonishing key changes and even tempo changes." But he reserved his highest praise for the lyrics: "What Janis has written is a short social document. Not a satire, not a protest, just a picture of a social trap. Of course, underneath it is the spirit of protest, which underlies so many of these pop songs. The implication is, and strongly, that this is not at all the way things ought to be." Less than two months after the Bernstein broadcast, "Society's Child" was peaking on the *Billboard* chart at number fourteen.

Ian's eponymous album was filled with more surprising, striking, and intense songwriting, fuzzy guitars, more of "that nasty electric organ," and liner notes by Robert Shelton, whose writing now sounds as if it is being telegraphed from a bygone era. Shelton can't be blamed—it was. Things were moving quickly now. It was not only *difficult* to keep up, it was impossible. The fact that Janis was only fifteen when she made this album is astonishing, but her age notwithstanding, the toughness of her stance, her confidence, and her attitude reframe gender roles and make it sound almost *post*-folk.

The tour that followed would also prove to be a study in mixed blessings. "On the one hand, I was getting to work with Janis Joplin and Jimi Hendrix and the Stones and hang out backstage and run into them at airports or play after-hours in the Village. And, on the other hand, a lot of the time, groups of ten and twenty people would buy tickets to my concert and sit together, and when I'd hit "Society's Child," they would start screaming: '*Kill the n———-loving bitch!' or 'N——— lover!*' and start chanting that, and try to drive me off the stage," she said on *Speaking Freely*. Still, she persevered. "There's a great Rainer Maria Rilke quote," Janis continued. "He said, 'I don't want to be a poet, I want to change your life.' I read that when I was thirteen, and I decided that was I wanted to do."

José Feliciano

"José Feliciano could walk into any world he wanted to," writer Elijah Wald told me. But although that would become true, that's not how things started out. One of eleven boys, José Feliciano and his family had emigrated from Lares, Puerto Rico, where his father was a farmer. In 1950, when José was five years old, the family moved to New York City, landing in Spanish Harlem, where the senior Feliciano found work as a longshoreman. Born blind due to congenital glaucoma, José had been drawn to music by the time he was three, was learning accordion by seven, and when he was nine, was playing guitar and performing at El Teatro Puerto Rico, in the Bronx. He listened to and practiced classical and jazz, but it was rock and roll that inspired him to sing. And sing he did, in a style that was, and is, distinctively soulful——with tonal hints of Sam Cooke and Ray Charles——and multilingual. But in the Village, it would be his unique, flamenco-fueled guitar playing that would set him apart.

By 1962, seventeen-year-old José Feliciano had made his way downtown and was performing at the sawdust-floored Café Id, one of the smaller basket houses on MacDougal Street. "It reminded me of a butcher shop but, gosh, it was where it all began for me in Greenwich Village," José told me. Even for a virtuoso guitarist and engaging performer, and even though Dave Van Ronk and Terri Thal had appealed to the musicians' union for help to improve the situation for folksingers on MacDougal Street, it was still impossible to make any money in the basket houses. "But I didn't care about that," he insisted. "I just wanted to be part of the music scene." Feliciano developed a signature style that merged genres, languages, and cultures effortlessly——a superfast "Flight of the Bumble Bee" one minute, Ray Charles's "I Got a Woman" the next, followed by "Walk Right In" sung in *Yiddish*. I asked José if he felt he fit in with the others on the coffeehouse circuit. "No, not really," he answered. "Part of the time I did, even though I knew I didn't play like them so much. . . . I'm sure it was mostly just 'me.' I always wanted to fit in, so who knows, really? I've met up since then with a lot of people with whom I'd played in those days, like John Sebastian and others, and it's always a great experience, reminiscing about that magical time." I can vouch for that; I was there for one of those happy reunions when I produced the 2018 *Music + Revolution* concert at SummerStage in Central Park. "Richard, let me warn you. They hate me!" José told me when I invited him to participate. The truth was just the opposite——Sebastian and the others on the bill all loved him. But back in the mid-1960s, José's talent and ease of showmanship must have been at least somewhat intimidating. While most were Carter-picking three chords, José was playing classical and flamenco masterpieces, bringing down the house, and getting standing ovations. José was keenly aware and familiar with the others in the Village scene and was able to create his own space among them. "I loved Doc Watson, a blind guitarist. I really liked Len Chandler and Fred Neil. And Joan Baez.

But then again, *everybody* loved her! I really enjoyed the tune she did, 'Gospel Ship.' Harry Belafonte was revered at that time, too, and I loved him, as well . . . as I do to this day. And I liked Phil Ochs's writing a lot. 'There But for Fortune' . . . What a great song. What a troubled man."

"Referring to José Feliciano, Van Ronk said, 'Once in a while someone would come along and you knew they would not be in Greenwich Village very long,'" Elijah Wald told me. José's talent could not be contained by the Café Id or any of the coffeehouses. By 1964, José was invited to perform at the Newport Folk Festival and had graduated to Gerde's Folk City, where he was discovered and signed on the spot by RCA Records producer Jack Somer. Somer had been producing Latin, big band, and jazz albums for RCA as well as signing and producing Odetta, including her brilliant *Odetta Sings Dylan* in 1965. Robert Shelton was at the Gerde's show and, writing in the *New York Times*, called Feliciano a "ten-fingered wizard." Dave Van Ronk didn't hold back either. "He blew me away. . . . I said, 'My God, *you can't do that* with a guitar.'"

"Signing with RCA, and Jack Somer who found me at Gerde's, was my real birth as an artist," José told me. "Everyone was so excited for me . . . everyone, that is, except for my dad. But because of RCA, I had a career. First in South America, then back in the States, with [producer] Rick Jarrard and 'Light My Fire,' 'California Dreamin','' and 'Feliz Navidad,' among others." Feliciano also displayed a particularly off-the-cuff (and at times off-color) sense of humor. He famously did a Bob Dylan impersonation one evening at Gerde's, unknowingly when Dylan was in attendance. "After I was finished, somebody asked if I knew he was in the audience, and I cringed. He didn't come up to me, so I'm still wondering! Seriously, other times though, when he'd come up to me, he'd give me a hug—he was always nice to me." As well he should have been. Feliciano recorded several insightful covers of Dylan songs beginning with "Don't Think Twice, It's All Right" on his 1965 debut *The Voice and Guitar of José Feliciano*, and a stark, stunning reading of "Masters of War" on his 1966 album *A Bag Full of Soul*.

"Greenwich Village was a place where people didn't care if you had some condition that may have held one back in the 'real world,' so to speak," José told me. "Everybody has something going on with themselves, either physical or emotional or whatever. But if you were smart and had the passion, you were in an environment where you could excel and really make it happen for yourself. I love Greenwich Village and bless the day my friend, Vera Perret, 'introduced us' when I was just a kid. It was Mecca for a musician in those days and one thing's for sure—I never looked back."

RCA Records did well with, and for, José, beginning with the very first release. Produced by Somer and showing off José's remarkable musical range, José's debut was a collection that stands as a perfect snapshot of that moment in the Village. Over the next three years, an impressive succession of releases followed, both for the Latin American and general markets. Then, in 1968, having already achieved fame in Latin America, he would experience, with his album *Feliciano!*——produced by RCA producer Rick Jarrard——the kind of commercial breakthrough in the States that changes lives and creates mainstream legends. Even on that album, with its lavish orchestrations, Feliciano still improvised like crazy, on vocal and guitar, just as he might have done in the Village coffeehouses. The album garnered four Grammy nominations and two wins, including for Best New Artist. Suddenly, he was everywhere. It seemed the whole world was in love with José Feliciano. But in the midst of it all, 1968 would throw him a politically pitched curve ball, and it would happen in the middle of the World Series.

Like the concurrent releases of Phil Ochs, Buffy Sainte-Marie, Bob Dylan, Janis Ian, Tim Hardin, Fred Neil, José Feliciano, and many of the others, Eric Andersen's 1966 album *'Bout Changes 'n' Things* (Vanguard Records), produced by Patrick Sky, was a glorious snapshot of its time and place. You can almost hear, feel, and see MacDougal Street when you listen. As I write tonight, here on Waverly Place with the first light of dawn just beginning to come in through my window, I wonder if there is any album being made now, anywhere in the world, that will reflect its time and place as perfectly as the albums that were made in Greenwich Village during the mid-1960s. Surely some will. But I wonder which, and from where? Does a music scene exist in which artists perform, praise, and record each other's songs with such frequency? Where they can capture the genuine interest of the media and take turns in the national spotlight? Where the songs are written and first played in intimate spaces for each other, shared and traded like secrets in a conversation? In which the artists, producers, and accompanists are all friends who hang out together and fight and argue and love? And where history and the surroundings themselves become a mystical, musical element? Though it is impossible to put the peel back on the orange, and nostalgia for eras past is pointless, it's worth a moment of reflection, for musicians, to consider the factors that created such a wealth of music. It must have seemed at the time that it would go on forever.

Thirsty Boots

Hot on the heels of his 1965 debut, *Today Is the Highway*, Eric Andersen had come up with at least three eternal gems on his second album. "Close the Door Lightly When You Go" and "Violets of Dawn" were widely covered in various ways, "Close the Door" becoming a bluegrass standard (even though the original recording is far from bluegrass) and "Violets" being immediately picked up by the Blues Project, the Chad Mitchell Trio, and others. But perhaps most admired was "Thirsty Boots," a song Andersen wrote about the civil rights marches. It would be recorded by the Kingston Trio, later Dylan, but perhaps most famously at the time by Judy Collins, on her own classic snapshot of the era, *Fifth Album*.

Andersen recalled, "It was Phil Ochs who had told Judy Collins about 'Thirsty Boots.' I was supposed to meet her at seven o'clock that evening, and she was about five subway stops down from *Broadside* where I was living at the time. I was in a panic because I knew the song wasn't really finished. I only had two verses. So I wrote another verse on the train, on a matchbook cover. When I got there, I went into the bathroom and wrote it all out on a piece of paper. So by the time she got it, it was a finished song, and she thought it had been this way all along."

> *You've long been on the open road you've been sleepin' in the rain*
> *From dirty words and muddy cells your clothes are soiled and stained*

Although Andersen himself had not marched, he wrote "Thirsty Boots" as a compassionate tribute to those who had and he did participate in other protests and actions. "Phil and I drove down to Hazard, Kentucky, to sing for and support the coal miners on strike. Our future music manager, Arthur Gorson, was the union organizer, and Phil knew him. Bullets flew. A scary time to be trying to enlighten folks about justice in deep Appalachia. The coal mine owners didn't much take to it. The other scary time was that same year, when Debbie [Green] and I accompanied *Village Voice* writer Jack Newfield to Amite County in Mississippi on the Louisiana border to try and enlist people to vote. Bullets flew then too."

True to form, Phil Ochs would put the miners' strike action to words and music, in his song "Hazard, Kentucky."

> *Well, minin' is a hazard in Hazard, Kentucky,*
> *And if you ain't minin' there, well, my friends, you're awful lucky*

A dividend of the topical song movement of the 1960s is that we were left with a diary of the decade.

Summer in the City

The sometimes brutally cold winters of New York City are balanced by often mercilessly hot summers. The concrete-and-brick buildings and streets retain, contain, and amplify the heat. As uncomfortable as it can sometimes be, I have long felt that the extreme changes of season that occur in New York is another factor that finds its way into the music that's created here. Growing up in my home state of seasonless Florida, where the difference between July and November is barely perceptible, is a very different experience. Besides the physical and mental aspects of contending with temperature extremes, and the unifying feeling of knowing that everyone you see around you, rich or poor, is dealing with the same conditions, it is also a marker and reminder of the passing of time. As seasons change, so might the urgency to get things done.

The summer of 1966 was the hottest in nearly one hundred years. The temperature was ninety degrees or higher for thirty-four days in a row in New York City. As Julie Besonen wrote in the *New York Times* on August 9, 2018, "The conflict in Vietnam was also heating up, with 382,010 men drafted into service that year, 151,019 more than the previous year." Domestically, clashes and race riots were breaking out everywhere. It was in that climate that the Lovin' Spoonful had their genre-defying, number one hit, "Summer in the City," a masterstroke of writing, performing, arranging, and producing. In her excellent *Times* piece, Besonen rightfully refers to the song as "apolitical." It brought people together by reminding them of that summer's shared experience, and offered a ray of hope in the lyric "despite the heat it'll be alright." Of course, it was not the first record to address a hot summer, but it did so uniquely, with a sound that spoke to the moment, and it elevated the status of the band artistically. Legendary musician and producer Quincy Jones himself would create a funky, orchestrated cover of the song in 1973; it was, in turn, sampled by at least seventy-eight hip-hop artists in the 1990s, 2000s, and 2010s.

Released on July 4, 1966, "Summer in the City" owed its beginnings to John Sebastian's fourteen-year-old brother Mark, who lived in the family's apartment at 29 Washington Square West, on the fifteenth floor. His bedroom had a view of the Hudson River and, as Mark told Julie Besonen, "I wanted to run away, go down by the docks, dreaming of whatever this romance thing was, having a band of my own." Grabbing a pencil, Mark wrote in his notebook, "Hot town, summer in the city . . . but at night it's a different world," the heart of the song. When he showed it to older brother John, who was visiting, the lyrics got John's attention. Bringing it to the rest of the band, he and bassist Steve Boone col- laborated to complete Mark's song. The arrangement was ambitious, even avant-garde, with its choppy keyboards, stops, edits, Gershwinesque interludes composed by Boone—and sound effects of traffic and a jackhammer, irritations of city life. The opening, with its two-note organ riff that now seems eerily close to John Williams's main title theme of the movie *Jaws* (1975), sets an ominous tone and leads to a minor key, descending chord progression accompanying lyrics kvetching about the oppressive heat. Then it shifts to the major key for "but at night it's a different world," accompanied by bright autoharp strumming. Ahhh, it's gonna be alright after all, the song seems to say. We'll get through this. If this record couldn't make you believe in magic, nothing could.

Admittedly, the Beach Boys had released *Pet Sounds*, a blueprint for orchestral pop, in May, a little less than two months before "Summer in the City." I asked John Sebastian about its influence. "*Pet Sounds* affected all of us playing music at that time," John said. "But I can't say the album opened the idea of using sound effects for us. A much closer influence was *An American in Paris*, in which Gershwin uses the orchestra to imitate traffic." But a difference is that the Lovin' Spoonful was able to create a complex, engaging, pop symphony by themselves—not by using a forty-piece orchestra or the Wrecking Crew but simply with their own rock and folk instrumentation and an additional electric keyboard, played by Artie Schroeck. It hit the top spot on the chart on August 13, 1966, and was the Spoonful's biggest hit. The commercial success of "Summer in the City" signaled yet another musical trend, toward more complex forms of rock that maximized the possibilities of the recording process instead of merely capturing live a performance in the studio. The Beach Boys, in the United States, and the Beatles, in the UK, were two leaders in that charge.

By 1966, the Beatles had inspired but had themselves been strongly influenced by the Greenwich Village scene, and not only by Dylan. The folky, acoustic tones of *Rubber Soul* (1965) had given way to the electric, experimental, and varied sounds of *Revolver* (August 1966), which included a tip-of-the-cap to the Lovin' Spoonful in "Good Day Sunshine," a song that McCartney credits as being inspired by the Spoonful's early 1966 hit "Daydream." On April 18, 1966, John Lennon and George Harrison, on a night off from recording *Revolver*, went to see the Spoonful perform at the Marquee Club in London. Before you knew it, Lennon was wearing Sebastian's signature round, wire-rimmed glasses and had grown the same thick "mutton chop" sideburns. Looking at Lennon on the picture sleeve of the Beatles' March 1968 single, "Lady Madonna," you would think that Sebastian had actually joined the Beatles.

But even with all the admiration and success—a number one single, three hit albums, and no less than nine hits in the top twenty in barely two years—the Lovin' Spoonful found the summer of 1966 to be the beginning of a disharmonious time. In May, Zal Yanovsky and Steve Boone had been arrested in San Francisco for possession of marijuana. Zal, who was Canadian, was threatened with immediate deportation unless he revealed his source. The pressure was intense, and Zal cooperated with police. Although it was kept quiet for a while, sometime after "Summer in the City" had run its course, the story broke in California's burgeoning underground press. Seen as counterculture traitors, the Spoonful lost much of the credibility they had earned. It is also said that Yanovsky had also begun to be disillusioned with the group's direction. When I spoke with their producer Erik Jacobsen, he cited that the group's work on two film scores, Francis Ford Coppola's *You're a Big Boy Now* and Woody Allen's *What's Up, Tiger Lily?*, both in 1966, as distractions that ate up a lot of their time and stalled their momentum. Allen, whom the group knew from performing at the Bitter End and the Café Au Go Go in the Village, was making his directorial debut. But the film was actually a preexisting Japanese spy film to which Allen overdubbed completely unrelated English dialogue. It was not a commercial success and received mixed reviews. "I said, listen, we're working on a third album. We're trying to show we're building a career here, and to put out a goofball album like this. I mean, Sebastian wrote great songs for it, but that's not what the people wanted. They should have been focusing on their own next album, *Hums*, which was an absolutely fabulous album." *Hums of the Lovin' Spoonful* was released in November 1966, over four months after the success of "Summer," and yielded a total of three top-ten hit singles. But, after the disappointing reaction to the *What's Up, Tiger Lily* soundtrack LP, preorders were diminished. By 1967, both Yanovsky and Jacobsen would be out of the picture, and the band would never be the same.

Get Together

Another friend in Erik Jacobsen's circle was Jesse Colin Young. While it's true that Jesse may have landed in the Village at a perfect time, just as the scene was beginning to take off in 1961, by the time he had dropped out of NYU and was playing the basket houses, the twenty-two-year-old found himself in an already overcrowded field. It got me thinking about all the others, all the other Perry Millers who came to the Village whose names we'll never know. That alchemic combination of persistence and luck was never needed more than here. "A lot of serendipitous things needed to happen," Young told me. Luckily, a yearlong rent strike in his East Village apartment building allowed Jesse to live rent-free while he got his act together, and he had gotten a job at the Rockefeller Foundation. But he was getting anxious. If anything was to materialize for him, in his words, "I needed a miracle." Through a connection Jesse's brother-in-law made for him with Walter Bishop, music supervisor at CBS News, he met the renowned and versatile jazz musician Bobby Scott, who was working for Bobby Darin's publishing company at the Brill Building. At the time, Roger McGuinn was also working with Darin, playing twelve-string guitar for the pop star in his folk incarnation. Scott brought Young into Phil Ramone's legendary A & R Recording studio, in the middle of Music Row on West Forty-Eighth Street above Manny's instrument store, for a four-hour session. McGuinn was on hand as a backup but ended up just hanging out, as the record was cut with just Young's vocal and guitar. This one session, produced by Scott, resulted in Young's debut album, *Soul of a City Boy*, released on Capitol Records in 1964. It should be noted that any folksinger releasing a debut in 1964 on Capitol Records, the Beatles' US label, would not have had an easy time getting the label's attention. A second release produced by Scott, *Young Blood* (Mercury Records, 1965), followed, featuring John Sebastian on harmonica, quintessential jazz drummer Grady Tate, and bassist George Duvivier. With his angelically soulful voice and fine acoustic guitar stylings, and under Scott's mentorship, Young got a gig at Club 47 in Cambridge, and his track "Four in the Morning" was picked up by WBZB AM Radio in Boston. Once he was back home in the Village, however, seeing all the new bands starting up, Young wanted to start one of his own. "McGuinn was there doing Beatles impressions. This was the beginning of all the folksingers saying, 'Thanks to the Beatles, we gotta have a band.' That's what gave us the Lovin' Spoonful, the Byrds, Buffalo Springfield, the Youngbloods, a bunch of others. It was a great time," Young remembered.

The angelic intervention that Young is convinced had drawn him to the Village in the first place was still with him. In 1965, he met Cambridge bluegrass musician, folksinger, and ragtime guitar-picker Jerry Corbitt. The duo began performing together, calling themselves the Youngbloods. Along the way they picked up Lowell Levinger on electric Wurlitzer piano and electric guitar (Levinger's full, original, rather arbitrary folksinger nickname, Harmon N. Banana, had by then been shortened to "Banana"), and drummer Joe Bauer. Young told me that it was on a Canadian tour, including two freezing weeks in Winnipeg, that the Youngbloods really got started. "The venues were not yet set up for electric music," Young recalled, "so the sound was *so bad*. People who ran folk clubs were not always ready for a *band*." Back in the Village, the Youngbloods made their debut at Gerde's Folk City and, a few months later, they began alternating with the Blues Project as the house bands at the Café Au Go Go, opening for other acts. "If we were lucky, we'd get twenty dollars apiece for opening. But we had free rehearsal space," Young told me. And that's when angelic intervention once again came into play.

One Sunday afternoon in the fall of 1965, raga-rock vibraphonist and Village fixture Buzzy Linhart was singing a particular song in his trademark style at an open mic Café Au Go Go, when Jesse Colin Young happened to walk in, curious to see if the space was available that day for the Youngbloods to rehearse. Linhart was playing a song that had been written by another star of MacDougal Street, Chet Powers, also known by a number of pseudonyms, including Dino Valenti. Powers/Valenti had played with Fred Neil, Karen Dalton, and most of the Village regulars and was now bicoastal. The song Young heard was an instant, eternal anthem. "I was in love," Young told me. "The heavens opened. I felt as if my life had changed." The song was called "Get Together."

Young then went backstage, introduced himself, and asked Linhart about the song. "Buzzy wrote down the lyrics for me, and I scribbled out the chord changes. I took it into rehearsal with the Youngbloods *the next day*," he recalled to me. By the spring of 1966, the Youngbloods were signed to

RCA Records and were planning their first album. The band chose Felix Pappalardi, now an in-demand session musician and producer whose reputation in the Village had continued to grow, to produce. Within a year, Pappalardi would produce Cream's *Disraeli Gears*—the textbook for psychedelic, heavy blues-rock—and went on to produce their next two albums before cofounding his own heavy rock band, Mountain, with Leslie West.

The Youngbloods album would include songs by Fred Neil, Jimmy Reed, Mississippi John Hurt, and others, along with Young and Corbitt. "Get Together" was beautifully arranged and performed; Pappalardi's unobtrusive production and minimal overdubbing made it one of the *purest* examples of folk-rock. The Youngbloods retained a bit of Buzzy Linhart's raga feel in Banana's guitar soloing, and the tempo, which slightly increases throughout the song, gave the end choruses an even stronger sense of confidence and urgency.

> *Come on, people now, smile on your brother*
> *Everybody get together, try to love one another right now*

But ultimately, what makes the record a classic is Jesse Colin Young's spectacularly understated vocal performance. "Jesse was really the best singer of them all," Erik Jacobsen told me. Once, when I was texting with Dion, who himself is considered one of the best male vocalists of the rock era, he told me that Jesse Colin Young was his favorite singer from the Village scene of the 1960s. "And tell him I said so," Dion added. It's easy to agree. The gentle masculinity of Young's vocal tone is one of the most natural, unaffected, and perfectly pitched voices of *any* era. Because the sincerity and understatement of his singing is anything but preachy or aggressive, the song becomes a call to action *of the heart*. Regardless of other renditions of the song, by the Kingston Trio, Jefferson Airplane, and others, Jesse owns it.

Yet for all the record's perfection, when it was released along with their debut album, *The Youngbloods*, the reaction was far from spectacular. Yes, it was a regional hit in San Francisco during the Summer of Love, but it was not a national hit and stalled well below the midchart point in the *Billboard* Hot 100. The album's opening song, "Grizzly Bear"—actually the 1928 ragtime tune "This Morning She Was Gone" by Jim Jackson—initially saw *slightly* better chart action with its Lovin' Spoonful–style, jug-band vibe than did the stately "Get Together." Until two years later, that is, during the week of February 17, 1969, when the National Conference of Christians and Jews put out a series of public-service television and radio ads using "Get Together" to promote National Brotherhood Week. Though RCA Records was resistant to his efforts to rerelease the two-year-old single, the head of promotion, Augie Bloom, went to bat for the Youngbloods. "He said, 'I want this record out, or I'm leaving the company.' He put his job on the line," Young recalled. Relenting, RCA rereleased the record in June 1969, just a matter of weeks before the Woodstock Festival. This time it was a smash, reaching number five on *Billboard*.

"From the moment I heard those words, I knew I had found my path forward," Jesse would write in the liner notes of his 2019 album, *Dreamers* (BMG Records). And he has always lived up to the lyrics of "Get Together." At the end of the 1970s, he joined forces with Jackson Browne, Bonnie Raitt, Graham Nash, and others to perform in the No Nukes concerts at Madison Square Garden and elsewhere, raising awareness for alternative energy. Of course, he sang "Get Together."

Motorpsycho Nightmare

On July 29, 1966, three months after Richard Fariña's motorcycle accident, Bob Dylan would himself, on a Woodstock road one sunny morning, crash his beloved Triumph Tiger 100. Or something. It was a month after the release of *Blonde on Blonde*, the first double LP from a major rock artist. Four days after the incident, the *New York Times* wrote, "Dylan Hurt in Cycle Mishap" and little else, in a two-sentence, tiny box near the bottom of page 30, just above an ad for dance lessons. Unlike the fatal certainty of Fariña's accident, Dylan's was and is still shrouded in mystery. No medical records or police reports exist, and his own comments were, then and now, minimal. "I had been in a motorcycle accident and I'd been hurt, but I recovered," is all he wrote in *Chronicles*. From that moment and for the next several years, Dylan retreated from public view, a rock-and-roll Greta Garbo, holed up in Woodstock and quietly recording with his backing band from recent tours, the Hawks, now known as the Band. Rick Danko, Richard Manuel, Garth Hudson, and Robbie Robertson, who had been the backing band for his friend John Hammond Jr., backed Dylan on well over one hundred songs—traditional; blues; songs by Tim Hardin, Ian & Sylvia, and John Lee Hooker; and about half originals—recorded in a casual, live style that was the complete antithesis of the current recording trend, often with keyboardist Garth Hudson manning the tape machine. Tiny Tim was summoned to visit, and he performed some Rudy Vallee and other songs from the 1920s and '30s for Dylan and friends. "Mr. Dylan was so nice," Tiny once told me. "I told him, 'Mr. Dylan, you're the Rudy Vallee of your day!' and he told me, 'Tiny, would you like a banana before you go to bed?' I told him, 'No thank you, Mr. Dylan. I brought my own fruit.'" Some of the recordings made with the Band would be released by Columbia in the following decade as *The Basement Tapes* (1975). The remaining tracks were distributed as bootlegs among fans for years and were subsequently released officially by Columbia in 2014 as *The Bootleg Series Vol. 11: The Basement Tapes Complete*. During his self-exile, Dylan became even more of an enigma, a kind of ghost of Village past, present only on records and endless cover versions of his songs, in rumors, photos, and stylized art. He would not tour again for eight years.

Jimi

If the folksingers of the 1950s or early '60s had been teleported into the future, to MacDougal Street in 1966, they would have not have believed their ears. Between the Blues Project, the Magicians, the Fugs, and the Velvet Underground, the jarring dissonance of fuzz-drenched sounds emanating from venues once dominated by fingerpicked acoustic guitars and banjos would been unrecognizable.

Richie Havens was living at 61 Jane Street in the West Village when he met a guitarist who had been playing with the Isley Brothers, Little Richard, and Ike and Tina Turner. After months of touring with these and other R&B bands down South, the guitarist had left the chitlin circuit, was living in Harlem, and was looking to launch his own career with unique interpretations of blues and rock. "I actually sent him to Greenwich Village," Richie Havens said in a 1994 interview with Gary James. At the time, the guitarist was playing with Curtis Knight and the Squires at the Cheetah nightclub uptown, on Broadway at Fifty-Third Street. "He wasn't Jimi Hendrix when I met him. He was a guitarist for a band. I met him right after I made my first album. The whole incident was about him getting his own band and not having to get a job through the union to play for somebody else. That's what the gist of the conversation was about. I thought he could do his own thing and sent him to the Cafe Wha? Three months later, I was asked by a friend to go hear this great player down at the Café Wha? who turned out to be Jimmy James (stage name for Hendrix) and the Blue Flames. So we were friends from the beginning."

Originally from Seattle, Jimi Hendrix——whose genealogy included African American, Chero-kee, and Irish——had a difficult, unstable childhood that would later be expressed in the lyrics to some of his most haunting songs, like "Castles Made of Sand" and "Angel," which, according to his brother Leon, was written about their young mother Lucille, who had died in 1958. In 1961, Hendrix joined the army and was assigned to the 101st Airborne Division, stationed at Fort Campbell, Kentucky. Apparently, not readily adapting to army life, he was honorably discharged in June 1962 and, when his army friend Billy Cox was discharged the following year, they moved to Tennessee and began performing in Nashville. Years later, the two were to reunite, and Cox would accompany Hendrix on his legendary Woodstock set.

Performing at the Cheetah as guitarist for the Squires, Jimi Hendrix caught the eye of British model Linda Keith, then-girlfriend of Rolling Stone Keith Richards, who immediately spotted Hendrix's potential and became an early champion. "It was so clear to me. I couldn't believe nobody had picked up on him before because he'd obviously been around," Linda recalled to *The Guardian* in 2013. "He was astonishing—the moods he could bring to music, his charisma, his skill and stage presence. Yet nobody was leaping about with excitement. I couldn't believe it." According to the 2014 film *Jimi: All Is by My Side*, Linda Keith also was the first to turn Hendrix on to LSD, as they listened to Dylan's then-current *Blonde on Blonde* album. Later, Hendrix would create a supremely psychedelic recording of "All Along the Watchtower," one of the songs from Dylan's decidedly *un*-psychedelic, late-1967 album *John Wesley Harding*, asking Richie Havens for help transcribing it. "Can you write it down for me?" Hendrix asked Havens. After several misfires, when she invited record exec Seymour Stein and Stones manager Andrew Loog Oldham to see Hendrix sets at the Café Au Go Go, Linda succeeded in getting Chas Chandler, bassist for the Animals, who was leaving the group to focus on producing, to see Hendrix one night at the Café Wha? There, Richie Havens had secured Hendrix and the Blue Flames a monthlong residency. As Jimi opened his set with his soon-to-be iconic rendition of "Hey Joe," based on Tim Rose's slow arrangement, Chandler was sufficiently blown away. He arranged to bring Jimi to England where the Jimi Hendrix Experience was formed; strategic gigs, management, and a new record label were put into place; and, well, where the first psychedelic superstar was born.

A Legendary Bike Ride

The influx of psychedelic music—and drugs—in the Village had changed the landscape. LSD was not particularly new. It was first synthesized in a Swiss laboratory in 1938 by chemist Albert Hofmann, working for the Sandoz chemical company. Hofmann was attempting to create a compound, based on the substance lysergic acid, that could stimulate circulation and respiration. Ultimately, Hofmann combined the chemical with the ammonia derivative diethylamine, naming the resulting solution LSD-25. But his experiment was deemed an utter failure: the results "aroused no special interest in our pharmacologists and physicians." Five years later, however, in 1943 and in the midst of World War II, Hofmann recalled the compound's effect on laboratory animals at the time of his early work and went back to it, at first accidentally dosing himself and then returning for more research. "I perceived an uninterrupted stream of fantastic pictures, extraordinary shapes with intense, kaleidoscopic play of colors," Hofmann would write in a company memo after a particularly memorable—and now legendary—bicycle ride home from the lab.

Jump-cut to the 1950s and early 1960s: the CIA had launched a secret mind-control program called MK-Ultra that involved experimenting with LSD-25 on volunteers and unwitting subjects in universities and elsewhere, with the intent of creating a weapon to use in the Cold War effort. Through this surreptitious testing, which caused public outrage when finally revealed in the 1970s, LSD would escape from the laboratory into the general population. Starting in 1959, author Ken Kesey, then a grad student at

Stanford, began participating in government-sponsored testing and, in 1962, would publish his international best-selling novel, *One Flew Over the Cuckoo's Nest*. With his gang of "Merry Pranksters" and music by the Grateful Dead, Kesey instigated a series of LSD-fueled, blacklight-and fluorescent paint–enhanced parties in the San Francisco Bay area known as "acid tests." Tom Wolfe's 1968 nonfiction book *The Electric Kool-Aid Acid Test* chronicled their adventures, including attending a Beatles concert while tripping. The Beatles, in turn, mimicked the Merry Pranksters' wildly colorful school bus exploits in their 1967 film *Magical Mystery Tour*. Harvard psychology professors Timothy Leary and Richard Alpert began administering the then-legal LSD and psychedelic mushrooms to students before both men were dismissed from the faculty. With his phrase "Turn on, tune in, drop out" (which he actually attributed to philosopher Marshall McLuhan), Leary was encouraging people to embrace cultural change through the use of psychedelics and disconnect from the conventions of society.

Like Leary, some users were positively evangelistic in getting others turned on. "Barbara Rubin and Allen Ginsberg wanted people to try LSD," Chuck Smith told me. "Timothy Leary gave it to Allen to share with 'all the cool people' very early on." And the list of songs written and performed under its influence would fill these pages. The only problem was that LSD, as all drugs, had an antithetical downside. Inventor Hofmann was later to write, "The unpredictability of effects is the major danger of LSD." In his 1980 book *LSD: My Problem Child*, Hofmann would write, "A feeling of happiness can be heightened to bliss, a depression can deepen to despair. It is dangerous to take LSD in a disturbed, unhappy frame of mind, or in a state of fear. The probability that the experiment will end in a psychic breakdown is then quite high."

As I continued to write this book, I began to wonder about Paul Clayton. Like some of the others, he seemed to drop out of the picture. After making over twenty albums in the 1950s and early '60s, suddenly everything stopped. But why? I had to call Terri Thal again, to ask. She told me that Clayton hadn't been the same ever since he returned from that cross-country road trip with Bob Dylan in the blue Ford station wagon way back in 1964. "Paul had a bad dope experience," Thal told me. "Was it LSD?" I asked. "Yes," she answered, quickly and quietly. Clayton had been in the Village since the beginning, a true believer, and as Terri spoke to me, my heart sank. "Pablo (the Van Ronks' affectionate pet nickname for Paul) started having episodes right after that tour with Dylan," Thal told me. "He wasn't around. I don't know what happened. He disappeared often. It was very, very unpleasant." Quoted in *Hoot! A 25-Year History of the Greenwich Village Music Scene* (1986) by Robbie Woliver, Barry Kornfeld who, like Terri, had seen the whole story unfold, said, "Paul lived on dexies (Dexedrine). After his system was weakened, he took a little bit of acid, and that pushed him off the deep end. He sold his writer's share of 'Gotta Travel On.' When he got crazy, he sold his shares." The song had been covered by dozens of country artists and was surely one of the most valuable copyrights Clayton owned.

But so many things must have chipped away at Paul Clayton. Struggling with his sexuality, his (what Kornfeld calls) "tremendous" and "horrible" crush on Dylan and the betrayal over "Don't Think Twice, It's All Right" back in 1962, and the shifting tone and timbre of the Greenwich Village music scene——as it moved farther away from the purity of the folk tradition he loved so much into cults of personality, ten-minute guitar solos, music copyright battles, and greed——it must have all become too much. He became more and more alienated, especially from Dylan. "I believe that 'It Ain't Me, Babe' was written for Paul Clayton," Kornfeld said.

> *Go away from my window, leave at your own chosen speed*
> *I'm not the one you want, babe, I'm not the one you need*

Terri Thal, too, was there to witness to Clayton's decline, which reached its sorrowful conclusion on March 30, 1967. "Paul came to our apartment on Waverly Place one Friday. He stayed until Sunday morning. It was an awful weekend. Paul was ranting. Dave couldn't handle it emotionally and went to bed, leaving me there with Paul. I stayed up all night with Paul, not knowing what to do other than to just listen," Thal remembered. She paused, and took a breath. "Paul killed himself the following weekend."

Paul had electrocuted himself, by dragging an electric heater into his bathtub. He had just turned thirty-six.

The Human Be-In, a celebration of LSD, poetry, and politics in Golden Gate Park, had kicked off the year 1967 on January 14, shifting the focus to San Francisco. Showcasing "All of San Francisco's Rock Bands," that massive psychedelic gathering set the stage for what many consider to be the official beginning of the "Summer of Love," the Monterey Pop Festival, on June 16, 1967. The three-day festival embodied the San Francisco vibe and was organized by the Mamas & the Papas' John Phillips, producer Lou Adler, and brilliant publicist Derek Taylor. Jimi Hendrix (who famously lit his Fender Stratocaster on fire for his finale), Janis Joplin, the Grateful Dead, soul singer Otis Redding, and others rose to instant stardom at the proto-Woodstock. But just as importantly, the event was an open invitation to the counterculture to make the move to California. As Phillips's anthem "San Francisco," sung by Scott McKenzie and released to promote the festival, recommended, "Be sure to wear some flowers in your hair." I'm sure many did. Quickly, psychedelia went viral, affecting fashion, art, music, and thought, across all media. It was a joyful thing—the hypercolorful artwork and matching music with all manner of sounds and expression. The black-and-white film noir movie set of Bleecker and MacDougal Streets at night had switched suddenly to garish, Day-Glo technicolor, plastered over with psychedelic concert posters; Dorothy had stepped out her doorway into an acid-drenched Oz. The flamboyant costumes musicians wore, scarves and feathered hats, were about as far as you could possibly get from Woody Guthrie's workman's clothes, and the ornateness of the music and lyrics seemed of another realm entirely than Pete Seeger's earnest banjo and plaintive words. Yet it *was* still all about freedom. To use another phrase from Marshall McLuhan, the medium was now the message. And for a brief moment, it seemed the emphasis was not so much on the struggles of reality as on the boundless possibilities of *love*: a feeling of oneness that, while triggered by LSD, had taken on a life of its own. Like Dr. Hofmann's first dosing, it was as if the whole world was suddenly experiencing a contact high. And though ground zero was now San Francisco, much of the music and imagery heard and seen that summer, wherever you were, had at least one foot in the Village—from the Jefferson Airplane's cover of Fred Neil's "The Other Side of This Life," to the Blues Project and Simon & Garfunkel on the stage at Monterey, to the front cover of the Beatles album *Sgt. Pepper's Lonely Hearts Club Band* (1967), an eternal symbol of that summer. Designed and built by pop artists Peter Blake and Jann Haworth, the collage surrounding the Beatles contained life-size images of several Greenwich Village residents or frequenters of the past, like Oscar Wilde and Mae West, and more recent ones: Lenny Bruce, Dylan Thomas, William Burroughs, Dion. Oh, and Bob Dylan—while the real one was still hiding out upstate in Woodstock. Yet for all its psychedelic majesty, the cover of *Sgt. Pepper* also had the somber appearance of a funeral service. But . . . for whom? Or . . . for what?

Chapter Twelve

anot

her age

Eric Andersen and Patti Smith, photographed
on a balcony of the Chelsea Hotel in 1971.

It's all the streets you crossed not so long ago.
—Lou Reed, "Sunday Morning"

Like all great parties, from the bacchanals of ancient Rome to the excesses of the Roaring Twenties, the Summer of Love was followed by a monumental hangover.

In early 1967, the Beatles' manager Brian Epstein became interested in managing Eric Andersen. Impressed with Andersen's songwriting and, no doubt, his handsome good looks, Epstein believed that the time was right for the rise of the solo balladeer. Once again, his instincts were right on the money, as the careers of countless singer-songwriters in the late 1960s and early '70s would affirm. Epstein had already signed American pop trio the Cyrkle, whose 1966 hit "Red Rubber Ball" was cowritten by Paul Simon. Epstein reportedly also had an interest in the Velvet Underground and met with Lou Reed, though nothing came of it. With Eric Andersen, however, plans were discussed, letters were written, and promises were made. Epstein brought Eric to London and invited him to visit the Beatles in the recording studio during sessions for *Sgt. Pepper*. The irony can be lost on no one that Andersen himself, the artist whom Robert Shelton had once called "an antidote to the Beatles," was to become their manager's latest client. Having the Midas touch of Brian Epstein as his manager would surely have elevated Andersen in ways that are now, and were then, unfathomable.

On August 27, 1967, Andersen was backstage at the Philadelphia Folk Festival, preparing for his set and talking with John Denver, when he heard an announcement from the stage made by the festival's founder and host, esteemed folklorist, producer, and academic Kenneth Goldstein. According to Steve Katz, who was also at the event, Goldstein told the audience, "I have some *good news* for you: Brian Epstein has died." The audience cheered wildly. Fueled by their response, Goldstein continued, insisting that Epstein "had never done anything for folk music." The audience cheered more. It was a macabre reaction that echoed Dylan's booing folk crowd at Newport in 1965, but more hateful, inappropriate, and shocking. Andersen was later to write, "John Denver and I just looked at each other in shock. It was a sad day for us who knew Brian, and worked with him." While Ken Goldstein's words were appalling, they exemplified the threat and fear of lost status that the traditional folk community must have been feeling. But they had become deaf to their own message. The old road, as Dylan had once sang, was rapidly aging. Was the "peoples' music," once so easily traded and so freely shared, now the exclusive domain of a kind of folk elite who were ready to punish any artist who dared to diverge from the rigid norms of folk music? Or those who dared to cross the thin line from obscurity to fame? David Amram often mentions "folk Nazis" when we speak; they exist today. The baffling and distasteful experience at the Philadelphia Folk Festival in reaction to Brian Epstein's death influenced Eric Andersen to distance himself from the folk scene, as Dylan had long since done. Though Andersen would continue to make stunning, poetic music, the music industry itself never seemed to align with him. But perhaps that's the very thing that has allowed him to remain a true artist and poet through the decades.

A little over a month later, on October 3 at Creedmore Psychiatric Center in Queens, Woody Guthrie finally passed away from Huntington's disease at fifty-five years of age. Hospitalized since 1952, Guthrie, like Lead Belly who had died in 1949, was never able to fully participate in the folk boom he had helped to instigate. Even as a patient, Guthrie was kept under observation by the FBI because of his prior connection to the Communist Party of America and was still considered a security risk. Regardless, Guthrie was widely revered, and his presence was felt through his songs and indelible persona. Tribute concerts were held in 1968 at Carnegie Hall and in 1970 at the Hollywood Bowl. Dylan broke his eighteen-month self-imposed exile and made an appearance on January 20, 1968, at Carnegie Hall, backed by members of the Band. As Guthrie had been physically absent from the scene for a decade and a half, and not by choice like Dylan, his passing might have seemed more symbolic than actual—a sign of the beginning of the end of the second wave of the folk revival.

Of the original triumvirate, only Pete Seeger was able to experience firsthand the music they championed become commercialized, exploited, and embedded in American popular culture. But even Seeger, because of the blacklist, had limited access to the kind of national exposure and recognition he deserved. As was his nature, Seeger had turned to grassroots methods, movements, and causes, most famously and perhaps most successfully in the realm of environmental activism. In 1966, Pete and Toshi founded the Hudson River Sloop Clearwater organization, using advocacy and education to clean up the badly polluted Hudson River. For years, the river had been used as a literal dumping ground for industrial pollutants—especially from the General Electric company—that had severely contaminated the water. In 1968, Seeger's organization launched the sloop *Clearwater*, a 106-foot wooden sailing vessel, designed in the style of eighteenth- and nineteenth-century Dutch sailing sloops, as a symbol of their cleanup efforts and the river's natural, historic beauty. Seeger was cited as a major contributor to the passing of the Clean Water Act in 1972, one of the most influential, modern environmental laws in American history. According to fisherman, conservationist, and academic John Cronin, speaking to *The Guardian* on March 28, 2019, "There's no question that the Hudson is a cleaner river. It's an environmental success story. But it's an incomplete job, the work isn't over." Of course, Seeger knew that conservation work was an ongoing process. With the experience gained from their work with the Newport Folk Festival, Pete and Toshi instituted the Clearwater Festival, an annual fundraiser also known as the Great Hudson River Revival. The festival, which began in 1966, is held in Croton Point Park, near Seeger's home in Beacon, New York, and continues as of this writing.

Folksinging comedy duo the Smothers Brothers had landed a weekly CBS variety show in early 1967 and, for the premiere of their second season on September 19, 1967, told the network that they would like to book Pete Seeger. Ratings for the first season had been high, so the brothers, Tom and Dick, were permitted to break Seeger's seventeen-year ban from national television by having him perform on the program. Pete performed the Weavers' hit "Wimoweh," "Where Have All the Flowers Gone?," and a new song, "Waist Deep in the Big Muddy." The first two went off without a hitch, but the last one caused problems. Though the lyrics were set in World War II, the last verse seemed to refer to the mire of America's current involvement in Vietnam and appeared to be critical of the sitting president.

> *We're, waist deep in the Big Muddy*
> *And the big fool says to push on.*

CBS censors were skittish because the phrase "the big fool" appeared to parody President Lyndon B. Johnson. According to the *Washington Post* in 2019, LBJ had himself once phoned up CBS head William Paley at 3:00 a.m. from the White House to complain about the Smothers Brothers' anti-war humor. CBS demanded that Seeger omit the final verse. But Pete refused, insisting that it was the very point of the song. When the show aired, "Big Muddy" was completely cut from the broadcast. Regardless, Pete had finally returned to national television, freed from the blacklist. He never stopped performing, advocating, and marching for the causes he believed in. Pete Seeger would pass away on January 27, 2014, at ninety-four years old.

On October 17, 1967, Gerome Ragni, James Rado, and Galt MacDermot's self-described "American Tribal Love-Rock Musical" *Hair* opened as the first show produced at Joseph Papp's Public Theater, located at 425 Lafayette Street in the East Village. The loose, Village-centric storyline was a celebration of all things hippie, covering every pertinent topic from burning draft cards to dropping acid, and would spawn a slew of hit singles by a variety of artists.

LBJ took the I.R.T. down to 4th Street, USA
When he got there, what did he see? The youth of America on LSD.

After a brief, interim run at the Cheetah nightclub uptown, *Hair* opened at the Biltmore The-atre on Broadway on April 29, 1968, where it ran for 1,750 performances. As multiple, simultaneous productions opened all over the country, in London, and subsequently around the world, and its songs were covered by artists ranging from the Cowsills and the Fifth Dimension to Nina Simone, *Hair* became big business. In the June 27, 1970, issue of *Billboard*, Mike Stewart, president of United Artists Music, called *Hair* "the most successful score in history as well as the most performed score ever written for the Broadway stage." But what was actually happening on the street was another story.

By 1967, the changes taking place in the Village continued to be more and more pronounced. The Cham-bers Brothers had veered from gospel music and were forging a proto-funk, psychedelic-rock-meets-R&B sound at the Electric Circus—the former Dom—on St. Mark's Place. Meanwhile, the garage-blues-rock Blues Magoos had been rocking the Night Owl on West Third. But Dylan was out of the picture and rarely seen, Phil Ochs had moved to California and signed with A&M Records, and Tom Paxton had moved to Long Island. As *Rolling Stone* writer David Browne puts it, "The leading lights were physically gone, and the bands—the Lovin' Spoonful and Blues Project—were breaking up. Fred Neil was living in Florida. John Sebastian and Joni Mitchell had headed to California. Jimi Hendrix had to go to England to 'make it.' The Village wasn't cool anymore. It was overrun with tourists, and it had become a carnival atmosphere." Mitchell Cohen told me, "The scene shifted west, and the Village bands were overshadowed by the Cali-fornia and British groups. In the post–*Sgt. Pepper* world, the Village was not the thing." One of those who moved to California, singer Judy Henske, speaking in the Phil Ochs documentary *There But for Fortune*, recalled, "It was turning into something else. It was turning into something that was a real *drag*."

I asked producer Erik Jacobsen why *he* left the Village: "Well, the vicissitudes of living in New York City. Basically, you're never more than fifty feet away from anybody. In your apartment there's somebody twelve feet above you and twelve feet below you. And up and down the hallway. It's like cave dwelling. In California, we can breathe. And we have mountains, the ocean, the bay, the scent of salt air—the beautiful ocean breezes." While the beauty and allure of the Pacific coast is undeniable, the brick-and-cobblestone concentration of life in Greenwich Village, and the proximity to others, surely had something to do with the energy and intensity of the music that was generated here. But for some, it was now passé.

In "Tape from California," Phil Ochs would write,

New York City has exploded
And it's crashed upon my head

David Fricke and I have engaged in numerous conversations about this period. In Fricke's words, "1967 was a turning point year in so many ways. I think one of the issues for the Village is that the perspective was turned elsewhere. Suddenly, everything that had been happening in the Village that informed the changes in songwriting—in what singers could be and could do—had all been disseminated and taken root in San Francisco, and to some degree, Los Angeles. And you had these perspectives coming from London, because of Dylan's impact on songwriting there. When you have that kind of impact, there's going to come a time when ground zero is not the focus anymore." Yet many remained, including Carolyn Hester, Peter Stampfel, and of course, Dave Van Ronk. Jimi Hendrix began plans for his recording studio, Electric Lady, on West Eighth Street, although he would not live to record there.

I was emailing with Buffy Sainte-Marie after attending her concert in Brooklyn in August 2021 and asked about the changes that took place in the Village during the later 1960s. Buffy replied, "I wonder whether you've considered the transition out of that real innocent student, coffeehouse entertainment/activism of the early sixties—that youth phenomenon supported by caffeine communication . . . into the drift toward liquor licenses and thus older audiences and bigger money, alcohol vs. coffee consciousness (and lack thereof), addiction, and big-time management's impact on the whole scene which, in my opinion, kinda killed it. The Mamas and the Papas and cocaine in Laurel Canyon was a different thing altogether from Phil Ochs at the Gaslight."

Ochs himself hired his younger brother Michael as manager, signed with L.A.-based A&M Records, and reinvented his sound with the ambitious, orchestral pop Pleasures of the Harbor. Anyone coming to the album expecting "I Ain't Marching Anymore" or "Too Many Martyrs" would have been in for a major shock when they dropped the needle to the groove. The sound they'd have heard was positively cinematic. Neither folk nor rock, it merged classical arrangements and counterpoint, honky-tonk piano, and satirical social commentary, ending with Ochs's eight-minute, forty-five-second magnum opus "Crucifixion"—widely interpreted as a depiction of the life and assassination of President John F. Kennedy. "Well, here's a song that New York isn't ready for yet. Won't be for another century or so. But I'll do it anyway. At the risk of life and limb . . . and psyche. It's a song about Christ-killing, how all America and even, especially, New York loves to create heroes to moralize to them and then kill them violently, bloodily, and dig the death so much, every detail of the death," Ochs said when introducing the song in an early performance. "It's a song about Jesus Christ. It's called 'The Crucifixion.' It's a song about Kennedy. And maybe a song about Dylan." On Ochs's album, the song received boldly experimental, adventurous orchestration and production that are intriguing. But it did not serve the lyrics and melody as well as Ochs's own, spare acoustic guitar accompaniment did in live performance, or Jim & Jean's sweeping, harmonized version, released in 1966.

Ultimately, the album did not chart and received but a smattering of FM radio play, especially when one of its most popular tracks, "Outside a Small Circle of Friends" was banned from some stations because of its reference to pot.

> *Smoking marijuana is more fun than drinking beer,*
> *But a friend of ours was captured and they gave him thirty years*

"*Pleasures of the Harbor* was two years ahead of the singer-songwriter movement," David Fricke suggested. "The album showed up at the wrong moment." And yet Phil Ochs himself showed up at precisely the right moment. Moreover, it was a moment he had helped to create. But it must have been heartbreaking for him not to have been able to connect commercially in the way some of his peers did, in the way he knew he deserved. In the way Dylan had.

1968 began innocently enough. NBC, certainly inspired by the success of the *Smothers Brothers Comedy Hour* on CBS, had concocted *Rowan & Martin's Laugh-In*. Less overtly political but equally as topical, *Laugh-In* was structured as a stylized series of comic sketches set in the visual imagery of mod/hippie counterculture. Both shows were hosted by two males—one bright and one dumb—except that the tuxedo-clad Rowan & Martin were nightclub performers in their midforties while Tom and Dick Smothers were folk musicians, one barely thirty and the other in his late twenties, respectively. *Laugh-In* debuted on January 22, 1968, and that debut show gave the country its first real glimpse of idiosyncratic Greenwich Village stalwart Tiny Tim.

Tiny Tim had recently signed with Warner Bros. Records' Reprise label and was currently in the midst of a residency uptown at Steve Paul's the Scene, at 301 West Forty-Sixth Street. In a case of the stars aligning in his favor, Tiny's meticulously crafted debut album, *God Bless Tiny Tim*—produced by Richard Perry and featuring a bizarre cameo appearance by the Velvet Underground's Nico as the voice of actress Tuesday Weld—would be released in April. Amid his regular national exposure on *Laugh-In*, Tiny landed himself an indelible hit single with an old-timey, orchestrated rendition of "Tiptoe Through the Tulips." Suddenly, the falsetto-singing, long-haired, ukulele-wielding musical misfit was catapulted from gigging at Greenwich Village gay bars to being one of the highest-paid performers in the world and performing at the legendary Isle of Wight Festival in England for an estimated audience of over six hundred thousand people. The particular kind of fame that Tiny Tim achieved was impossible to sustain for long, but at its peak, his wedding to seventeen-year-old fan Miss Vicki on the *Tonight Show with Johnny Carson* on December 17, 1969, was viewed by more than twenty-one million households—making it one of the most-viewed television events of the sixties, after the first moon landing. Years later, when I met and became friends with Tiny, he allowed me to produce an album for him, *Rare Moments Vol. 1: I've Never Seen a Straight Banana*, released posthumously in 2009, that included some select stories from his unbelievable showbiz odyssey in the sixties. More than any other artist of his time, Tiny Tim brought the conversation of sexual identity to the mainstream and helped shatter the boundaries of gender conformity for countless artists who followed. Just as important, Tiny served as an affable, lovable, and diverting comic relief during a time when it was needed the most.

The war in Vietnam had been raging on, and opinion polls showed that public support for the conflict had been steadily declining. But on January 30, 1968, it was the Tet Offensive—a twenty-six-day battle that resulted in heavy losses on both sides—that finally tipped the scales and drove American popular opinion against the war. What Phil Ochs, Buffy Sainte-Marie, Tom Paxton, Donovan, and Pete Seeger had been singing about for years was now seen in its most graphic, bloody reality. CBS News anchor Walter Cronkite, then considered "the most trusted man in America," traveled to Vietnam to capture live footage. Images of wounded or slain nineteen-year-old boys on tanks and stretchers were being seen on television and in newsmagazines by millions of Americans who had been led to believe that we were winning the war. It was in the midst of the Tet Offensive that Pete Seeger was invited to return to the *Smothers Brothers* show on February 25, 1968. This time he was permitted to perform "Waist Deep in the Big Muddy" in its entirety. But, the Smothers Brothers' problems with censors were far from over. Lobbying for First

Amendment protections, Tom Smothers in particular found himself perpetually at odds with the network, and the *Smothers Brothers Comedy Hour* was finally cancelled on June 8, 1969. The brothers sued CBS for breach of contract and won, in a settlement worth $776,300, or $5,786,650.19 in 2021 dollars.

On February 27, 1968, just two days after Pete Seeger sang "Big Muddy" on the *Smothers Brothers Comedy Hour,* Walter Cronkite, in a prime-time special "Report from Vietnam," looked straight into the camera and told his twenty million viewers that the war could not be won. "It seems now more certain than ever, that the bloody experience of Vietnam is to end in a stalemate," he reported on the *CBS Evening News*. Lyndon Johnson saw the writing on the wall. "If I've lost Cronkite, I've lost Middle America," he reportedly said. A few weeks later, with anti-war protests breaking out all over the country, the president announced that he would not run for reelection, a stunner that would put the Democratic Party and the presidential election of 1968 in a tailspin. As unpopular as the Vietnam War had become, it—and the draft—were to continue until April 30, 1975—nearly twenty years after the war began. Demonstrations heated up in 1968 after the Tet Offensive, and the climate of civil unrest was beginning to reach a boiling point.

Then, just after 6:00 p.m. on April 4, 1968, in a devastating blow to the civil rights movement, Dr. Martin Luther King was assassinated at the Lorraine Motel in Memphis, Tennessee. For all he had accomplished, including receiving the Nobel Peace Prize in 1964, King was only thirty-nine years old. That evening, Senator Robert F. Kennedy, who was then running for president in the Democratic primaries, broke the news of Dr. King's death to a predominantly Black audience at a campaign rally in Indianapolis, Indiana. Wearing an overcoat that had belonged to his brother, President Kennedy, Bobby Kennedy delivered his most eloquent address—an extemporaneous, six-minute speech honoring Dr. King and calling for peace in the streets by invoking the assassination of his brother less than five years prior, noting that he also was killed at the hands of a white man: "But we have to make an effort in the United States, we have to make an effort to understand, to go beyond these rather difficult times." There was no rioting in Indianapolis that night, while shock waves of violent protest were felt and riots erupted in more than one hundred other US cities. With intelligence and compassion, Robert Kennedy had shown he could lead. But it was not to be.

Just two months later, on June 5, 1968, Robert Kennedy was himself shot and killed at the Ambassador Hotel in Los Angeles. As he lay wounded on the hotel's kitchen floor, it seemed that the violence and polarization happening all over America would never end. With so many people, including Dr. King, under constant surveillance by the FBI, one would think that these assassinations would have been somewhat preventable. J. Edgar Hoover's FBI seemed to be more intent, however, on collecting dirt and gossip than on preventing actual crimes. Is it any wonder that Americans became more and more distrustful and suspicious of their institutions of government? This trend would become even worse in the years that followed. Speaking to the *Washington Post* in 2018, on the fiftieth anniversary of the killings, legendary activist and US congressman John Lewis said, "When Bobby Kennedy was assassinated and when Dr. King was assassinated, I think something died in all of us." Allan Pepper who, with partner Stanley Snadowsky, promoted shows at Gerde's Folk City before later co-owning the Bottom Line on West Fourth Street, summed up the decade in four words: "We lost our innocence."

Dion, who had signed with Columbia Records in 1962 as the label's first rock and roll artist, had been hanging out in Greenwich Village, jamming with Tim Hardin, John Sebastian, and Tom Paxton. In 1968, it had been more than nine years since the day Buddy Holly's plane had crashed, but the memory continued to haunt him. "I felt guilty for a long time for turning that seat over," Dion told Leslie Gray Streeter in the *Palm Beach Post* in 2009. "When that plane went down, killing all three of those guys, I was wondering who am I? Where am I? What's life all about? Where am I going? Why am I here?" he told *Billboard* in 2017. After John Hammond turned him on to the music of Robert Johnson, Dion had recorded numerous blues and folk-rock tracks for Columbia, such as the *Kickin' Child* album, produced by Tom Wilson and featuring songs written by Dylan, Tom Paxton, and Mort Shuman alongside his own songs. But it was to remain unreleased—until 2017—and hits were elusive. Less elusive were drugs, and Dion had fallen into heroin addiction.

But in 1968, Dion would kick drugs. He returned to his original record label, Laurie Records—and to the top ten—sending through the nation's transistor radios a comforting, almost prayerful tribute to Dr. King and the slain Kennedy brothers, as well as to Abraham Lincoln, in "Abraham, Martin, and John," written by Dick Holler. The gently orchestrated folk-rock arrangement and Dion's immaculate vocal performance spoke for the grieving nation and gave Dion a number four spot on the *Billboard* Hot 100, on December 14, 1968.

In a conversation in October 2021, Dion would talk to me about the inherent spirituality of rock and roll, as a musical form that began as an extension of gospel with Sister Rosetta Tharpe, Little Richard, and others. But as comforting as Dion's voice could be coming through the airwaves, the violence and chaos in America was still far from over, and 1968 wasn't done with us yet.

Another victim of violence that year was none other than Andy Warhol. On June 3, 1968, only two days before Robert Kennedy was assassinated, Andy was shot point-blank at the Factory, 33 Union Square West, by radical feminist playwright Valerie Solanas, author of the *S.C.U.M. Manifesto*. The acronym stood for Society for Cutting Up Men. Solanas's book argues that men have ruined the world and that it is up to women to fix it. Though Andy recovered from the horrific shooting, his chest remained a patchwork of scars for the rest of his life. When Solanas turned herself in to police, she famously told them that Warhol "had too much control in my life." Though Warhol continued to be one of the most important artists of the twentieth century, he was never the same after the shooting. When I first visited the Factory a decade later, it was a high-security operation, with bulletproof doors and then-uncommon closed-circuit surveillance. Andy gave me a copy of his most recent book, *The Philosophy of Andy Warhol*, drew his signature Campbell's tomato soup can for me, and signed the title page. Chapter 8 is called "Death"; this is the entire chapter:

I don't believe in it, because you are not around to know that it's happened. I can't say anything about it because I'm not prepared for it.

After Andy died on February 22, 1987, from a botched gall bladder operation, former Velvets Lou Reed and John Cale reunited to write and perform a tribute song cycle, *Songs for 'Drella* (1990, Sire Records).

People said to lock the door and have an open house no more
They said the Factory must change and slowly slip away

As for the Velvet Underground themselves, January 30, 1968, had seen the release of their second Verve album, *White Light/White Heat*, a title that *could* have included the phrase "white noise." Produced by Tom Wilson, it was a solid blast of rock and roll that pushed the limits of distortion and chaos; a sonic mirror of the year ahead. With explicit sexuality and explosions of manic guitar improvisation, the Velvets had delivered another—eventual—game changer, though, again, it was hardly a blip on *Billboard*, peaking at number 199 on the top 200. In fact, none of the four primary studio releases by the Velvet Underground cracked the top 100, and yet each could be said to have presaged elements of seventies rock—from glam to punk—and laid the groundwork for almost every type of what would later be called "alternative." As if that were not enough, the solo careers of Lou Reed, John Cale, and Nico were guideposts of art rock during subsequent decades.

Enigmatic blues singer Karen Dalton had drifted away from the Village to Colorado in the early years of the decade, and then to Los Angeles, but wound her way back to the Village to give it one more shot in 1968; this time with a newfound desire to record an album. Her timing was such that she had left town just as things were beginning to pick up steam, and she returned just as things were winding down. As portrayed in the 2021 documentary *Karen Dalton: In My Own Time*, Dalton's newly formed friendship with Tim Hardin was a creative match made in heaven—her interpretations of Hardin's songs equaled or surpassed his own. But the liaison also proved hellishly disastrous, enhancing her propensity for self-destructive behavior, drinking, and intravenous drug use. While she created two stunning, haunting albums, she became wildly unreliable, alienating even her most ardent supporters, including the jovial, genial Peter Stampfel, with whom Dalton had collaborated in the Holy Modal Rounders. Her renditions of Fred Neil's "Little Bit of Rain" and Hardin's "Reason to Believe" endure as supreme examples of a singer completely embodying a lyric. It's not only as if the songs had been written *for* her but that they coursed through her bloodstream before she sang them. Though her next, final drift was into obscurity, recent artists who have discovered her, such as Nick Cave, Devendra Banhart, and Vanessa Carlton, cite Dalton as an influence.

1967–1968 saw a lot of reshuffling, as the bands that broke up splintered in a number of directions. After the demise of the Blues Project, Al Kooper and Steve Katz, along with jazz trumpeter/flugelhornist Randy Brecker and others formed the jazz-rock band Blood, Sweat & Tears, a kind of rock big band that, according to Kooper, was inspired by the Maynard Ferguson Orchestra and the brass-heavy early pop-rock hits of the Buckinghams. Debuting their full lineup at the Café Au Go Go on November 17, 1967, Blood, Sweat & Tears were to become immensely popular. According to Marc Myers, regular contributor to the *Wall Street Journal* and founder of the daily blog *JazzWax*, the success of B, S & T affected what jazz clubs began booking. "Clubs were switching from Miles Davis to Blood, Sweat & Tears," Myers told me. Their second, eponymous album released in late 1968 even beat out the Beatles' *Abbey Road* for the Album of the Year Grammy award. By that point, however, Al Kooper had left the group, becoming a producer for Columbia Records. Katz would finally leave the group in 1973, also to produce others, and then joined the supergroup American Flyer in 1976. Peter Stampfel and Steve Weber had joined forces with the Fugs, cofounded by Ed Sanders and poet Tuli Kupferberg, who had become widely known for their satirical political songs. "CIA Man," written by Kupferberg for the group's 1967 album *Virgin Fugs* (ESP Disk), parodied Johnny Rivers's 1966 hit "Secret Agent Man."

Who can kill a general in his bed? Overthrow dictators if they're Red?
Fucking-a man! CIA Man!

FBI files on the Doors from 1969 revealed correspondence that referred to the Fugs as the "most vulgar thing the human mind could possibly conceive." While the blacklist was no longer spoken of, the threat of censorship, arrest, or worse was still prevalent. The House Un-American Activities Committee had mutated into a more subtle surveilling mechanism that hovered around the Greenwich Village scene—which was now scattered all over the country. Buffy Sainte-Marie, speaking in *Greenwich Village: Music That Defined a Generation*, said, "Their next incarnation were a lot smarter about it. They didn't let you know that you were under surveillance. They didn't drag you before Congress and question you. They'd just put you out of business." Sainte-Marie herself found herself unwelcome on network television due to her outspoken views on Native American rights. "Was I blacklisted because of 'Universal Soldier'? No. I was blacklisted because I'm an outspoken person," she told Rick Rubin in 2020. "I was a woman on television, pointing out the fact that they were stealing Indian land—the particular parts of Indian land that contained uranium. You don't say that!" Regardless, Buffy Sainte-Marie has continued to write and create important, successful music to this day and was the first Indigenous woman to win an Oscar, for her song "Up Where We Belong" from the film *An Officer and a Gentleman* in 1983.

Even José Feliciano, riding high on the charts with his signature cover of the Doors' "Light My Fire," was not exempt from the wrath of 1968 and the threat of blacklisting. When José performed a soulful, Latin jazz–flavored rendition of "The Star-Spangled Banner" at game 5 of the World Series in October at Detroit's Tiger Stadium, he was greeted by a now-familiar combination of booing and applause from the divided audience. Feliciano was immediately criticized and reprimanded in the media for taking liberties with the song. How *dare* a Puerto Rican, an American citizen raised in New York City, interpret his national anthem in a way that reflected his cultural heritage? José was temporarily banned from commercial radio at that crucial moment in his career climb. "They stopped playing me. Like I had the plague, or something," Feliciano told NPR's Karen Grigsby Bates in 2017. But José's rendering of the anthem opened the door for the many interpretations of the song performed at sports events and other gatherings that followed—including renditions by Marvin Gaye in 1983, Whitney Houston in 1991, and Lady Gaga in 2016—and perhaps inspired Jimi Hendrix's incendiary performance at the close of the Woodstock festival less than a year later. "The only thing I can say about all these versions is they wouldn't have done it if I hadn't done it," said Feliciano, "and I'm glad that I did."

Janis Ian, who had been under surveillance since she was a teenager because of her parents' leftist leanings, made an album called *God & the FBI* in 2000. Speaking on NPR's *All Things Considered* on July 23, 2008, Ian said 1968 "was the beginning of the end. It might as well have been the end of the decade, because it sort of wrapped up everything that had begun in the '60s, and I think for those of us who had been active in civil rights and been active in the Vietnam War protests, it really became a very clear indicator that we had totally underestimated the powers that be." Nothing made that clearer than the Democratic National Convention of 1968 in Chicago.

The Whole World Is Watching

Phil Ochs had aligned himself with radical activists Jerry Rubin and Abbie Hoffman. As early as his October 1, 1967, concert at Carnegie Hall, Ochs began announcing plans for gathering in Chicago. On tour, and at student demonstrations, Ochs continued to invite audiences to join him at the convention to protest the Vietnam War. The city of Chicago's Democratic mayor Richard Daley and his police force had a lead time of nearly eleven months to strategize a defense, during which time Daley spoke to the media of their preparedness to combat youthful protesters. It was a battle between the old and the young—a violent manifestation of the generation gap. By December, Rubin and Hoffman, along with Ed Sanders, of the Fugs, activist Jim Fouratt, Hugh Romney a.k.a. Wavy Gravy, WBAI Radio's free-form *Radio Unnameable* host Bob Fass, and others, including Ochs, would form the Youth International Party, or "Yippies." They held their first press conference at the Americana Hotel on March 17, 1968, at which Judy Collins performed, five months before the August convention.

The Democratic Party of 1968, not unlike that of the early 2020s, was divided and in disarray. The gulf between anti-war progressives and moderates was widened by the lack of an obvious front-runner. First, their incumbent president, LBJ, refused to run for reelection and withdrew in March. Then Robert F. Kennedy, on his way to becoming the Democratic pick, was assassinated. The field now included the current vice president, Hubert Humphrey—who represented the current, unpopular administration, the status quo—and US senator Eugene McCarthy, who appealed to younger voters dissatisfied with government. Even without what was about to happen, there was trouble afoot.

Phil Ochs, back in the Village, invited Dave Van Ronk to join the planned festivities in Chicago. Van Ronk, forever the pragmatist, firmly declined. "It's a mistake, Phil," Van Ronk replied, according to biographer Marc Eliot. "If I were you, I would steer clear. It's a trap." Ochs disagreed, shaking his head, but Van Ronk continued. "It's a trap," he repeated. "They'll use this to discredit the Left. Phil, [Mayor] Daley's releasing hourly communiqués to the press about his ability to preserve law and order. It's a trap."

Not surprisingly, Van Ronk was right. When Ochs performed "I Ain't Marching Any More" during the protests outside the convention—inspiring hundreds of young men to burn their draft cards—he described it as the highlight of his career. But it was all downhill from there. Mayor Daley had deployed twelve thousand police officers and called in another fifteen thousand state and federal officers, ostensibly to "contain" the protesters. The massive, militaristic police presence only intensified and agitated the several thousand who had gathered in Lincoln Park, and containment quickly turned into a full-scale riot. Police severely beat up and teargassed demonstrators, journalists, and medics in a scene that—at a quick glance on the evening news—could have been mistaken for a battle in the very war being protested. The media coverage of the head-to-head spectacle was a devastating blow to the Left that served to further divide the country politically. Ochs famously said he had witnessed "the death of America." In "Another Age" Ochs would write,

> We were born in a revolution and we died in a wasted war
> It's gone that way before.

Images of the chaos and violence in Chicago helped secure the election of the Republican candidate for president, Richard M. Nixon, who proclaimed he could restore order.

What happened in Lincoln Park only spawned more violence and further divided the country. Less than two years later, on May 4, 1970, four students were killed and nine injured at Kent State University, when the Ohio National Guard opened fire on student protesters at an anti-war rally. Kent State students Chrissie Hynde, future frontwoman of the Pretenders, and Gerald Casales, later of DEVO, witnessed their friends getting shot and killed. "I stopped being a hippie and I started to develop the idea of devolution. I got real, real pissed off," Casales said in a 2010 interview in the *Vermont Review*. Neil Young was moved to write the song "Ohio," with its refrain of "four dead in O-hi-o," recorded by Crosby, Stills, Nash & Young and released a few weeks later.

No More Songs

Phil Ochs never fully recovered from Chicago in 1968. The following year, he was one of the witnesses called to testify at the historic trial of the Chicago 7, including Rubin and Hoffman, who were tried for conspiring to incite a riot. Outside the courthouse each day, protesters repeatedly chanted, "The whole world is watching! The whole world is watching!" For the cover of his subsequent album, *Rehearsals for Retirement* (A&M Records), released in May 1969, Ochs had his own tombstone made, proclaiming his death in Chicago. "He was writing his own obituary," David Fricke told me. Despite some brilliant songs and stellar performances, it would be Ochs's poorest-selling album. Next, resurrected in an Elvis-inspired gold lamé suit singing Elvis and Buddy Holly songs at Carnegie Hall and elsewhere, Ochs released the ironically titled, country-flavored *Greatest Hits* album—produced by Van Dyke Parks and including the decidedly downcast "No More Songs"—in 1970. But the irony only further distanced Ochs from his fan base. Audiences yelled, "Phil Ochs is dead!" and "Bring back Phil Ochs!"

On a trip to Africa in 1972, Ochs was mugged and strangled by robbers in Dar es Salaam, Tanzania. The attack, which Ochs was convinced had been carried out by the CIA, left his vocal cords permanently damaged, caused the loss of the top three notes in his vocal range, and increased his severe paranoia. Drinking heavily, Ochs continued to spiral mentally and emotionally, yet with flashes of brilliance and moments of true determination—especially when he heard the call to action, to organize.

The democratically elected Chilean president Allende was overthrown in a US-backed coup d'état on September 11, 1973. Ochs had recently visited Chile and befriended the beloved Chilean folksinger Victor Jara. In the coup, Jara was rounded up along with professors and students, tortured, and assassinated. Allende himself committed suicide while the presidential palace was being bombed. Upon hearing the news, Ochs was devastated. On May 9, 1974, in a show of support for Chile and to raise funds for the Chilean people, he organized the *Friends of Chile Concert: An Evening with Salvador Allende*, at Madison Square Garden's Felt Forum, gathering Pete Seeger, Arlo Guthrie, Melanie, Dave Van Ronk, Beach Boys Dennis Wilson and Mike Love, and actor Dennis Hopper. Ticket sales were slow, however, and Ochs knew he had to ask Bob Dylan to be on the bill for the evening to be a success. When, finally, Dylan agreed to perform and it was announced, ticket sales took off. The concert served as a reunion for the two frenemies—nearly a decade after those heated, humiliating exchanges at the Kettle of Fish, being kicked out of the car, and all the intricacies and social dynamics of the MacDougal Street scene. They embraced onstage and spoke of collaborating on a club tour, an idea that Ochs proposed. Dylan was to revise and use the idea when he mounted the *Rolling Thunder Revue* in 1975. But although it was discussed between the two, Ochs was not included on the tour.

Fulfilling the prophecy and political theater of Ochs's "The War Is Over" song and rallies in 1968, the Vietnam War finally, officially ended for real on April 30, 1975. Ochs staged a final "War Is Over" rally in Central Park on May 11, gathering, among others, Harry Belafonte, Odetta, Pete Seeger, and Joan Baez, who gave Ochs a kiss on the cheek after their duet of his "There But for Fortune." But from that joyful day, with the war ended, there was no turning back. No climbing back up. It was as if his work here was done.

By midyear in 1975, Phil Ochs began assuming an alternate, violently erratic personality—named John Butler Train—who he claimed had murdered Phil Ochs. Drinking constantly, he was ejected from all of the Village venues that had once welcomed him. Even Mike Porco at Gerde's Folk City refused to serve him and ejected him from the premises. Still worse, Train (Ochs) constantly carried weapons: a hammer, lead pipe, knives. Native American folksinger and friend of Pete Seeger, Roland Mousaa, who arrived in the Village in 1968, told me he grabbed a knife from Ochs at Folk City, on October 23, 1975, at Mike Porco's sixty-first birthday party. The gang was all there and performed after the main set: Dylan, Baez, Ramblin' Jack Elliot, Eric Andersen, Patti Smith, Buzzy Linhart, Ochs—even Bette Midler was there. Mousaa described seeing Ochs wielding the nine-inch blade with a black, square handle and grabbing it from him before any damage could be done. "Phil was also stopped at Carnegie Hall for carrying weapons," Mousaa told me. "They found a knife on him—and a hammer." Ochs had attempted suicide and spoke of it constantly, and his brother Michael tried, unsuccessfully, to have him committed to a psychiatric hospital. Defeated, dejected, disconnected, Ochs moved in with his sister Sonny in Far Rockaway, New York. He was diagnosed with bipolar disorder and was prescribed medication. But it was no use. On April 9, 1976, Phil Ochs was found dead by his young nephew. He had hanged himself in his sister Sonny's home. He was thirty-five.

The Felt Forum, where Ochs had staged the Concert for Chile two years prior, was also the home of his own memorial tribute concert on May 28, 1976. From the point of view of the post-Watergate mid-1970s, it was an evening that looked back to an era that seemed by then long passed. The concert brought together Ochs's friend, former attorney general Ramsey Clark, activist lawyer William Kunstler (who had defended the Chicago 7 and called Ochs to testify), Allen Ginsberg, and Jerry Rubin, along with Pete Seeger, Melanie, Jack Elliott, Tim Hardin, Tom Rush, Peter Yarrow, David Blue, Pat Sky, Jim & Jean, Bob Gibson, Eric Andersen, and Len Chandler. Dave Van Ronk delivered perhaps the evening's most poignant message, singing a deliberate and pensive rendition of "He Was a Friend of Mine." Speaking to *People* magazine at the time, Jerry Rubin said of Ochs, "He's one of the people most responsible for ending the Vietnam war. He was the anti-war movement's troubadour." Quoted in the same *People* concert review, Ochs's traveling companion, David Ifshin, said, "I felt so sad for him at the end. People were laughing behind his back, playing with him, and he couldn't see it. Dylan really rubbed it in." At the memorial concert, Bob Dylan did not appear.

If the summer of 1967 was the Summer of Love, and the summer of 1968 was the summer of chaos and despair, then the summer of 1969 was a summer of completion. Just as the 1950s had done, the sixties were cramming to tie up as many loose ends as possible before the clock struck midnight on New Year's Eve.

Fred Neil, who had hosted the afternoon shows at the Café Wha? all those years ago, achieved a massive hit with his song "Everybody's Talking," when Brooklynite Harry Nilsson's version was used as the central, recurring theme in the 1969 film *Midnight Cowboy*, directed by John Schlesinger. In spite of the film's X rating, it won the Oscar for Best Picture of Year, and Nilsson received a Grammy for his performance of Neil's song. While Bob Dylan, Randy Newman, and even Nilsson himself were in a race to have their songs in the film, this was to be Fred Neil's moment. Yet Neil kept a low profile for the next, and last, thirty years of his life. Profoundly interested in the protection of dolphins, he cofounded the Dolphin Research Project in 1970 and spent most of this time in Florida, giving only sporadic performances—usually with John Sebastian on harmonica.

> *I'm going where the sun keeps shining, through the pouring rain*
> *Going where the weather suits my clothes.*

On June 28, 1969, at 1:20 a.m., the Mafia-owned Stonewall Inn at 51 and 53 Christopher Street, filled with its Saturday night crowd of over two hundred patrons, was raided by the New York Police Department's Sixth Precinct, as it had been routinely—on a monthly basis—along with all the other gay and lesbian bars in New York City. But this night was different. The raid didn't go smoothly when men refused to show their IDs to police officers, who barricaded the doors. Nor when the lesbian women resisted being physically assaulted and frisked inappropriately. When patrons were roughly herded outside the bar onto the sidewalk of Christopher Street—directly across Sheridan Square from where Billie Holiday and Josh White had performed at the long-since-gone Café Society thirty years prior—violence began to break out. Beer cans, bottles, and bricks were thrown, and the growing crowd tried to overturn the police paddy wagon. Learning that the reason for the raid was that the corrupt cops, like Officer Fitzgerald, who had tried to shake down Joe Marra at the Night Owl, had not been paid their extortionate "gayola," coins were tossed at them, accompanied by shouts of "Pay 'em off!" Trans women refused to go into the patrol wagon, and fights broke out with the police. The crowd sang, "We Shall Overcome." By that point, as if on cue, Dave Van Ronk, who was then living at 15 Sheridan Square and had been in the neighboring Lion's Head bar, got into the fray. Considering the Trotskyite theory of permanent revolution, it only made sense that the Mayor of MacDougal Street would be where the action was and get involved. Van Ronk was one of the thirteen people ultimately arrested. Legend has it that it took three cops to restrain the hulking folksinger. The uprising would last for nearly one week and made all the papers. "HOMO NEST RAIDED, QUEEN BEES ARE STINGING MAD," blared the *New York Daily News*. On the second night of rioting, Allen Ginsberg appeared on the scene. "Gay power! Isn't that great?! It's about time we did something to assert ourselves." The events of that week, and the media coverage it generated, catalyzed the gay rights movement like nothing before. The annual LGBTQ+ pride parade that happens every year at the end of June, not just in New York but around the world, is a celebration of that rebellion. Stonewall was a culmination, and along with the "Beatnik Riot" of 1961, it framed a decade of protests in Greenwich Village.

It was barely three weeks later, on July 20, 1969, that the first manned space mission, Apollo 11, landed on the moon, with the words "The Eagle has landed," and Commander Neil Armstrong ceremoniously planted the US flag. President Kennedy's challenge to get there before the end of the decade—an undeniable, stunning, technical feat and a crowning achievement of Kennedy's legacy—was fulfilled. The space race with the USSR was ostensibly over, even though the Cold War between the two countries would continue until December 3, 1989, with the tearing down of the Berlin Wall and opening of the borders. But just as the Apollo 11 spacecraft was hurtling toward the moon, on July 18–19, the youngest Kennedy brother, Senator Ted Kennedy, found himself implicated in a devastating scandal involving a suspicious car accident after a party on Chappaquiddick Island, in Massachusetts, and the death of Mary Jo Kopechne, a secretary and campaign worker for his brother Robert's 1968 presidential campaign. The incident ensured that the next Kennedy in line would never successfully run for president, though he would remain in the Senate for nearly forty-seven years.

Woodstock, which began as a three-day music and art fair, was held in Bethel, New York, August 15–18, 1969. It transformed into the ultimate, four hundred-thousand-plus-strong, hippie love-in, be-in, celebration that no one could have fully anticipated. In all its trippy, muddy, sometimes naked glory, the Woodstock festival was also the fulfillment of the promise of that little scene that grew from the Gaslight and the other basement clubs at the beginning of the decade. Like Apollo 11 reaching the moon, this Eagle, too, had landed: the mission was complete. Bookending the festival were two Greenwich Village friends: Richie Havens, who opened the event with a lengthy, improvised, star-making set, and Jimi Hendrix, who closed the event in the 9:00 a.m. slot on Monday morning. Though most of the audience had left, Hendrix's interpretation of the "Star-Spangled Banner" raised the national anthem to high art. John Sebastian was hanging out, making the scene, and not scheduled to perform. He wandered backstage, and ended up onstage himself for a solo set, dressed head-to-toe in spectacular tie-dye of his own creation. Tim Hardin, Melanie, Joan Baez, Blood, Sweat & Tears . . . they were all there—except for Bob Dylan, who lived nearby but declined to perform. However, Dylan's friends the Band delivered a memorable performance, just months after their first show using that name. In all, thirty-two acts performed, and the sheer size of the audience, the remarkable performances, the success of the multiple live album releases, and the Academy Award–winning documentary *Woodstock* (1970), changed the entertainment industry. The so-called counterculture was now mainstream.

Trends, by definition, come and go. But a lot of what the folk revival brought with it came and stayed. And it wasn't just the music. In a June 2018 *GQ* magazine article entitled "The Hippies Were Right After All," Devin Friedman wrote, "The hippies may not have won immediately . . . but they won. Their most cherished obsessions—sustainability, solar panels, yoga, mindfulness, mushroom masks, farm-to-table, biodynamism in wine and all else—are all the ideological and practical offspring of what was considered a threat to regular America in the '60s."

Also in 1969, Dylan returned to the Village after a long hiatus in Woodstock. According to the *New York Times* on October 18, 2016, "Despite Mr. Dylan's notoriety, he remembered, he was relatively unbothered by those in the neighborhood, and purchased a 19th-century townhouse at 94 MacDougal Street." But that was not to last. The street, in part by his own doing, had become a bona fide tourist attraction, and the privacy-seeking Dylan was now one of the most famous people in the world. Soon obsessive fans "paraded up and down in front of it chanting and shouting," Dylan wrote in *Chronicles*. And, poof. Once again, he was gone. In 1970, Dylan cut more ties with his past by dissolving his business relationship with manager Albert Grossman after discovering Grossman, as the result of a hastily signed contract, had been pocketing an additional fifty percent of Dylan's publishing royalties.

The singer-songwriter movement flourished in the 1970s. Greenwich Village alumni James Taylor, of the Flying Machine, Janis Ian, who returned with another signature song titled "At Seventeen," Paul Simon, Bob Dylan, Joni Mitchell, and Carly Simon, who had sung in the Village with sister Lucy as the Simon Sisters, dominated singles and album charts, even coexisting for a time with disco. Ever since the "new song" movement had begun to replace traditional folk songs circa 1962, listeners expected artists to write their own material, and that in itself was a revolution in the music industry, changing the roles of A&R departments at labels and song publishers, forever.

As far as protest or topical songs, that is a different story. From the late 1960s through the 1970s, with singer-songwriters making music that was more and more introspective, the mantle was picked up by R&B artists: Stevie Wonder, Marvin Gaye, the Last Poets, the Isley Brothers, War, Gil Scott Heron, Melvin Van Peebles, and many others. In the 1980s, Grandmaster Flash, with "The Message," would do the same as hip-hop took over.

The Beatles had purposely avoided politics. But once they broke up in 1970, John Lennon as a solo artist, and especially in collaboration with Yoko Ono, positively embodied politics, with songs like "Power to the People" and "Give Peace a Chance." At the height of his solo success with the hit single and album *Imagine* in 1971, John Lennon and Yoko Ono moved to Greenwich Village. "I regret profoundly that I was not an American and not born in Greenwich Village," Lennon was to proclaim. The couple rented a modest, one-bedroom apartment atop a house at 105 Bank Street, owned by Lovin' Spoonful drummer Joe Butler. There, visited constantly by Jerry Rubin and Abbie Hoffman, Lennon and Ono composed their most politically charged album, the somewhat Phil Ochs–like *Sometime In New York City*, and the perennial "Happy Xmas (War Is Over)." The Lennon-Onos immersed themselves in the Village scene, producing an album for Lower East Side street-rock performer David Peel after hearing him perform in Washington Square Park, and working with Elephant's Memory, a Village-based, politically active street band.

While Lennon had been admittedly influenced by Dylan in the previous decade, by 1972, he appeared to be more in Ochs's singing journalist territory. However, Lennon's political outspokenness, support of the Black Panthers, and attendance at anti-war demonstrations were to cause problems, including the threat of deportation and constant FBI surveillance, as documented in the film *The U.S. vs. John Lennon* (2006).

Teenagers Terre Roche and sister Maggie arrived in the Village in 1968 to audition for Izzy Young at Folklore Center, in hopes of performing Maggie's fabulously idiosyncratic—some might say "quirky"—songs on Izzy's folk music show on WBAI radio. They soon found themselves being taken under the wing of Dave Van Ronk, who was at the audition, and being managed by Terri Thal. Van Ronk turned them on to albums by Joni Mitchell, Tim Buckley, Tim Hardin, and Tom Rush. "These were all friends of theirs," Terre told me.

"When I wandered into this scene, I had no idea that this was a significant thing that had been brewing since the beginning of the sixties. I was fifteen years old and still in high school in New Jersey. And when I'd go back there, nobody knew who Joni Mitchell or Tim Hardin and all these people were. I remember feeling out of step with others at school. It was like opening up into a whole new world." During this time, Dave Van Ronk and Terri Thal were splitting up. But Thal remained Maggie and Terre's manager, and Van Ronk continued to give performance advice. "Don't be afraid to flop," he told them.

In 1970, with Simon & Garfunkel having split up, Paul Simon was teaching a songwriting class at NYU. Thal recommended the class to Maggie and Terre, who went to the university to meet Simon. "Maggie found out where the class was and went there. She waited in the lobby and approached Paul when he came in. He invited her to come back the next week with me and play for him," Terre recalled. "When we did, he invited us to join the class."

"We played at the hoots at the Gaslight and at the Bitter End. That's where we were introduced by Terri Thal to Marilyn Lipsius, who put us on the coffeehouse circuit," Terre told me. She continued her high school lessons on the road while touring the national circuit with Maggie. Upon returning to New York two years later, they reconnected with Paul Simon and ended up at the session for his next, blockbuster solo album *There Goes Rhymin' Simon* (1973) in Muscle Shoals, Alabama—where they arrived uninvited—and signed with Simon and his attorney Michael Tannen's publishing company, De-Shufflin Inc. That led to Maggie and Terre making their debut duo album *Seductive Reasoning* (1975) for Columbia Records.

"After we made *Seductive Reasoning*, we quit the music business and went down to Hammond, Louisiana. That's where Maggie wrote 'The Hammond Song.' After a year we came back to New York. Suzzy [Maggie and Terre's younger sister] was in college at SUNY Purchase, studying acting. She and Maggie moved into an apartment together, and that's when we started singing together as a trio." As the 1980s approached, now with Suzzy, the Roches would sign with Warner Bros. records and continue to make beguiling recordings. Though comfortable performing folk music, the Roches had a particular knack for moving with ease in progressive rock and avant-garde circles, with artists like Robert Fripp and Philip Glass. They defied genre or category with a unique songwriting perspective and a rare sense of humor, writing songs like "Face Down at Folk City" and Terre's "Mr. Sellack," a song about begging to return to her old job at the Waverly Inn restaurant. Sadly, Maggie passed away in 2017. Terre and I became good friends starting in the 1990s, and we have collaborated on many shows and recordings. She has explored multiple styles and genres in her solo work, and both she and Suzzy continue to perform and record music that defies category, each possessing exquisite musicality and a signature sense of humor.

Dave Van Ronk was never to leave Greenwich Village. Quoted by Lawrence Block in the foreword of his memoir, "Why should I go anywhere?" Dave said of the Village. "I'm already here." I never met Dave. For no good reason, because we were neighbors. But while writing this book, it was his presence I felt the strongest. Late at night, if I'd put on one of his records or pick up my guitar to play one of his arrangements, I would sense his particular mix of witty criticism and tremendous support. Known more for his interpretations, one of the handful of songs that Dave Van Ronk wrote was "Last Call," first appearing on his 1973 album *Songs for Aging Children*.

And so we've had another night, of poetry and poses,
And each man knows he'll be alone, when the sacred ginmill closes.

Van Ronk passed away in 2002 at age sixty-five. Hero to Dylan, champion of Joni Mitchell— his version of her song "Clouds (Both Sides Now)" was her favorite—and mentor to countless others, it's no wonder that a section of Sheridan Square is named Dave Van Ronk Street in his honor. His memoir, *The Mayor of MacDougal Street*, was completed by Elijah Wald and published in 2005.

On New Year's Eve of 1972, proto-punk poetess Patti Smith opened for Phil Ochs at Max's Kansas City on Union Square—which was then booked by Gaslight manager Sam Hood. She returned to Max's on a bill with Ochs for six subsequent nights in 1973. With her 1960s rock sensibilities (her first single was "Hey Joe," backed with her own masterful Beat poem set to music, "Piss Factory," in 1974), and just as Carolyn Hester had bridged the fifties and sixties, Smith became a bridge between the sixties and seventies. Inspired by Beats and rock and roll, Smith's career has been one of the most enduring and consistent in the rock pantheon.

Though the sound may have been considerably different, the punk scene of the 1970s from which Patti Smith emerged—born in East Village and Bowery venues, particularly CBGB and Max's—can itself be seen as a continuation of the revolution that began with the folk revival and the MacDougal Street coffeehouses. Woody Guthrie and Pete Seeger's unrelenting messaging, Dylan's unyielding arrogance, and the Velvet Underground's uncompromising, amped-up street wisdom all played a part in punk.

By the mid-1980s, a new, acoustically driven Greenwich Village folk scene was thriving, at venues like the relocated Gerde's Folk City, now on West Third Street, and the Speakeasy, on MacDougal, right across from the old Kettle of Fish. That's where Cynthia Gooding and Dave Van Ronk would meet for a drink, checking out and critiquing the newer acts in town—Suzanne Vega, Christine Lavin, Cliff Eberhardt, Shawn Colvin—as Gooding's daughter, Leyla Spencer, bartended. The cycle had begun yet again.

In subsequent years, skyrocketing rents for apartments and venues, changes in musical tastes, and the increasing number of entertainment options elsewhere took their toll on the Village. Jazz clubs like the Half Note and the Five Spot were shuttered. The Night Owl became a head shop, selling smoking supplies, T-shirts, and souvenirs. And artists, no longer able to afford apartments in the Village, moved away. Terre Roche and I had a game we would play while walking around the Village—trying to name the previous occupants as we'd pass each storefront—that we put to words and music.

> *Walk through the city*
> *on any clear night*
> *There are signs you will see there*
> *that may never seem right.*
> *At first glance, or last glance,*
> *or by light of the day*
> *Something else used to be there that must have*
> *faded away. . . .*
>
> *What used to be there?*
>
> *Somebody asked me to drop in and see*
> *But the door was different, and you needed a key*
> *The person inside who was no longer me*
> *said the person who died lived in number 2B.*
>
> *Slowly returning the gravity pull*
> *I wanted to find those responsible*
> *for turning Times Square into a video game*
> *and Folk City into the Kettle of Fish*
> *and so on, and so on, and so on.*

What used to be there?

I'm a no more neighbor in my neighborhood
standing in the spot where Bob Dylan once stood
Before he shot out the cannon and landed in Hollywood
scratching the back of his head, and feeling real good
Feeling real good.

Who are those people in the window pane
with a vague recollection of some reason they came?
It's me with a grin and you with a blank stare
Come lookin', come lookin', come lookin' for what used to be there

What used to be there?

Coda

In fall 2021, I was teaching my class, Music + Revolution: Greenwich Village in the 1960s, at the New School here in the Village for the fourth consecutive year. In our classroom on West Thirteenth Street, we were talking about the so-called "Beatnik Riot" that had happened a few blocks away, in Washington Square Park, and what it meant at the time. 2021 marked its sixtieth anniversary. We watched nineteen-year-old Dan Drasin's 1961 film *Sunday* and talked about how Izzy Young and those folksingers went to battle with their voices, guitars, and autoharps so that people can play music in the park today. Happy Traum had just spoken to the class via teleconference call, as we were still in the throes of the pandemic. He had been in the park that day in '61 and was roughed up by cops—all captured in Drasin's film. As we talked with Happy onscreen, a student in the front row, Sophia, raised her hand. "Can we go?" she asked. "Where?" I replied. "Can we bring our guitars and play folk music in the park on a Sunday?" I responded with an unequivocal "yes."

We made plans to gather in the park on October 17, 2021, just as I was writing the final chapter for this book. I invited Happy to join us. Sophia and I contacted the Sixth Precinct of the NYPD to inquire about permits to play music in the park and were told that none would be needed. We both posted about our plans on social media and immediately got hundreds of shares.

It was a beautiful, sunny fall afternoon as I walked with my friend Abraham along Waverly Place to the park. Past the Washington Square Hotel, past the "hanging tree." Just one glimpse of the luminescent, white arch from a distance, and all the history came gushing forth. Marcel Duchamp climbing to the top with his friends and declaring the Village a free and independent republic . . . echoes of the voices raised in protest for workers' rights in the aftermath of the Triangle Shirtwaist Factory fire, and for women's suffrage . . . the anti-Nazi rallies in the thirties, anti–Vietnam War rallies in the sixties, Bette Midler singing at a Gay Pride rally in the seventies, Occupy Wall Street drum circles in 2011, Madonna singing in support of Hillary Clinton's 2016 presidential campaign, Black Lives Matter protests in the summer of 2020 . . . and people making music or just hanging out on the grass or by the fountain. All happening on top of what had been a graveyard, still with an occupancy of roughly twenty thousand souls.

I recalled a scene in the Tennessee Williams film *The Fugitive Kind* (1960), based on his play *Orpheus Descending*. In the film, Joanne Woodward as Carol Cutrere and Marlon Brando as Valentine "Snakeskin" Xavier, a guitar-playing folksinger, are talking in a dark cemetery, the "local bone orchard." Carol says to Snakeskin,

> *"You hear the dead people talking?"*
> *"Dead people don't talk," Snakeskin replies.*
> *"Sure they do. They chatter away like birds. But all they can say is one word.*
> *And that word is 'live.' Live. Live. Live. Live. Live. That's all they know.*
> *That's the only advice they can give."*

Even police barricades and curfews have never stopped people from being drawn to Washington Square Park. Maybe they are hearing—and heeding—the simple word of advice from all those spirits that linger there. It's a place where people come to live. Music is a pure expression of life—crystallized yet fluid. It lives.

We gathered by the fountain at 2:00 p.m., facing the arch, and played music together in the park that day. "If I Had a Hammer," "This Land Is Your Land," Donovan's "Colours," "Blowin' in the Wind," "House of the Rising Sun," "Goodnight, Irene." The sound echoed through the park as people listened and sang along. Two cops watched from a distance. One of the spectators made a FaceTime call to filmmaker Dan Drasin, now seventy-nine, so he could watch. I said hello and thanked him for his film. Happy Traum came by with his wife, Jane, and their daughter. Some Hare Krishna followers were chanting nearby, with bells and singing. The strains of a jazz combo's saxophone echoed from one corner of the park, the sounds of hip-hop from another. My friend, in a tie-dyed hoodie and shoulder-length hair, was skateboarding around, while my students continued singing, casting long shadows in the fall sun. A ray of deep-gold sunlight flashed on my guitar as I handed it to Happy. He smiled, looking around at the scene, taking it in. When he started playing, he was young again. Time stood still. Not a second had passed.

acknowledgments

I am indebted to John Cerullo, whose belief in this project gave it wings. I am grateful for his editorial contributions and his friendship. And I was fortunate to work with a dream team that included Laurel Myers, Barbara Claire, Jessica Thwaite, Chris Chappell, and others at Backbeat Books and Rowman & Littlefield—all of whom helped bring *Music + Revolution* to life.

I could not have written this book without the continuous help, advice, suggestions, and encouragement from my lifelong friend Jon Klages. Thank you, Jon, for always being there for me.

Special thanks to Jean Slobodow, another lifelong friend, who was instrumental in formatting the book and putting everything in order.

I've been a fan of Donovan all my life. His help, encouragement, and poetry has been a tremendous gift throughout the writing of this book. Thank you, Donovan.

Special thanks to Carolyn Hester, Terri Thal, Barry Kornfeld, Steve Katz, Happy Traum, and David Amram for going way beyond the call of duty. Thank you to all the interviewees for making this book breathe with your own lives, insights, and beautiful histories.

Thanks to Anthony DeCurtis, David Fricke, Stephen Petrus, and Andrew Berman for historical perspectives that laid the foundation for this work.

Appreciation to Bob Ward for kindly helping facilitate the use of David Gahr's iconic images, and to Roger Gorman, whose brilliant design concepts never cease to excite me.

Thanks to Sophia Bondi and to Abraham Spencer for being a part of the final scene, and for helping with the book's completion.

I am surrounded by brilliance: musicians, writers, and friends who inspire me with their talent and

permissions

"Lyndon Johnson Told the Nation"
Words and music by Tom Paxton. © EMI U Catalog,
Inc./Sony ATV Music Publishing.

"I Ain't Marchin' Anymore"
Words and music by Phil Ochs. © Barricade Music,
Inc./ALMO Music Corp./Rondor Music International, Inc.

"It's All Over Now, Baby Blue"
Words and music by Bob Dylan. © Universal Tunes/
Universal Music Publishing Group.

"To Sing for You"
Words and music by Donovan Leitch. © Donovan Music,
LTD/Songs of Peer, LTD.

"The Ballad of a Crystal Man"
Words and music by Donovan Leitch. © Songs of Peer,
LTD.

"Handsome Johnny"
Words and music by Richie Havens. © EMI Unart Catalog,
Inc.

"Heroin"
Words and music by Lou Reed. © Oakfield Avenue Music,
Ltd./EMI Blackwood Music, Inc.

"Don't Make Promises"
Words and music by Tim Hardin. © Allen Stanton
Productions.

"There But for Fortune"
Words and music by Phil Ochs. © Barricade Music, Inc./
ALMO Music Corp./Rondor Music International, Inc.

"Positively 4th Street"
Words and music by Bob Dylan. © Universal Tunes/
Universal Music Publishing Group.

"Chords of Fame"
Words and music by Phil Ochs. © Barricade Music, Inc./
ALMO Music Corp./Rondor Music International, Inc.

"Season of the Witch"
Words and music by Donovan Leitch. © Donovan Music,
LTD./Peer International Corp.

"House Un-American Blues Activity Dream"
Words and music by Richard Fariña. © Warner Chappell
Music, Inc.

"Birmingham Sunday"
Words and music by Richard Fariña. © Songs of
Universal/Universal Music Group.

"Society's Child"
Words and music by Janis Ian. © Taosongs Two.

"Thirsty Boots"
Words and music by Eric Andersen. © EMI U Catalog,
Inc./Sony ATV Music Publishing.

"Hazard, Kentucky"
Words and music by Phil Ochs. © Barricade Music,
Inc./ALMO Music Corp./Rondor Music International, Inc.

"Summer in the City"
Words and music by John Sebastian, Mark Sebastian, and
Steve Boone. © Alley Music Corp./Trio Music Company/Mark
Sebastian Music.

"Get Together"
Words and music by Chet Powers. © Irving Music.

"It Ain't Me, Babe"
Words and music by Bob Dylan. © Universal Tunes/Univer-
sal Music Publishing Group.

sources

Interviews

(In alphabetical order. All dates 2021, unless noted)

Steve Addabbo (8/16)

David Amram (9/21)

Eric Andersen (7/6, 7/8)

Jack Baker (8/1)

Steve Berkowitz (6/11, 6/12)

Andrew Berman (1/26, 9/13, 9/14)

David Browne (5/13, 7/21)

David "Lapis" Cohen (2/9, 8/6)

Mitchell Cohen (7/6)

Anthony DeCurtis (5/12)

Dion DiMucci (10/12)

Delores "Dee" Dixon (4/30/2022)

Donovan (5/15, 7/20, 7/21)

Cliff Eberhardt (7/29)

Marc Eliot (8/31)

Jose Feliciano (8/7)

Benjamin Filene (10/7, 10/28)

David Fricke (10/4)

Will Friedwald (7/1)

Jim Glover (5/3, 8/29)

John Heller (4/8)

Carolyn Hester (4/17, 8/21)

Erik Jacobsen (8/18)

Steve Katz (6/14, 6/22, 7/16)

Al Kooper (8/9)

Barry Kornfeld (4/28, 6/23)

Arthur Levy (8/10)

Andre Marcell (7/29)

Justin Martell (7/7)

James K. Moran (6/5)

Roland Mousaa (7/30)

Maria Muldaur (6/26)

Marc Myers (7/29)

Jared Michael Nickerson (10/18)

Rob Norris (5/5)

Sonny Ochs (2/3)

Walter Parks (8/16)

Tom Paxton (4/29)

Allan Pepper (2/26)

Stephen Petrus (4/26, 10/7, 11/1)

Bob Porco (4/12)

Terre Roche (8/29, 10/26)

Steve Rosenthal (3/3)

Buffy Sainte-Marie (8/18)

Michael Schumacher (8/4)

John Sebastian (7/5, 8/28)

Marc Silber (7/23)

Chuck Smith (7/16)

Leyla Spencer (8/8)

Peter Stampfel (2/5)

Terri Thal (1/29, 4/10, 4/19, 5/2, 8/15)

Pat Thomas (7/9)

Happy Traum (5/24, 6/24, 10/5)

Elijah Wald (2/27)

Douglas Yeager (6/2)

Jesse Colin Young (5/19)

Personal Conversations

(Pre-2021)

Tom Chapin

David Gahr

Lenny Kaye

Jonas Mekas

Lou Reed

Melanie Safka

Pete Seeger

Herbert Khaury (Tiny Tim)

Lorre Wyatt

Selected Bibliography

(In order of publication)

Guthrie, Woody. *Bound For Glory*. E. P. Dutton, 1943.

Gahr, David, and Robert Shelton. *The Face of Folk Music*. Citadel Press, 1968.

Eliot, Marc. *Death of a Rebel: A Biography of Phil Ochs*. Anchor Books, 1979.

Warhol, Andy, and Pat Hackett. *Popism: The Warhol Sixties*. Harcourt Brace Jovanovich, 1980.

Bockris, Victor, and Gerard Malanga. *Up-Tight: The Velvet Underground Story*. Omnibus Press, 1983.

Spitz, Bob. *Dylan: A Biography*. McGraw-Hill Publishing Company, 1989.

Schumacher, Michael. *There But for Fortune: The Life of Phil Ochs*. Hyperion, 1996.

Wein, George, with Nate Chinen. *Myself Among Others: A Life in Music*. Da Capo Press, 2003.

Dylan, Bob. *Chronicles: Volume One*. Simon & Schuster, 2004.

Leitch, Donovan. *The Hurdy Gurdy Man*. Century Books/ Random House, 2005.

Van Ronk, Dave, and Elijah Wald. *The Mayor of MacDougal Street*. Da Capo Press, 2005.

Rotolo, Suze. *A Freewheelin' Time*. Broadway Books, 2008.

Cohen, Ronald D., and Stephen Petrus. *Folk City: New York and the American Folk Music Revival*. Oxford University Press, 2015.

Martell, Justin, with Alanna Wray McDonald. *Eternal Troubadour: The Improbable Life of Tiny Tim*. Jawbone Books, 2016.

DeCurtis, Anthony. *Lou Reed: A Life*. Little, Brown and Company, 2017.

Cohen, David. *I'm Gonna Say It Now: The Writings of Phil Ochs*. Backbeat Books, 2020.

Other Sources

Folk City: New York and the Folk Music Revival (2015). Exhibition, curated by Dr. Stephen Petrus at the Museum of the City of New York; June 17, 2015 to January 10, 2016. Sources such as radio, film, television, and print interviews are credited within the text of this book.

In Memoriam

The following people, integral to the story of this book and whose names appear on its pages, passed away in 2021. Sincere condolences to their families and friends.

Alix Dobkin (August 16, 1940–May 19, 2021)

Nanci Griffith (July 6, 1953–August 13, 2021)

Patrick Sky (October 2, 1940–May 26, 2021)

Greg Tate (October 14, 1957–December 7, 2021)

George Wein (October 3, 1925–September 13, 2021)

index
of songs

"A Little Bit of Rain" (Fred Neil), 202, 273, 293

"A Poem on the Underground Wall" (Paul Simon), 179

"A Thousand Years Ago" (Traditional), 110, 172

"Abraham, Martin, and John" (Dick Holler), 271

"All Along the Watchtower" (Bob Dylan), 256

"All I Really Want to Do" (Bob Dylan), 183

"All My Trials" (Traditional), 70

"An American In Paris" (George Gershwin), 250

"Ananais" (Buffy Sainte-Marie), 169

"Angel" (Jimi Hendrix), 255

"Baby Let Me Follow You Down" (Bob Dylan), 107

"Ballad in Plain D" (Bob Dylan), 183

"Beans in My Ears" (Len Chandler), 72

"Benedictus" (Orlando di Lasso; Arr. Paul Simon), 178

"Birmingham Sunday" (Richard Fariña), 241, 294

"Black Is the Color of My True Love's Hair" (Traditional), 44

"Black Sheep Boy" (Tim Hardin), 227

"Bleecker Street" (Paul Simon), 179

"Blowin' in the Wind" (Bob Dylan), 136-39, 292

"Born This Way" (Stefani Germanotta, Jeppe Laursen), 170

"Bound for Glory" (Phil Ochs), 173

"Buddy, Can You Spare A Dime" (Jay Gorney/ Yip Harburg), 109

"California Dreamin'" (John Phillips & Michelle Phillips), 197, 198, 214

"Castles Made of Sand" (Jimi Hendrix), 255

"Catch the Wind" (Donovan Leitch), 219, 231

"Catfish Blues" (McKinley Morganfield aka Muddy Waters), 231

"Chimes of Freedom" (Bob Dylan), 183

"CIA Man" (Tuli Kupferberg), 274

"Cindy, Oh Cindy" (Robert Barron, Burt Long), 33

"Close the Door Lightly When You Go" (Eric Andersen), 247

"Clouds (Both Sides Now)" (Joni Mitchell), 284

"Cod'ine" (Buffy Sainte-Marie), 169

"Coffee Blues" (Mississippi John Hurt), 199

"Colours" (Donovan Leitch), 287

"Come Back Baby" (Walter Davis), 99, 106

"Country Boy" (Fred Neil), 202

"Crucifixion" (Phil Ochs), 160, 267-68, 292

"Crying, Waiting, Hoping" (Buddy Holly), 45

"Daily News" (Tom Paxton), 171

"Daydream" (John Sebastian), 219, 250

"Day-O (The Banana Boat Song)" (Traditional; Arr. Harry Belafonte, William Attaway, Lord Burgess), 32, 41

"Dazed and Confused" (Jake Holmes), 231

"Dear Companion" (Traditional; Arr. Jean Ritchie), 105

"Deutschland Uber Alles" (Joseph Haydn/ August Heinrich Hoffman von Fallersleben), 93

"Diamonds and Rust" (Joan Baez), 75

"Do You Believe In Magic" (John Sebastian), 200, 293

"Don't Make Promises" (Tim Hardin), 226-27, 293

"Don't Think Twice, It's Alright" (Bob Dylan), 149, 151, 168, 246, 258

"Don't Worry Baby" (Brian Wilson/Roger Christian), 213

"Everybody's Talking" (Fred Neil), 279, 295

"Face Down At Folk City" (Maggie, Terre, Suzzy Roche), 283

"Feliz Navidad" (José Feliciano), 246

"Flight of the Bumblebee" (Nikolai Rimsky-Korsakov), 245

"Flute Thing" (Al Kooper), 231

"Four in the Morning" (Jesse Colin Young), 254

"Freight Train Blues" (John Lair), 118

"Freight Train" (Elizabeth Cotten), 54, 118, 167

"Gates of Eden" (Bob Dylan), 194

"Get Together" (Chet Powers), 252-53, 294

"Go Tell It on the Mountain" (Traditional), 179

"Gone Again" (Fred Neil), 202

"Good Day Sunshine" (John Lennon/ Paul McCartney), 219, 250

"Goodnight Irene" (Huddie Ledbetter aka Lead Belly), 26, 30, 169, 287

"Gospel Ship" (Traditional), 246

"Gotta Travel On" (Paul Clayton), 68, 89, 257, 291

"Grizzly Bear" (Jerry Corbitt; from "This Morning She Was Gone" by Jim Jackson), 253

"Hair of Spun Gold" (Janis Ian), 243

"Handsome Johnny" (Richie Havens), 221, 293

"Happy Together" (Garry Bonner/ Alan Gordon), 201

"Happy Xmas (War Is Over)" (John Lennon/ Yoko Ono), 283

"He Lived Alone In Town" (Buffy Sainte-Marie), 170

"He Was A Friend Of Mine" (Traditional), 278

"He Was My Brother" (Paul Simon), 177-78

"Heroin" (Lou Reed), 222-23, 293

"Hesitation Blues" (Traditional), 192, 293

"Hey Joe" (Billy Roberts), 196, 256

"Hey School Girl" (Paul Simon & Art Garfunkel), 177

"House of the Rising Sun" (Traditional), 107-8, 214, 287

"House Un-American Blues Activity Dream" (Richard and Mimi Fariña), 241, 294

"How Much Is That Doggie in the Window?" (Bob Merrill), 41

"I Ain't Marching Anymore" (Phil Ochs), 171, 204, 221, 267, 291
"I Call Your Name" (John Lennon/ Paul McCartney), 213
"I Can't Help But Wonder Where I'm Bound" (Tom Paxton), 73-74
"I Enjoy Being A Girl" (Rogers and Hammerstein), 190
"I Got A Woman" (Ray Charles/ Renald Richard), 245
"I Should Have Known Better" (John Lennon/ Paul McCartney), 182, 202
"I Want To Hold Your Hand" (John Lennon/ Paul McCartney), 167, 183, 185
"I Was Born Ten Thousand Years Ago" (Traditional), 110, 291
"I'll Be Your Mirror" (Lou Reed), 224
"I'll Fly Away" (Traditional), 105
"I'll Keep It With Mine" (Bob Dylan), 88
"I'm On My Way" (Traditional), 157
"If I Were A Carpenter" (Tim Hardin), 227
"If the River Was Whiskey" (Charlie Poole), 192
"Imagine" (John Lennon/Yoko Ono), 283
"It Ain't Me Babe" (Bob Dylan), 183, 214, 258, 294
"It's All Over Now, Baby Blue" (Bob Dylan), 206, 207, 218, 293
"It's Alright Ma (I'm Only Bleeding)" (Bob Dylan), 195

"John Henry" (Traditional), 32

"Keep On Keepin' On" (Len Chandler), 71-72, 291
"Kisses Sweeter Than Wine" (Traditional; Arr. Seeger/Hays), 30

"Lady Madonna" (John Lennon/Paul McCartney), 251
"Last Call" (Dave Van Ronk), 284, 295
"Last Night I Had the Strangest Dream" (Ed McCurdy), 63, 179
"Leader of the Pack" (Shadow Morton, Jeff Barry & Ellie Greenwich), 243
"Learning the Game" (Buddy Hollly), 45
"Light My Fire" (The Doors), 246, 276
"Like A Rolling Stone" (Bob Dylan), 204-6, 207, 214, 233
"Lyndon Johnson Told the Nation" (Tom Paxton), 203, 293

"Maggie's Farm" (Bob Dylan), 194, 206
"Masters of War" (Bob Dylan), 150, 246
"Mississippi Train" (Fred Neil), 202
"Misty Roses" (Tim Hardin), 226-27
"Morning Dew" (Bonnie Dobson), 114-15, 135, 151, 197, 291
"Moscow Nights" (Mikhail Matusovsky), 74
"Motorpsycho Nitemare" (Bob Dylan), 183
"Mr. Sellack" (Terre Roche), 283
"Mr. Spaceman" (based on "Mr. Bass Man" by Johnny Cymbal; Arr. Weber/Stampfel), 193
"Mr. Tambourine Man" (Bob Dylan), 194, 206, 213-14
"Murder Most Foul" (Bob Dylan), 159, 292
"My Back Pages" (Bob Dylan), 183

"Nature Boy" (Eden Ahbez), 190
"Nine Inch Will Please a Lady" (Robert Burns; Paul Clayton), 69, 291
"No More Songs" (Phil Ochs), 276-77
"Not Fade Away" (Buddy Holly, Norman Petty), 44
"Now that the Buffalo's Gone" (Buffy Sainte-Marie), 169

"Oh, Boy!" (Sonny West, Bill Tilghman, Norman Petty), 44
"Oh, Freedom" (Traditional), 156-57
"Oh! Susanna" (Stephen Foster), 196
"Ohio" (Neil Young), 276
"On Top of Old Smoky" (sometimes spelled "Smokey") (Traditional), 30
"One More Parade" (Bob Gibson/ Phil Ochs), 173
"Only A Pawn In Their Game" (Bob Dylan), 156, 292
"Outside A Small Circle of Friends" (Phil Ochs), 268, 294

"Pack Up Your Sorrows" (Richard Fariña), 241
"Peggy Sue" (Jerry Allison, Norman Petty), 44
"Pioneer Women" (John Phillips), 197
"Piss Factory" (Patti Smith, Richard Sohl), 284
"Polly Wolly Doodle" (Traditional), 172
"Positively 4th Street" (Bob Dylan), 233, 293
"Power and the Glory" (Phil Ochs), 5, 173, 292

"Reason to Believe" (Tim Hardin), 226, 273
"Red Rubber Ball" (Paul Simon/Bruce Woodley), 263
"Remember (Walking in the Sand)" (Shadow Morton), 243
"Rock Island Line" (Huddie Ledbetter aka Lead Belly), 32, 143, 167

"Season of the Witch" (Donovan Leitch), 236-37, 241, 295
"Secret Agent Man" (Johnny Rivers), 273
"Seltzer Boy" (Alan Sherman), 158
"September Fifth" ["Steve's Song"] (Steve Katz), 231
"Society's Child" (Janis Ian), 242-45, 294
"Song For Bob Dylan" (David Bowie), 90, 291
"Song To Woody" (Bob Dylan), 89, 107, 291

"Sparrow" (Paul Simon), 179
"Stay Away from the Girls" (Traditional), 69
"Strange Fruit" (Abel Meeropol), 15, 99
"Subterranean Homesick Blues" (Bob Dylan), 194, 218, 293
"Summer In the City" (John Sebastian, Mark Sebastian, Steve Boone), 248-51, 294

"Talkin' New York" (Bob Dylan), 107, 291
"Talking Birmingham Blues" (Phil Ochs), 154
"Talking John Birch Paranoid Blues" (Bob Dylan), 116
"Tape From California" (Phil Ochs), 267, 294
"That'll Be the Day" (Buddy Holly, Norman Petty, Jerry Allison), 44
"The Ballad of a Crystal Man" (Donovan Leitch), 221, 293
"The Banjo Song" (Tim Rose; based on "Oh! Susanna" by Stephen Foster), 197
"The Battle Hymn of the Republic" (William Steffe/Julia Ward Howe), 93
"The Bells" (Phil Ochs), 173
"The Hammer Song" (Pete Seeger, Lee Hays), 5, 29, 31, 157, 291
"The Hammond Song" (Maggie Roche), 283
"The Lady Came From Baltimore" (Tim Hardin), 227
"The Last Thing On My Mind" (Tom Paxton), 171
"The Lonesome Death of Hattie Carol" (Bob Dylan), 168
"The Marvelous Toy" (Tom Paxton), 74
"The Other Side Of This Life" (Fred Neil), 85, 202, 259, 291
"The Patriot Game" (Dominic Behan), 168-69
"The Sounds of Silence (The Sound of Silence)" (Paul Simon), 178-80, 214-15
"The Star Spangled Banner" (Francis Scott Key/John Stafford Smith), 93, 274, 281

"The Titanic" (Huddie Ledbetter aka Lead Belly), 22-23
"The Universal Soldier" (Buffy Sainte-Marie), 127, 169, 204, 221, 274, 291
"The War Drags On" (Mick Softley), 220
"The War Is Over" (Phil Ochs), 277
"There But For Fortune" (Phil Ochs), 171, 231-32, 246, 277, 293
"Thirsty Boots" (Eric Andersen), 183, 247-48, 294
"This Land Is Your Land" (Woody Guthrie), 21-22, 67, 93, 170, 287, 291
"This Little Light of Mine" (Traditional), 36
"This Morning She Was Gone" (Jim Jackson), 253
"Tiptoe Through the Tulips" (Al Dubin & Joe Burke), 269
"Tom Dooley" (Traditional; Arr. Frank Proffitt), 52-53, 169
"Too Many Martyrs" (Bob Gibson/Phil Ochs), 173, 267, 292
"Turn! Turn! Turn!" (Pete Seeger; adapted from the Book of Ecclesiastes), 111, 214-15
"Twelve Thirty (Young Girls Are Coming to the Canyon)" (John Phillips), 198, 214, 246
"Two Trains Running" (McKinley Morganfield aka Muddy Waters), 231

"Venus in Furs" (Lou Reed), 222-23
"Venus" (Robbie van Leeuwen), 196
"Violets of Dawn" (Eric Andersen), 182, 230, 247

"Waist Deep in the Big Muddy" (Pete Seeger), 265, 269, 294
"Walk Right In" (Gus Cannon/Hosea Woods), 143-45
"Water Boy" (Traditional), 34, 158

"We Shall Overcome" (Adapted from "I'll Overcome Some Day"; Arr. Pete Seeger, Zilphia Horton, Guy Carawan, Frank Hamilton), 137, 155-56, 279
"What Used to Be There?" (Terre Roche and Richard Barone), 285-86
"When the Ship Comes In" (Bob Dylan), 156
"When the World's on Fire" (A. P. Carter), 22
"Where Have All the Flowers Gone?" (Pete Seeger and Joe Hickerson), 110-11, 127, 265
"Who's Gonna Buy You Ribbons" (Paul Clayton), 151, 169, 293
"Wimoweh" (Solomon Linda; Arr. Pete Seeger), 30, 265

"You Can Tell the World" (Traditional; Arr. Bob Gibson & Hamilton Camp), 178
"You Were On My Mind" (Sylvia Fricker), 129, 214

index
of subjects

ABC *(television network)*, 165, 166

ABC-TV Hootenanny *(magazine)*, 165.
    See also Hootenanny

Abbey Road (album), 273

ACLU, 33

Actor's Playhouse, 55

Adams, Derroll, 88

Addabbo, Steve, 205, 297

Adler, Lou, 258

Ahbez, Eden, 190

Ain't That News!, 203

Albert Hotel, 199, 229

Alexis Korner's Blues Incorporated *(band)*, 230

All the News that's Fit to Sing (album),
    172, 173

All Things Considered (radio program), 275

Allan Block's Sandal Shop, 91, 100, 229.
    See also Allan Block

Allen, Ray, 54

Allen, Woody, 95, 197, 251

Allende, Salvador, 277

Allison, Jerry, 44. *See also* The Crickets

Allison, Mose, 147, 229

AllMusic Guide, 52

Almanac Singers, The *(folk group)*, 25, 26,
    28, 29, 30, 36, 107, 115, 158

Alpert, Richard, 257

American Communist Party, 24, 29, 36, 47,
    55, 116, 156, 166, 266

American Flyer *(band)*, 273

American Labor Party, 116

American Youth for Democracy, 51

Amram, David, 34, 239, 264, 289, 297

Animals, The *(band)*, 108, 256

Andersen, Eric, 133, 180-82, 225, 230-32,
    240, 247, 262-64, 278, 294, 297

Anderson, Marian, 156

Anohni, 84. *See also* Antony Hegarty

Another Side of Bob Dylan (album), 195,

229, 283

Anthology of American Folk Music, 31, 48,
    84, 87, 107, 155, 192. *See also* Harry Smith

Appalachian dulcimer, 35, 67, 150-51

Arista Records, 194

Armstrong, Louis, 63

Armstrong, Neil, 280

Aronowitz, Al, 184-85, 222-23

Asch, Moses, 23

Ashley, Clarence "Tom," 107

Aspinall, Neil, 184

Associated Press, 173

Astral Weeks (album), 226

Atlantic Records, 123, 243

Audubon Ballroom, 195

A&M Records, 277

Bacharach, Burt, 111

Baez, "Big Joan," 175

Baez, Joan, 34, 42, 51-52, 64, 70, 75, 77,
    107, 114, 123, 144, 150, 152-53, 156,
    166, 169-70, 175-76, 181, 184, 195,
    219, 231, 240-42, 245, 277, 281

Baez, Mimi, 51, 175-76, 240-42. *See also*
    Mimi Fariña

Baez, Pauline, 242

Bag Full of Soul, A (album), 246

Baker, Ginger, 230. *See also* Cream

*Ballads from her Appalachian Family Tradition
    (album)*, 150

Band, The *(band)*, 254, 264, 281

Banhart, Devendra, 273

Bangs, Lester, 239

Banjo Joe, 145. *See also* Gus Cannon

Baraka, Amiri, 48. *See also* LeRoi Jones

Bare, Bobby, 129

Barrett, Syd, 231. *See also* Pink Floyd

Basement Tapes, The (album), 254

Basie, Count, 106

Bastone, Joe, 61-62

Baudelaire, Charles, 180

Bauer, Joe, 252

Bay of Pigs, 83, 113, 135

Beach Boys, The *(band)*, 53, 213-14, 250, 277

Beat Generation, 33, 134. *See also* Beatniks

Beat Poetry, 33, 43, 48, 134, 151, 180

Beatles, The *(band)*, 24, 147, 167-68,
    181-82, 184-85, 191, 195-96, 198, 202,
    213-14, 219, 226, 250-52, 257, 259, 263,
    273, 282. *See also* The Quarrymen

Beatnik Riot, 5, 92, 94, 280, 286

Beatniks, 49, 91-92, 94, 134. *See also*
    Beat Generation

Behan, Dominic, 168

Belafonte, Harry, 26, 31-34, 41-42, 53,
    73, 123-124, 129, 156-57, 242, 246, 277

Bell, Vinnie, 214

Belmonts, The *(vocal group)*, 24. *See also* Dion
    DiMucci; Dion

Benny, Jack, 166

Bergman, Ingmar, 133

Berkowitz, Steve, 12, 27, 115, 205, 297

Berlin, Irving, 11

Berlin Wall, 57, 58, 141

Berman, Marshall, 97

Bernstein, Leonard, 35, 244

Berry, Chuck, 42, 44

Besonen, Julie, 249

Bibb, Eric, 165

Bibb, Leon, 55, 165

Biden, Joe, 21

Big Sur Folk Festival, 240

Big 3, The *(folk trio)*, 169, 196-97

Bikel, Theodore "Theo," 55, 70, 109, 153,
    155, 173

Billboard Hot 100 *(singles chart)*, 144,
    168, 205, 253, 271, 272

Billboard magazine, 8, 28, 32, 41, 118, 125,

128, 144, 168, 177, 185, 195, 205, 219, 234, 244, 253, 254, 266, 271, 272
Bill Haley and the Comets *(band)*, 30
Billy, Matthew, 132
Biltmore Theatre, 266
Biograph (box set), 118
Bishir, Jane, 86
Bishop, Walter, 251
Bitter End, The *(venue)*, 11, 87, 110, 124, 130, 147, 196, 198, 201, 213, 251, 283. *See also* the Cock 'n Bull
Black Lives Matter, 287
Black Panther Party, 282
Black Rock Coalition, The, 228
Blaine, Hal, 214
Blake, Peter, 259
Błaszczak, Jan, 223
Bleecker & MacDougal (album), 85, 201, 202
Bleecker Street, 11, 13, 48, 51, 55-57, 62, 71, 77, 85, 90, 110, 113, 117, 131, 179, 191, 197, 201, 202, 213, 220, 230, 259, 293
Block, Allan, 91, 100, 229. *See also* Allan Block's Sandal Shop
Block, Lawrence, 283
Block, Rory, 91
Blonde on Blonde (album), 254, 256
Blood, Sweat & Tears *(band)*, 273, 281
Blood, Sweat & Tears (album), 273
Bloody Ballads: British and American Murder Ballads (album), 67
Bloom, Augie, 254
Bloomfield, Mike, 204, 206. *See also* Paul Butterfield Blues Band
Blue Angel, The *(venue)*, 31, 176
Blue, David, 136-38, 232, 278
Blues Magoos, The *(band)*, 268
Blues Project, The: A Compendium of the Very Best on the Urban Blues Scene (album), 228
Blues Project, The *(band)*, 75, 224, 227-31,

247, 252, 255, 259, 273
Blumenfeld, Roy, 229
Bobby Burns' Merry Muses of Caledonia (album), 69
Bogarde, Dirk, 133
Boggs, Dock, 153, 177
Boguslav, Raphael "Ray," 77
Bon Soir *(venue)*, 87
Bondi, Sophia, 286, 289
Bongos, The *(band)*, 11, 222
Bonner, Garry, 201
Bonnie Dobson at Folk City (album), 114
Booker, Steve, 227
Boone, Steve, 199, 249, 250, 294. *See also* The Lovin' Spoonful
Bootleg Series Vol. 11: The Basement Tapes Complete (album), 254
Bottom Line, The *(venue)*, 271
'Bout Changes 'n' Things (album), 247
Bouchillon, Chris, 131
Bound For Glory (album), 88
Bound For Glory (book), 88, 136-37, 298
Bowie, David, 11, 90, 291
Boyd, Joe, 207
Brand, Oscar, 20, 31, 55, 94, 106, 129. *See also* Oscar Brand's Folksong Festival
Brando, Marlon, 112, 117, 234, 287
Brecker, Randy, 273
Brend, Mark, 226
Brevoort, The *(building)*, 44-45
Brill Building, 43, 84, 94, 132, 177, 225, 251
Brickman, Marshall, 95, 197
Bringing It All Back Home (album), 193-95, 204, 213-14
British Invasion, 33, 108, 167-68, 185
Broadside magazine, 115, 116, 126, 138, 182, 239, 243
Broadway Central Hotel, The, 95
Brothers Four *(vocal group)*, 129, 165

Brown, Jim, 109
Brown, Peter, 185
Brown v. Board of Education, 41
Browne, David, 266, 197
Browne, Jackson, 254
Bruce, Jack, 166. *See also* Cream
Bruce, Lenny, 26, 189, 191-92, 217, 230, 259
Brumley, Albert E., 105
Buckinghams, The *(band)*, 272
Buffalo Springfield *(band)*, 252
Burns, Ric, 97
Burroughs, William S., 33, 134, 180, 222, 259
Burton, Gary, 226
Butler, Artie, 226, 243
Butler, Joe, 199, 282
Byrds, The *(band)*, 129, 198, 213-15, 252

Café au Go Go *(venue)*, 11, 191, 230, 251, 252, 256, 273
Café Bizarre *(venue)*, 55, 125, 189, 199, 221-23
Café Bohemia *(venue)*, 56
Café Id *(venue)*, 245, 246
Café Raffio *(venue)*, 113, 131
Café Reggio, 56
Café Society *(venue)*, 15, 26-27, 30, 99, 155, 156, 279
Café Wha? *(venue)*, 55, 84-85, 90, 189, 201, 220, 255, 256, 279
Cage, John, 133
Cale, John, 222-23, 272, 294. *See also* The Velvet Underground
Callier, Terry, 213
Cameo-Parkway Records, 172
Camp, Bob (Hamilton Camp), 51, 178
Campbell, Alex, 175
Cannon, Gus, 144-45. *See also* Banjo Joe
Cannon's Jug Stompers *(band)*, 143, 145-46
Capitol Records, 52, 111, 251

Capote, Truman, 133

Caravan (fanzine), 47

Cardin, Pierre, 167

Caricature, The *(venue)*, 90

Carl, Jan, 199

Carlton, Vanessa, 273

Carnegie Hall *(venue)*, 35, 60, 73, 76,
   106, 133, 136, 137, 146, 151, 164, 224,
   264, 275, 277, 278

Carolina Chocolate Drops, The *(band)*, 145

Carson, Johnny, 146, 196

Carter, A. P., 22. *See also* The Carter Family

Carter Family, The, 22, 48, 54, 129, 219, 245

Carter, Maybelle, 54. *See also* The
   Carter Family

Casales, Gerald, 276

Cash, Johnny, 74, 113, 165

Cassady, Neal, 180-81

Castro, Fidel, 55, 78, 174

Cataldo, Joseph "Joe the Wop," 201

Catlin, Roger, 213

Cavalier Magazine, 60, 239

Cavallo, Bob, 198-99

Cave, Nick, 273

CBGB *(venue)*, 284

CBS *(television network)*, 20, 24, 112,
   148, 166-68, 244, 251, 265, 268-70

Celebrations for a Grey Day (album), 240

Chad Mitchell Trio *(folk trio)*, 74, 124, 129,
   139, 165, 174, 213, 248

Chain Gang (album), 27

Chambers Brothers, The *(band)*, 268

Chandler, Chas, 258. *See also* The Animals;
   Jimi Hendrix

Chandler, Len, 71-73, 130, 232, 245, 278, 291

Chaney, James, 178

Chapman, Colin, 117

Charles, Ray, 245

Charles River Valley Boys *(bluegrass group)*, 175

Charters, Samuel "Sam," 143-45, 147

Cheetah, The *(venue)*, 255, 266

Chelsea Hotel, 147, 207, 262

Cherry Lane Music Publishing, 73, 133

Cherry Lane Theatre, 35, 55, 73, 133

Christ, Jesus, 47, 268

Christgau, Robert, 193

CIA, 83, 195, 256, 273-74, 277, 295

Cinematheque, The, 216-17, 222-23

Circle in the Square *(venue)*, 55

City Lights Books, 33, 181

City Winery, New York *(venue)*, 199

Civil Rights Act of 1957, 22, 42

Civil Rights Act of 1964, 203

Civil Rights Movement, 19, 33, 41, 130,
   157, 182, 195, 228, 241, 270

Clancy Brothers *(folk group)*, 34-35, 50,
   55-56, 63-65, 75, 94, 98, 168, 203, 240

Clancy, Liam, 34, 75, 168-69, 176. *See also*
   Clancy Brothers

Clancy, Paddy, 34, 65. *See also* Clancy Brothers

Clancy, Tom, 34-35. *See also* Clancy Brothers

Clark, Gene, 213. *See also* The Byrds

Clark, Ramsey, 278

Clarke, Michael, 214

Clapton, Eric, 228. *See also* Cream

Clayton, Paul, 40, 67-69, 76, 89, 134, 151-154,
   158, 168, 180, 182, 184, 257-58, 291-92

Clearwater Music Festival, 265

Cock 'n Bull *(venue)*, 87. *See also* The Bitter End

Coen Brothers, 72, 109

Cohen, Bob, 138

Cohen, David "Lapis," 239, 297

Cohen, John, 53, 95. *See also* The New Lost
   City Ramblers

Cohen, Mitchell, 11, 194-95, 227, 266, 297

Cold War, 26, 31, 55, 74, 97, 112, 113,
   127, 136, 256, 280

Cole, Bernard, 124

Coleman, E., 158

Collins, Judy, 70, 153, 154, 165, 170, 203,
   213, 227, 241, 248, 275

Columbia Records, 12, 15, 27, 56, 77, 98-100,
   106, 107, 115, 118, 123, 131, 134, 138,
   148, 158, 177, 180, 194, 205, 207, 214-15,
   224, 229, 230, 240, 254, 271, 273, 283

Columbia University, 71, 95, 177, 180

Colvin, Shawn, 285

Commons *(venue)*, 55, 72, 75

Communist Party, 24, 29, 36, 47, 55, 116,
   156, 166, 264

Communist Party U.S.A., 24, 28

Como, Perry, 117

Congress of Racial Equality (CORE), 86, 96,
   130, 156

Cooke, John, 175

Cooke, Sam, 245

Corbitt, Jerry, 252

Corso, Gregory, 48

Cousin Emmy, 206

Country Blues, The (album), 143. *See also*
   Samuel Charters

Cotten, Elizabeth, 54, 167

Cox, Billy, 255

Cray, Ed, 54

Cream *(band)*, 76, 230, 253

Creem Magazine, 239

Crickets, The, 43, 45. *See also* Buddy Holly

Cronkite, Walter, 269, 270

Crosby, David, 198, 213, 276. *See also*
   Crosby, Stills, and Nash

Crosby, Stills, and Nash *(band)*, 87, 276

Cuban Missile Crisis, 135-36, 151

Cuban Revolution, 55, 76, 78, 86, 113

Cunningham, Agnes "Sis," 115, 126,
   173, 181, 182

*Cutting Edge 1965-66, The: The Bootleg Series
   Vol. 12 (album)*, 205

Cyrkle, The *(band)*, 263

Daley, Richard, 275
Dalton, Karen, 77, 83-85, 202, 252, 273
Damned, The (film), 133
Dane, Barbara, 166
Danko, Rick, 254. *See also* The Band
Darin, Bobby, 213, 251
Darling, Erik, 35, 62, 94, 143-45. *See also*
  The Tarriers; The Rooftop Singers; The Weavers
Dave Clark Five, The *(band)*, 168
*Dave Van Ronk and the Ragtime Jug
  Stompers (album)*, 75, 147
Davis, Clive, 201
Davis, Miles, 56, 87, 273
Davis, Reverend Gary, 55, 63, 70, 72, 75,
  95, 123, 125, 153, 219, 243
Day, Doris, 213
Dean, James, 32, 35, 88, 112, 151
Decca Records, 30-31, 44
DeCurtis, Anthony, 8, 11, 42-43, 57, 105,
  134, 222-23, 226, 289, 297-98
Democratic National Convention of 1968,
  275-76
Denisoff, Serge, 132
Denver, John, 263
Devo *(band)*, 115, 276
di Prima, Diane, 48
Dickson, Jim, 213
Diddley, Bo, 222
Didion, Joan, 133
Dietrich, Marlene, 111
DiMucci, Dion, 46, 253, 259, 271, 297.
  See also Dion; The Belmonts
Dion, 46, 253, 259, 271, 297. *See also*
  Dion DiMucci; The Belmonts
Disraeli Gears (album), 253
Dixon, Delores "Dee," 137-39. *See also* New
  World Singers

D'Lugoff, Art, 51, 94
Dobkin, Alix, 76, 298
Dobson, Bonnie, 114-15, 128-29, 135,
  151, 196, 291
Doherty, Denny, 197
Dom, The *(venue)*, 11, 266. *See also*
  The Electric Circus
Donegan, Lonnie, 32, 143, 167, 203
Donovan (Donovan Leitch), 7, 11, 127,
  210, 212, 218-20, 224-25, 230, 240,
  269, 287, 289, 293-95, 297-98
Dont Look Back (film), 218
Doors, The *(band)*, 87, 225, 274
Drake, Nick, 226
Drasin, Dan, 92-94, 286-87
Dreamers (album), 254
Duchamp, Marcel, 15, 133, 286
Dulcimer Songs and Solos (*album*), 69
Dust Bowl, 21, 25, 83
Dutch West India Company, 12
Duvivier, George, 252
Dylan, Bob, 34, 43, 50-51, 53, 56, 75-77,
  83, 85, 87-91, 94-95, 98-100, 104, 106-8,
  113, 116-18, 126, 128-29, 136-39,
  146, 148-59, 170-75, 177-78, 180-85,
  189, 193-95, 201, 204-8, 212-14, 218-19,
  224-29, 232-34, 246-47, 250-51, 254,
  256-59, 271, 277-79, 281, 286, 291-94,
  298. *See also* Robert Zimmerman

Earle, The, 75, 128, 182, 197, 214. *See also*
  Washington Square Hotel
East of Eden (film), 35, 88
Eberhardt, Cliff, 221, 284, 297
Ed Sullivan Show, The (television show), 8,
  147-48, 167-68, 196
Eder, Bruce, 52, 77
Eisenhower, Dwight D., 42, 78
El Teatro Puerto Rico *(venue)*, 245

Electric Circus, The *(venue)*, 266. *See also*
  The Dom
Electric Lady Studios, 267
Elektra Records, 42, 67, 70, 75, 85, 146-47,
  148, 171-72, 201, 203-4, 228, 242
Eliot, Marc, 113, 177, 180, 239, 297-98
Elizabeth Irwin High School, 109
Elliot, Cass, 168, 196-97, 199. *See also*
  The Big 3; The Mamas and the Papas
Elliot, Ramblin' Jack, 63, 70, 88-89, 90-91,
  95, 112, 153, 166, 218, 278
EMI Records, 167, 291-94
Empire State Building, 7, 202, 216
English, Logan, 64, 66, 70, 94-95
Epstein, Brian, 167, 185, 263-64
Ertegun, Ahmet, 201
Evans, Bill, 182
Even Dozen Jug Band *(band)*, 87, 146-48, 229
Everly Brothers, 45, 116, 123, 128, 158, 178
Everly, Phil, 45
Evers, Medgar, 154, 157, 173
Exploding Plastic Inevitable, 223

Factory, The, 134, 205, 108, 223-35, 271-72.
  See also Andy Warhol
Fariña, Mimi, 175-76, 240-42. *See also*
  Mimi Baez
Fariña, Richard, 65, 98-99, 134, 174-76,
  240-42, 254-55, 294. *See also* Richard
  & Mimi Fariña
Fass, Bob, 275
Fat Black Pussycat *(venue)*, 136-37, 190
Faust, Luke, 55
FBI, 29, 31, 36, 195, 201, 264, 270, 274-75, 282
Feliciano! (album), 247
Feliciano, José, 158, 189, 245-47, 274, 297
Fellini, Federico, 223
Ferlinghetti, Lawrence, 33, 180-81. *See also*
  City Lights Books

Fields, Danny, 225

Fifth Album (album), 232, 248

Fifth Peg, The *(venue)*, 62-64. *See also* Gerde's Folk City

Filene, Benjamin, 23, 297

Fillmore East, The *(venue)*, 11

Fillmore West, The *(venue)*, 224, 231

Fitzgerald, Ella, 30

Five Spot Café *(venue)*, 117

Flanders, Tommy, 229-30

Flemons, Dom, 145

Flying Machine, The *(band)*, 229, 281. *See also* James Taylor

FM Records, 196

Folklore Center, 28, 56, 61, 64, 71, 90, 92-93, 109, 148, 229, 233, 282

Folk Festival at Newport (album), 70

Folksay, 28-29

Folksinger's Choice (radio program), 70, 129

Folksinger's Guild, 50, 68

Folksingers 'Round Harvard Square (album), 52

Folksong Festival, 20, 106

Folkways Records, 23, 31, 48, 54, 64, 66-67, 69, 110, 116, 139, 143, 151, 170, 221, 230-31, 291

Fosse, Bob, 192

Foster, Gwen, 107

Foster, Stephen, 196

Fouratt, Jim, 275

Frank, Robert, 34

Freedom Rides (Freedom Riders), 86, 96, 155

Freedom Highway (album), 241

Freedom Singers, The *(vocal group)*, 71, 138, 153, 155

Freewheelin' Bob Dylan, The (album), 139, 148-50

Fretted Instruments, 229

Fricke, David, 232, 267, 268, 277, 289, 297

Fricker, Sylvia, 128-29. *See also* Ian & Sylvia; Sylvia Tyson

Friedan, Betty, 133

Friedman, Devin, 281

Friedwald, Will, 87, 297

Friesen, Gordon, 115, 126, 173, 181, 232

Fripp, Robert, 283

Frizzell, Lefty, 113

Fugitive Kind, The (film), 287, 295

Fugs, The *(band)*, 84, 225, 273-75. *See also* Ed Sanders

Gabler, Milt, 30

Gahr, David, 4, 8, 28, 229, 289, 297

Gandhi, Mahatma, 157

Gabro, Greta, 191, 254

Garfunkel, Art, 158, 176-80, 214-15, 259, 283. *See also* Tom Graph; Tom & Jerry; Kane & Garr; Simon & Garfunkel

Garrick Theater, 191

Gaslight Poetry Cafe *(venue)*, 33, 48, 55, 66, 71-73, 75, 76, 85, 89, 108, 109, 127, 131, 136, 137, 151, 171-72, 177, 182, 191, 225, 228, 243, 267, 280, 283, 284

Gaslight Records, 171

Gate of Horn *(venue)*, 50, 75, 105, 108, 192, 213

Gaye, Marvin, 274, 282

Genet, Jean, 217

Gerde's Folk City *(venue),* 61-66, 75, 94, 96, 98-100, 110, 114, 138, 146, 177, 178, 181, 182, 197, 216, 220, 222, 246, 252, 271, 278, 284-85. *See also* The Fifth Peg

Gerry and the Pacemakers *(band)*, 168

Gibson Guitars (Gibson Brands, Incorporated), 21, 45, 75, 143, 229

Gibson, Bob, 51, 52, 53, 68, 108, 113, 153, 154, 165, 173, 179, 279, 292

Giddens, Rhiannon, 241. *See also* The Carolina Chocolate Drops

Gilbert, Ronnie, 29, 30, 184, 196, 207. *See also* The Weavers

Gillespie, Dizzy, 63

Gilliam, Michelle, 197-98. *See also* Michelle Phillips; The Mamas and the Papas

Ginsberg, Allen, 33, 36, 41, 48, 134, 179, 180-81, 195, 217, 218-19, 257, 278, 280

Glaser, Milton, 124, 191. *See also* Push Pin Studios

Glass, Philip, 283

Glover, Jim, 112-13, 116, 123, 125, 131, 201, 297. *See also* Jim & Jean

God & the FBI (album), 275

God Bless Tiny Tim (album), 269

Goldberg, Barry, 206

Goldstein, Kenneth, 263

Gooding, Cynthia, 52, 55, 56, 64, 69-71, 90, 94, 95, 129-31, 169, 206, 223, 285. *See also Folksinger's Choice*

Goodman, Andrew, 178

Goodman, Benny, 15, 106, 228

Gordon, Alan, 201

Gordon, Lou, 55

Gordon, Max, 26, 33, 147, 176

Gorgoni, Al, 215

Gorson, Arthur, 248

Gottlieb, Lou, 53

GQ magazine, 281

Graham, Bill, 224

Grammar, Billy, 68

Grammy Awards, 20, 158, 205, 247, 273, 279

Grand Ole Opry, The *(venue; radio program)*, 105

Graph, Tom, 179. *See also* Art Garfunkel; Tom & Jerry; Simon & Garfunkel

Grateful Dead *(band)*, 114, 115, 148, 231, 257, 258

Gravy, Wavy, 71, 191, 275. *See also* Hugh Romney

Gray, Michael, 137

Gray Streeter, Leslie, 271

Great Depression, 19, 21, 29, 88, 144, 156

Great Society, The, 203

Greatest Hits (Phil Ochs album), 277

Green, Debbie, 181, 248

Greenbrier Boys, The *(bluegrass group)*, 49, 95, 100, 130, 166

Greenhaus, Dick, 77

Greenwich Theater *(venue)*, 176

Gregg, Bobby, 204, 214

Gregory, Dick, 157

Griffith, Nanci, 106, 298

Grisman, David, 146

Grossman, Albert, 50, 52, 98, 104, 108-10, 118, 123, 128, 129, 155, 194, 198, 205, 206, 207, 218, 221, 225, 281

Grossman, Sally, 194

Grossman, Stefan, 146

Guardian, The (newspaper), 25, 255, 265

Guthrie, Arlo, 277

Guthrie, Woody, 21, 23-25, 26, 35, 67, 83, 86, 88, 90, 107, 112, 116, 117, 130, 131, 158, 164, 165, 170, 173, 182, 218, 259, 264, 284, 291

Haight-Ashbury, 181

Hair (musical), 265-66

Haley, Alex, 133, 195

Halifax Three, The *(folk trio)*, 168, 197

Hammond, John, 15, 27, 98-100, 106, 118, 148, 155, 174, 230, 271

Hammond Jr., John, 230, 254

Hansen, Barry, 228

Hardin, Tim, 87, 181, 199, 200, 220, 225-27, 231, 247, 254, 271, 273, 278, 281-83, 293

Harper, Josie, 45

Harrison, George, 24, 168, 213, 250. *See also* The Beatles

Havens, Richie, 164, 181, 189, 206, 210,

220-21, 255-56, 281, 293

Haworth, Jann, 259

Haynes, Todd, 225

Hays, Lee, 25, 28-29, 91, 291. *See also* Almanac Singers; The Weavers

Hegarty, Antony, 85. *See also* Anohni

Heller, John, 51, 297

Hellerman, Fred, 29, 77. *See also* The Weavers

Hendricks, Jim, 196-97

Hendrix, Jimi, 221, 244, 255-56, 259, 266, 267, 274, 281

Hendrix, Leon, 255

Hendrix, Lucille, 255

Henske, Judy, 153, 165, 266

Heron, Gil Scott, 283

Hester, Carolyn, 44-45, 52, 56-57, 61, 64-65, 70, 77, 96, 98-100, 105-9, 118, 166, 174-76, 223, 240-42, 267, 289, 297

Hickerson, Joe, 111

Highway 61 Revisited (album), 207, 223

Hill, Joe, 25

Hillman, Chris, 213. *See also* The Byrds

Hinds, William, 242

Hoboken, New Jersey, 11, 149

Hoffman, Abbie, 275, 282

Hoffman, Dustin, 192

Hofmann, Albert, 256-57, 259

Holbrook, Benjamin Scott, 133

Holiday, Billie, 15, 27, 83, 99, 106, 279

Holler, Dick, 271

Holly, Buddy, 43-46, 65, 68, 84, 89, 99, 106, 201, 271, 277, 291. *See also* The Crickets

Holy Modal Rounders *(band)*, 76, 84, 188, 192-93, 273

Holy Modal Rounders, The (album), 193

Holzman, Jac, 70, 146, 173

Hood, Sam, 76, 284

Hooker, John Lee, 70, 72, 94-95, 108, 153,

181, 254

Hootenanny, 26, 63, 138, 151, 165, 174, 177, 196, 243

Hootenanny (magazine), 146-47, 165. *See also ABC-TV Hootenanny*

Hootenanny (television show), 165-66, 203

Hootenanny Hoot (film), 165

Hoover, J. Edgar, 195, 271

Hopkins, Lightnin', 117, 182

Hopper, Dennis, 277

Hotel Delmonico, 184, 219, 222-23

House Un-American Activities Committee (HUAC), 31, 35-36, 51, 111, 274

Houston, Cisco, 25, 26, 63, 89, 90, 91

Howlin' Wolf, 130, 205

Hubert's Museum and Live Flea Circus, 189

Hudson, Garth, 254. *See also* The Band

Hudson River, 12, 97, 131, 149, 249, 264-65

Hudson River Sloop Clearwater, 264

Hughes, Langston, 156, 241, 292

Hums of the Lovin' Spoonful (album), 251

Humphrey, Hubert, 275

Hunstein, Don, 150

Hynde, Chrissie, 276. *See also* The Pretenders

I Love Lucy (television show), 86

Ian, Janis, 34, 116, 231, 242-43, 247, 276, 281, 295

Ian & Sylvia *(folk duo)*, 108, 128-30, 149, 153, 165, 214, 254. *See also* Sylvia Fricker; Ian Tyson; Sylvia Tyson

Ifshin, David, 278

Ike and Tina Turner, 255

Imagine (album), 282

Industrial Workers of the World, 25

Inman & Ira, 75. *See also* Leroy Inman; Ira Rogers

Inman, Leroy, 75. *See also* Inman & Ira

Inside Llewyn Davis (film), 72, 109

International Talent Associates, 129

Irish Republican Army, 174

Iron Curtain, 113

Isaacson, Miki, 96

Isle of Wight Festival, 269

Isley Brothers, The *(band)*, 255, 282

It's My Way! (album), 169-70

Ives, Burl, 20, 25, 31, 35, 62, 72-73, 86, 171

Jack Benny Program (television show), 167

Jackson, Mahalia, 63, 156

Jacobs, Jane, 94, 97, 98

Jacobsen, Erik, 118, 198, 226-27, 250-51, 253, 266, 297

James, Gary, 255

James, Jesse, 117

James-Younger Gang, 117

Jara, Victor, 277

Jarrard, Rick, 246-47

Jeff Beck Group *(band)*, 115

Jefferson Airplane *(band)*, 253, 259

Jefferson, Blind Lemon, 48

Jenkins, Gordon, 30

Jennings, Waylon, 45, 46, 129

Jim & Jean *(folk duo)*, 113, 123, 131, 231, 268, 278

Jimmy James and the Blue Flames *(band)*, 255

Joe's Pub *(venue)*, 216. *See also* Joseph Papp's Public Theater

John Birch Society, 74, 148

John Wesley Harding (album), 265

Johns, Jasper, 133

Johnson, Lady Bird, 159

Johnson, Lyndon, 203, 265, 270, 293

Johnson, Robert, 271

Johnson Reagon, Bernice, 157

Johnston, Bob, 207

Jones, Brian, 223, 230. *See also* The Rolling Stones

Jones, LeRoi, 48. *See also* Amiri Baraka

Jones, Quincy, 249

Joplin, Janis, 244, 256

Joseph Papp's Public Theater, 265

Josh White and the Carolinians *(band)*, 27, 155-56

Journal of American Folklore, The, 54

Journeymen, The *(band)*, 129, 165, 172, 196-98

Judson Memorial Church, 94, 133

Jug Bands, 87, 143, 145-47, 149, 192, 201, 253

Kalb, Danny, 75, 95, 147, 173, 179, 227-31

Kane & Garr, 177, 180. *See also* Simon and Garfunkel; Tom & Jerry

Kapp Records, 139

Karmon, Pete, 182

Katz, Steve, 96-97, 143, 146-47, 149, 224, 227, 229-31, 263, 273, 289, 297. *See also* Even Dozen Jug Band; The Blues Project; Blood, Sweat & Tears; American Flyer

Kaufman, Bob, 48

Kazan, Elia, 35-36

Keith, Linda, 255-56

Kelly, Paula, 99

Kennedy, John F., 24, 77-78, 83, 112, 115, 130, 135, 155, 159-60, 165-66, 181, 193, 267-68, 270-71, 281

Kennedy Onassis, Jacqueline, 159

Kennedy, Robert F., 270, 275

Kennedy, Ted, 280

Kent State Massacre, 276

Kerouac, Jack, 33-34, 48, 88, 134, 180

Kesey, Ken, 133, 256-57

Kettle of Fish, 90, 107-8, 128, 172, 216, 219, 232, 277, 284-85

Khrushchev, Nikita, 114, 135

Khuary, Herbert, 189. *See also* Tiny Tim

Kickin' Child (album), 271

King Dunaway, David, 111

King, Reverend Dr. Martin Luther, 34, 41, 72, 155, 270

Kingston Trio *(folk/pop trio)*, 52-54, 73-74, 77, 108, 110-11, 123, 128-29, 150, 168, 184, 220, 249, 253

Knight, Curtis, 255

Knob Lick Upper 10,000 *(band)*, 118, 198

Koch, Ed, 94

Koerner, Ray, & Glover *(band)*, 228

Kooper, Al, 204, 206, 230-31, 273, 297. *See also* The Blues Project; Blood, Sweat & Tears

Kopechne, Mary Jo, 280

Kornbluth, Jesse, 134

Kornfeld, Barry, 75-76, 78, 89-90, 147, 153, 171, 173, 179-80, 183-84, 215, 257, 259, 289, 297

Kramer, Daniel, 194, 207

Kramer, Stanley, 111, 114, 117

Ku Klux Klan (KKK), 74, 96, 178, 241

Kubrick, Stanley, 114

Kulberg, Andy, 229

Kunstler, William, 278

Kupferberg, Tuli, 273, 294. *See also* The Fugs

Kwait, Todd, 144

Kweskin, Jim, 145. *See also* Kweskin Jug Band

Kweskin Jug Band *(band)*, 146, 147, 148, 199

La Lanterna *(café)*, 28, 56

La MaMa Experimental Theatre Club, 133

Labor Unions, 19, 24

Lady Gaga, 170, 274

LaFarge, Peter, 138, 170, 182

LaMont, Paul, 180

Landis, Jerry, 179. *See also* Paul Simon; Tom & Jerry; Simon & Garfunkel

Langhorne, Bruce, 98, 105, 157, 174, 179, 195, 204, 240

Lankford Jr., Ronnie D., 145

Last Poets, The, 282

Launois, John, 174

Laurel Canyon, 198, 267

Laurie Records, 271

Lavin, Christine, 284

Le Figaro Café, 56, 225

Leacock, Richard, 92

Lead Belly, 22-26, 30-32, 89-90, 107, 112, 143, 167, 266. *See also* Huddie Ledbetter

Leary, Timothy, 257

Led Zeppelin *(band)*, 231

Ledbetter, Huddie, 22, 291. *See also* Lead Belly

Lee, Bill, 98-99, 105, 179

Lee, Harper, 133

Lee, Peggy, 30

Lee, Spike, 105, 195-96

Lenape *(North American indigenous people)*, 12

Lennon, John, 32, 184-85, 202, 250, 282. *See also* The Beatles

Lerner, Murray, 153, 206, 212, 220

Leslie, Alfred, 34

Leventhal, Harold, 166

Levinger, Lowell, 252

Levy, Arthur, 231, 297

Levy, Joe, 207

Lewis, John, 96, 156, 158, 271

Library of Congress, 4, 19, 20, 24, 53

Lichtenstein, Roy, 133

Life I'm Living, The (album), 174

Limeliters, The *(band)*, 53, 165, 213

Lincoln, Abraham, 13, 271

Linhart, Buzzy, 252, 253, 278

Lion, The *(venue)*, 87

Lipsius, Marilyn, 283

Little Red School House, 28, 109

Little Richard, 24, 42, 44, 89, 199, 255, 271

Little Rock Nine, 41

Little Sandy Review, The, 228

Live at the Café au Go Go (album), 230

Living Theater, the, 190

LSD (Lysergic acid diethylamide), 256-59, 266

Lomax, Alan, 19-21, 23, 25, 31, 43, 53, 94, 107, 146, 204-5, 291

Lomax, Bess, 26

Lomax, John, 22

Loog Oldham, Andrew, 256

Louisiana Red Hot Records, 193

Love, Mike, 277. *See also* The Beach Boys

Lovin' Spoonful, The *(band)*, 87, 188, 198-200, 202, 219, 223, 225, 228, 231, 249-53, 266, 283

Lownds, Sara, 207

Lulu, 115

Lyrichord Records, 143

Lyman, Mel, 148

MacDermot, Galt, 265, 295. *See also* Hair

MacDougal Street, 7, 8, 14, 28, 33, 43, 47, 48, 55-57, 62, 64, 66, 72, 77, 83-86, 88, 90, 97, 109, 117, 125, 131, 136, 143, 146, 151, 153, 165, 172, 177, 185, 189, 190, 191, 199, 201, 202, 215, 220, 225, 229, 245, 247, 252, 255, 259, 277, 281, 284, 298

Macho Jr., Joe, 204, 214

MacLise, Angus, 222. *See also* The Velvet Underground

Madison Square Garden *(venue)*, 254, 277

Mafia, the, 201, 279

Magicians, The *(band)*, 201, 255

Maharishi Mahesh Yogi, 219

Makem, Tommy, 35, 56, 63, 94, 105

Mamas and the Papas, The *(vocal group)*, 197-98, 215, 258, 267

Manuel, Richard, 254

Mapes, Jo, 165

Marcell, Andre, 201, 297

March on Washington, 155-58, 159

Margolis, George, 31

Marra, Joe, 199-201, 220, 226, 232, 279. *See also* The Night Owl

Marsh, Dave, 20

Martell, Justin, 190, 297, 298

Martí, José, 136

Martin, Vince, 33, 64, 85, 115, 201

Max's Kansas City *(venue)*, 284

Mayall, John, 230

Maymudes, Victor, 182, 225

Maynard Ferguson Orchestra, The, 273

Mayo, Margot, 27-28

Maysles, Albert, 92

McCarthy, Eugene, 275

McCarthy, Joseph, 31, 36

McClure, Michael, 180-81

McCurdy, Ed, 55, 63, 68, 179

McEwen, Alex, 176. *See also* McEwen Brothers

McEwen Brothers, 176. *See also* Alex McEwen; Rory McEwen

McEwen, Rory, 176. *See also* McEwen Brothers

McGhee, Brownie, 23, 26, 55, 63, 115, 153

McGuinn, Roger (Jim McGuinn), 198, 213-14, 220, 251, 252. *See also* The Byrds

McGuire, Barry, 199

McKenzie, Scott, 197-98, 258. *See also* The Journeymen

McKuen, Rod, 185

McLuhan, Marshall, 257, 259

McSorley's Ale House, 13

MC5 (Motor City Five) *(band)*, 225

Mekas, Adolfas, 215

Mekas, Jonas, 93, 190, 191, 215-18, 222-23, 225, 297

Melanga, Gerard, 223

Melanie (Melanie Safka), 277, 278, 281, 298

Melcher, Terry, 213-14

Memphis Jug Band *(band)*, 130, 145-46

Mercury Records, 75, 147, 198, 252

MGM *(film studio; record label)*, 165, 224, 230, 244

Midler, Bette, 278, 287

Miller, Perry, 116-17. *See also* Jesse Colin Young

Milton Berle Show, The, 53

Minetta Lane, 12, 14

Mingus, Charles, 56, 182

Miss Vicki, 269

Mississippi John Hurt, 48, 72, 87, 91, 117, 153-55, 177, 182, 199, 203, 253

Mister Rogers' Neighborhood (television show), 233

Mitchell, Joni, 234, 267, 281, 283, 284

Mixed Bag (album), 221

MK-Ultra, 257

Modern Folk Quartet, 124

Modern Hi-Fi & Stereo Review, 239

Mojo Magazine, 202

Monkees, The (television show; band), 193, 200

Monterey Folk Festival, 153

Monterey Pop Festival, 258-59

Montgomery Bus Boycott, 41

Montreal Gazette, 206

Moody, Reverend Howard, 94

Morris, Newbold, 92

Morrison, Sterling, 222. *See also* The Velvet Underground

Morrison, Van, 226

Morton, George "Shadow," 243-44

Moses, Robert, 61, 92, 97, 98

Mother McCree's Uptown Jug Champions *(band)*, 148. *See also* Grateful Dead

Mountain *(band)*, 76

Mousaa, Roland, 278

Moving (album), 157

Mugwumps, The *(band)*, 197

Muldaur, Geoff, 145, 147-48, 228. *See also* Kweskin Jug Band

Muldaur, Maria, 143, 146-48, 150, 297. *See also* Maria D'Amato; Even Dozen Jug Band; Kweskin Jug Band

Music Inn, The, 90-91, 100

Music Row, 91, 251

My Son, the Folk Singer, 158

Myers, Marc, 42, 273, 297

Myddle Class, The *(band)*, 222

NAACP (National Association for the Advancement of Colored People), 156

NASA (National Aeronautics and Space Administration), 55

Nash, Graham, 87, 255, 276. *See also* Crosby, Stills, and Nash

National Conference of Christians and Jews, The, 253

National Urban League, 156

NBC *(television network)*, 35, 200, 268

Neil, Fred "Freddy," 64, 84-86, 87, 90, 115, 181, 189, 201-2, 220, 225, 226, 245, 247, 252, 253, 259, 266, 273, 279, 291, 293, 295

Nelson, Paul, 228

Neuwirth, Bob, 207, 218-19, 225

New Christy Minstrels *(vocal group)*, 148, 198, 213

New Lost City Ramblers, The *(band)*, 53-54, 89, 91

New School, The, 7, 11, 44, 133, 286

New World Singers *(band)*, 77, 137, 138

New York: A Documentary Film, 97

New York Daily Mirror, 182

New York Daily News, 280

New York Magazine, 124, 134

New York Mirror, 94

New York Times, The, 19, 36, 65, 87, 88, 91, 92, 94, 106, 110, 130, 133, 153, 157, 166, 181, 190, 221, 233, 241, 246, 249, 254, 281

New York University (NYU), 13, 44, 61, 91, 92, 116-17, 229, 251, 283

Newfield, Jack, 248

Newman, Paul, 35

Newman, Randy, 279

Newport Folk Festival, 53, 54, 70, 75, 82, 96, 104, 108, 122, 142, 152-55, 182, 184, 205-8, 212, 219-20, 227, 240-41, 246, 263, 265

Newport Jazz Festival, 52, 152

Newsweek (magazine), 126, 158

Nico, 223-25, 269, 272. *See also* The Velvet Underground

Night Owl Café *(venue)*, 199-201, 220, 223, 226, 228, 229, 232, 266, 279, 285

Nilsson, Harry, 279

Nixon, Richard M., 31, 36, 78, 112, 276

Norris, Rob, 222, 224, 297. *See also* The Bongos

NPR (National Public Radio), 94, 274, 275

Numbers with Wings (album), 11

NYPD (New York Police Department), 93, 191, 201, 287

Obomsawin, Mali, 21

O'Brien, Conan, 185

Occupy Wall Street, 132, 287

Ochs, Adolph S., 172

Ochs, Alice, 131, 182. *See also* Alice Skinner

Ochs, Michael, 125, 267, 278

Ochs, Phil, 43, 51, 112-13, 116, 125-27, 131, 135, 138, 151, 153-54, 160, 171, 172-73, 178, 181-82, 189, 200, 204, 221, 226, 227, 231, 232-33, 238-39, 246, 247, 248, 266-68, 269, 275-76, 276-78, 282, 284, 291-95, 298. *See also* The Sundowners; The Singing Socialists

Ochs, Sonny, 112, 126, 278, 297

Odetta (aka Odetta Holmes; Odetta Felious), 34, 41, 50, 52, 55, 64, 98, 105, 108, 137,

156-57, 242, 246, 277

Okeh Records, 43, 154

Okun, Milton "Milt," 73-74, 124, 133, 139, 174

Ono, Yoko, 133, 282

Orbison, Roy, 84, 201

Original Rag Quartet *(band)*, 76

Orlovsky, Peter, 33

Oscar Brand's Folksong Festival (radio program), 20, 106

Oswald, Lee Harvey, 160

Owens, Frank, 204

Oxford American Magazine, 145

Page, Patti, 41

Page Three, The *(venue)*, 190-92

Paley, Tom, 49, 53. *See also* The New Lost City Ramblers

Paley, William, 265

Palm Beach Post, The (newspaper), 271

Pappalardi, Felix, 77, 171, 253. *See also* Cream; Mountain

Parker, Henry, 179

Parks, Gordon, 22

Parks, Rosa, 41

Parks, Van Dyke, 277

Parlophone Records, 167. *See also* EMI

Paul Butterfield Blues Band, 205-6, 230-31

Paul, Steve, 268. *See also* Steve Paul's The Scene

Paxton, Tom, 48, 65, 72-74, 75-76, 85, 90, 93, 95, 106, 116, 124, 154, 166, 171-72, 181-82, 201, 203-4, 266, 269, 271, 291-95, 297

PBS (Public Broadcasting Service), 41, 195

Peace Corps, The, 83

Peer, Ralph, 43, 145

Peer-Southern Music, 43, 145

Pennebaker, D. A., 92, 218-19

People (magazine), 278

People's Songs *(organization)*, 29, 53, 116

People's Songs, The (newsletter), 29, 53, 116

Pepper, Allan, 271, 297

Perls, Nick, 146

Perret, Vera, 246

Perry, Richard, 191, 269

Persuasion Song *(type of topical song)*, 133

Peter, Paul and Mary *(folk trio)*, 30, 51, 76, 85, 108-11, 122-25, 128, 132, 139, 152, 155, 156-57, 166, 174, 184, 191, 196, 220

Pet Sounds (album), 250

Peter Stampfel's 20th Century (album), 193

Petrus, Stephen, 23, 25, 129, 289, 297-98

Petty, Norman, 44-45, 98

Philadelphia Folk Festival, 263-64

Phillips, John, 197-98, 258-59. *See also* The Journeymen; The New Journeymen; The Mamas and the Papas

Phillips, Michelle, 197-98. *See also* Michelle Gilliam; The New Journeymen; The Mamas and the Papas

Phillips, Shawn, 219

Piaf, Edith, 169

Pierce, Webb, 113

Pilgrims, The *(band)*, 177, 179

Pink Floyd *(band)*, 231

Pioneer Women *(organization)*, 197

Pitman, Bill, 214

Plant, Robert, 115. *See also* Led Zeppelin

Pleasures of the Harbor (album), 267-68

Playboy Magazine, 51

Poe, Edgar Allan, 173

Pop, Iggy, 225

Porco, Bob, 62, 94-95, 297

Porco, John, 61

Porco, Mike, 61-64, 66, 94-95, 278. *See also* Gerde's Folk City

Powers, Chet, 252, 294

Prendergast, Tom, 61-63

Presley, Elvis, 32, 42, 182, 228, 241

Prestige Records, 114, 134, 193

Pretenders, The *(band)*, 276

Price, Alan, 108. *See also* The Animals

Proffitt, Frank, 53

Projections (album), 231

Propaganda Song *(type of topical song)*, 133

Protest Song *(type of topical song)*, 133

Provincetown Playhouse, 14

Pugh, Mike, 75

Pugliese, John Sebastian, 87

Pull My Daisy (film), 34

Purple Onion, The *(venue)*, 52

Push Pin Studios, 124, 191. *See also* Milt Glaser

Quarrymen, The, 32, 167. *See also* The Beatles

Queens College, 75, 177-78

Queer Eye (television show), 167

Rado, James, 265, 294. *See also* Hair

Ragni, Gerome, 265, 294. *See also* Hair

Ragtime Jug Stompers *(band)*, 75, 147, 227. *See also* Dave Van Ronk

Raitt, Bonnie, 254

Ramblin' Boy (album), 141

Ramone, Phil, 251

Ramones, The *(band)*, 225

Randall, Elliot, 221

Randolph, Philip, 155

Rare Moments Vol. 1: I've Never Seen A Straight Banana (album), 269

Rauschenberg, Robert, 133

Ray, Dave "Snaker," 228. *See also* Koerner, Ray & Glover

Ray, Jean, 113. *See also* Jim & Jean

RCA Records, 86, 158, 224, 246, 253

Reagon, Cordell, 71

Rebel Without A Cause (film), 88, 151

Redpath, Jean, 168

Reed, Jimmy, 253

Reed, Lou, 11, 222, 263, 272, 293-94, 298. *See also* The Velvet Underground

Reed, Susan, 44, 176

Red Scare, 29, 31, 41

Redding, Otis, 258

Rehearsals For Retirement (album), 277

Relix (magazine), 227

Reprise Records, 268

Reserve Officers' Training Corps (ROTC), 113, 127

Revolver (album), 250

Richards, Keith, 255. *See also* The Rolling Stones

Richardson, J. P., 46

Richmond, Fritz, 145, 199

Right to Sing Committee, 94

Rilke, Rainer Maria, 244

Rimbaud, Arthur, 180, 183, 194, 217

Rinzler, Ralph, 130

Ritchie, Jean, 35, 55-56, 67, 70, 150-51, 153, 293

Robertson, Robbie, 254. *See also* The Band

Robeson, Paul, 14, 33, 109, 137, 155

Roche, Maggie, 282. *See also* The Roches

Roche, Suzzy, 283. *See also* The Roches

Roche, Terre, 282, 285, 295, 297. *See also* The Roches

Roches, The *(band)*, 283

Rock and Roll, 20, 30, 32, 42-45, 72, 89-90, 106, 113, 118, 144, 167, 193-94, 196, 200, 228, 230, 240-41, 245, 254, 271-72, 284

Rockwell, Norman, 174

Rogers, Ira, 75. *See also* Inman & Ira

Rolling Stone (magazine), 8, 205, 207, 227, 266

Rolling Stones, The *(band)*, 223, 230, 255

Romney, Hugh, 48, 71, 190-91, 275. *See also*

Wavy Gravy

Rooftop Singers, The *(folk trio)*, 143-46, 153

Roosevelt, Eleanor, 86

Rose, Artie, 147

Rose, Charlie, 195

Rose, Tim, 115, 196, 256

Rosenberg, Stuart, 213

Rosenthal, Steve, 20, 297

Roth, David Lee, 84. *See also* Van Halen

Roth, Manny, 84

Rothchild, Paul, 171, 173

Rothschild, Charlie, 64, 98, 108

Rotolo, Carla, 106

Rotolo, Suze, 86, 88-89, 91, 95-96, 130, 149, 151, 154, 169, 183, 193-94

Rowan & Martin's Laugh-In (television show), 268

Rubber Soul (album), 219, 250

Rubin, Barbara, 195, 216-19, 222-25, 257

Rubin, Jerry, 275, 278, 282

Rubin, Rick, 127, 274

Rush, Tom, 240, 278, 282

Russian Revolution, 47

Russell, Leon, 214

Rustin, Bayard, 27, 96, 155-56, 158

Sainte-Marie, Buffy, 116, 127, 142, 169-71, 173, 181, 203, 204, 221, 243, 247, 267, 269, 274, 291, 292, 297

San Remo Café, 202

Sandberg, Carl, 24, 183

Sanders, Ed, 272, 275. *See also* The Fugs

Sandpipers, The *(vocal group)*, 136

Santiago, Maria Elena, 43-46, 65

Saturday Evening Post, The (magazine), 174

Scaduto, Anthony, 234

Schatzberg, Jerry, 232

Schlesinger, John, 279

Schumacher, Michael, 126, 154, 232-33,

297, 298

Schwartau, Bill, 124

Schwerner, Michael, 179

Scorcese, Martin, 208

Scott, Bobby, 251

Searchers, The *(band)*, 129

Sebastian, John, 84, 85, 86-87, 91, 109, 143, 145, 146-48, 168, 185, 189, 190, 196, 197, 198-200, 202, 220-21, 224, 226, 227, 228, 229, 245, 249-51, 252, 266, 271, 279, 281, 293-94, 297. *See also* The Lovin' Spoonful; The Mugwumps; Even Dozen Jug Band

Sebastian, Mark, 86, 249

Sedgwick, Edie, 223, 225

Seductive Reasoning (album), 283

Seeger, Charles, 24, 208

Seeger, Mike, 53-54, 91. *See also* The New Lost City Ramblers

Seeger, Peggy, 54

Seeger, Pete, 18, 20, 23, 24-26, 28-31, 35, 36, 42, 44, 47, 51, 52, 53, 54, 55, 56, 62, 68, 72, 73, 74, 106, 107, 109, 110-12, 115, 116, 117, 123, 126, 133, 136, 137-38, 151, 152, 153, 155, 157, 165, 166, 170, 171, 181, 182, 198, 203, 207, 208, 213, 214, 218, 219, 227, 241, 259, 264-65, 269, 270, 277, 278, 285, 291, 294, 298. *See also* Almanac Singers; The Weavers

Seeger (née Ohta), Toshi Aline, 28, 29, 30, 35, 203, 264

Sellers, Brother John, 63, 105

Sellouts, The *(band)*, 199

Serendipity Singers *(vocal group)*, 72

Sgt. Pepper's Lonely Hearts Club Band (album), 195, 259, 263, 267

Shanty Boys, 95

Shelton, Robert, 63, 64-66, 95, 100, 105, 111, 113, 130, 146, 147, 157, 158, 165, 181, 182, 190, 205, 229, 244, 246, 263, 298

Sherman, Allan, 158

Shocking Blue *(band)*, 198

Shuman, Mort, 271

Silber, Irwin, 29, 53, 116

Silber, Marc, 229, 297

Silverstein, Shel, 51

Simmons, Dave, 215

Simon and Garfunkel *(folk duo)*, 158, 176-80, 214-15, 259, 283. *See also* Kane & Garr; Tom & Jerry

Simon, Carly, 281

Simon, Paul, 43, 134, 158, 170, 176-80, 214-15, 259, 263, 281, 283, 292-93. *See also* Jerry Landis; Tom & Jerry; Kane & Garr; Simon & Garfunkel

Simone, Nina, 56, 147, 266

Sinatra, Frank, 30, 43

Sing Out! (magazine), 29, 116, 151

Singing Socialists, The *(folk duo)*, 112-13, 125. *See also* The Sundowners; Phil Ochs; Jim Glover

Skiffle, 32, 142, 144, 147, 167, 200

Skiffle in Stereo (album), 143

Skinner, Alice, 131. *See also* Alice Ochs

Sky, Patrick, 76, 155, 170, 181, 212, 247, 298

Sloan, John, 15

Smith, Bessie, 83, 87

Smith, Chuck, 217, 257, 297

Smith, Harry, 31, 48, 53, 84, 87, 107, 146, 155, 191, 192, 193, 204

Smith, Jack, 217

Smith, Jimmy, 182

Smith, Patti, 169, 262, 278, 284

Smothers Brothers, The, 112, 265, 268-70. *See also* Dick Smothers; Tom Smothers

Smothers Brothers Comedy Hour, 265, 268-70

Smothers, Dick, 265, 268. *See also* The Smothers Brothers

Smothers, Tom, 265, 268, 269. *See also* The

Smothers Brothers

Snadowsky, Stanley, 271

Solanas, Valerie, 272

Solomon, Maynard, 145, 181

Solomon, Seymour, 145

Somer, Jack, 246

Sometime In New York City (album), 282

Son House, 19, 87, 182

Song Swappers, The *(folk group)*, 109

Songs for Aging Children (album), 284

Songs for 'Drella (album), 272

Songs That Made America Famous (album), 76

Sony Music Entertainment (SME), 149

Sorrows & Promises (album), 7

Soul of a City Boy (album), 251

Soule, Howard, 150

Southern Illinoisan, The, 220

Soviet Union, 28-29, 55, 74, 97, 114, 135, 159

Spector, Phil, 213, 243

Spencer, Abraham, 286, 289

Spencer, Leyla, 70, 285, 297

Spitz, Bob, 50, 90, 95, 232, 298

Spivey, Victoria, 95, 146, 220

Spoelstra, Mark, 90, 95-96, 138

Sprung, Roger, 49, 95

Squires, The *(band)*, 255

St. Mark's Place, 117, 266

Stampfel, Peter, 76, 84, 189, 192-93, 267, 273, 293, 297. *See also* Holy Modal Rounders; The Fugs

Starr, Ringo, 185. *See also* The Beatles

State Supreme Court of New York, 94-96

Stax Records, 145

Stein, Seymour, 256

Steve Paul's The Scene *(venue)*, 268

Stewart, Mike, 266

Stonewall Inn, 191, 279-80

Stooges, The *(band)*, 225

Stookey, Noel "Paul," 85, 109-10, 123, 131, 167. *See also* Peter, Paul & Mary

Streisand, Barbra, 87, 196

Student Nonviolent Coordinating Committee (SNCC), 71, 96

Sullivan, Ed, 8, 147, 148, 167, 168, 196

Summer of Love, 253, 258, 263, 279

Sunday (film), 92-94, 286-87

Sundowners, The *(folk duo)*, 112-13, 125. *See also* the Singing Socialists; Phil Ochs; Jim Glover

Sunshine Superman (album), 240

Svanoe, William "Bill," 143-44. *See also* The Rooftop Singers

Tannen, Michael, 283

Tarriers, The *(folk trio)*, 32-33, 35, 49, 51, 53, 62, 63, 64, 76, 95, 143, 153, 165, 197

Tate, Grady, 252

Tate, Greg, 228, 298

Taylor, Derek, 258

Taylor, Elizabeth, 35

Taylor, James, 229, 281. *See also* The Flying Machine

Taylor, Lynne, 143. *See also* The Rooftop Singers

Terry, Sonny, 23, 26, 55, 63, 89, 115, 153

Tet Offensive, 269, 270

Thal, Terri, 49, 66, 68, 69, 70, 76, 88, 89, 91, 94, 96, 108, 115, 123, 125, 149, 168, 178, 183, 184, 192, 245, 257, 258, 282-83, 289, 297

Tharpe, Sister Rosetta, 42, 271

There Goes Rhymin' Simon (album), 283

Thomas, Dylan, 56, 89, 259

Thompson, Hunter S., 133

Thomson, Elizabeth, 205

Third Side, The *(venue)*, 87, 125, 189, 192, 199

Timber-r-r! Lumberjack Folksongs and Ballads (album), 67
Tim Hardin 1 (album), 226
Tim Hardin 2 (album), 227
Tim Hardin 3: Live in Concert, 227
TIME (magazine), 153, 196
Times They Are A-Changin', The (album), 168, 183
Tin Pan Alley, 92, 191
Tindley, Reverend Charles, 139
Tiny Tim, 85, 87, 124, 189-92, 216, 254, 268-69, 298. *See also* Herbert Khuary
To Kill A Mockingbird (novel), 133
Today Is the Highway (album), 247
Tom & Jerry *(pop duo)*, 158, 177, 179, 180. *See also* Kane & Garr; Simon and Garfunkel
Tonight Show With Johnny Carson, The, 146, 155, 197, 269
Tork, Peter, 193. *See also* The Monkees
Town Hall, The *(venue)*, 169, 227
Tradition Records, 34, 50, 64, 67, 98
Traum, Artie, 229
Traum, Happy, 56, 61, 76-77, 91, 93, 96, 97, 115, 138, 170, 229, 286-87, 289, 297. *See also* New World Singers
Travers, Mary, 108-11, 124-25, 194. *See also* Peter, Paul & Mary; The Song Swappers
Triangle Shirtwaist Factory Fire, 14, 287
Trotsky, Leon, 47
Tucker, Maureen "Moe," 223-24. *See also* The Velvet Underground
Turner, Gil, 96, 138. *See also* New World Singers
Turner, Ike, 42
Turtles, The *(band)*, 201, 214
Tyson, Ian, 128-29. *See also* Ian & Sylvia
Tyson, Sylvia, 128-29, 149. *See also* Sylvia Fricker; Ian & Sylvia

UHF Channel 47 *(television station)*, 203
Unblushing Brassiness (album), 145
UNESCO, 175
United Artists Music, 266
United Nations, 52, 112, 135, 175, 215
U.S. Army Soldiers' Chorus, 173

Valens, Ritchie, 46
Vallee, Rudy, 254
Van Halen *(band)*, 84
Van Peebles, Melvin, 282
Van Ronk, Dave, 46-50, 53, 55, 56, 63, 64, 65, 66, 67, 68, 70, 71, 72, 73, 75, 76, 82, 84, 88, 89, 90, 91, 94, 96-97, 99, 106, 107-8, 109, 113, 118, 123, 125, 129, 131, 134, 143, 145, 146, 147, 150, 151, 152, 153, 154, 168, 172, 173, 177, 178, 181, 192, 224, 227, 228, 229, 232, 245, 246, 257, 267, 275, 277, 278, 279, 280, 282-84, 295, 298
Vance, Vivian, 86. *See also* I Love Lucy
Vanguard Records, 35, 70, 127, 128, 144-45, 169, 181, 240, 247
Variety (magazine), 168
Vega, Suzanne, 284
Velvet Underground, The *(band)*, 11, 222-25, 231, 255, 263, 269, 272, 285, 298
Velvet Underground and Nico, The (album), 224
Vermont Review, The, 276
Verve Records, 147, 194, 221, 224, 226-27, 230-31, 244, 272
Victor Records, 43, 143
Vietnam War, 19, 127-28, 159, 173, 182, 196, 202-4, 220, 226, 249, 265, 269-70, 275, 277-78, 287
Village Gate *(venue)*, 18, 45, 51, 56, 94, 112, 182, 242-43
Village Vanguard *(venue)*, 26-27, 30, 33, 45, 63, 87, 147, 176, 182
Village Voice, The, 28, 64, 93, 190, 216-17, 239, 249
Virgin Fugs, 273
Visconti, Luchino, 133
Voice and Guitar of José Feliciano, The (album), 246
Von Schmidt, Eric, 99, 107, 228

Wald, Elijah, 42, 65, 71, 138, 207, 245-46, 284, 297-98
Walker, T-Bone, 117
Wall Street Journal, The, 42, 46, 273
Wallace, George, 241
Wallace, Henry, 29
Wanted for Murder: Songs of Outlaws and Desperados (album), 67
War *(band)*, 282
Warhol, Andy, 133, 205, 216, 223-25, 271-72, 298
Warner Brothers Records, 110, 123-24, 152, 158, 268, 283
Washington, George, 12, 14
Washington Post, The, 175, 176, 265, 271
Washington Square Hotel, 75, 128, 287. *See also* The Earle
Washington Square Park, 7, 11, 13-15, 27, 28, 31, 33, 44, 47, 48, 49, 53, 57, 61, 67, 71, 75, 77, 78, 86, 91, 92, 93, 94, 95, 97, 109, 133, 117, 146, 197, 198, 199, 221, 222, 249, 282, 286
Waters, Muddy, 19, 72, 231
Watson, Doc, 87, 91, 153, 245
Waverly Place, 7, 50, 61, 65, 72, 76, 96, 97, 108, 131, 168, 180, 247, 258, 286
Waverly Theater, 229
WBAI *(radio station)*, 70, 129, 275, 282
Wednesday Morning, 3 A.M. (album), 179
We Five *(vocal group)*, 128, 214

Weavers, The *(folk quartet)*, 29-31, 35, 52, 53, 54, 62, 63, 72, 74, 76, 77, 91, 107, 112, 123, 136, 158, 166, 172, 173, 176, 184, 186, 213, 265

Weavers at Carnegie Hall, The (album), 72, 136

Weber, Steve, 192-93, 293. *See also* Holy Modal Rounders; The Fugs

Webster Hall *(venue)*, 15

Wein, George, 52, 110, 152-53, 154, 155, 206, 207, 208, 298

Weissberg, Eric, 76, 153. *See also* The Tarriers

Weissman, Dick, 172, 197. *See also* The Journeymen

Weld, Tuesday, 269

Weller, Sheila, 198

West, Hedy, 123

West, Leslie, 253. *See also* Mountain

West, Mae, 259

West Side Story (musical), 57

West 4th Street, 14, 47, 61, 62, 90, 91, 98, 100, 149, 150, 177, 183, 233, 266, 271, 293

What's Bin Did And What's Bin Hid (album), 218

White, Bukka, 130

White Horse Tavern, 56, 65, 90, 97, 168, 240

White Light/White Heat (album), 272

White, Josh, 23, 25, 27, 31, 33, 47, 69-70, 76, 86, 99, 107, 155-56, 279. *See also* Josh White and the Carolinians

Whiteman, Paul, 228

Whitman, Walt, 13

Why Not? *(venue)*, 87, 220

Wild One, The (film), 117, 234, 295

Wilde, Oscar, 259

William Morris Agency, 228

Williams, Hank, 113, 130

Williams, Tennessee, 35, 287, 295

Wilson, Brian, 213. *See also* The Beach Boys

Wilson, Dennis, 277. *See also* The Beach Boys

Wilson, Nancy, 63

Wilson, Teddy, 15

Wilson, Tom, 148, 169, 177, 180, 183, 204-5, 214-15, 224, 229, 230, 271, 272

Winehouse, Amy, 84

WNYC-AM (radio station), 20, 22, 106

Wolf, Howlin', 130, 205

Wolfe, Tom, 133, 257

Woliver, Robbie, 257

Wonder, Stevie, 282

Woods, Hosea, 144-45. *See also* Cannon's Jug Stompers

Woodstock *(festival)*, 221, 227, 240, 254, 255, 258, 274, 280-81

Woodstock, NY, 194, 225, 240, 254, 259, 281

Woodward, Joanne, 287

Woody Guthrie's Blues (album), 88

WOR-FM *(radio station)*, 123

World War II, 28, 77, 111, 113, 256, 265

Worthy, William, 173, 293

Wrecking Crew, The *(L.A. studio musicians)*, 179, 214, 250

X, Malcolm, 133, 195-96

Yanovsky, Zal, 168, 196, 197, 198, 250. *See also* The Lovin' Spoonful

Yarrow, Peter, 76, 109-10, 123, 206-7, 240, 278. *See also* Peter, Paul & Mary

Young Blood (album), 252

Youngbloods, The (album), 253

Youngbloods, The *(band)*, 76, 252-54

Young Communist League, 24

Young, Faron, 113

Young, Israel "Izzy," 28, 56, 61, 63, 64, 66, 71, 92-94, 95, 106, 109, 148, 229, 233, 282, 286

Young, Jesse Colin, 117, 199, 200, 251-54, 297. *See also* Perry Miller

Young, LaMonte, 133

Young Man and a Maid Sing Love Songs of Many Lands (album), 70

Young, Neil, 129, 276. *See also* Buffalo Springfield

Younger, Cole, 117

Youth International Party (Yippies), 275

Youth March for Integrated Schools, 86

Zoo World (magazine), 231